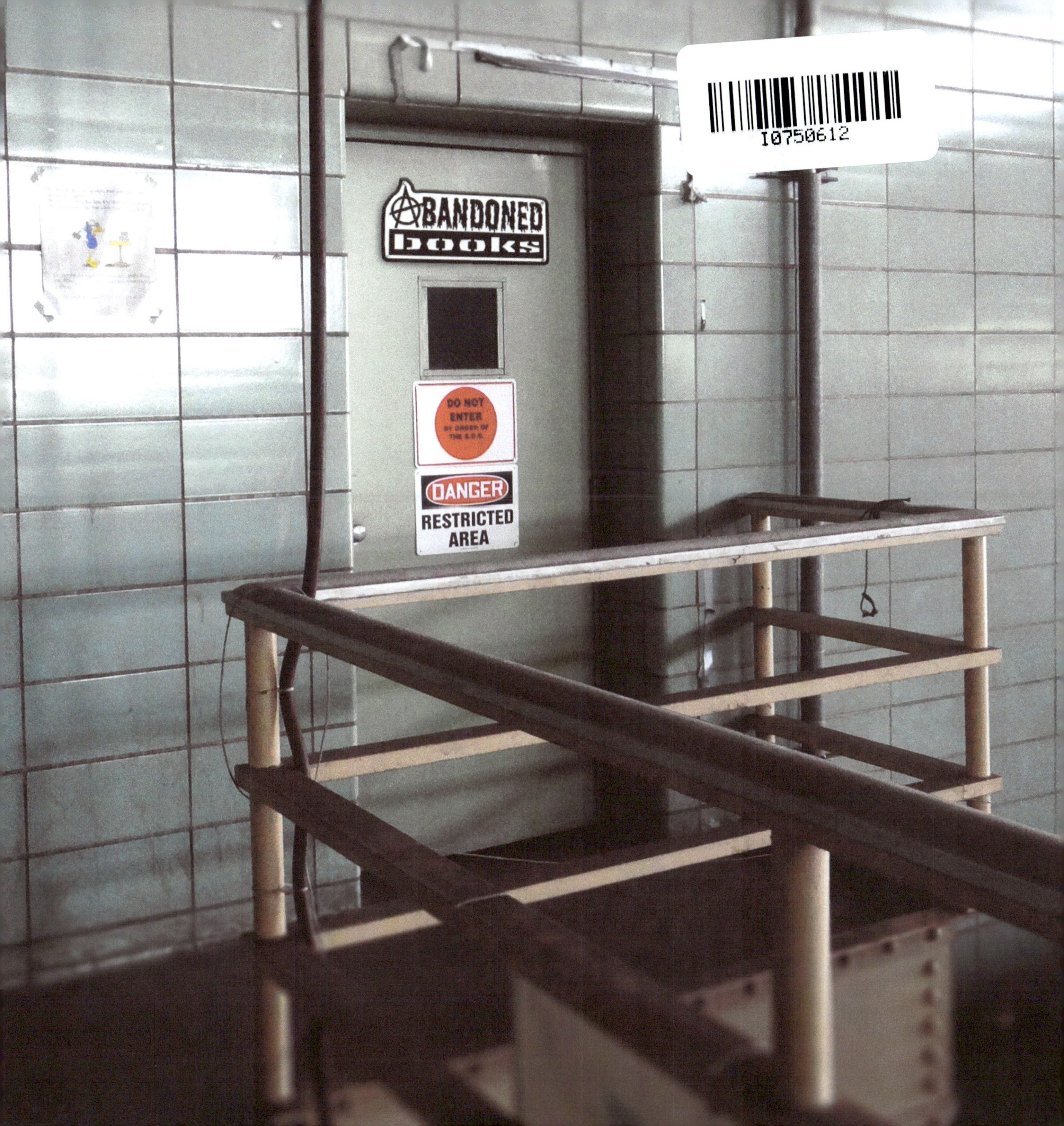
ABANDONED
books
DO NOT
ENTER
DANGER
RESTRICTED
AREA

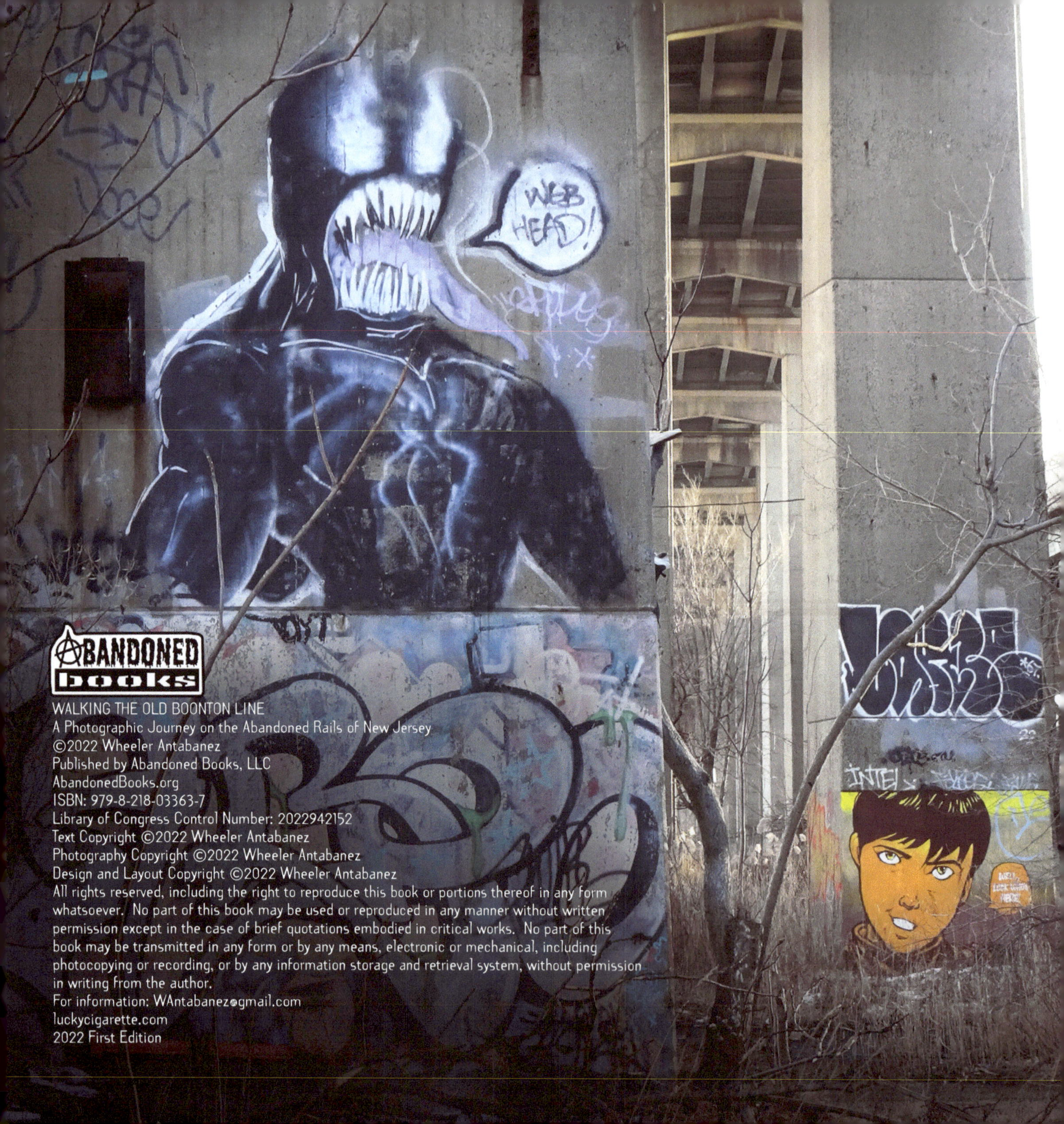

ABANDONED books

WALKING THE OLD BOONTON LINE
A Photographic Journey on the Abandoned Rails of New Jersey

Published by Abandoned Books, LLC
AbandonedBooks.org
ISBN: 979-8-218-03363-7
Library of Congress Control Number: 2022942152

For information: WAntabanez@gmail.com
luckycigarette.com
2022 First Edition

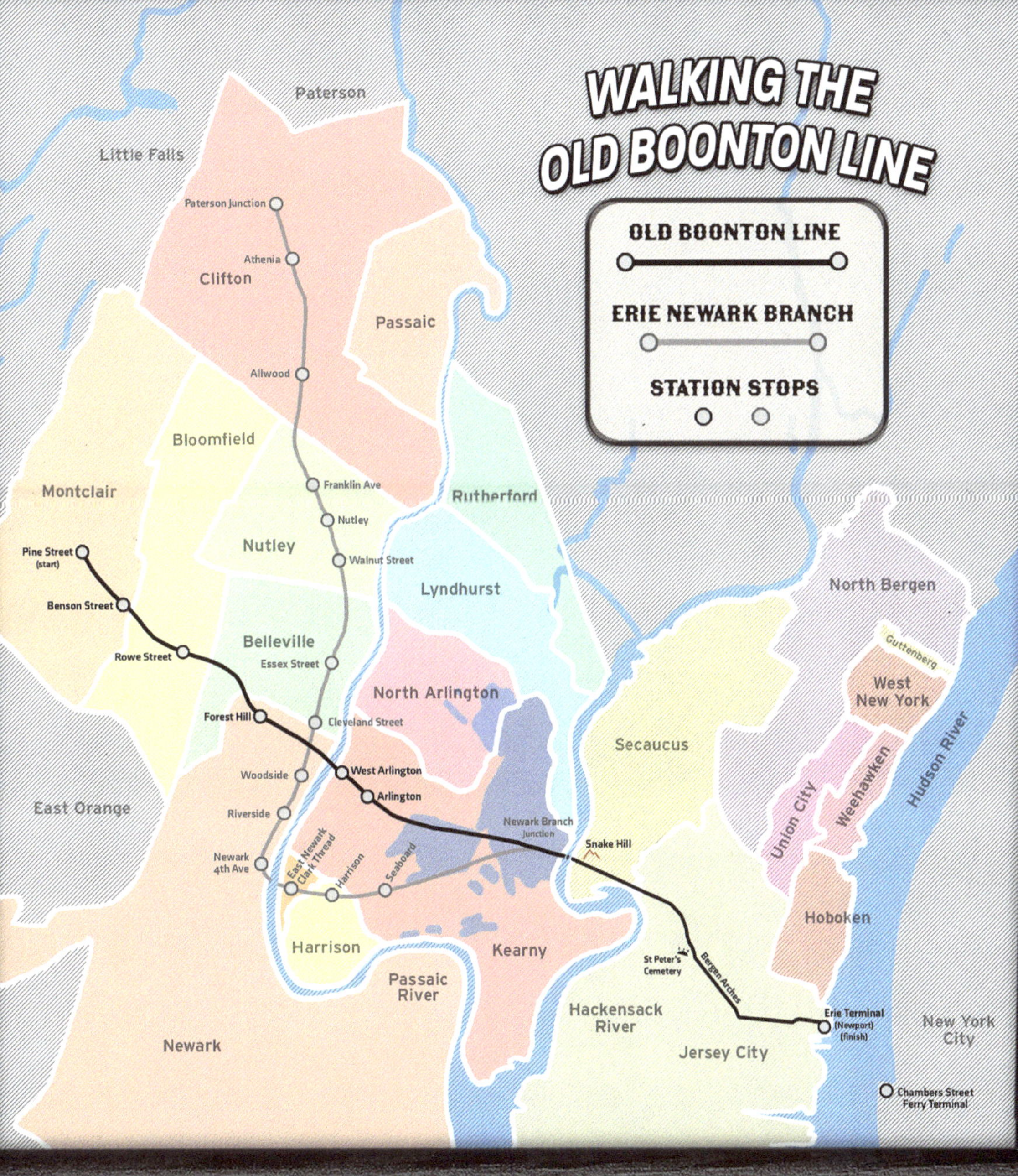
WALKING THE OLD BOONTON LINE
OLD BOONTON LINE
ERIE NEWARK BRANCH
STATION STOPS
Paterson
Little Falls
Paterson Junction
Athenia
Clifton
Passaic
Allwood
Bloomfield
Montclair
Franklin Ave
Nutley
Rutherford
Nutley
Walnut Street
Pine Street (start)
Lyndhurst
Benson Street
North Bergen
Rowe Street
Belleville
Essex Street
Guttenberg
West New York
North Arlington
Forest Hill
Cleveland Street
Secaucus
West Arlington
Woodside
Arlington
Union City
Weehawken
Hudson River
East Orange
Riverside
Newark Branch Junction
Snake Hill
Newark 4th Ave
East Newark Clark Thread
Harrison
Seaboard
Hoboken
Harrison
Kearny
St Peter's Cemetery
Bergen Arches
Passaic River
Hackensack River
Erie Terminal (Newport) (finish)
New York City
Newark
Jersey City
Chambers Street Ferry Terminal

WALKING THE OLD BOONTON LINE

INTRODUCTION

When my parents died two weeks apart in the spring of 2020, my method for coping with the loss was to take long walks on the abandoned railroad tracks near my home. The world was on Covid-19 lockdown, but I couldn't stand being cooped up inside. Lengthy, introspective rambles along the Old Boonton Line allowed me to be outdoors for extended periods while still maintaining social distancing.

My dad had been keeper of the family photos, but when he died, the archives were entrusted to me. One night, while browsing through old albums, I happened upon four pictures of my nerdy, six-year-old self, wearing glasses and riding the Santa train with childhood friends. Slipping the pictures out from under the protective plastic, I found that my Mom had dutifully inscribed the backs of the prints. Imagine my surprise when I discovered the pictures were snapped in 1983 on the Old Boonton Line at the Benson Street Station in Glen Ridge. Apparently, my history on these rails goes back further than I thought.

All of summer 2020 I walked the tracks, usually from Montclair to Bloomfield and back. Around that time, local papers began reporting on a proposed bike path called the Essex/Hudson Greenway that would pave the Old Boonton Line from Montclair to Jersey City. This was bad news for me but even worse news for the deer and other animals that live on the tracks. I have a long list of personal reasons for not wanting the abandoned rails to change, but my primary concern is for local wildlife. If people knew how many animals will be driven into the streets by this development, it would break their hearts.

When the Old Boonton Line was decommissioned in 2002, the right-of-way became a crucial urban habitat and wildlife corridor. I have seen coyote, fox, turkey, and numerous herds of deer living along the tracks because they simply have no other place to go. A bike path might be a lesser evil than a row of condominiums stretching from Montclair to Jersey City but calling it a "greenway" is a bit misleading. In my opinion, the "greenest" option would be to leave the tracks alone and let the right-of-way grow even wilder, but that's not how we do things in Dirty Jersey.

Whether I like the idea or not, it looks like the bike path might actually happen. With this in mind, I set out on a cold winter day in December 2021 to walk the Old Boonton Line one last time before they pave over my favorite set of abandoned tracks. It took nine separate trips, but I made it from Montclair to Jersey City,

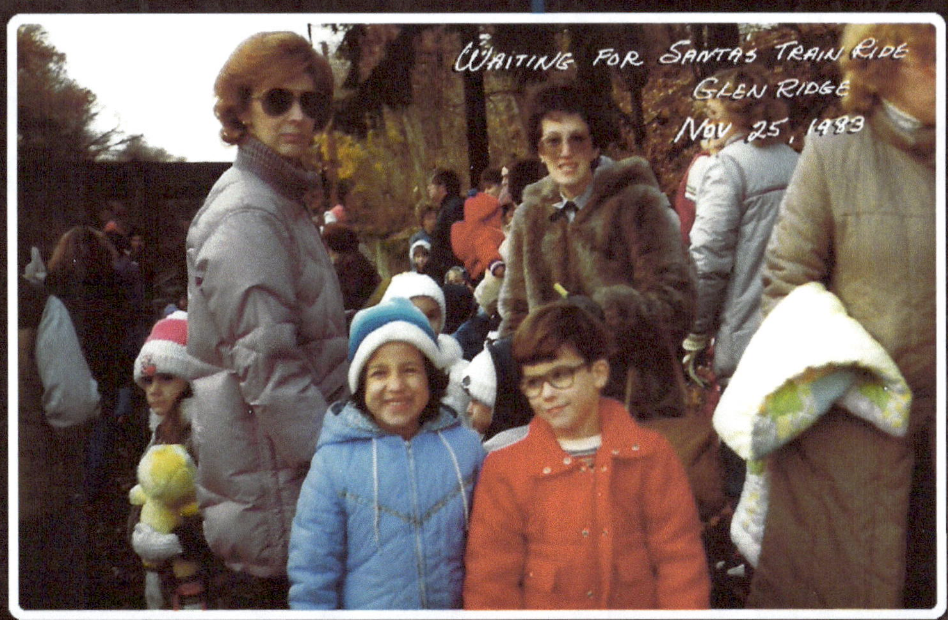

through the Bergen Arches, and into Jersey City proper, where I followed ghost rails to the Hudson River Waterfront. Upon reaching this milestone, I was lucky to have the opportunity to fly in a helicopter and capture aerial photos of the landscape I had just traversed. It was extremely cold taking a doors-off helicopter ride in the middle of winter, but what a rush and what a view!

My journeys along the tracks became a form of meditation that helped me get my head right during troubled times. The adventures along the way set my heart racing and helped me feel alive when the whole world seemed to be dying. If it were up to me, the tracks would remain untouched. I love the rails as they are: forlorn, overgrown, beautiful. They probably won't stay that way for long, but I hope this book will serve as a marker for that gorgeous winter of 2021/2022 when the Old Boonton Line was still perfectly abandoned, wild, and free.

-Wheeler
October 31, 2022

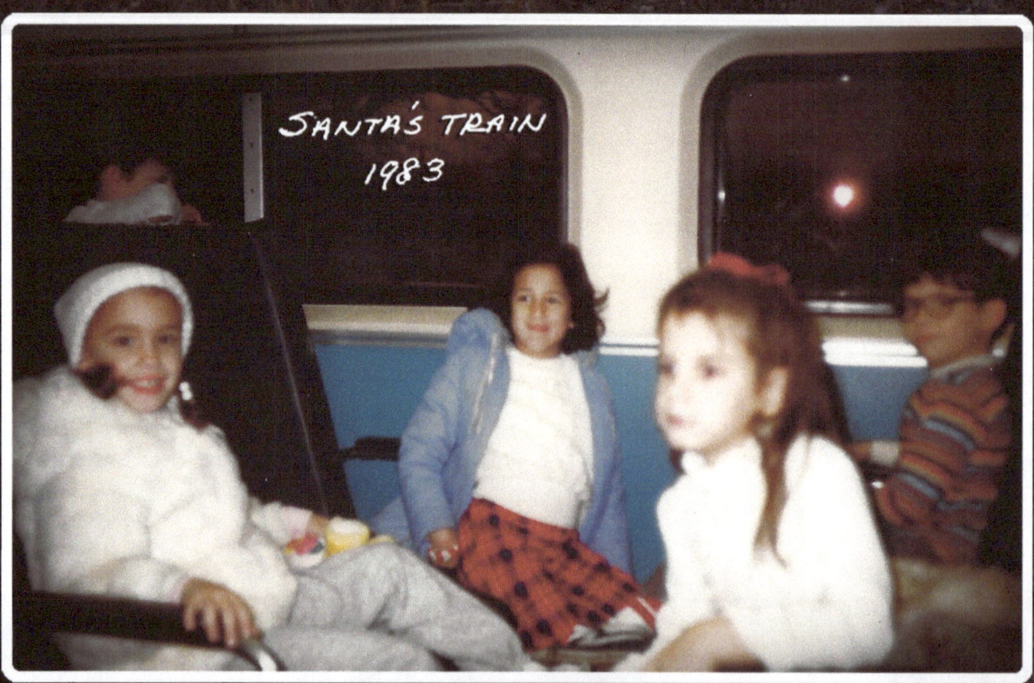

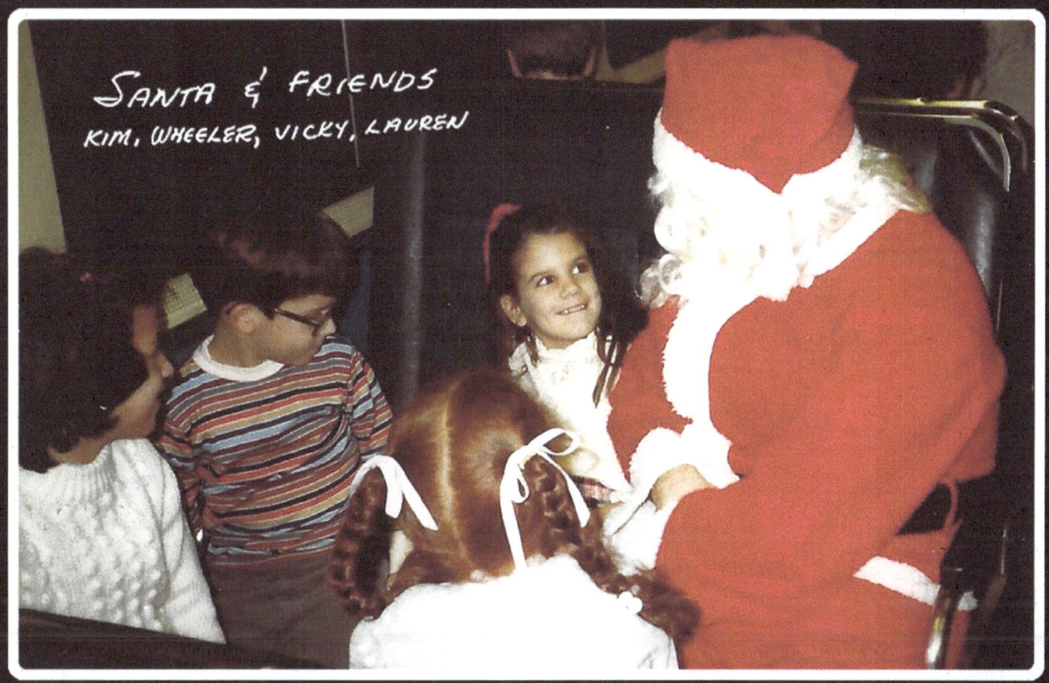
SANTA & FRIENDS
KIM, WHEELER, VICKY, LAUREN

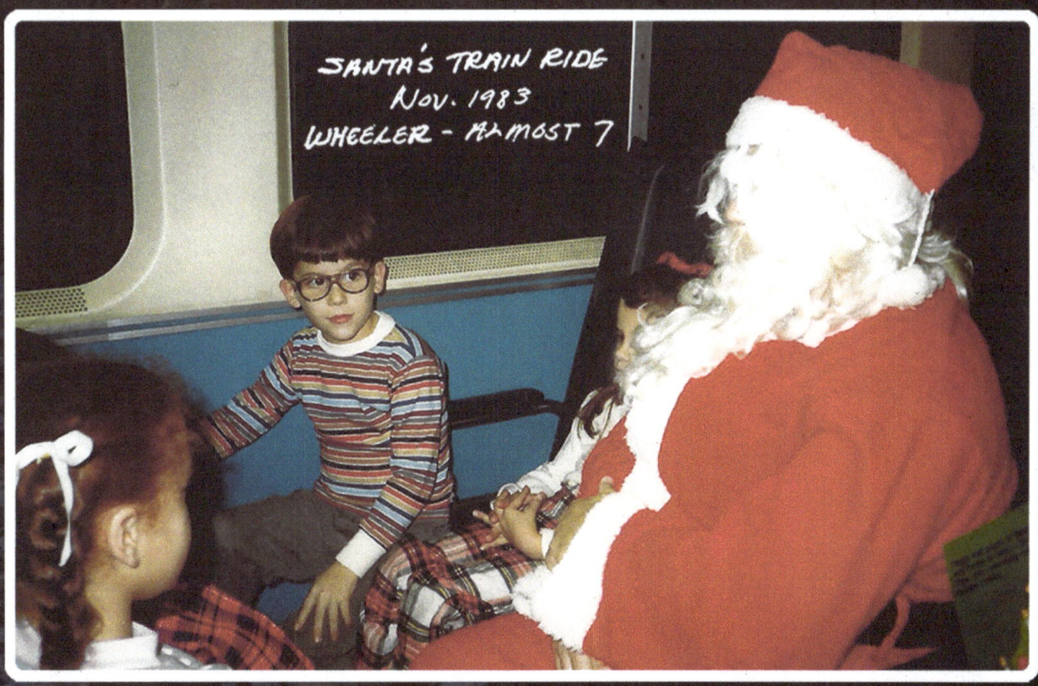
SANTA'S TRAIN RIDE
NOV. 1983
WHEELER - ALMOST 7

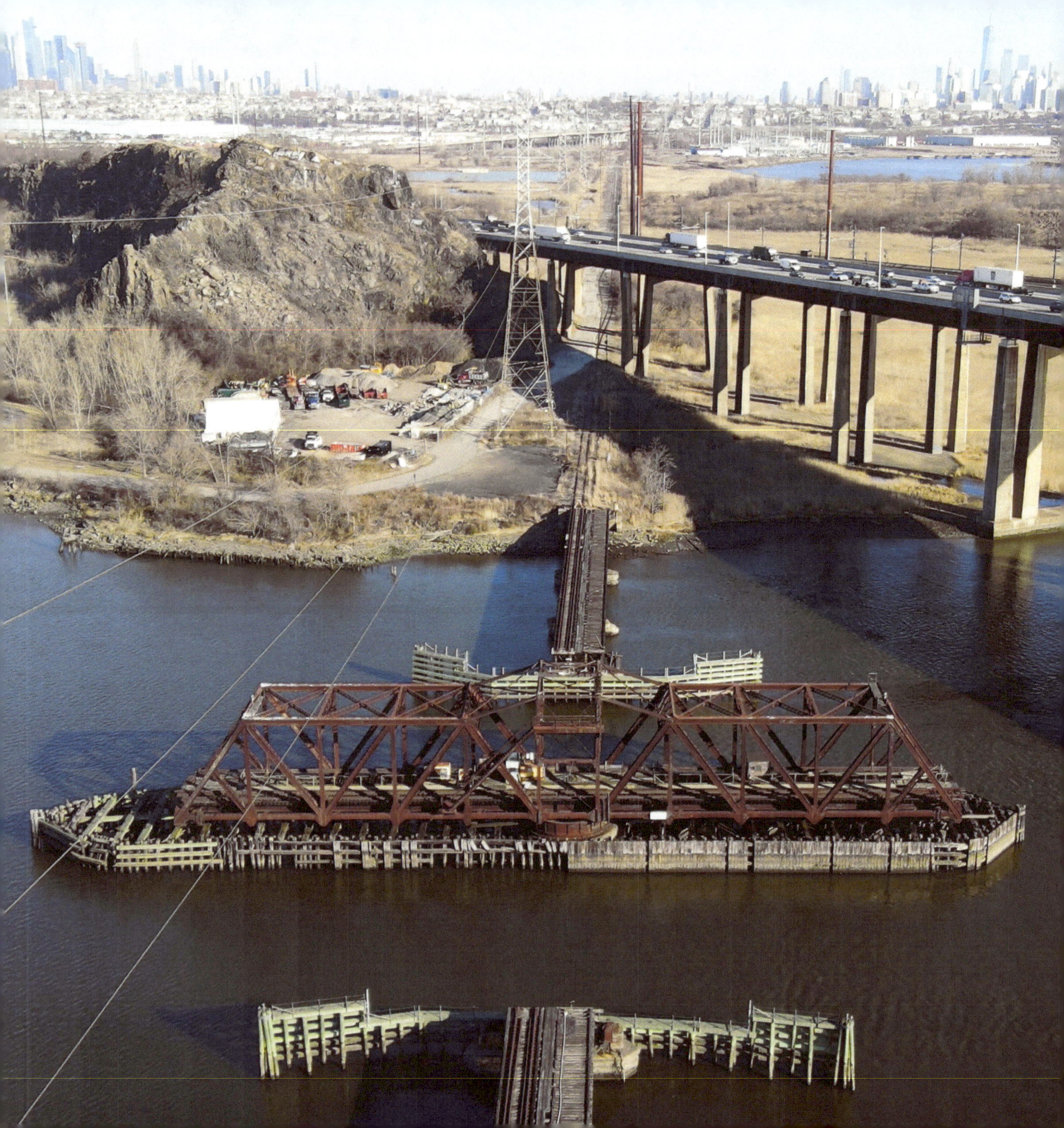

WALKING THE OLD BOONTON LINE

CONTENTS

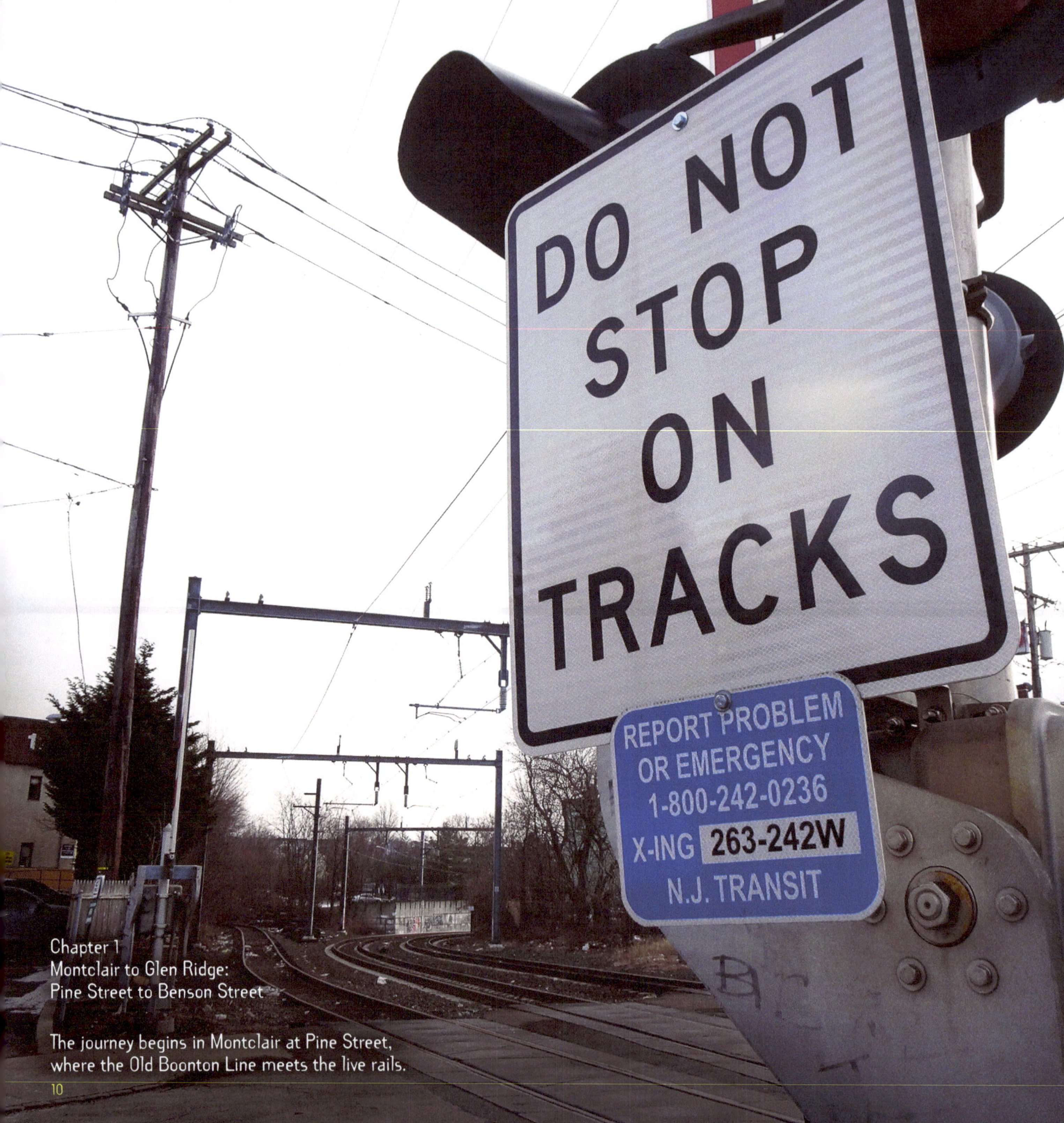

Chapter 1
Montclair to Glen Ridge:
Pine Street to Benson Street

The journey begins in Montclair at Pine Street, where the Old Boonton Line meets the live rails.

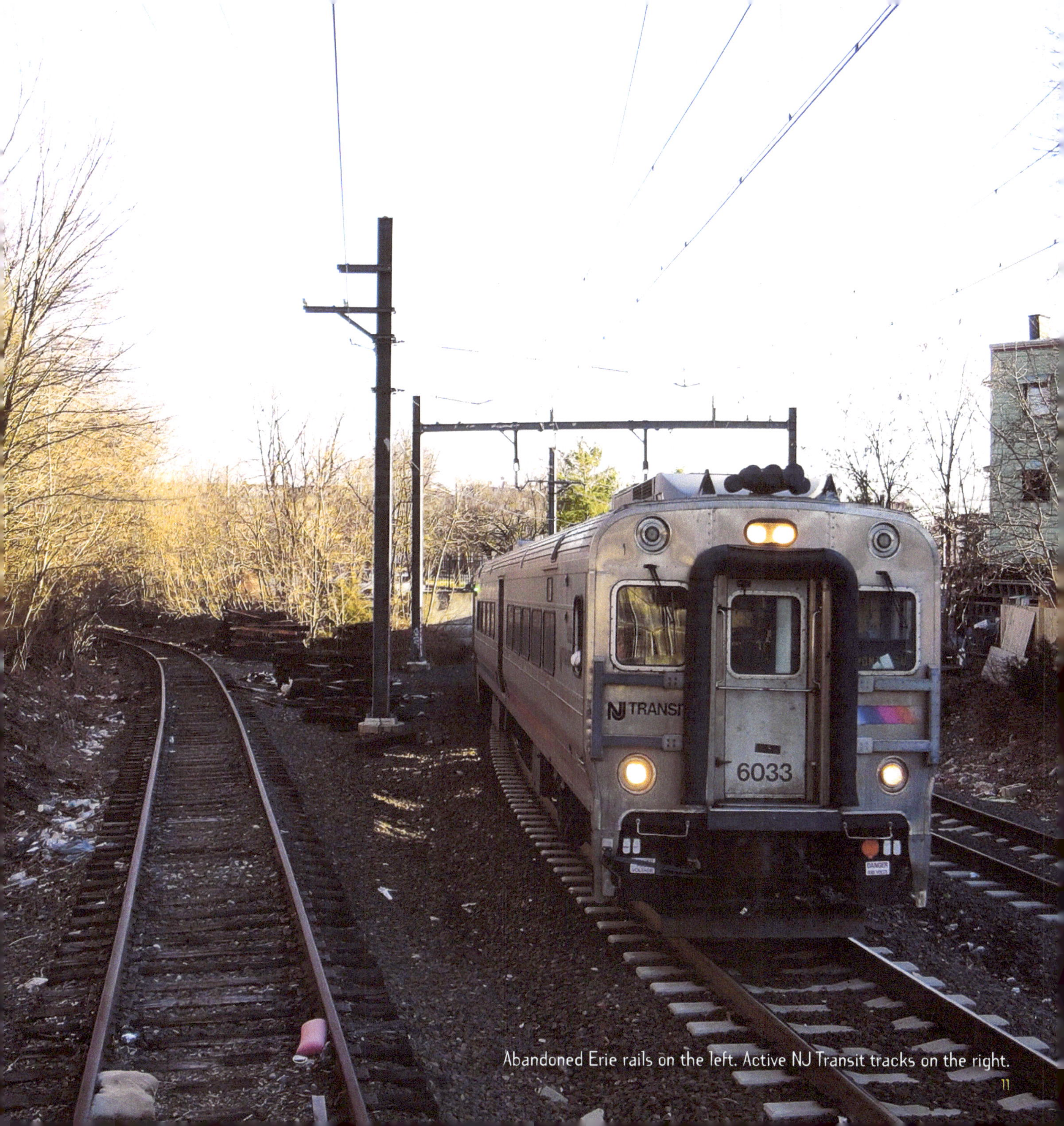

Abandoned Erie rails on the left. Active NJ Transit tracks on the right.

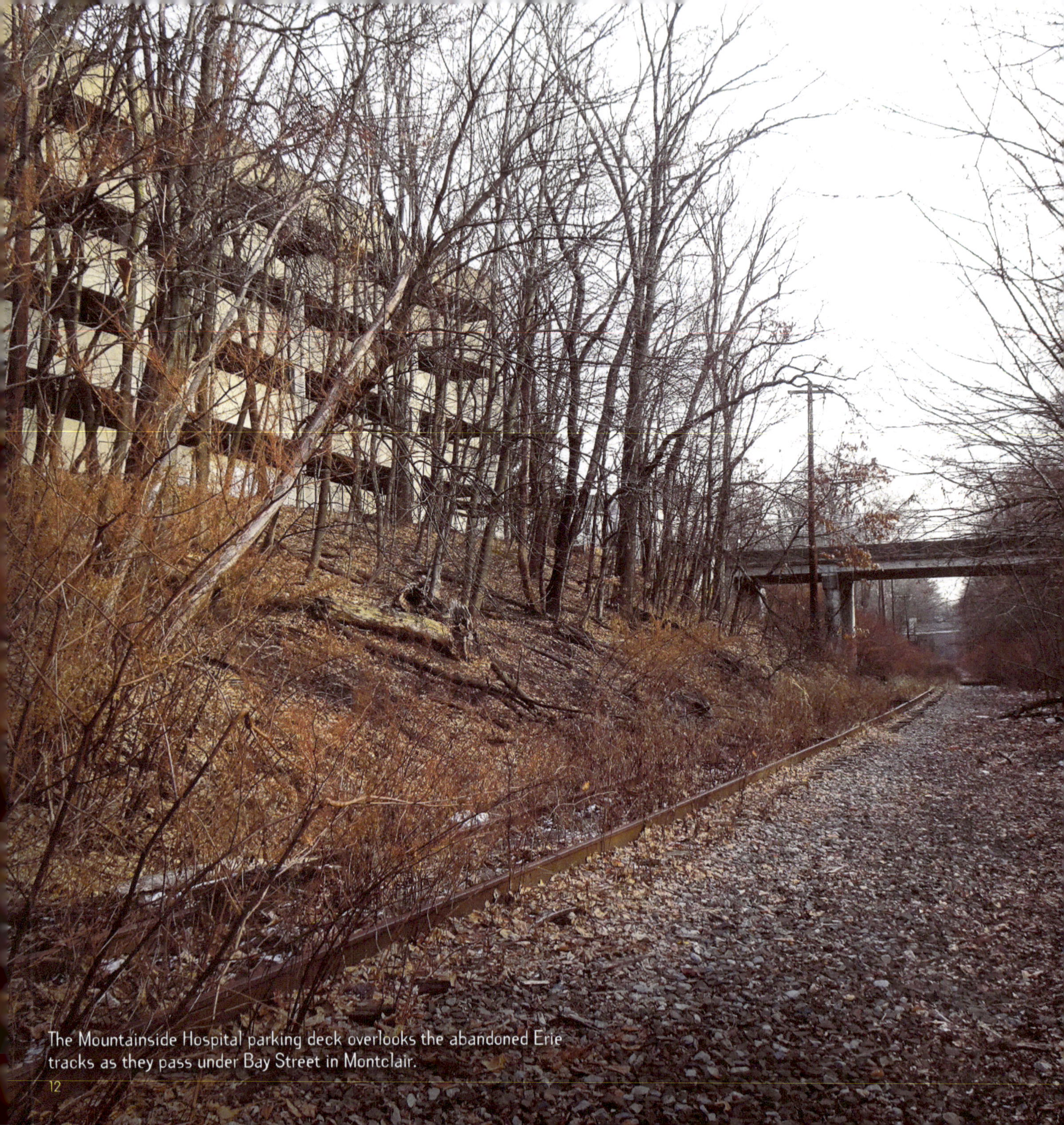

The Mountainside Hospital parking deck overlooks the abandoned Erie tracks as they pass under Bay Street in Montclair.

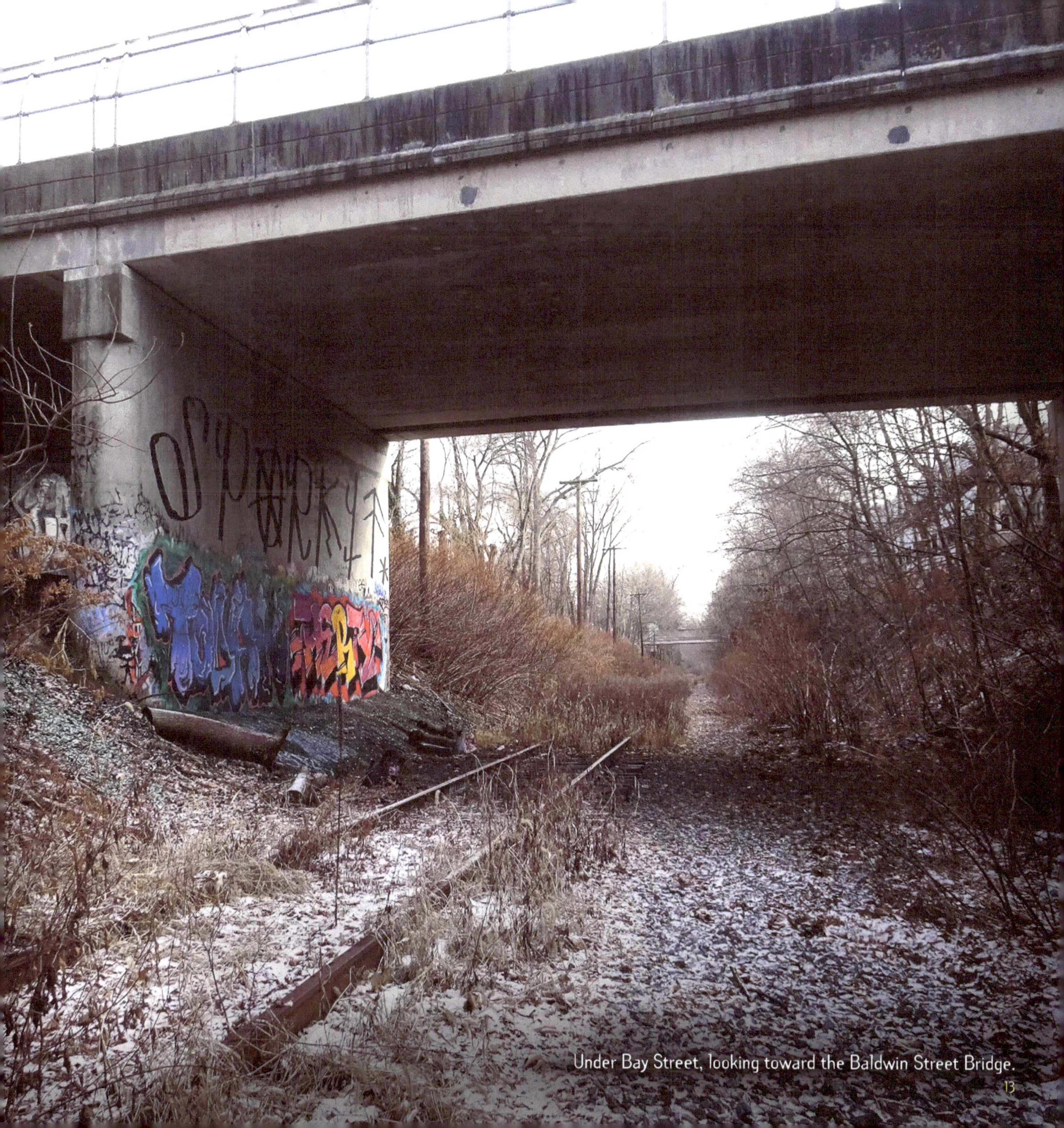

Under Bay Street, looking toward the Baldwin Street Bridge.

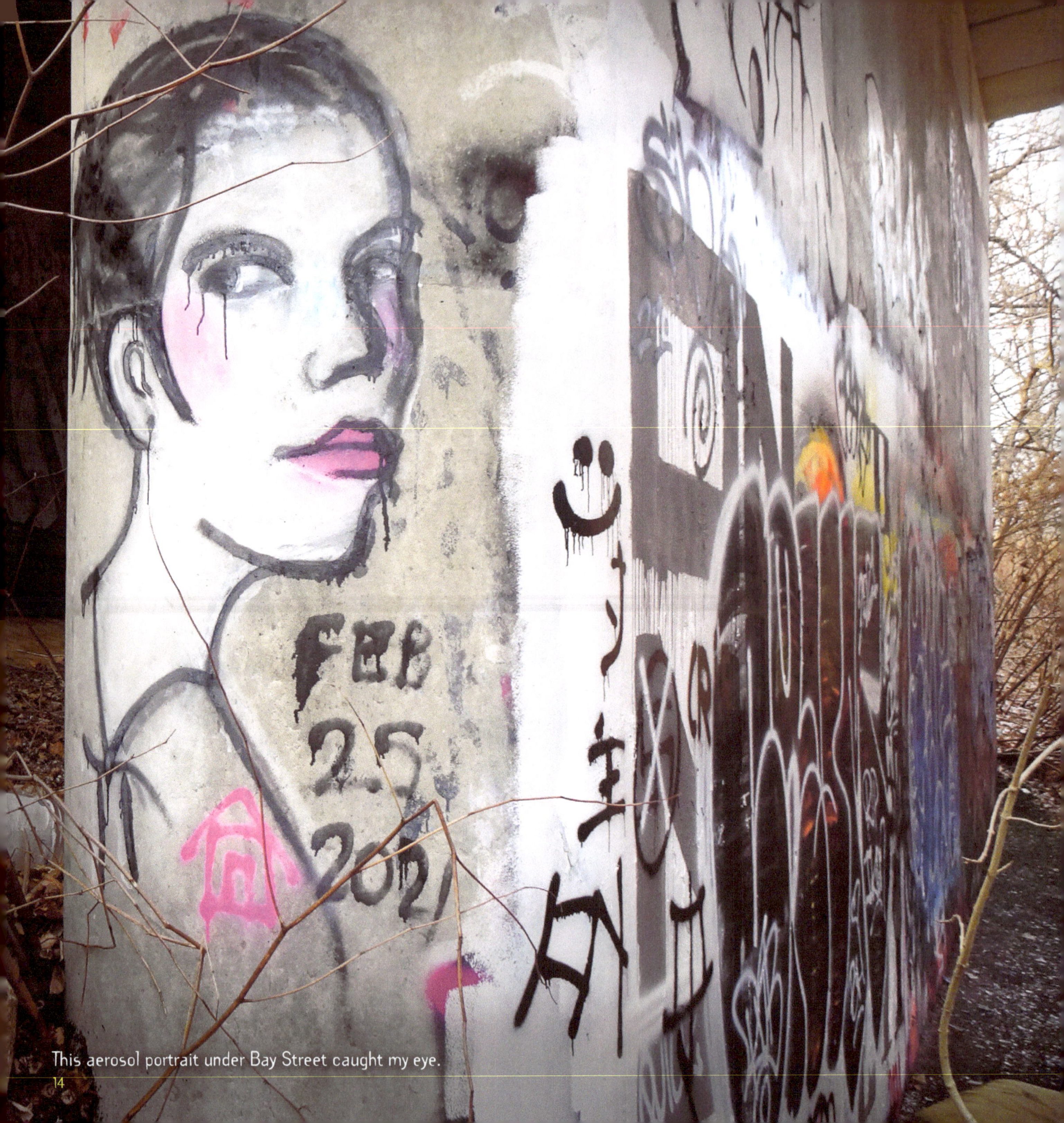

This aerosol portrait under Bay Street caught my eye.

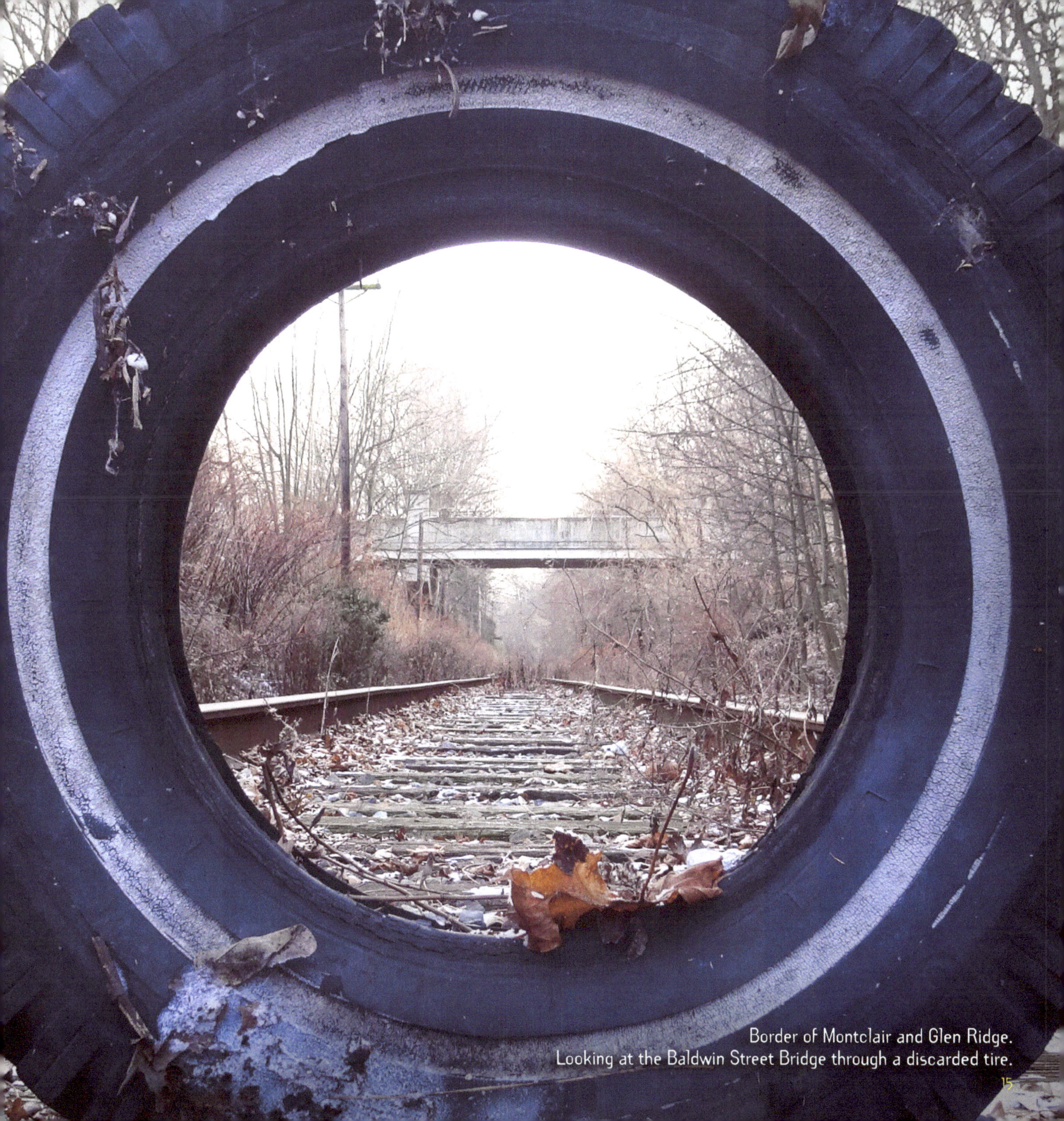
Border of Montclair and Glen Ridge.
Looking at the Baldwin Street Bridge through a discarded tire.

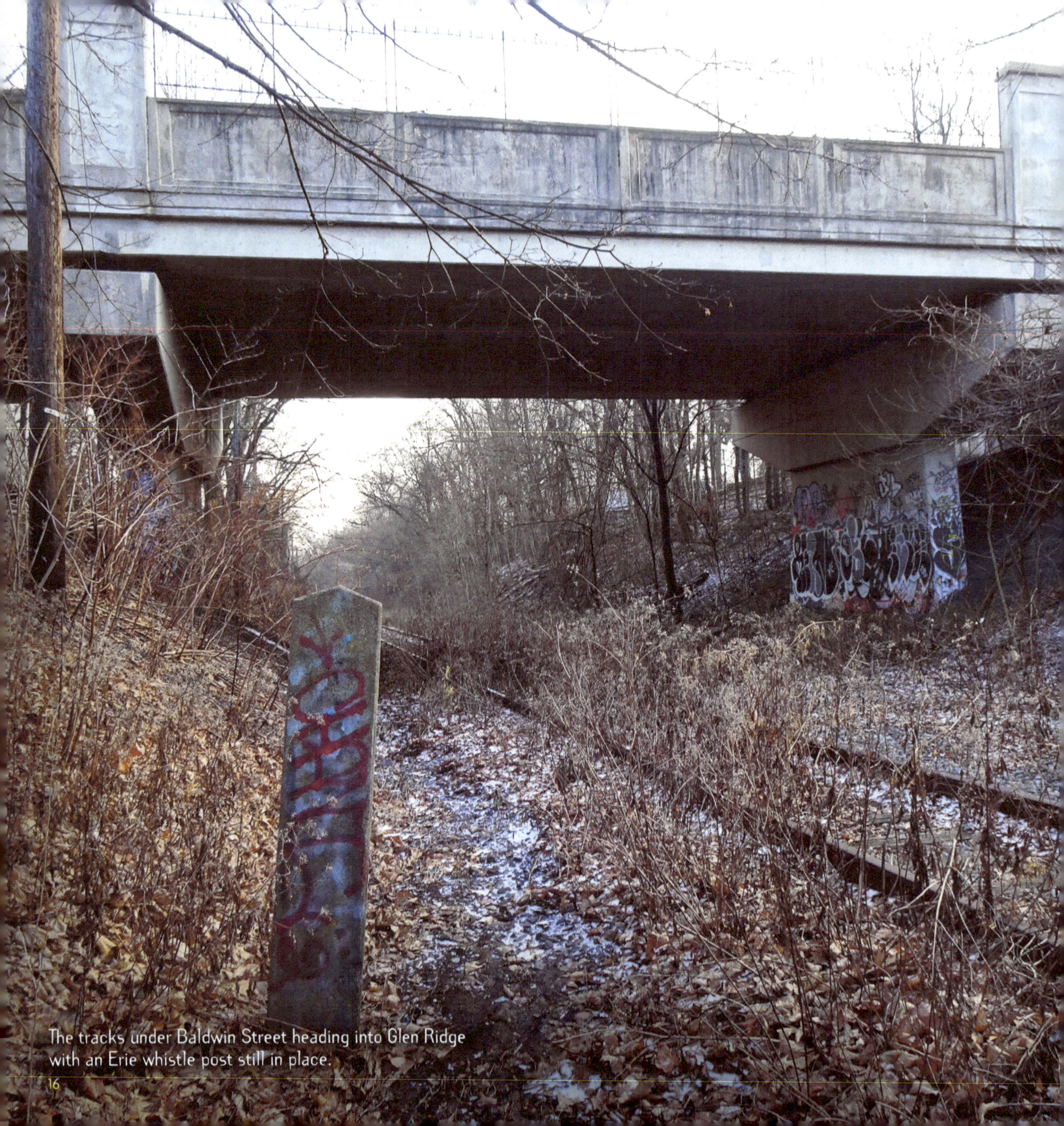

The tracks under Baldwin Street heading into Glen Ridge with an Erie whistle post still in place.

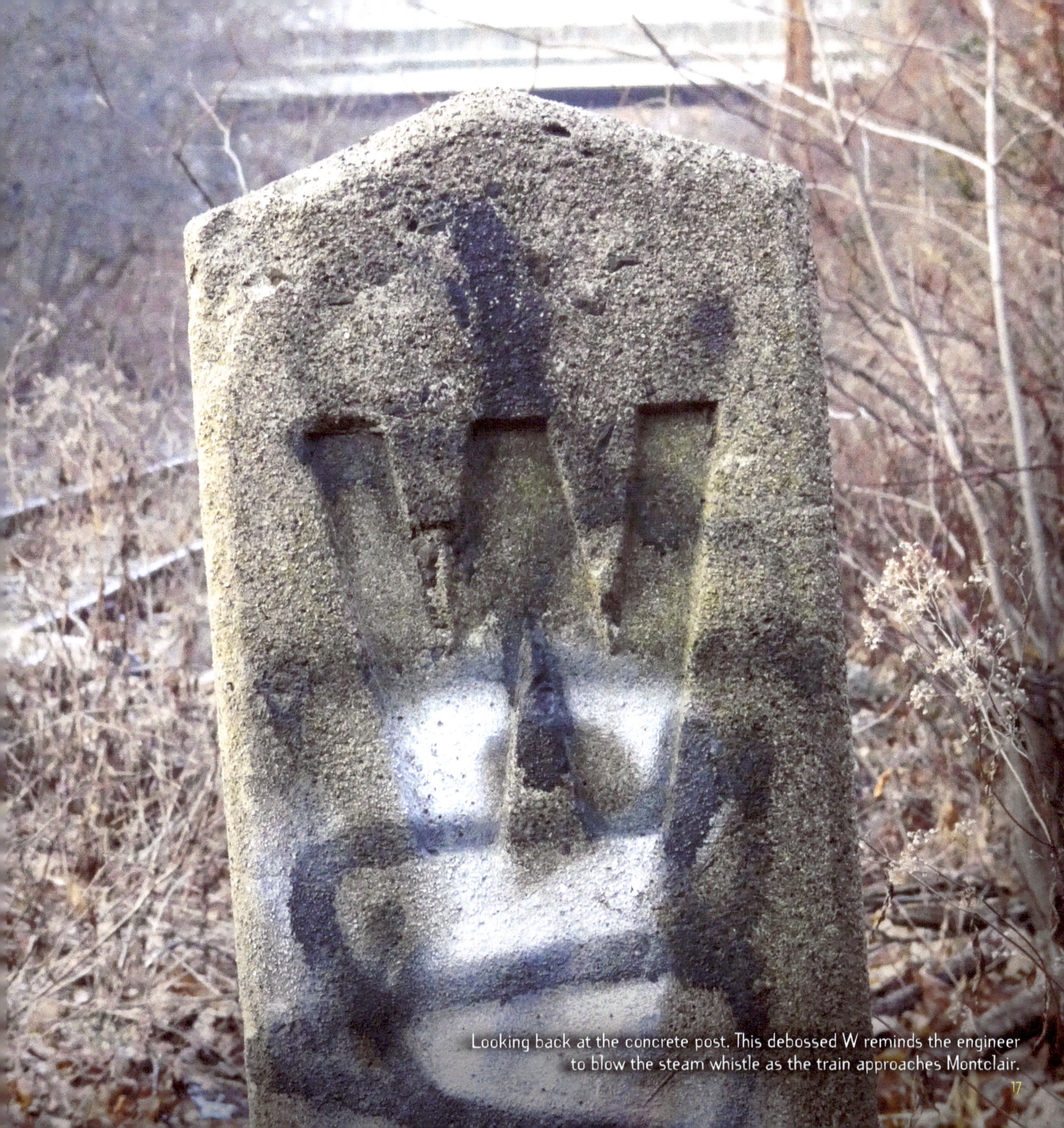

Looking back at the concrete post. This debossed W reminds the engineer to blow the steam whistle as the train approaches Montclair.

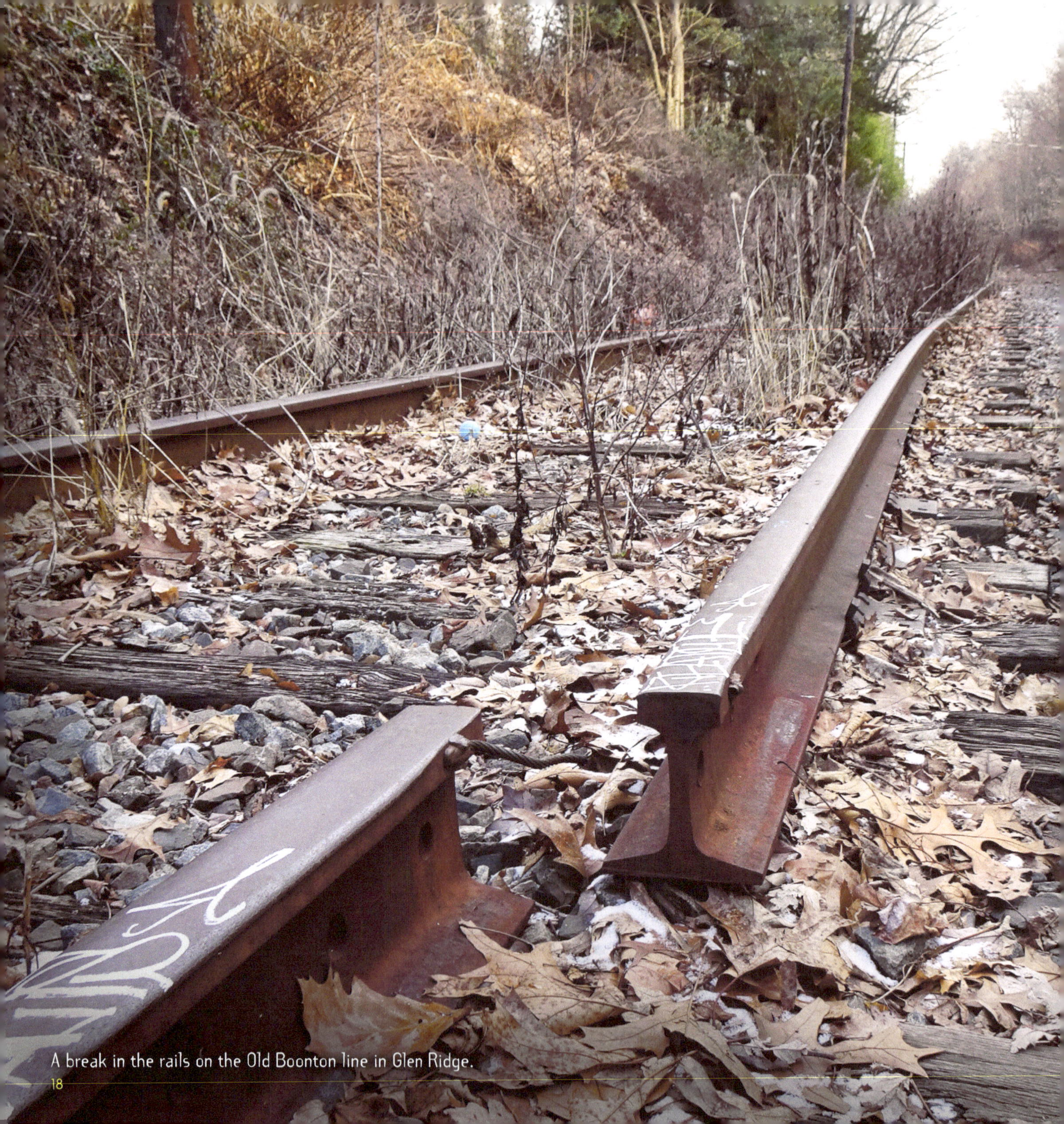

A break in the rails on the Old Boonton line in Glen Ridge.

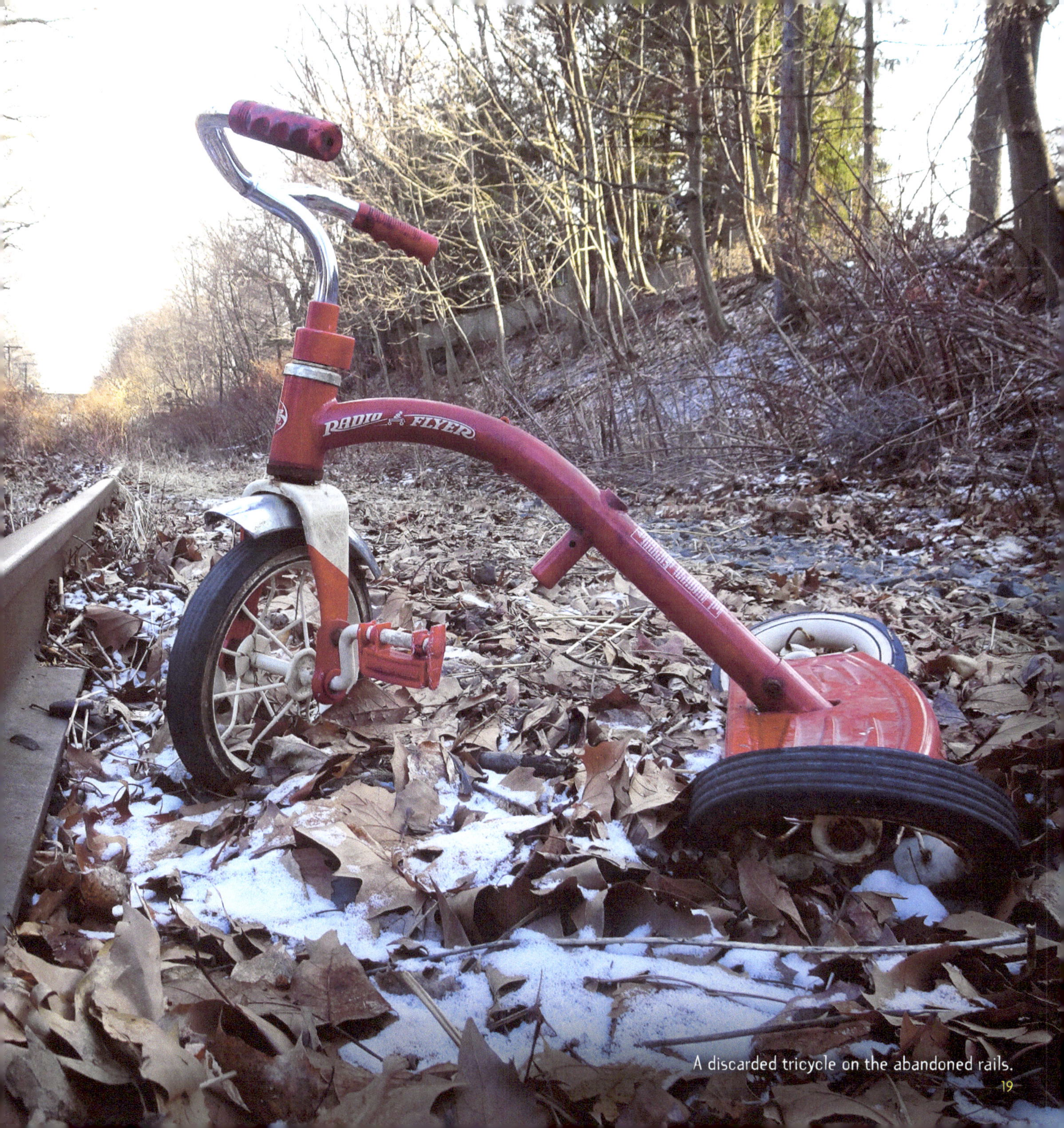

A discarded tricycle on the abandoned rails.

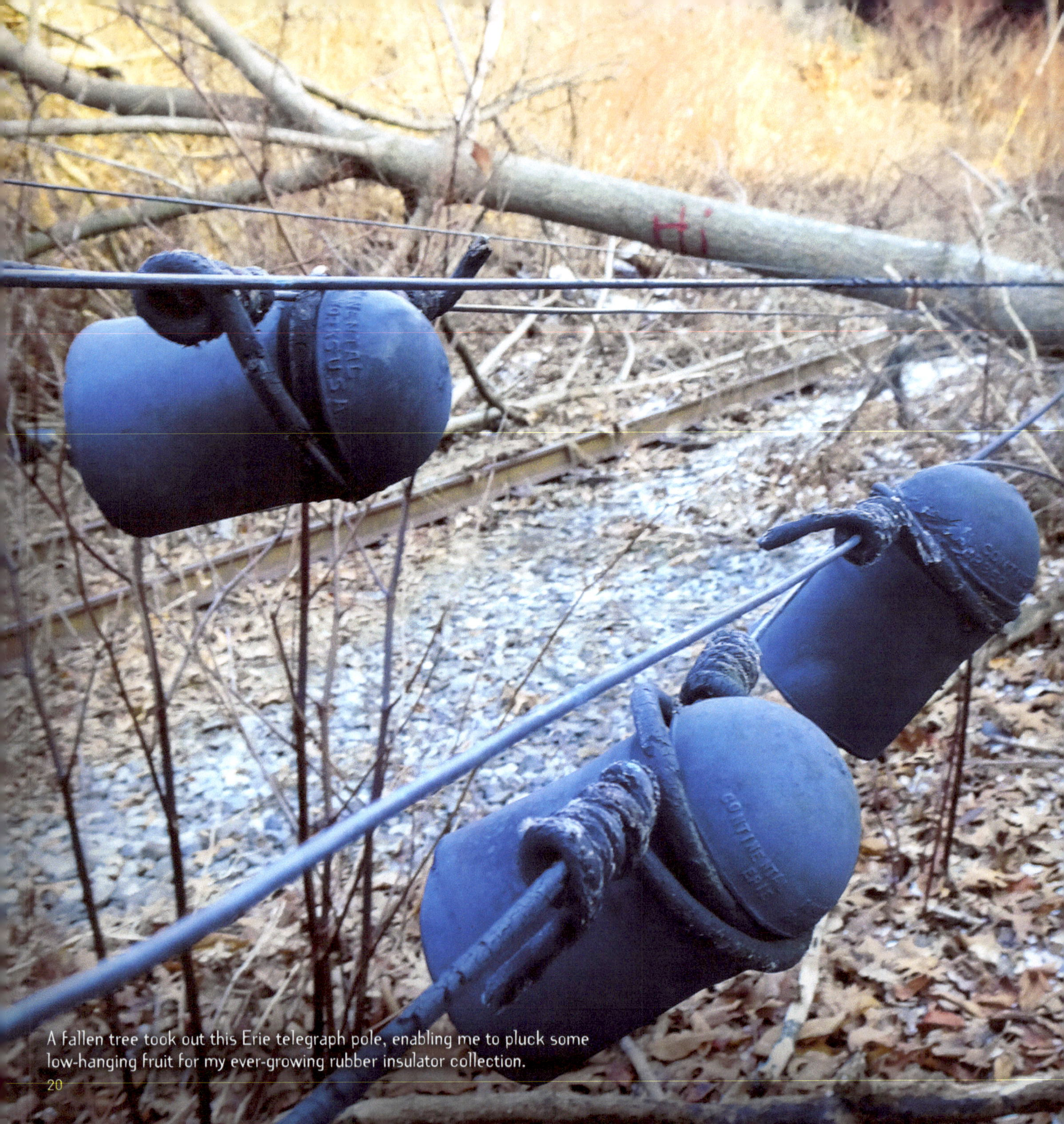

A fallen tree took out this Erie telegraph pole, enabling me to pluck some low-hanging fruit for my ever-growing rubber insulator collection.

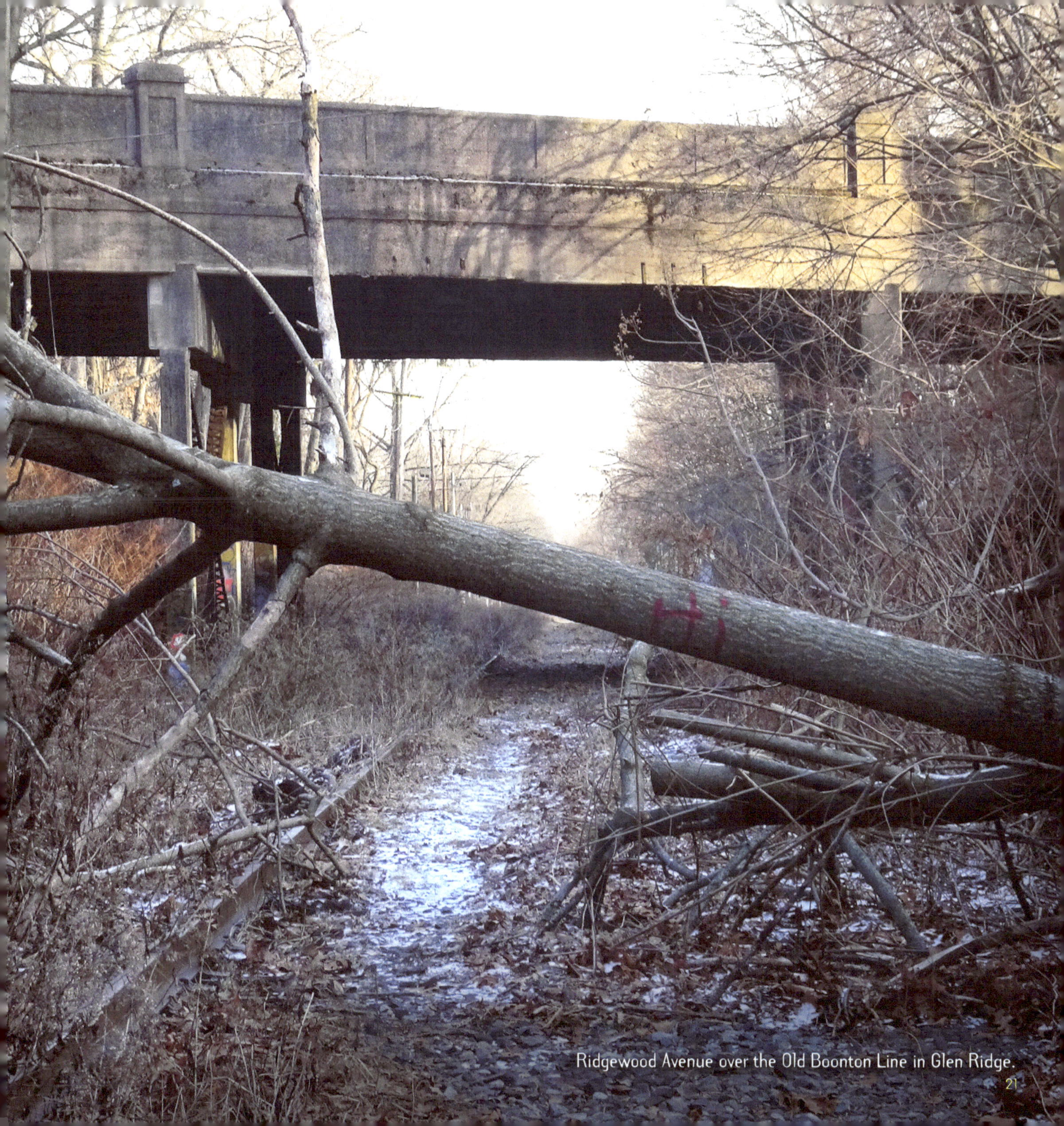

Ridgewood Avenue over the Old Boonton Line in Glen Ridge.

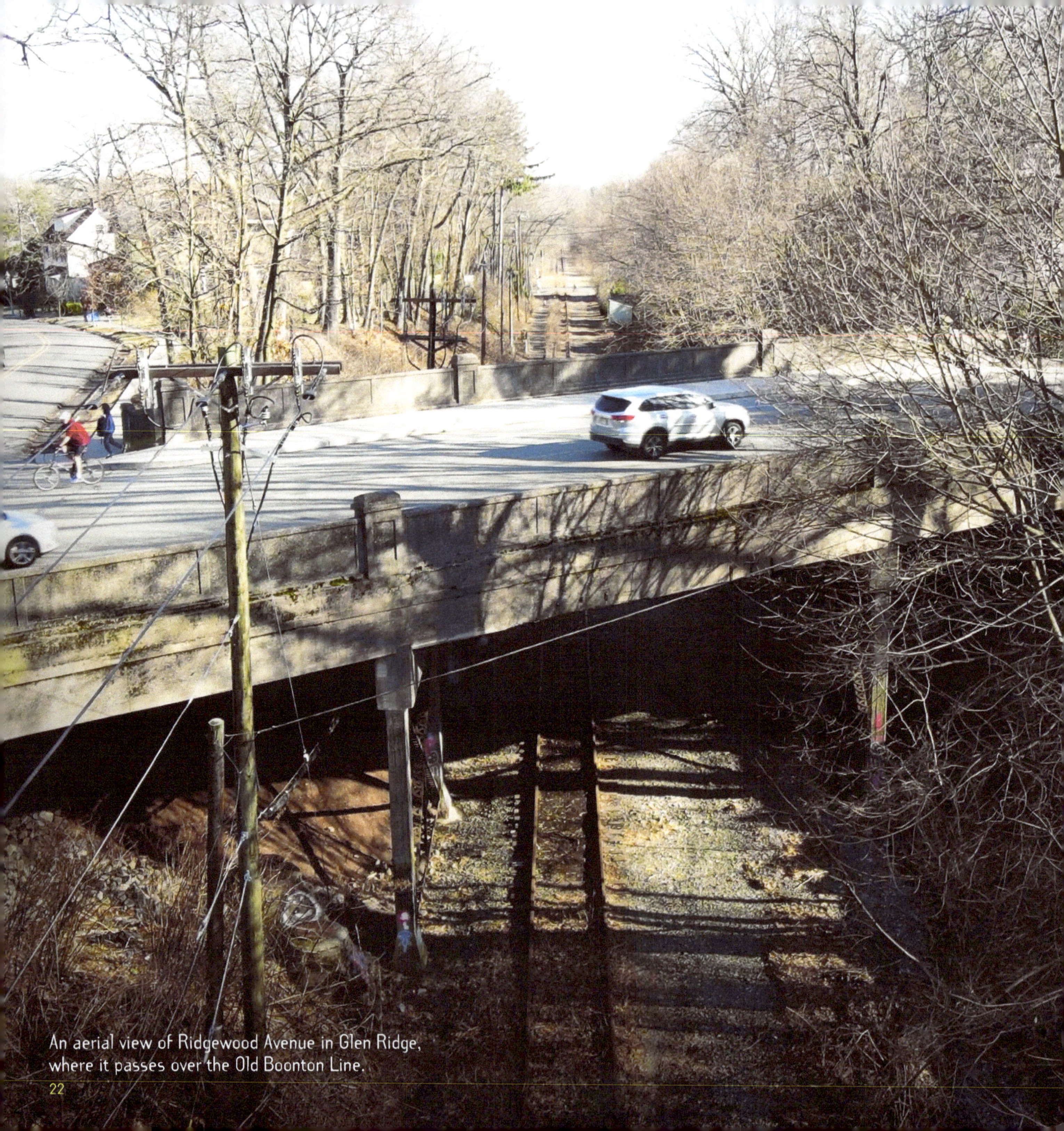

An aerial view of Ridgewood Avenue in Glen Ridge, where it passes over the Old Boonton Line.

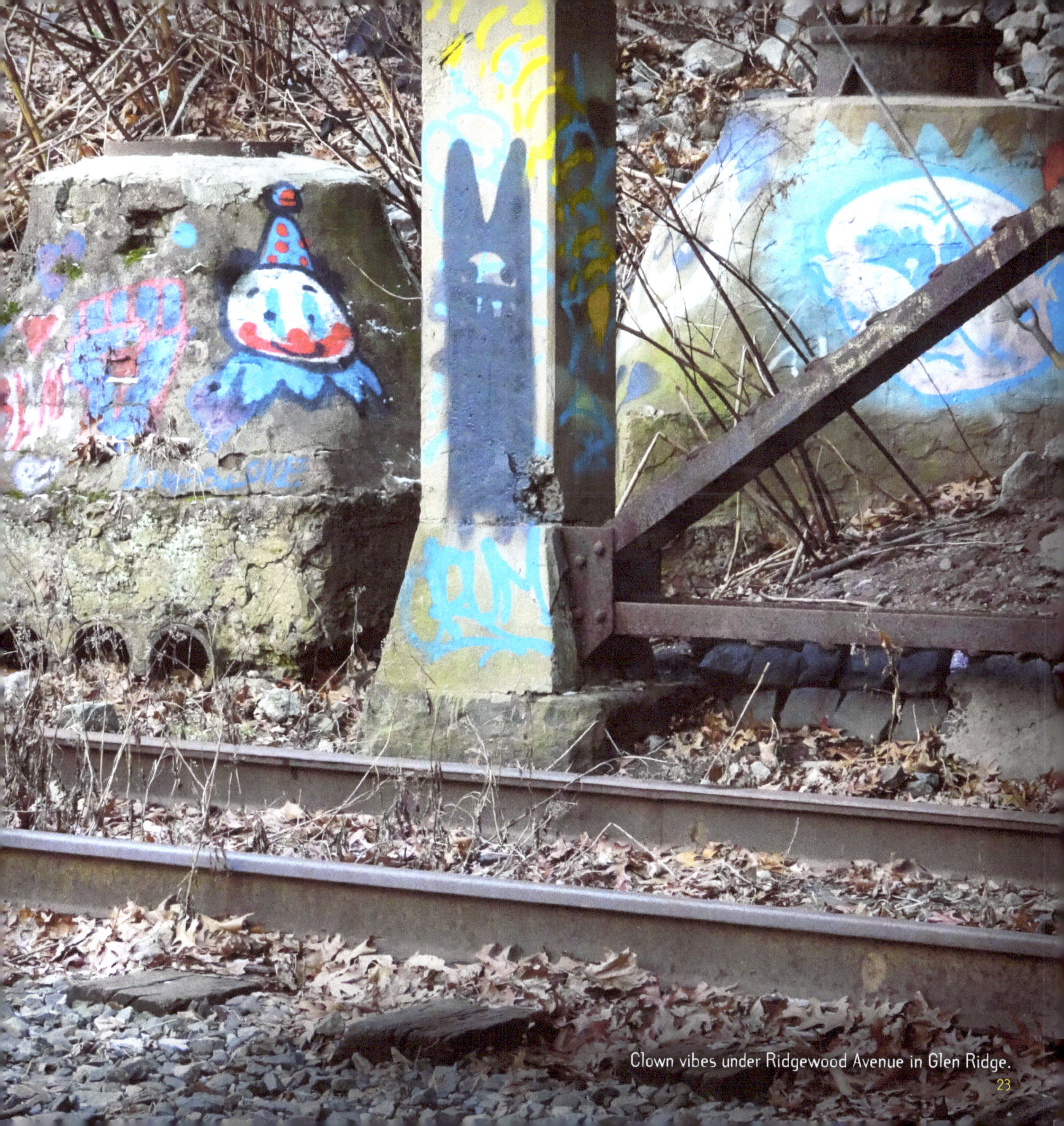

Clown vibes under Ridgewood Avenue in Glen Ridge.

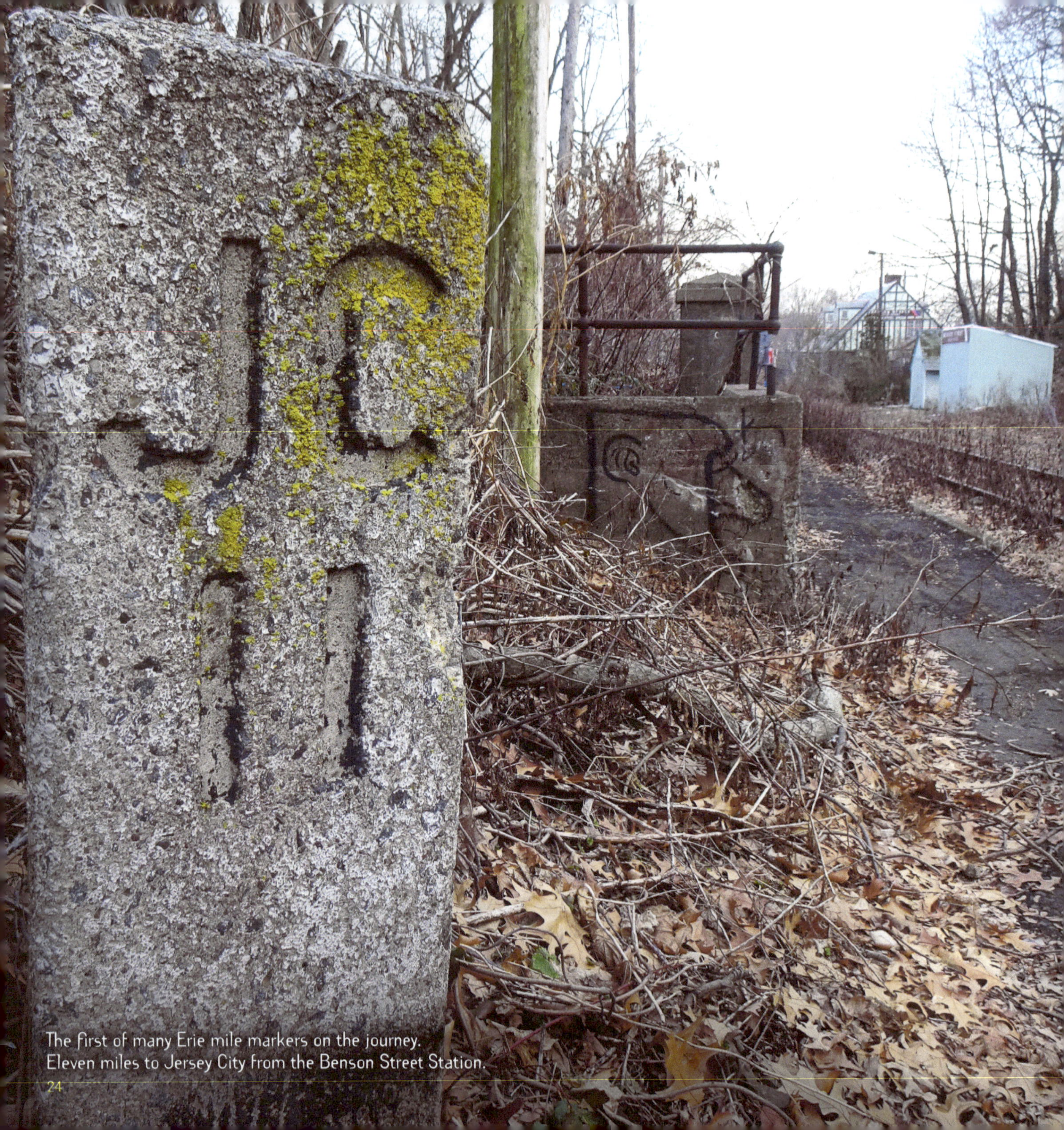

The first of many Erie mile markers on the journey.
Eleven miles to Jersey City from the Benson Street Station.

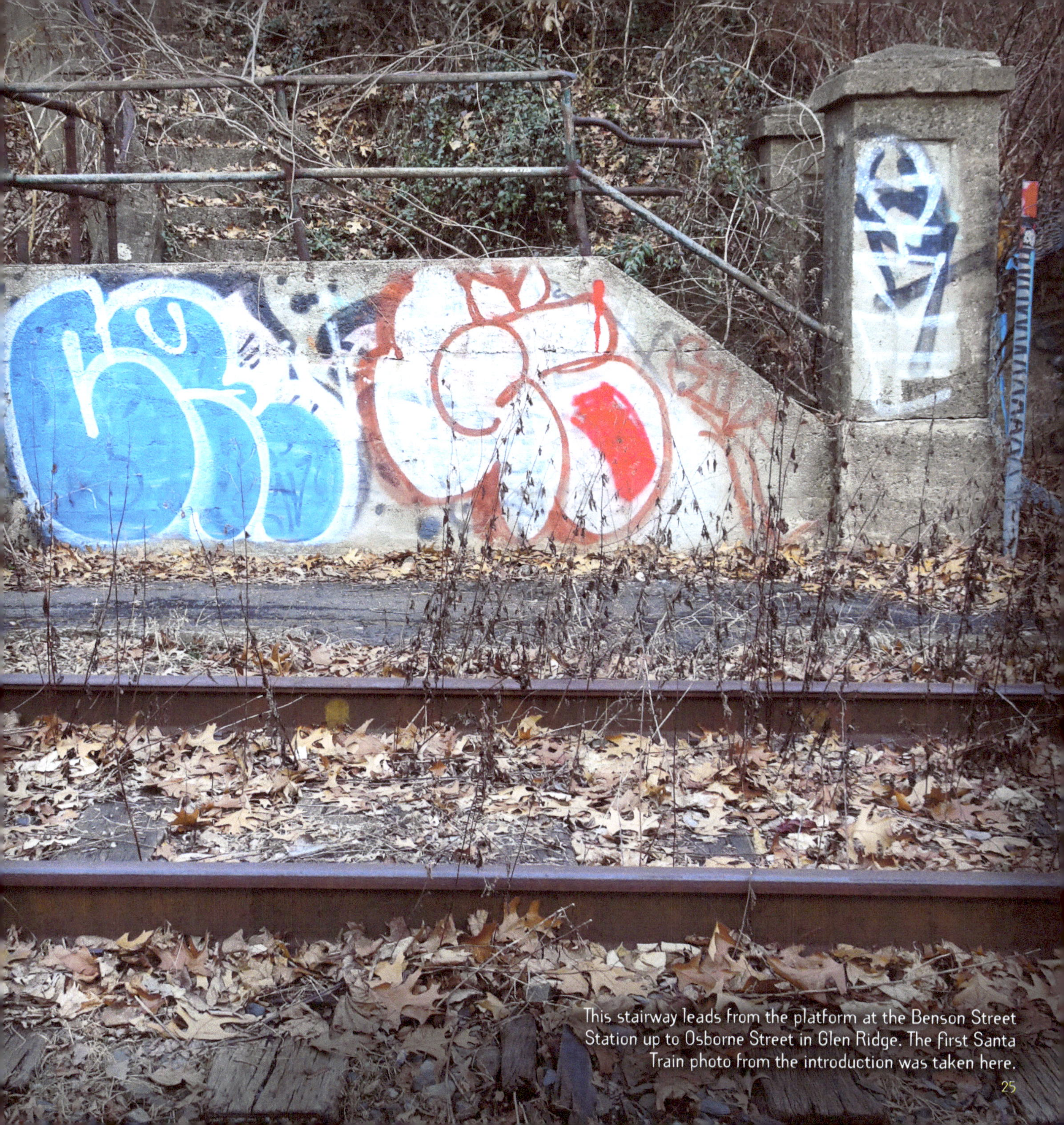

This stairway leads from the platform at the Benson Street Station up to Osborne Street in Glen Ridge. The first Santa Train photo from the introduction was taken here.

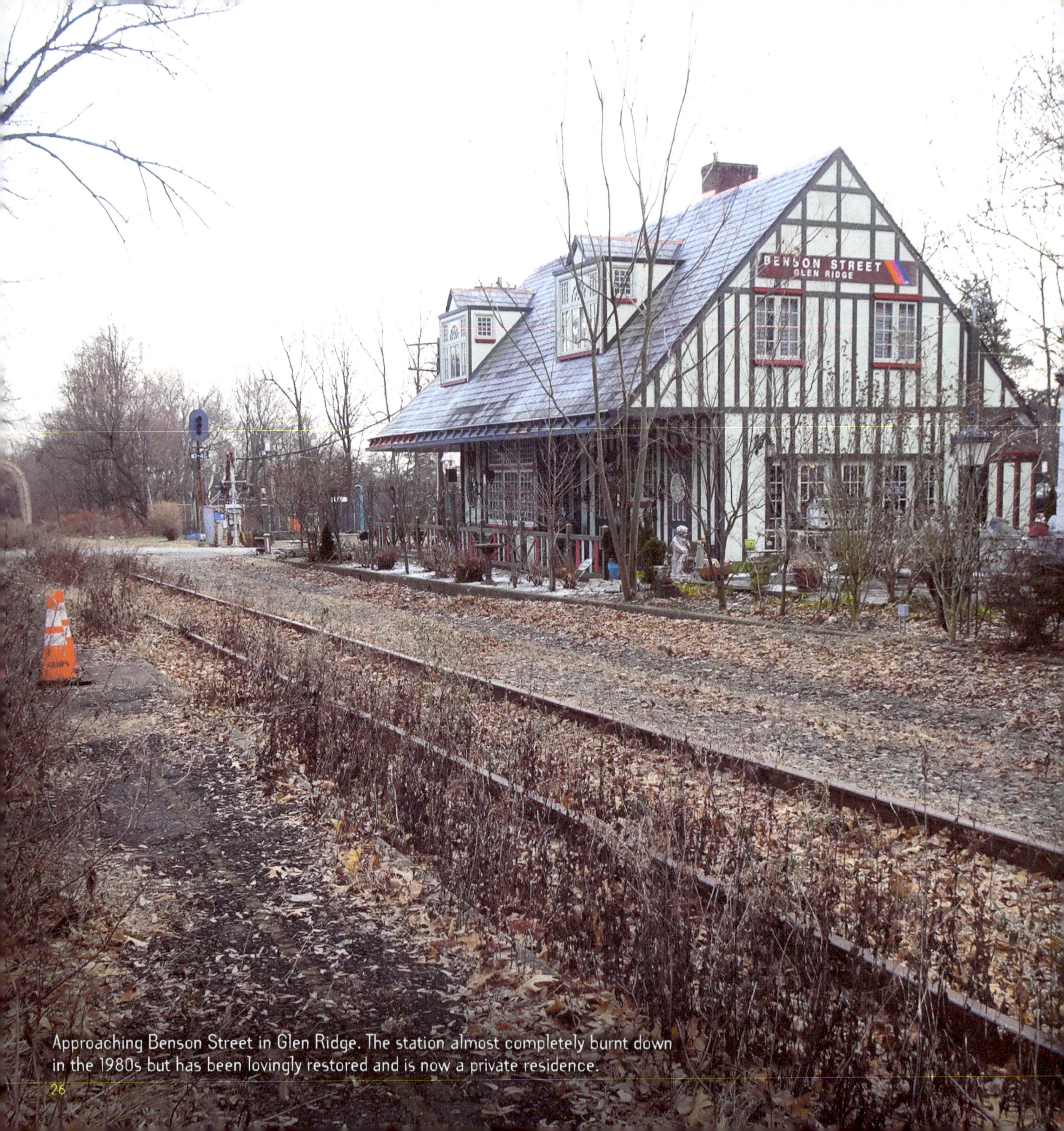

Approaching Benson Street in Glen Ridge. The station almost completely burnt down in the 1980s but has been lovingly restored and is now a private residence.

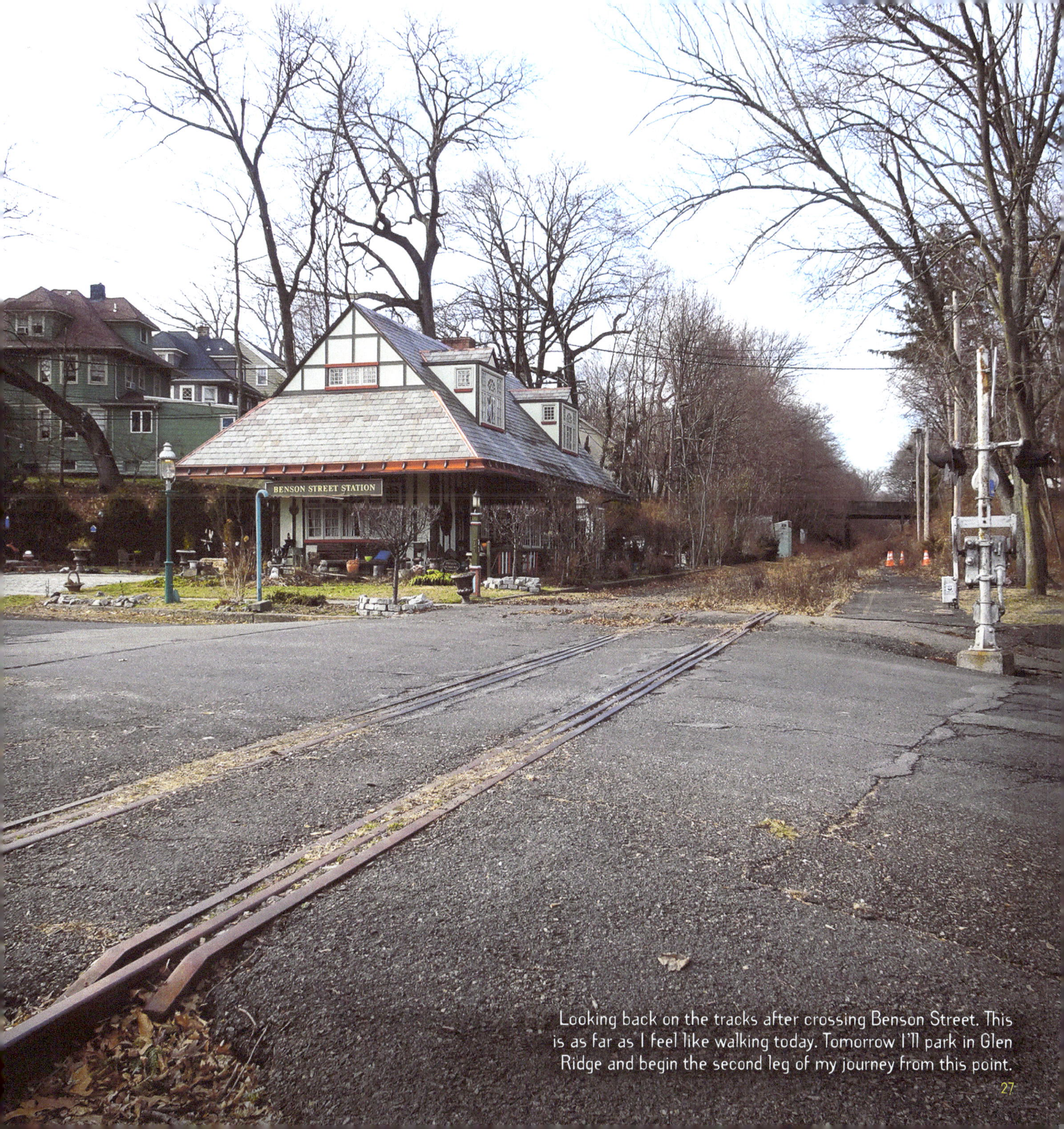

Looking back on the tracks after crossing Benson Street. This is as far as I feel like walking today. Tomorrow I'll park in Glen Ridge and begin the second leg of my journey from this point.

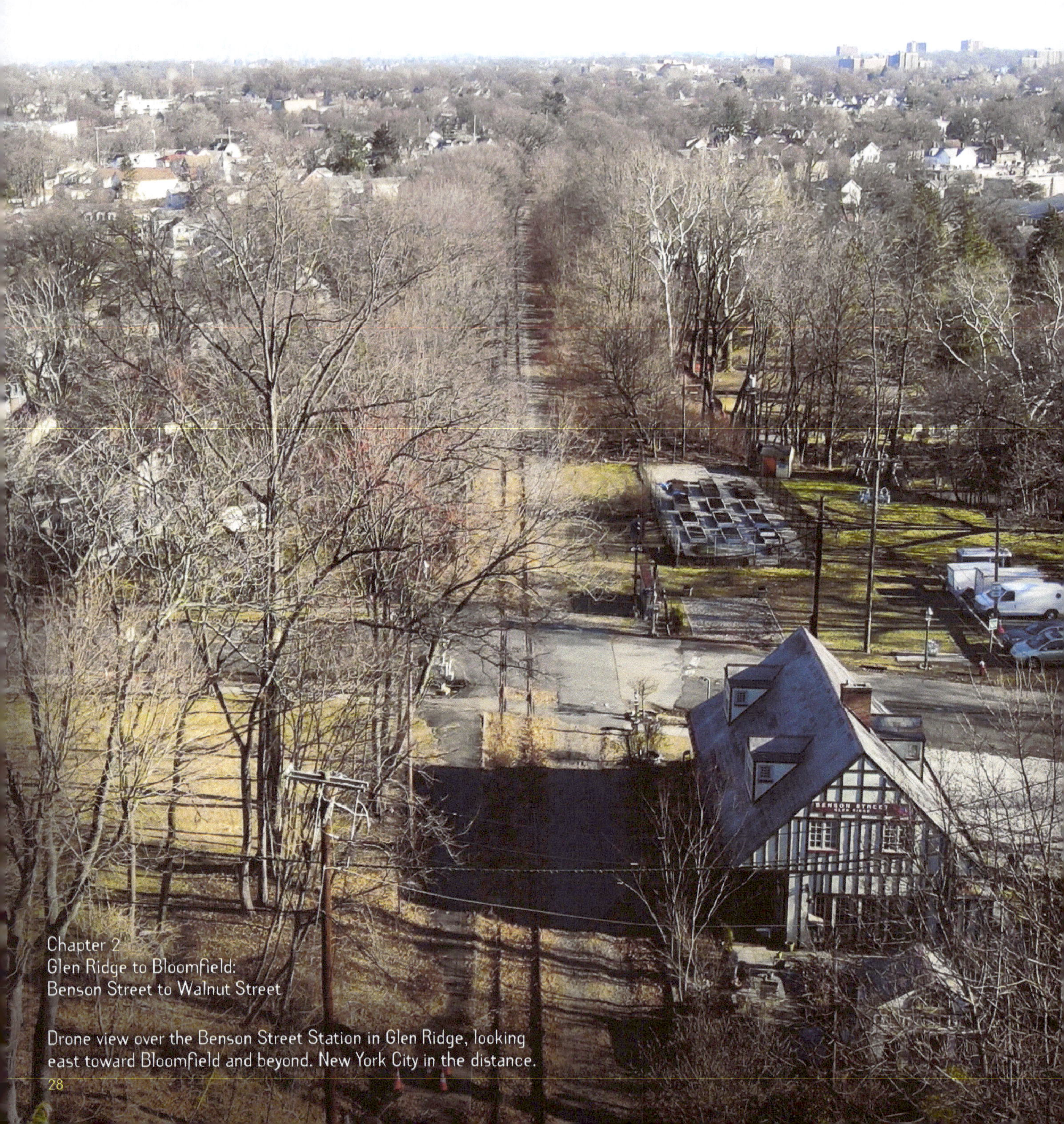

Chapter 2
Glen Ridge to Bloomfield:
Benson Street to Walnut Street

Drone view over the Benson Street Station in Glen Ridge, looking east toward Bloomfield and beyond. New York City in the distance.

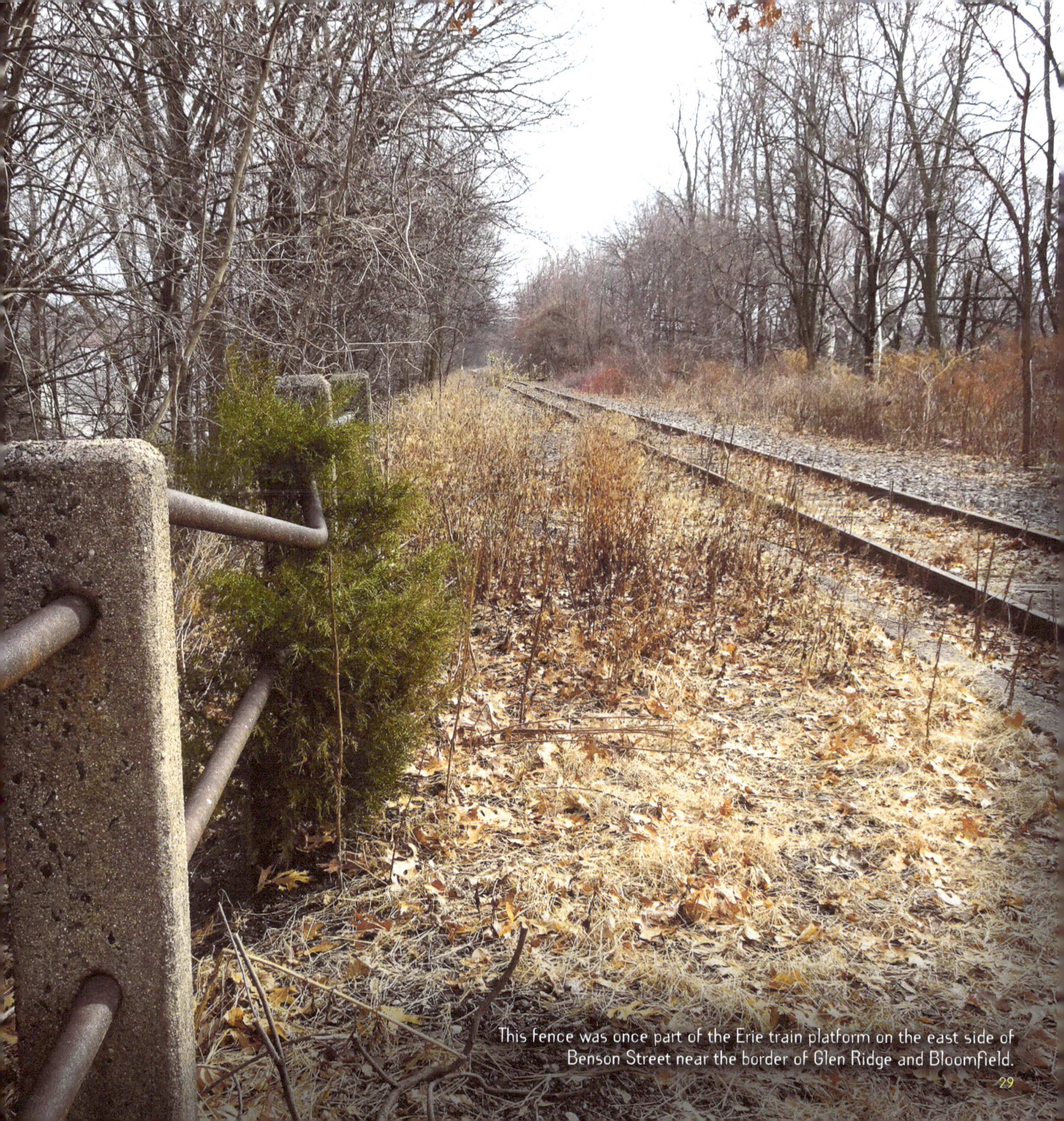

This fence was once part of the Erie train platform on the east side of Benson Street near the border of Glen Ridge and Bloomfield.

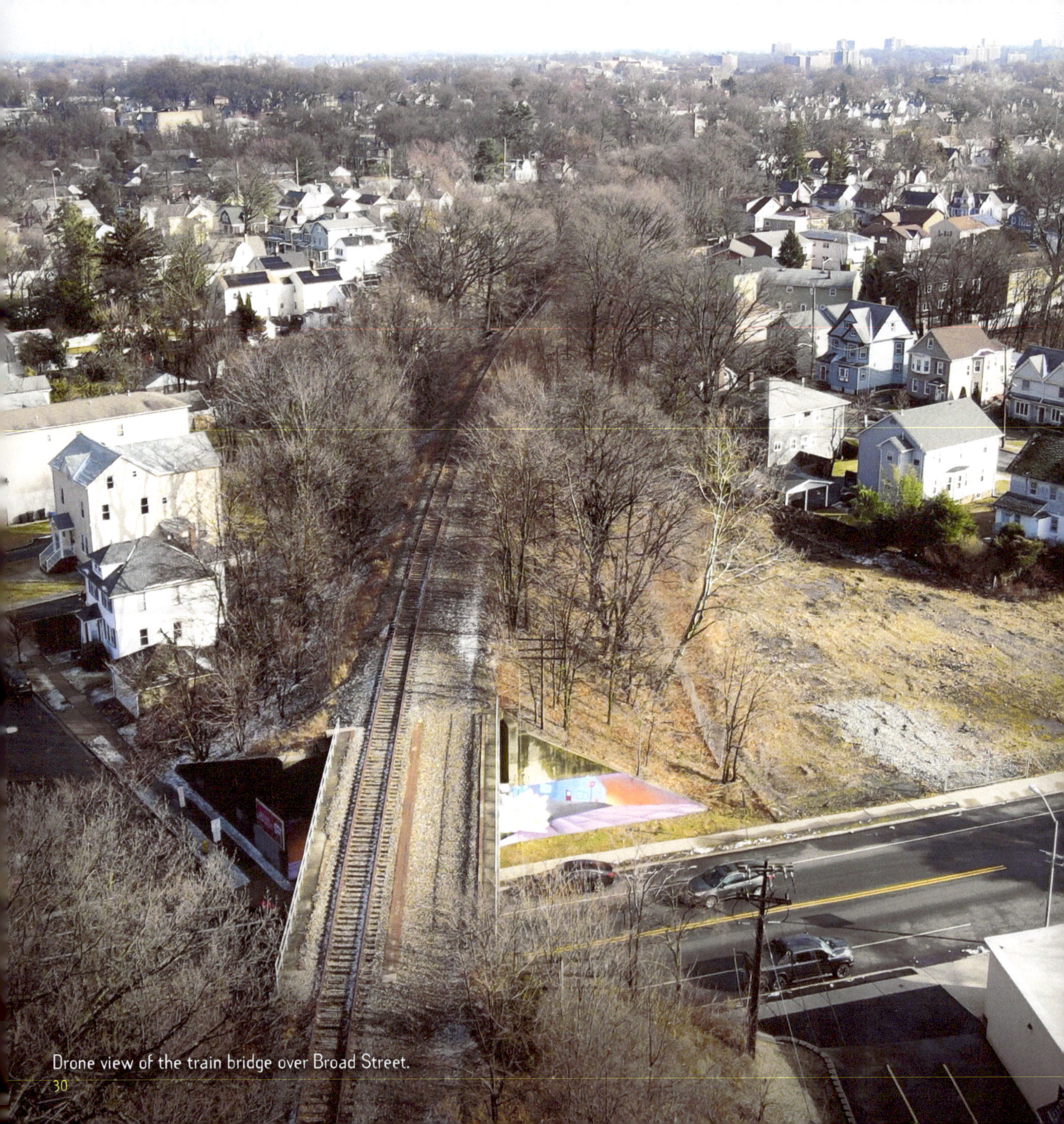

Drone view of the train bridge over Broad Street.

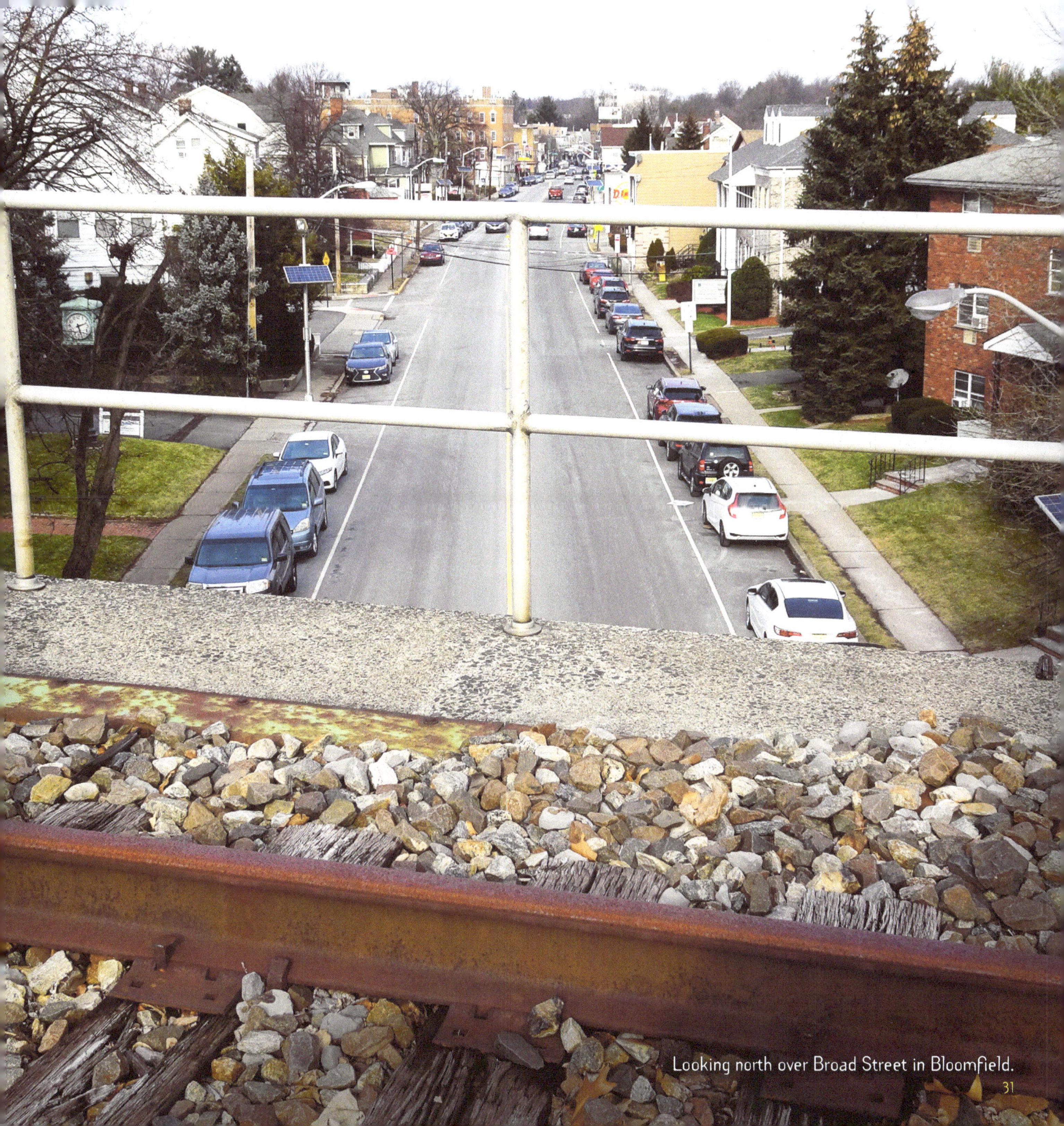

Looking north over Broad Street in Bloomfield.

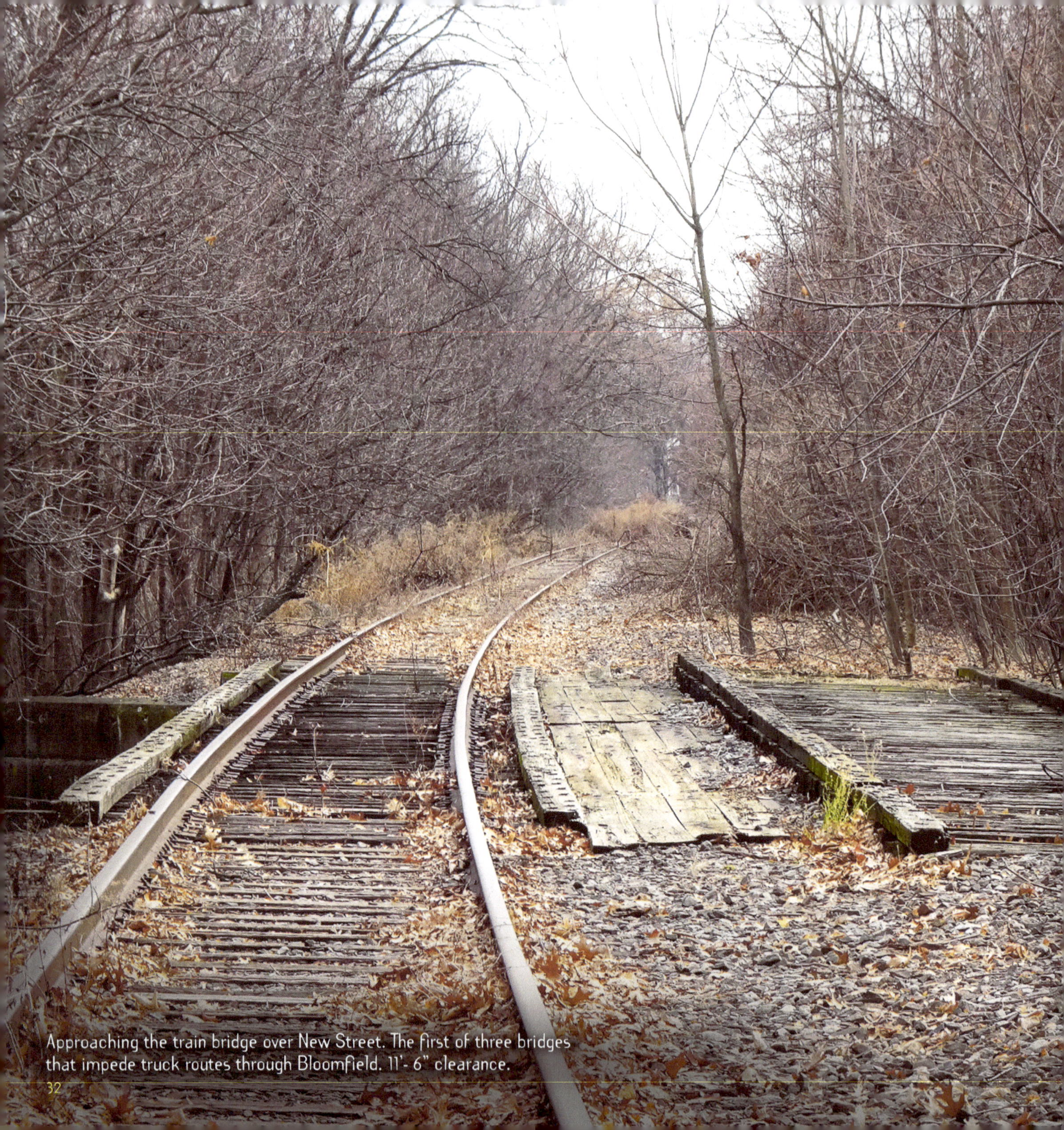

Approaching the train bridge over New Street. The first of three bridges that impede truck routes through Bloomfield. 11'- 6" clearance.

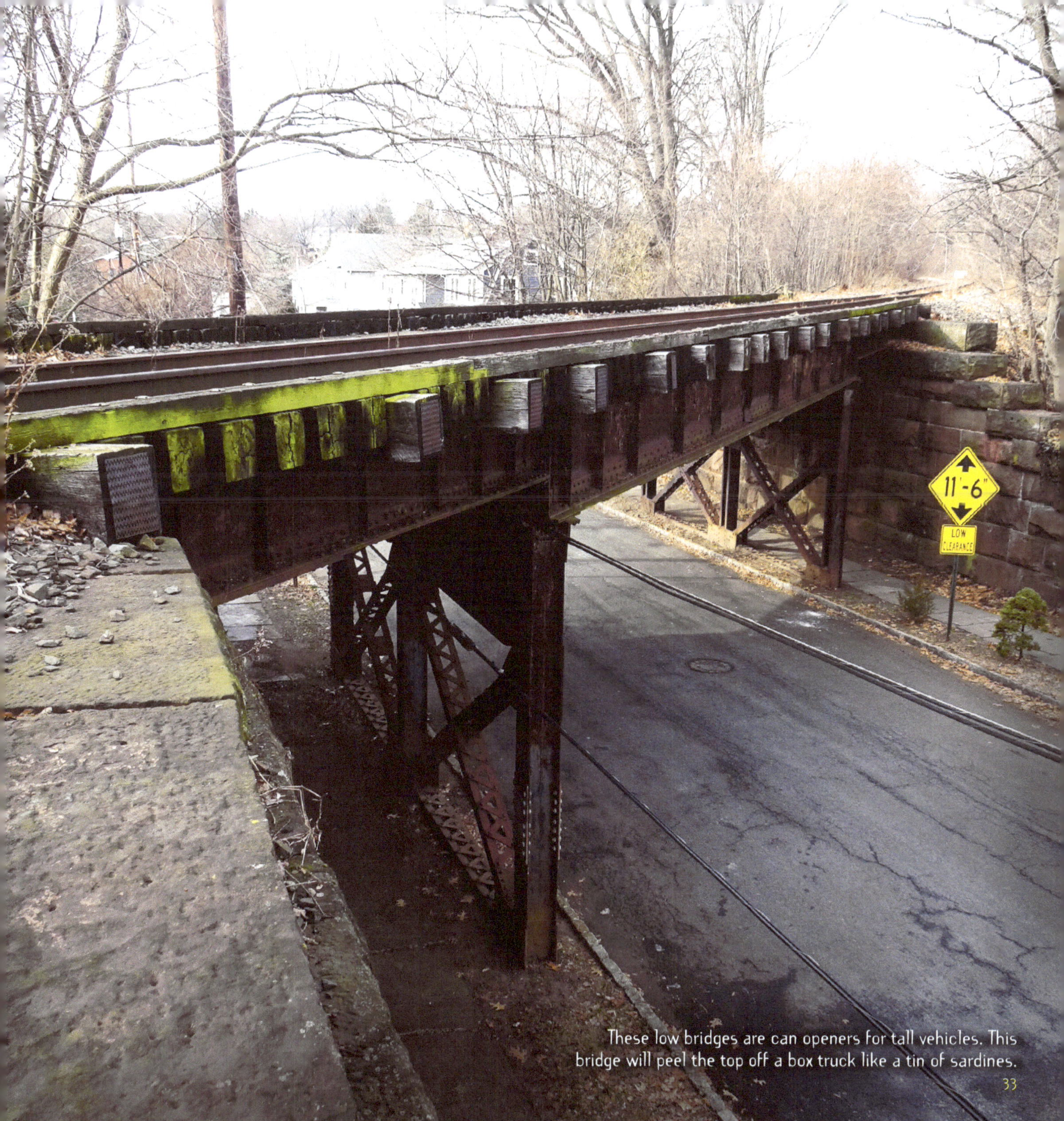

These low bridges are can openers for tall vehicles. This bridge will peel the top off a box truck like a tin of sardines.

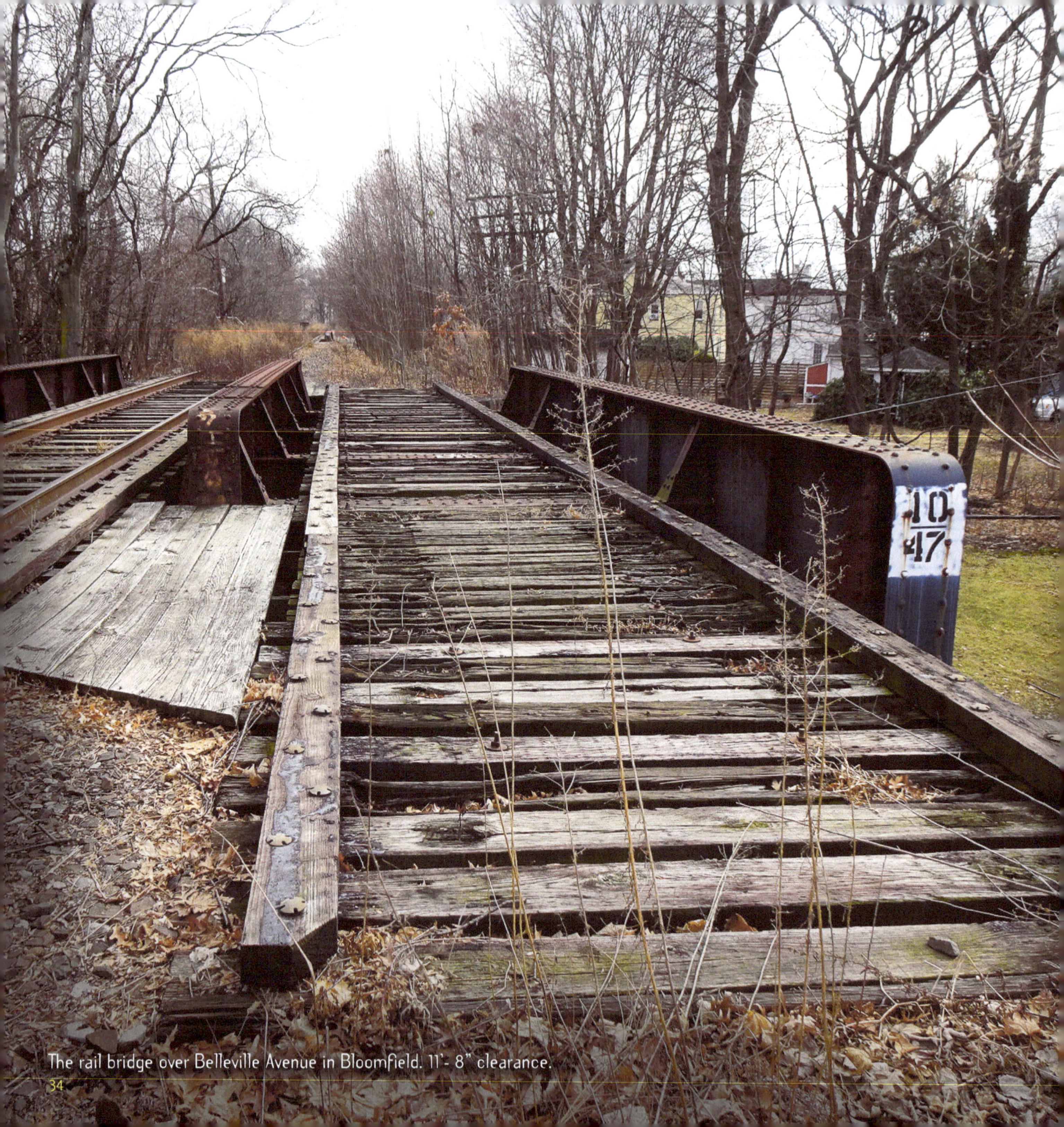

The rail bridge over Belleville Avenue in Bloomfield. 11'- 8" clearance.

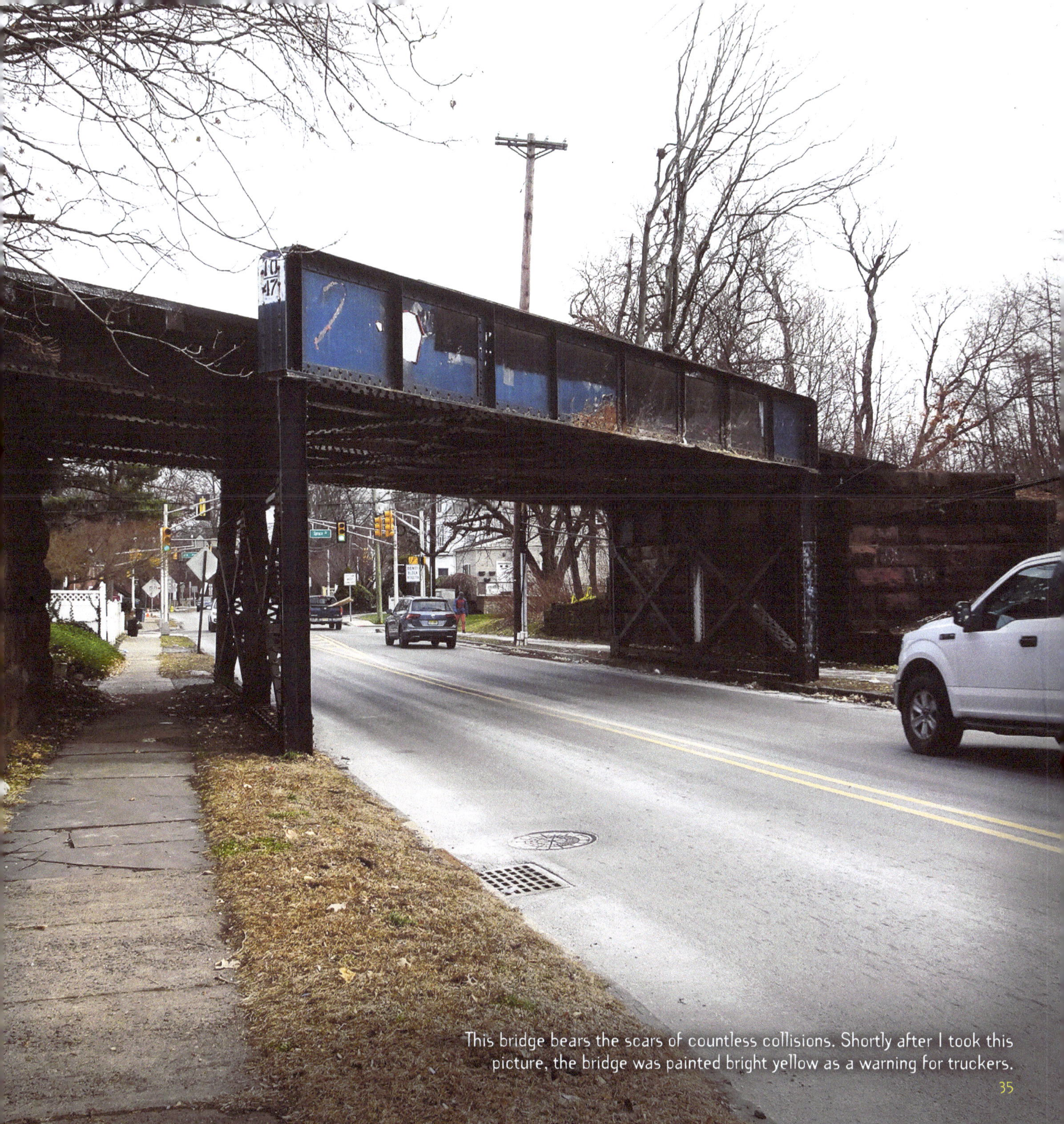

This bridge bears the scars of countless collisions. Shortly after I took this picture, the bridge was painted bright yellow as a warning for truckers.

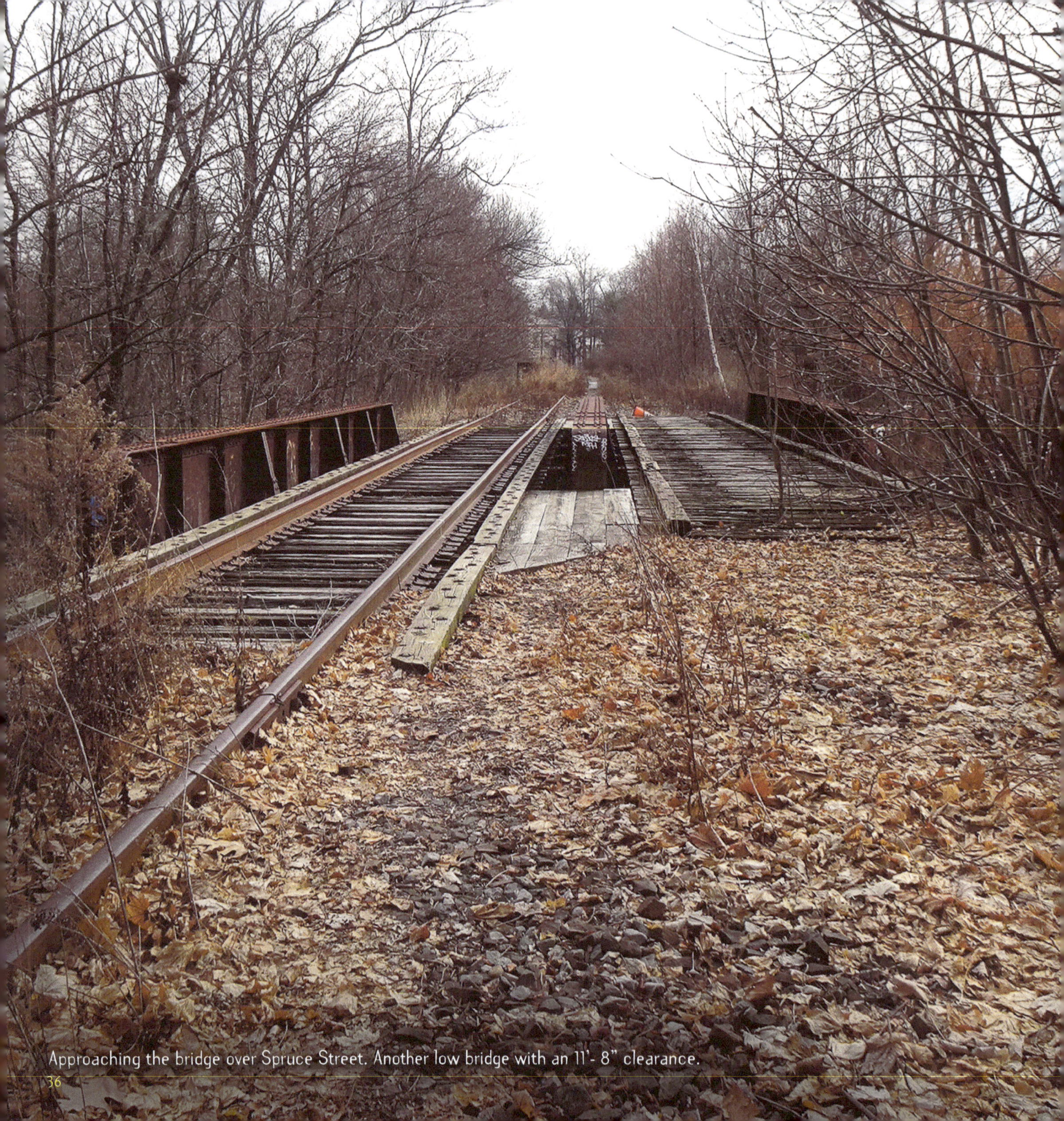

Approaching the bridge over Spruce Street. Another low bridge with an 11'- 8" clearance.

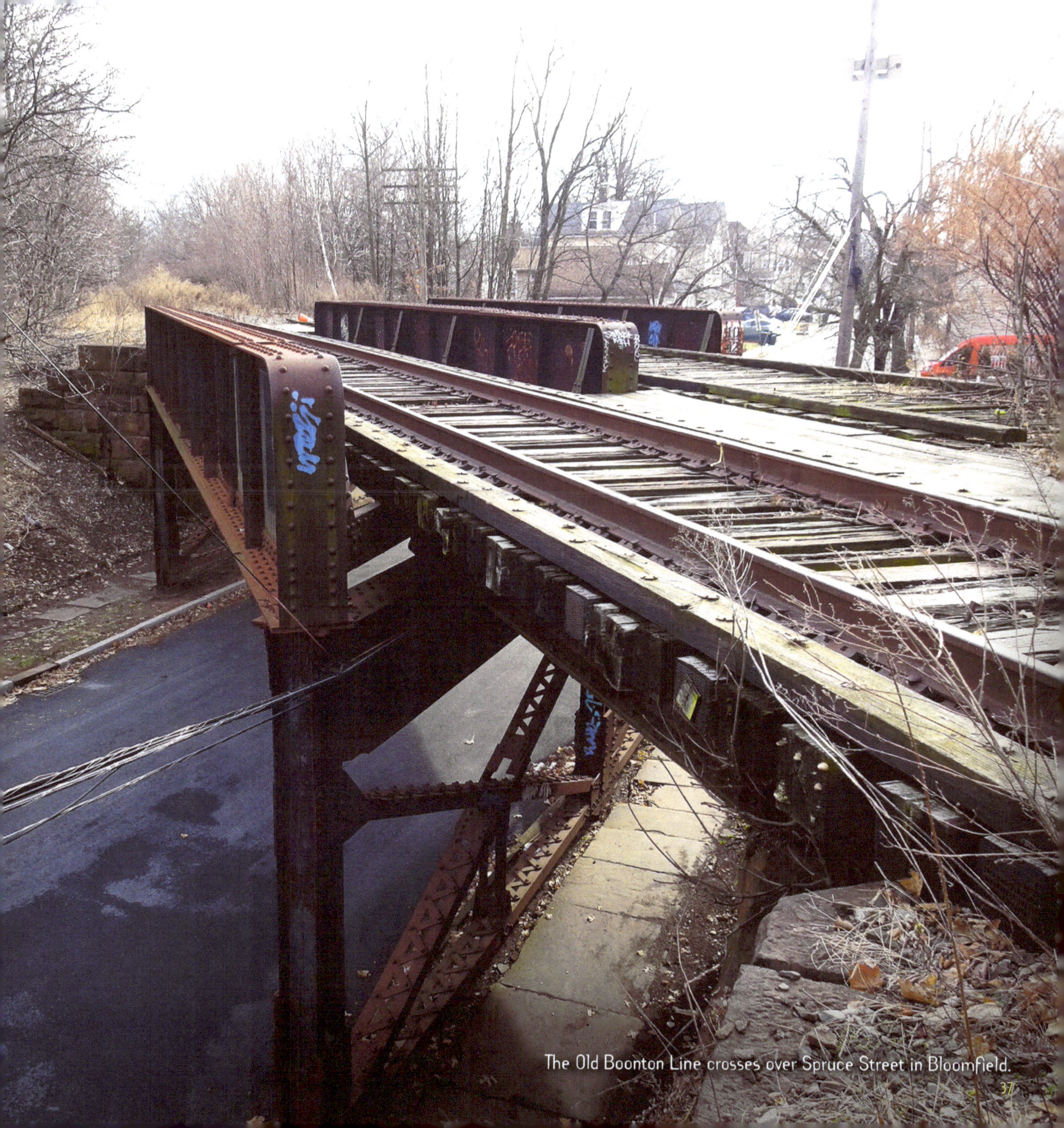

The Old Boonton Line crosses over Spruce Street in Bloomfield.

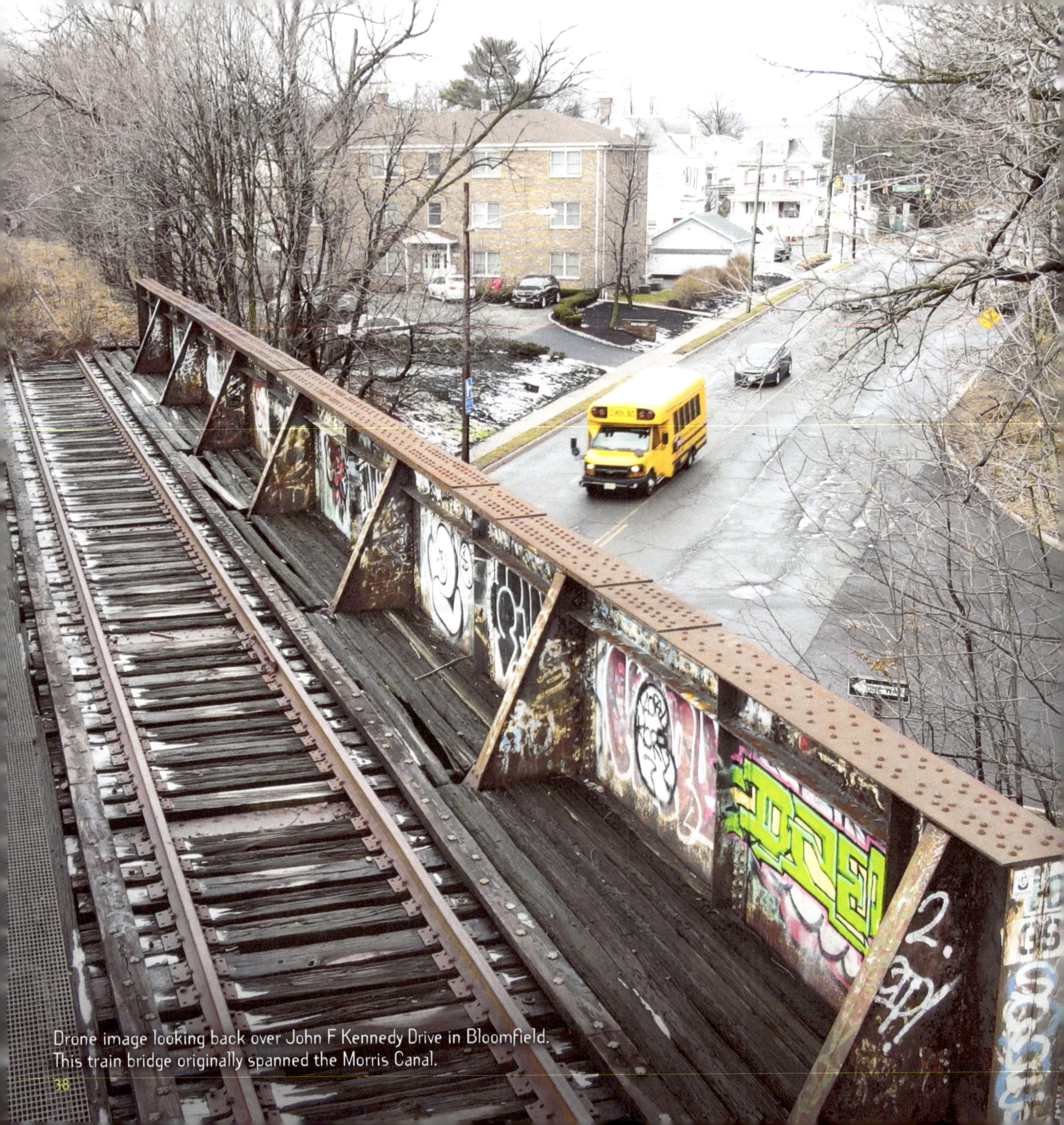

Drone image looking back over John F Kennedy Drive in Bloomfield. This train bridge originally spanned the Morris Canal.

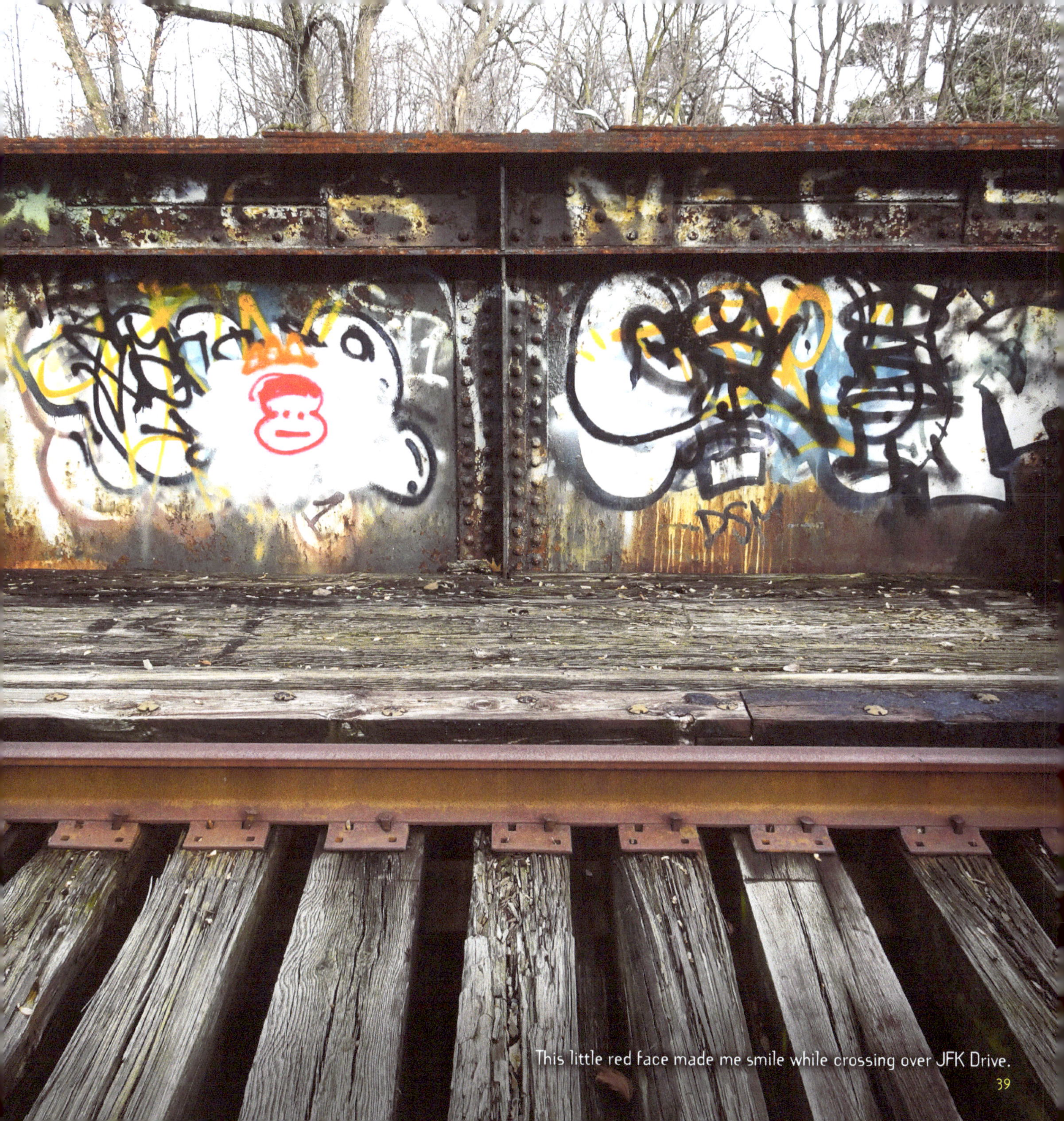

This little red face made me smile while crossing over JFK Drive.

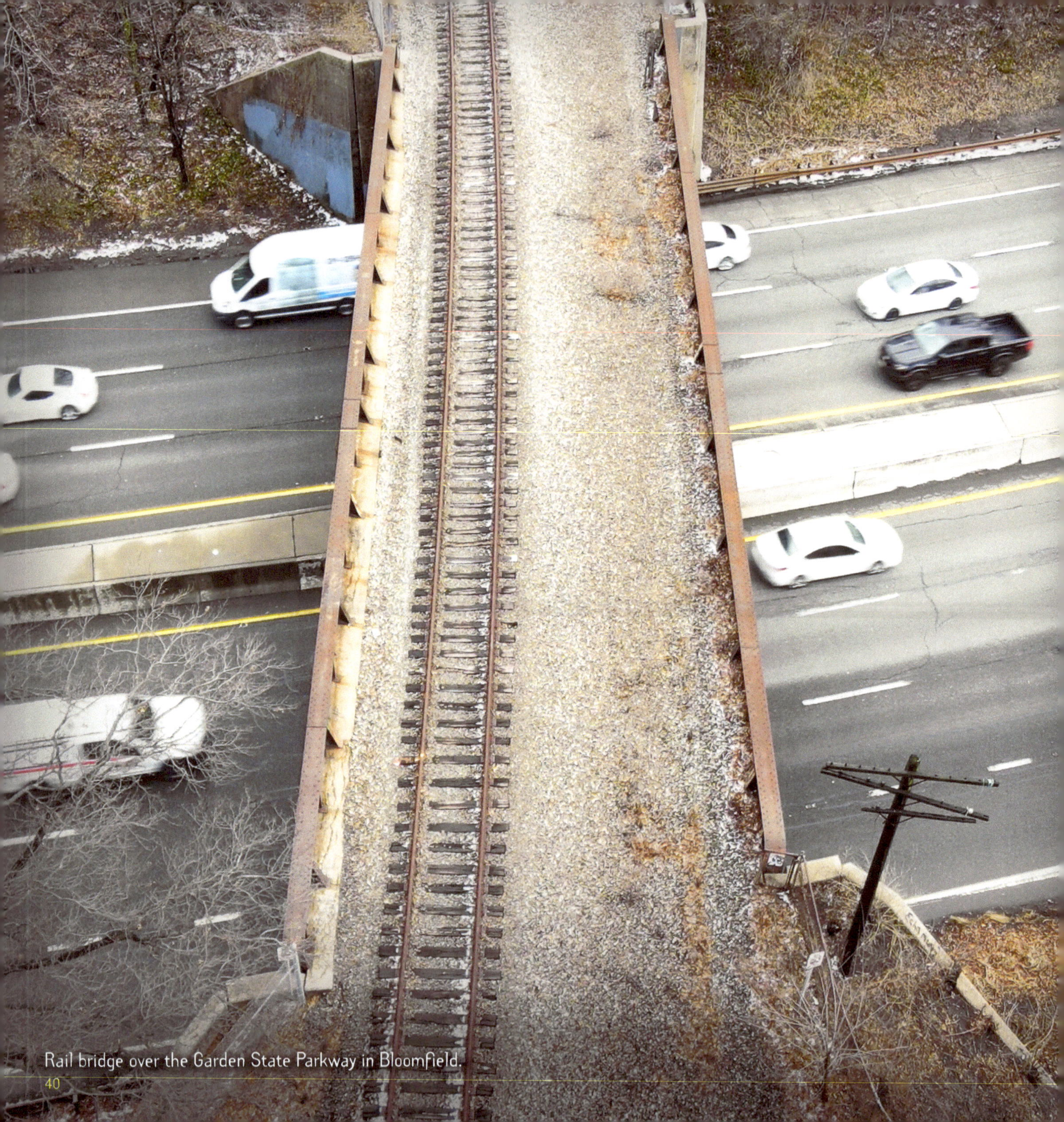
Rail bridge over the Garden State Parkway in Bloomfield.

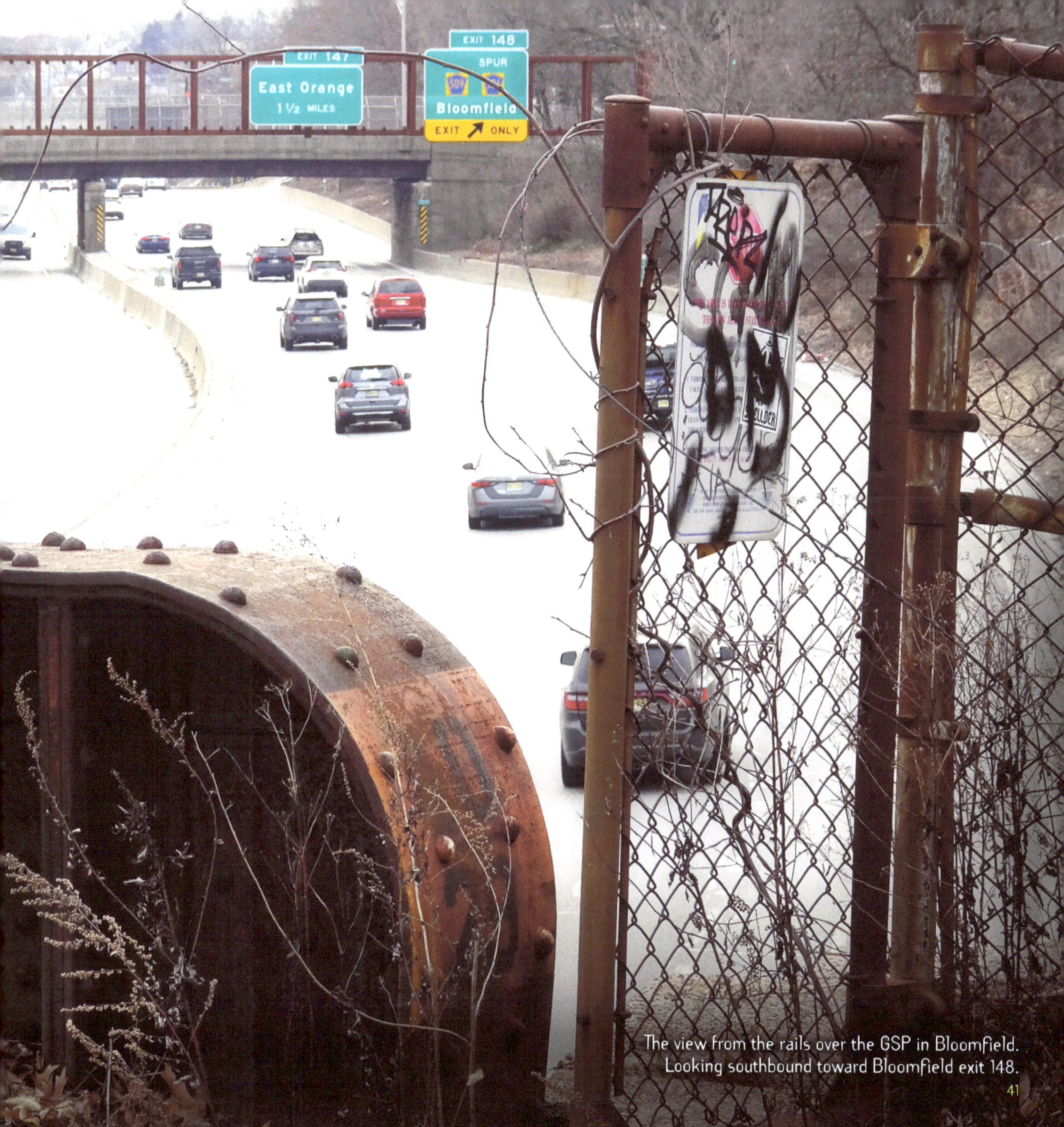

The view from the rails over the GSP in Bloomfield.
Looking southbound toward Bloomfield exit 148.

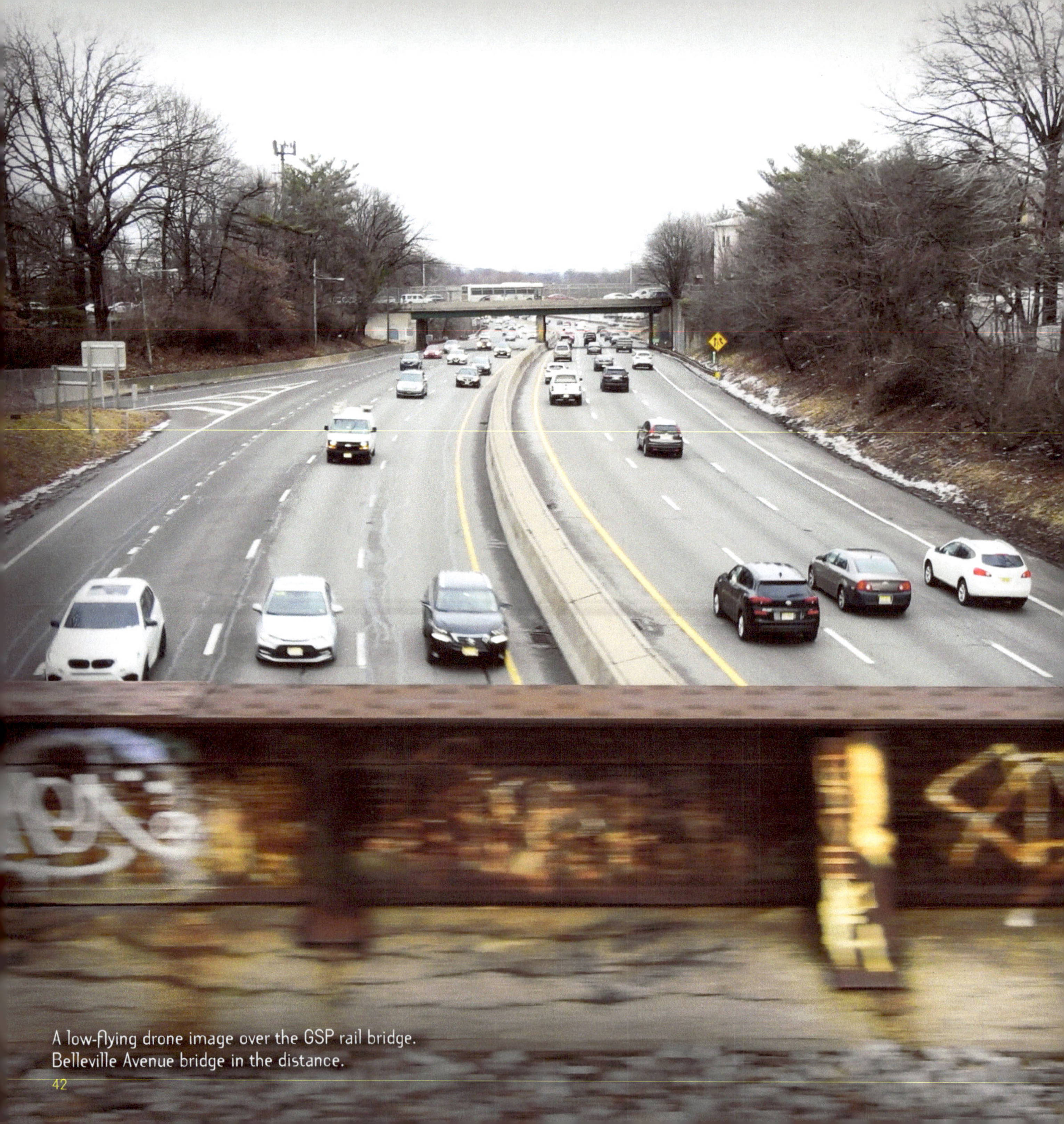

A low-flying drone image over the GSP rail bridge.
Belleville Avenue bridge in the distance.

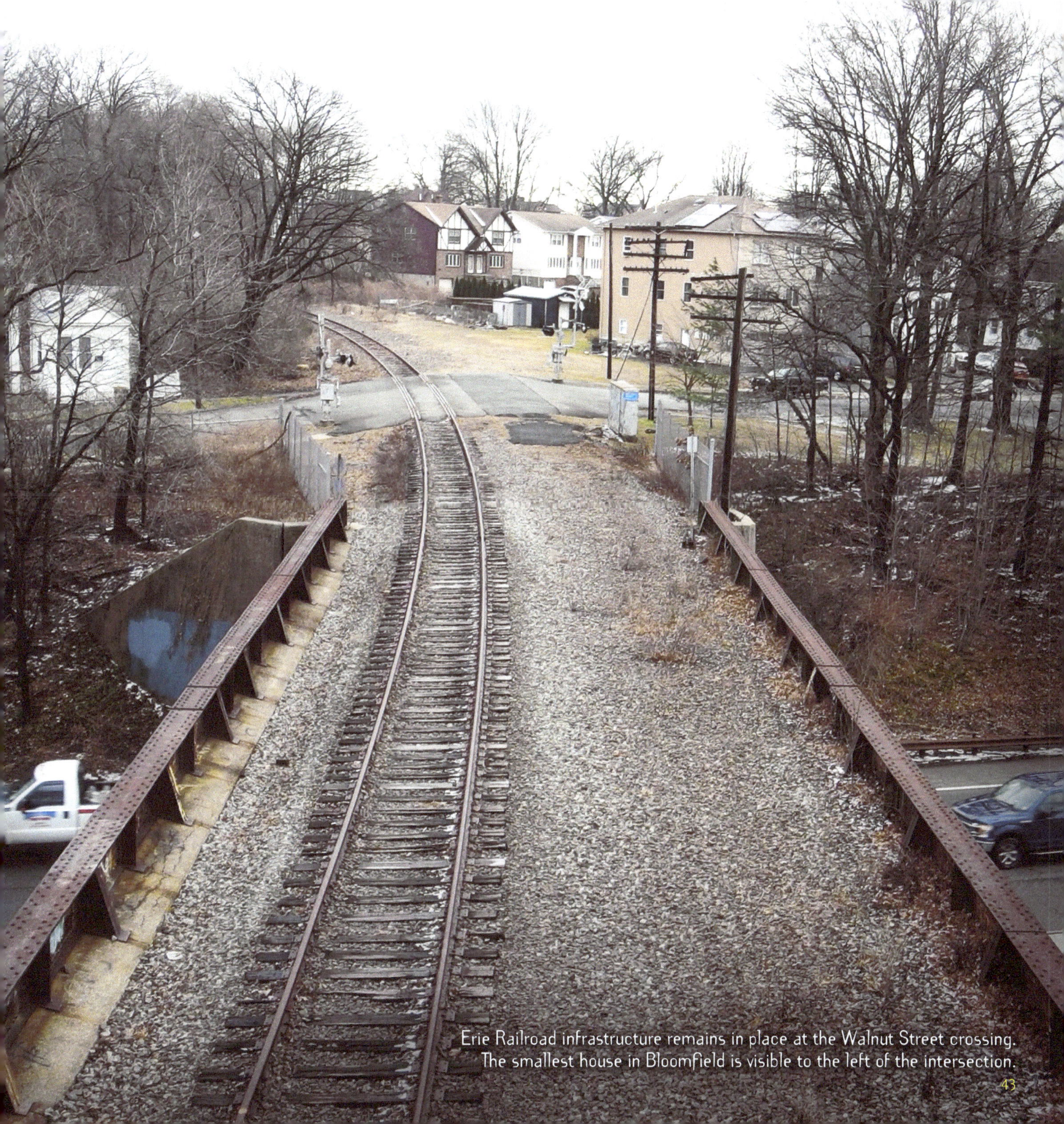

Erie Railroad infrastructure remains in place at the Walnut Street crossing. The smallest house in Bloomfield is visible to the left of the intersection.

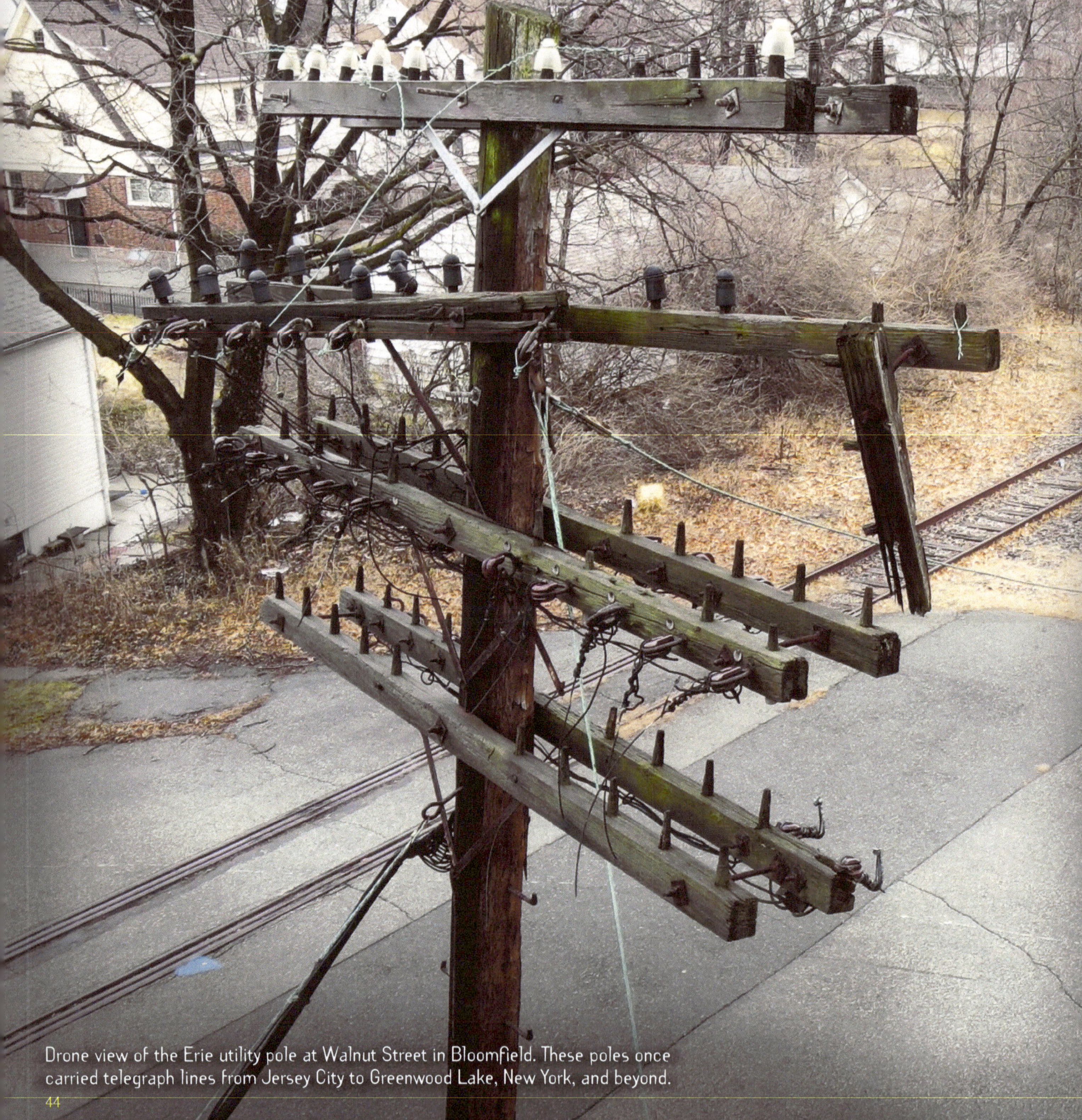

Drone view of the Erie utility pole at Walnut Street in Bloomfield. These poles once carried telegraph lines from Jersey City to Greenwood Lake, New York, and beyond.

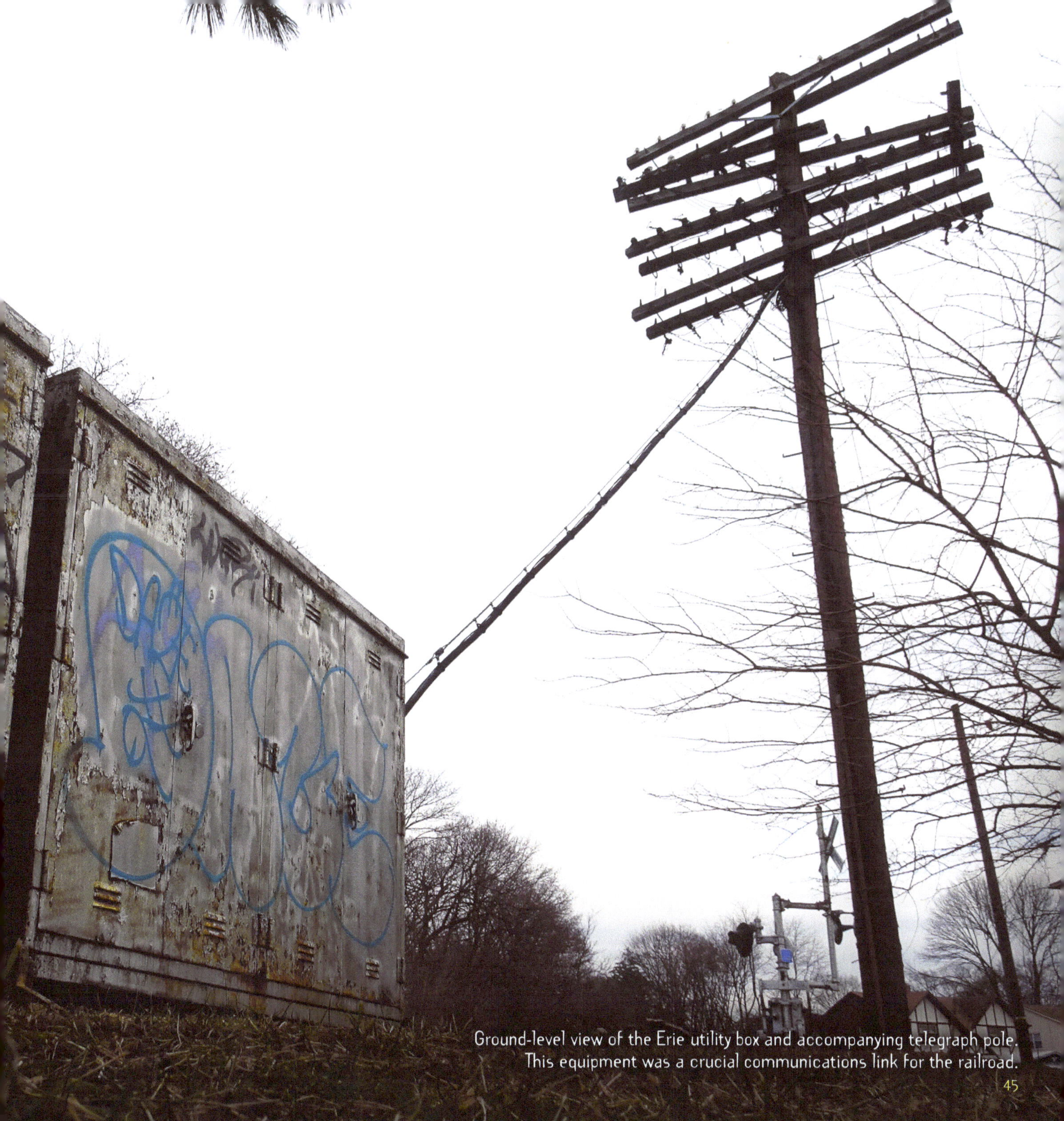

Ground-level view of the Erie utility box and accompanying telegraph pole. This equipment was a crucial communications link for the railroad.

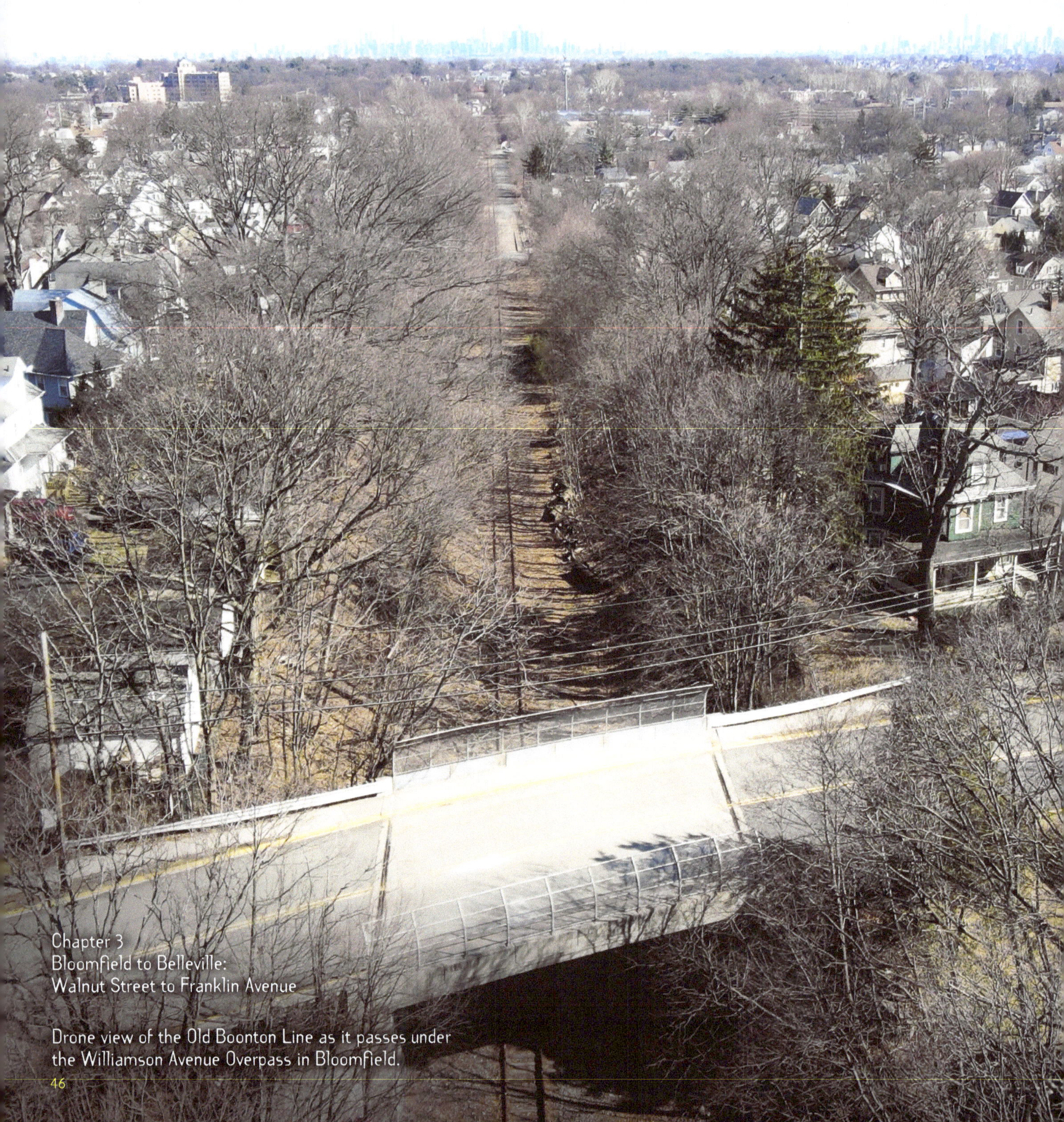

Chapter 3
Bloomfield to Belleville:
Walnut Street to Franklin Avenue

Drone view of the Old Boonton Line as it passes under the Williamson Avenue Overpass in Bloomfield.

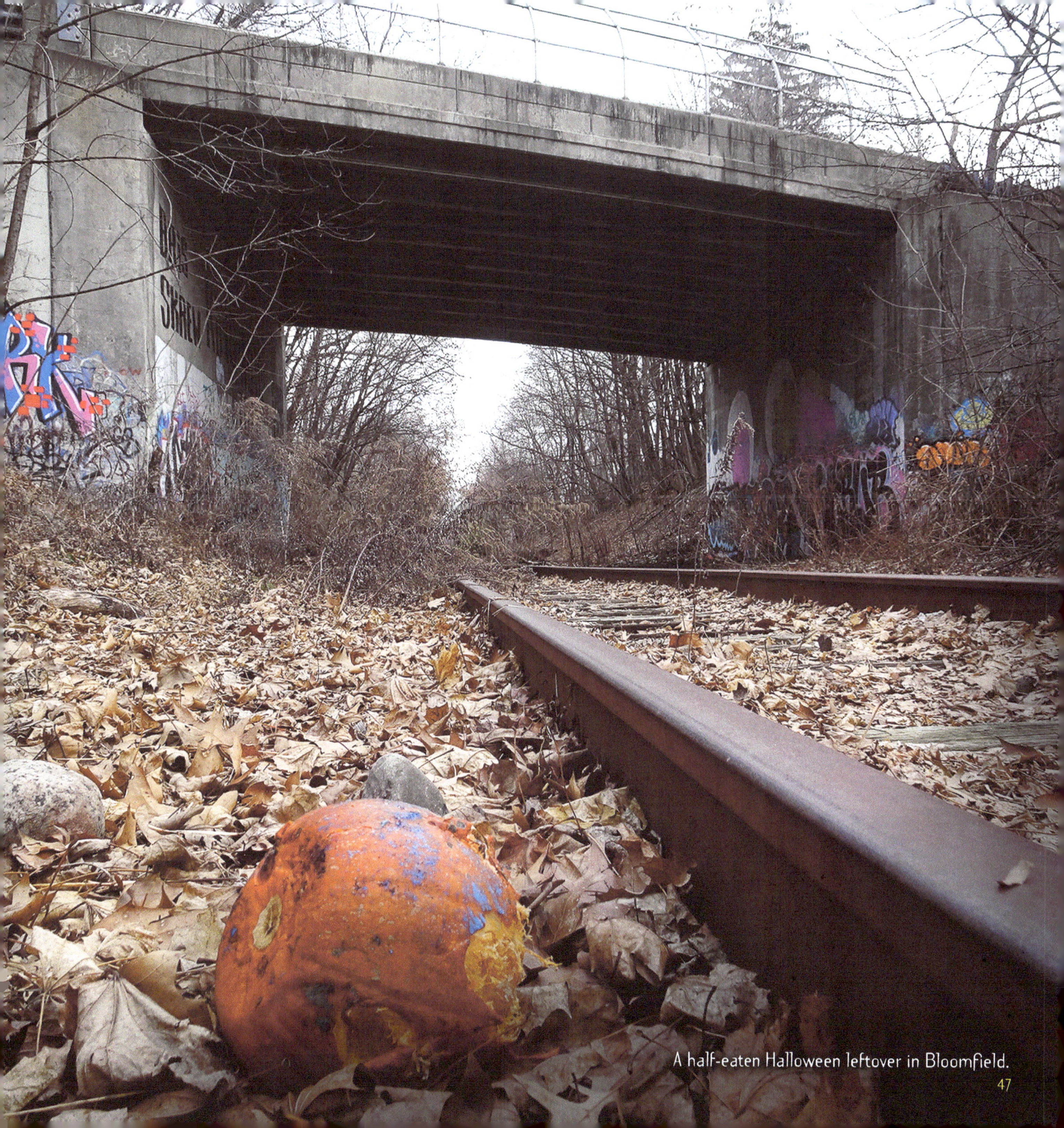

A half-eaten Halloween leftover in Bloomfield.

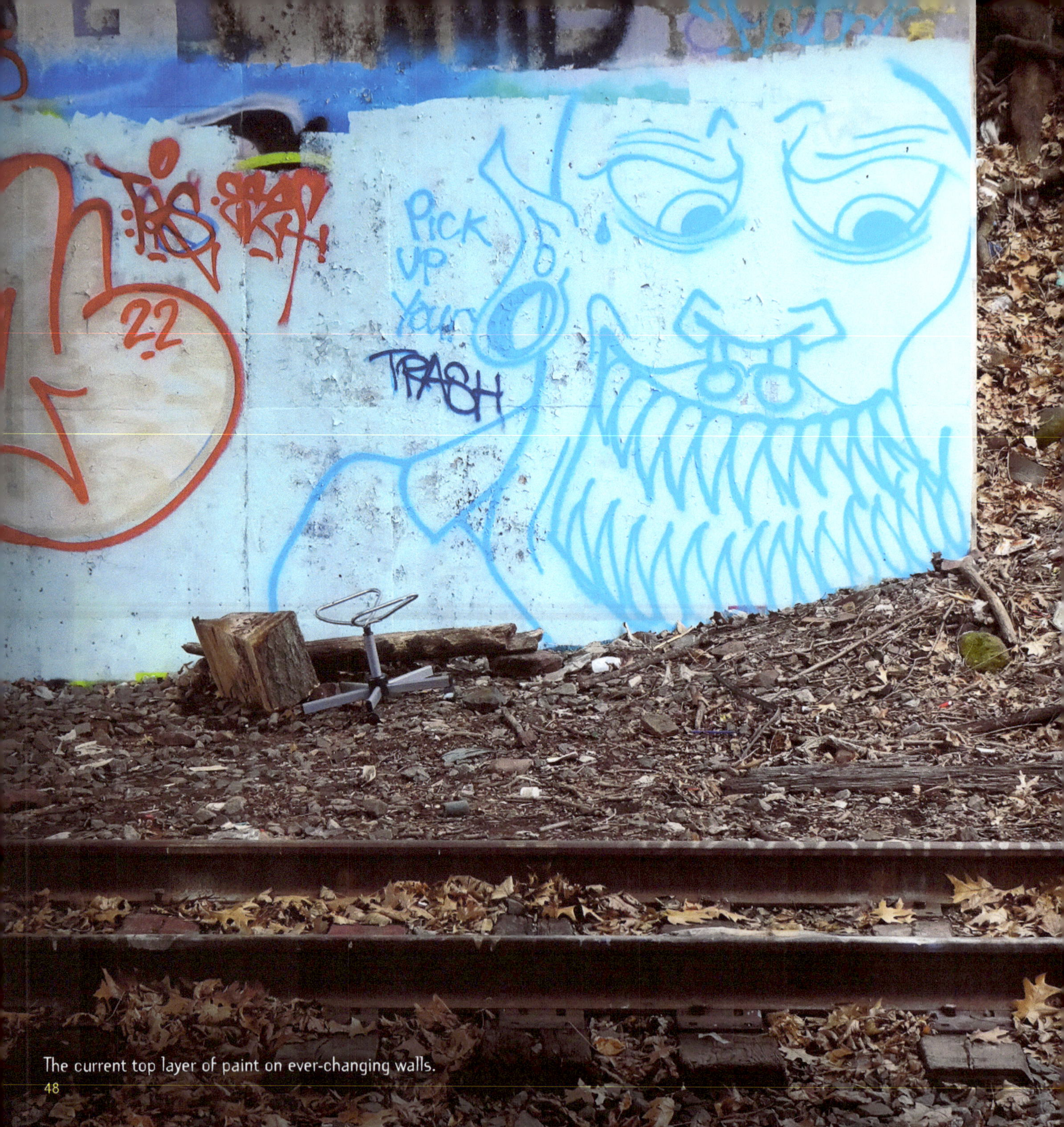

The current top layer of paint on ever-changing walls.

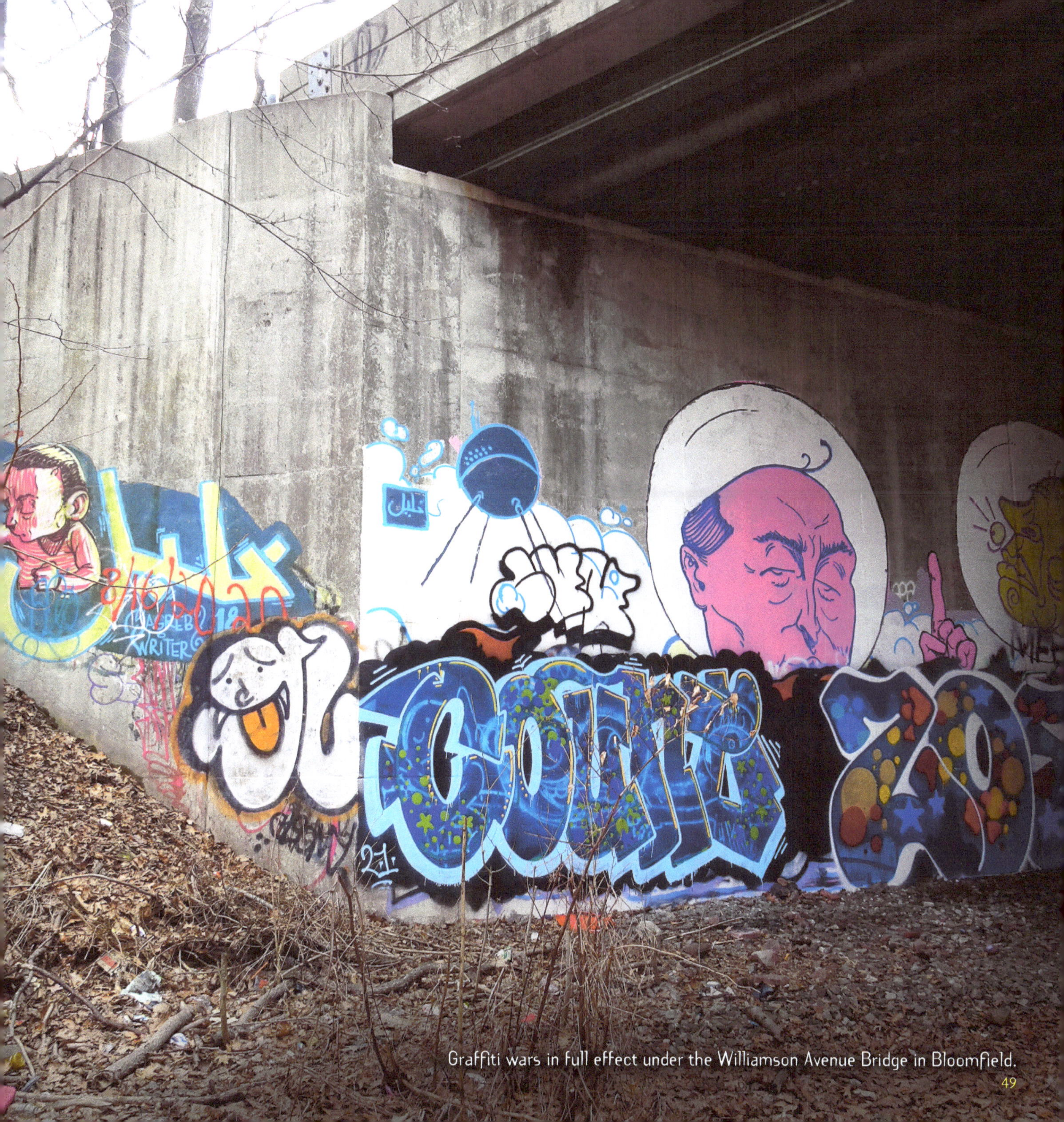

Graffiti wars in full effect under the Williamson Avenue Bridge in Bloomfield.

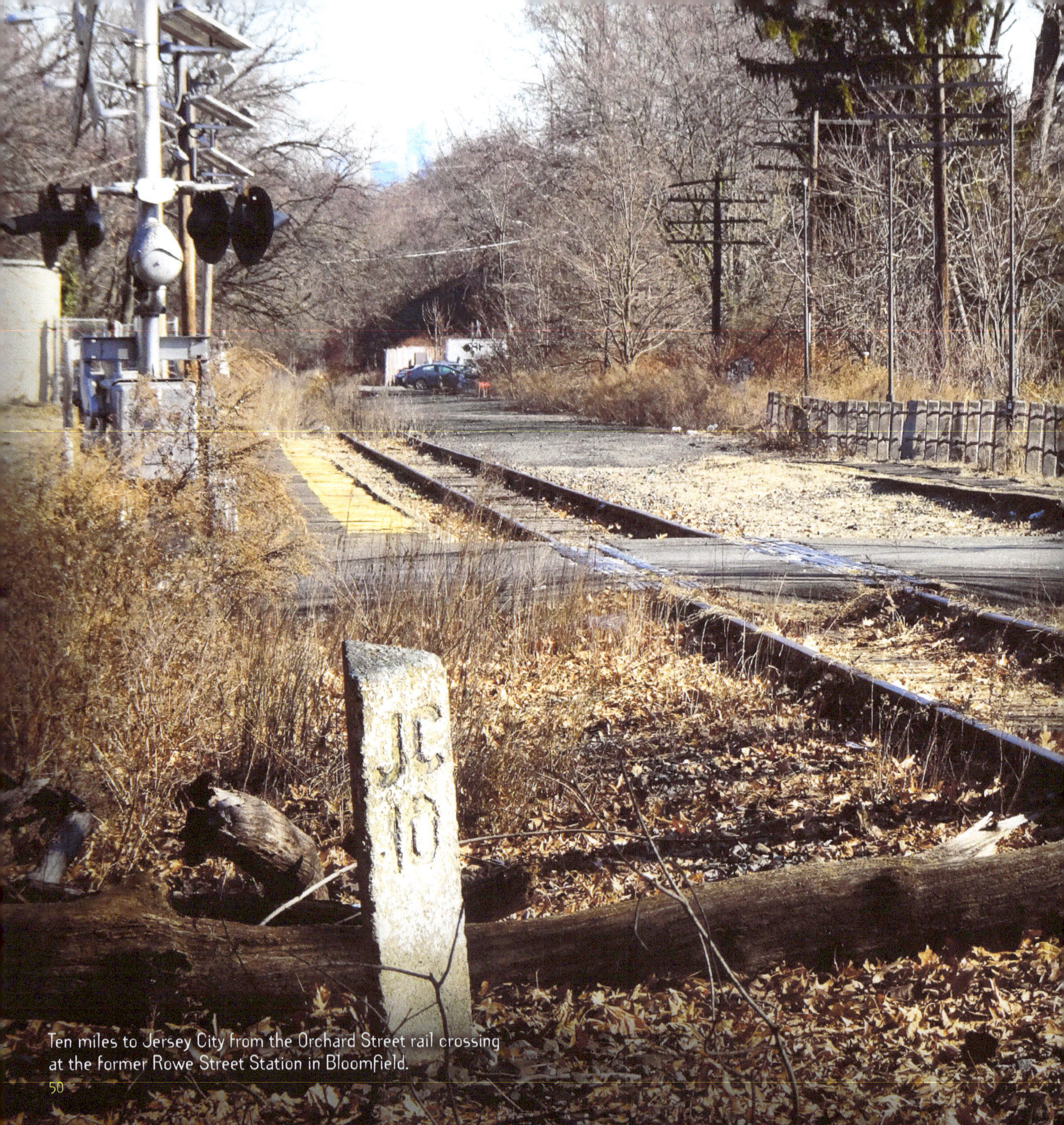

Ten miles to Jersey City from the Orchard Street rail crossing at the former Rowe Street Station in Bloomfield.

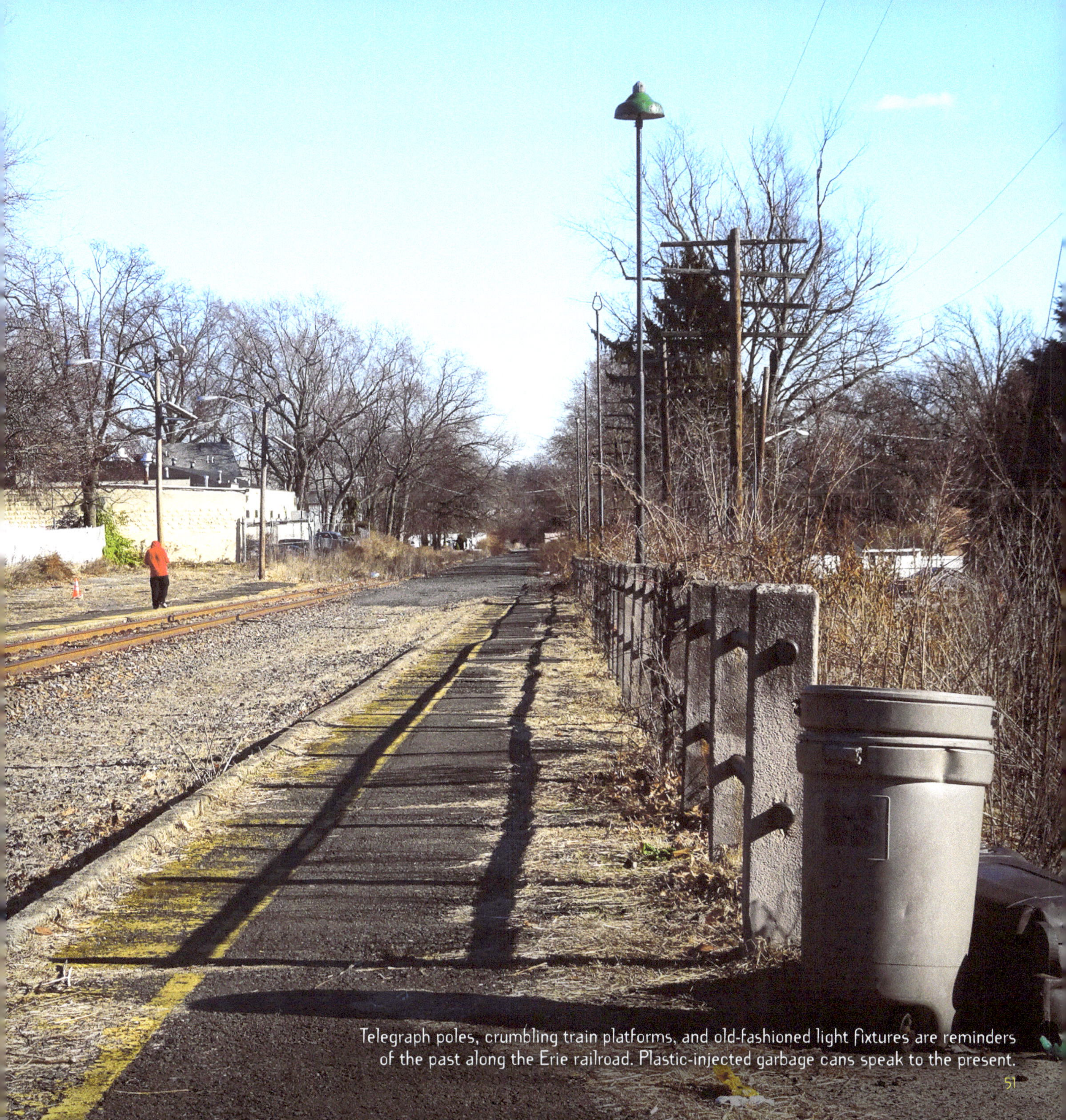

Telegraph poles, crumbling train platforms, and old-fashioned light fixtures are reminders of the past along the Erie railroad. Plastic-injected garbage cans speak to the present.

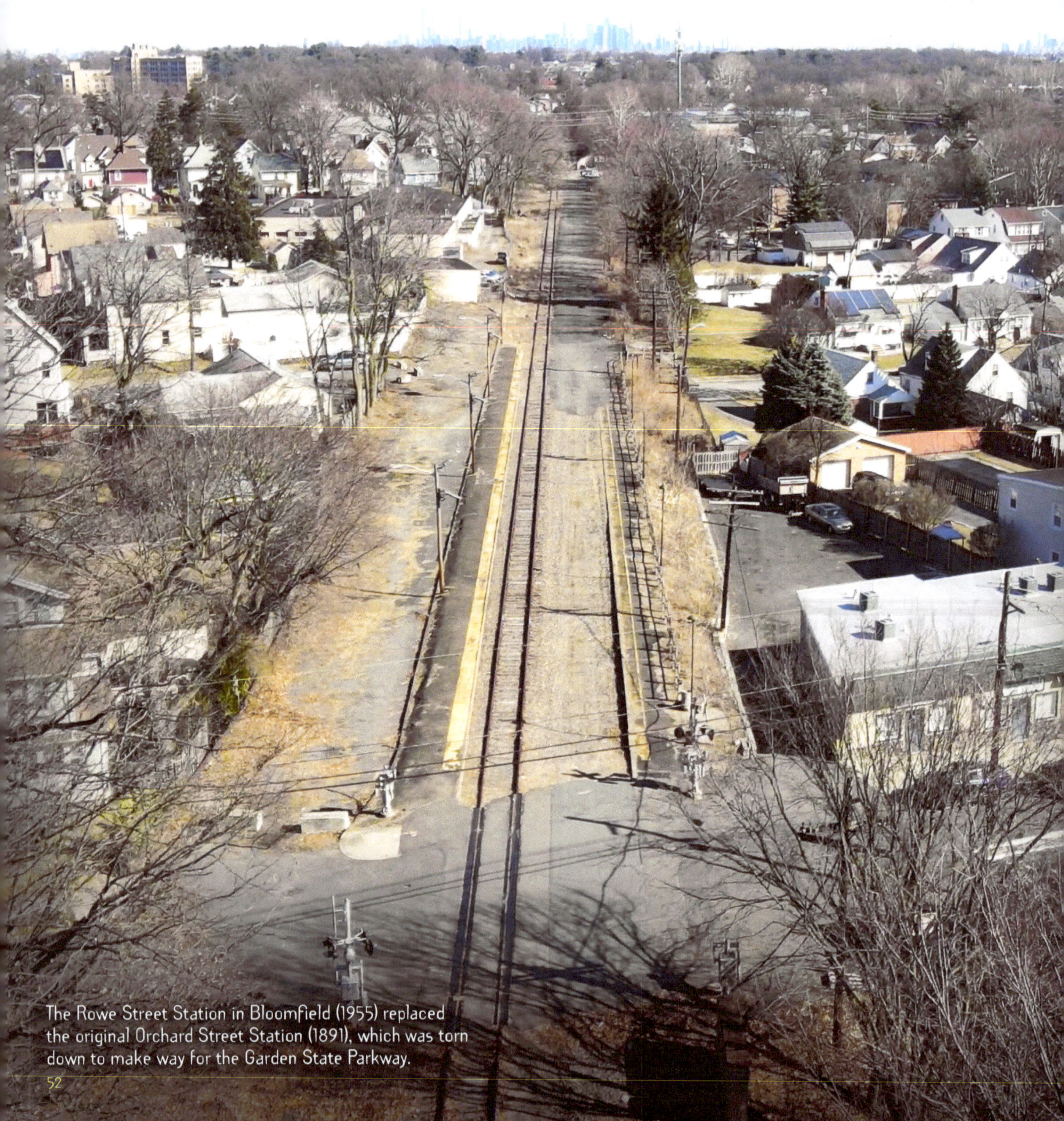

The Rowe Street Station in Bloomfield (1955) replaced the original Orchard Street Station (1891), which was torn down to make way for the Garden State Parkway.

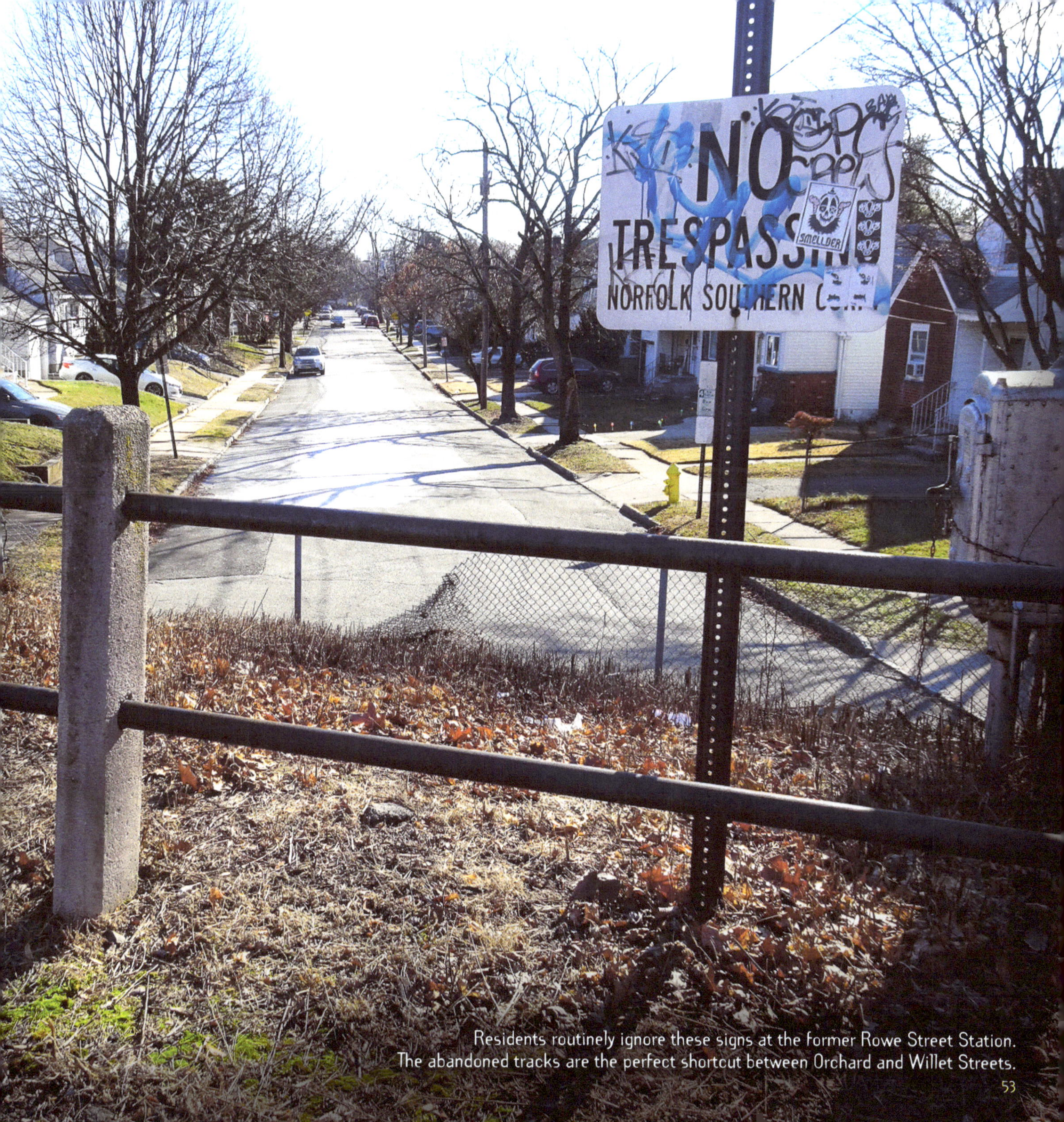

Residents routinely ignore these signs at the former Rowe Street Station.
The abandoned tracks are the perfect shortcut between Orchard and Willet Streets.

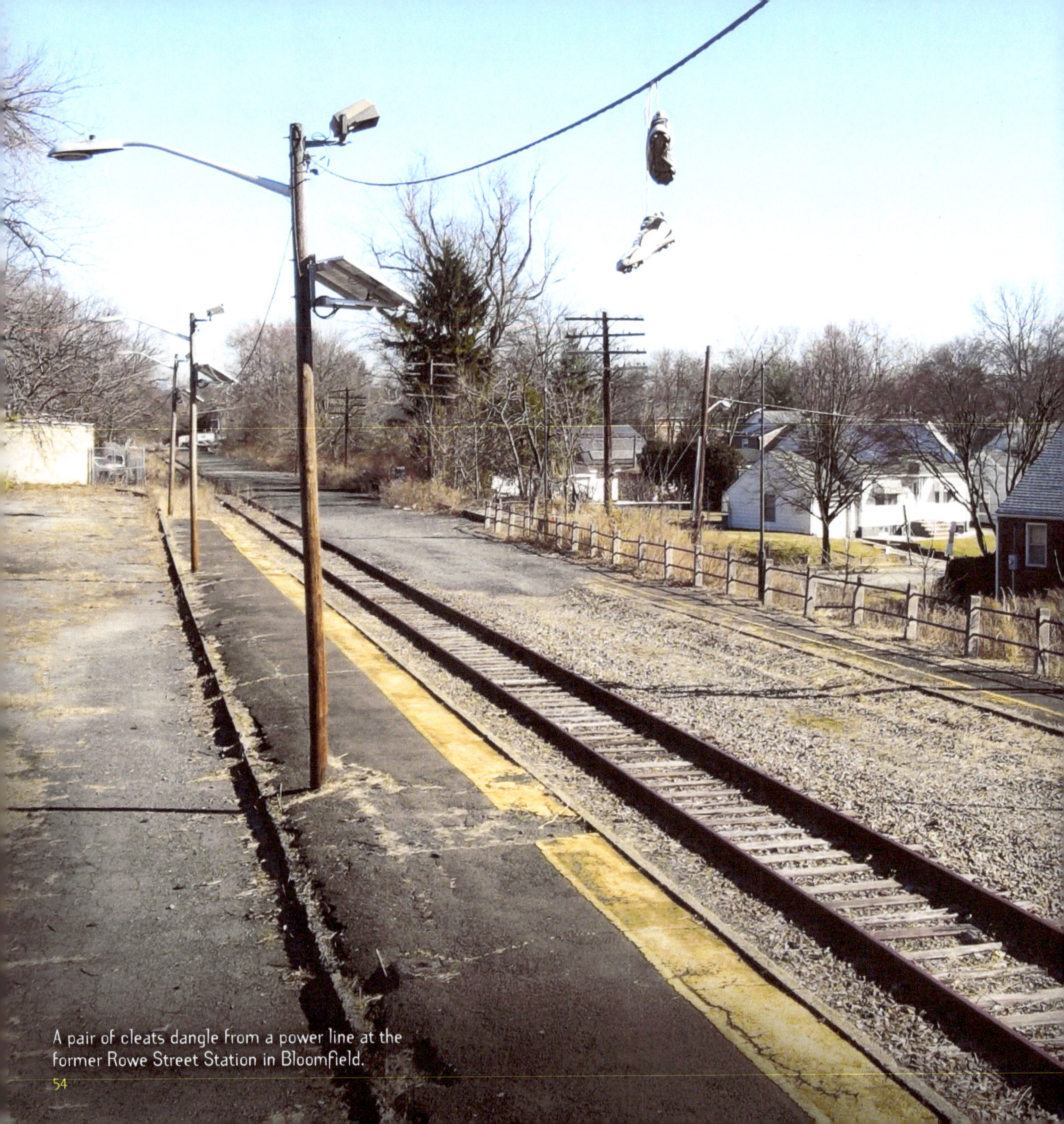

A pair of cleats dangle from a power line at the former Rowe Street Station in Bloomfield.

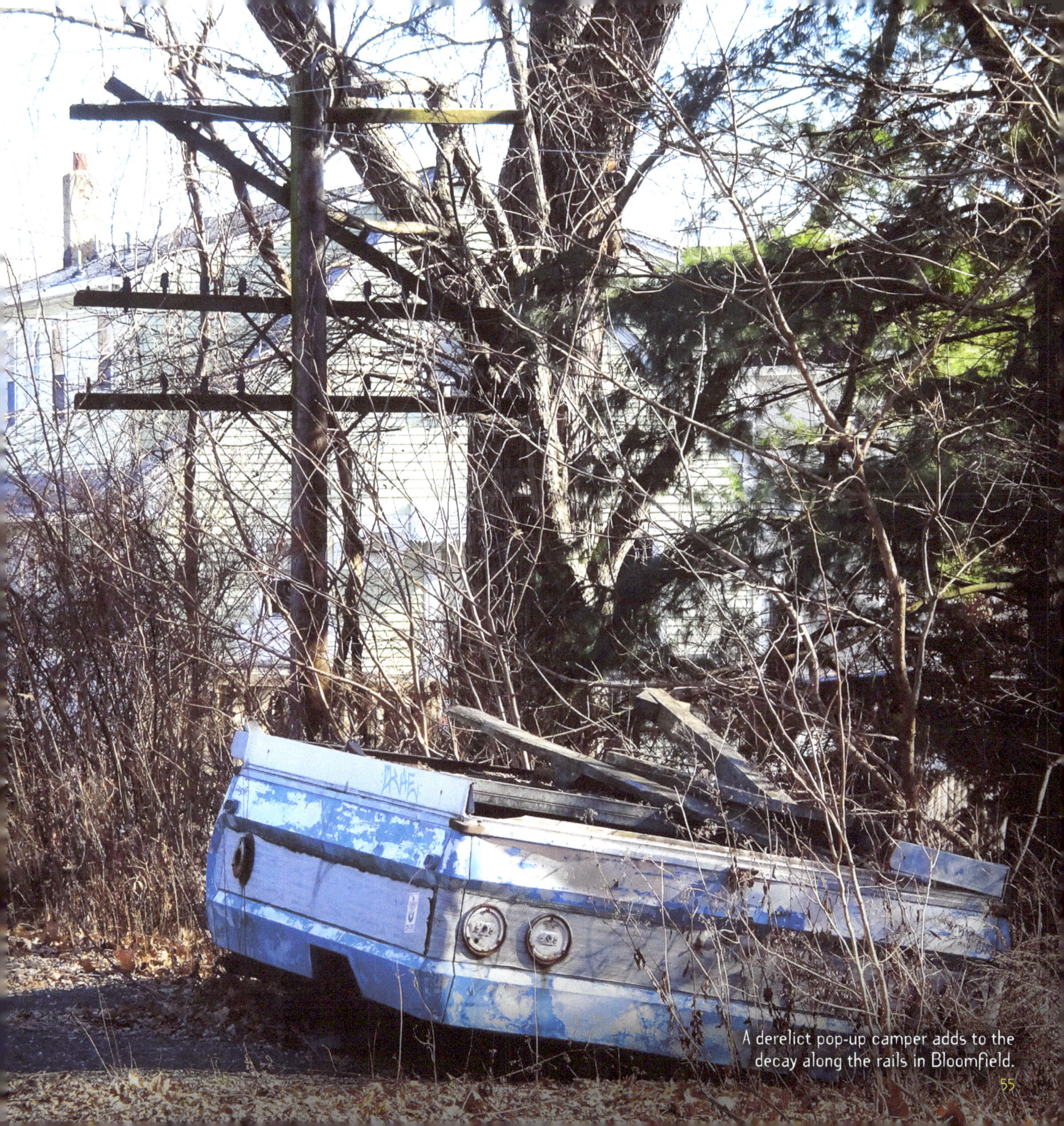

A derelict pop-up camper adds to the decay along the rails in Bloomfield.

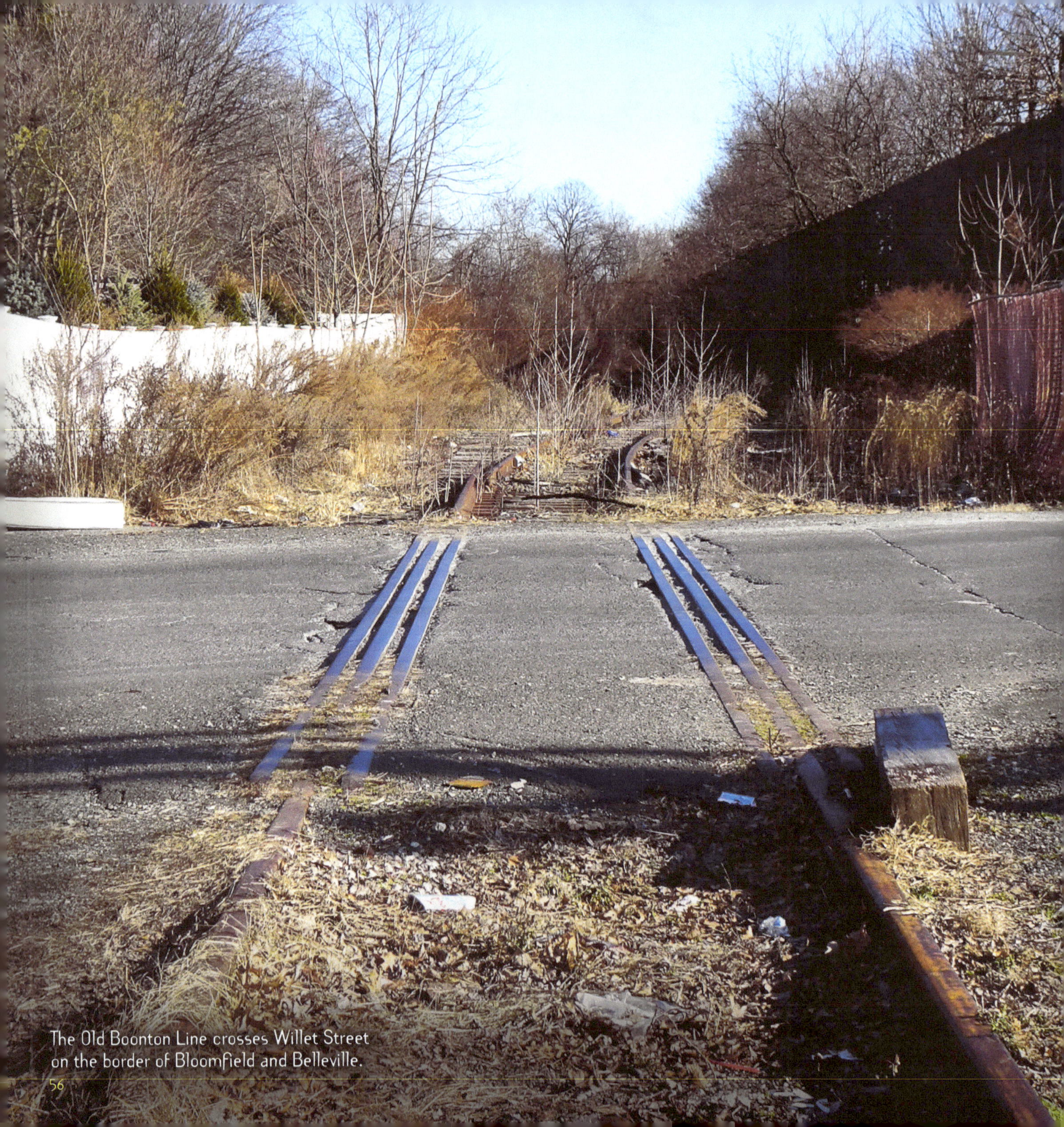

The Old Boonton Line crosses Willet Street on the border of Bloomfield and Belleville.

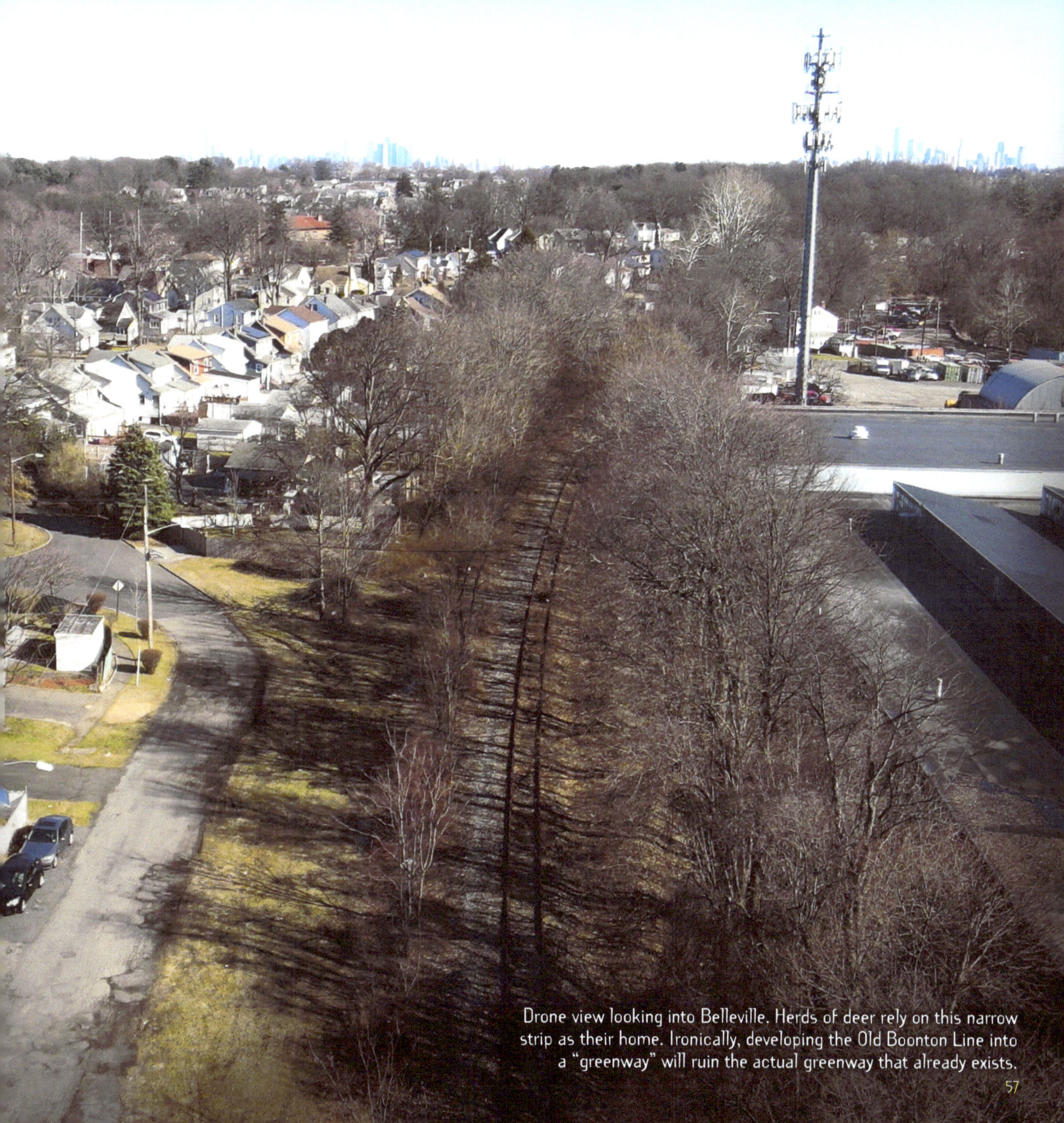

Drone view looking into Belleville. Herds of deer rely on this narrow strip as their home. Ironically, developing the Old Boonton Line into a "greenway" will ruin the actual greenway that already exists.

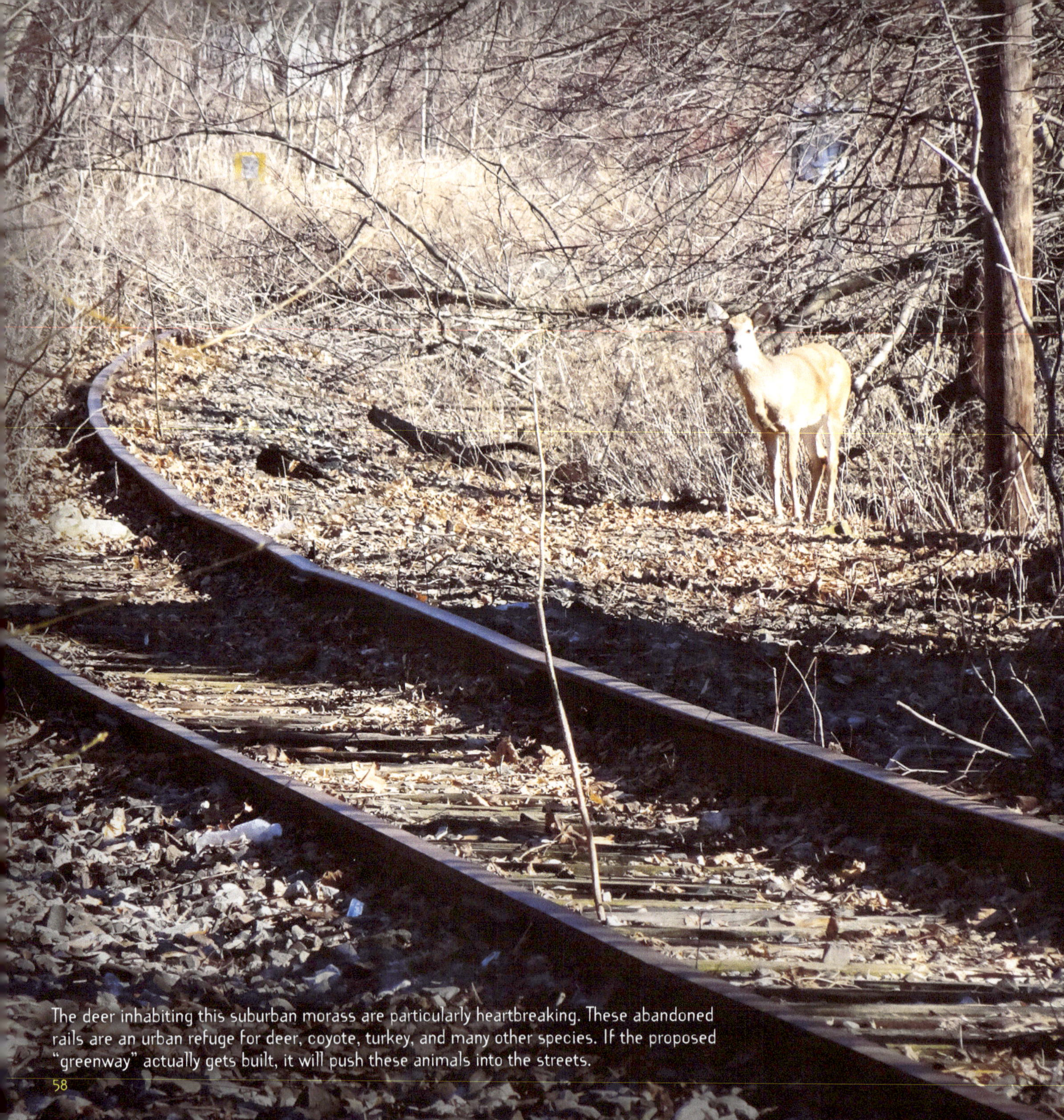

The deer inhabiting this suburban morass are particularly heartbreaking. These abandoned rails are an urban refuge for deer, coyote, turkey, and many other species. If the proposed "greenway" actually gets built, it will push these animals into the streets.

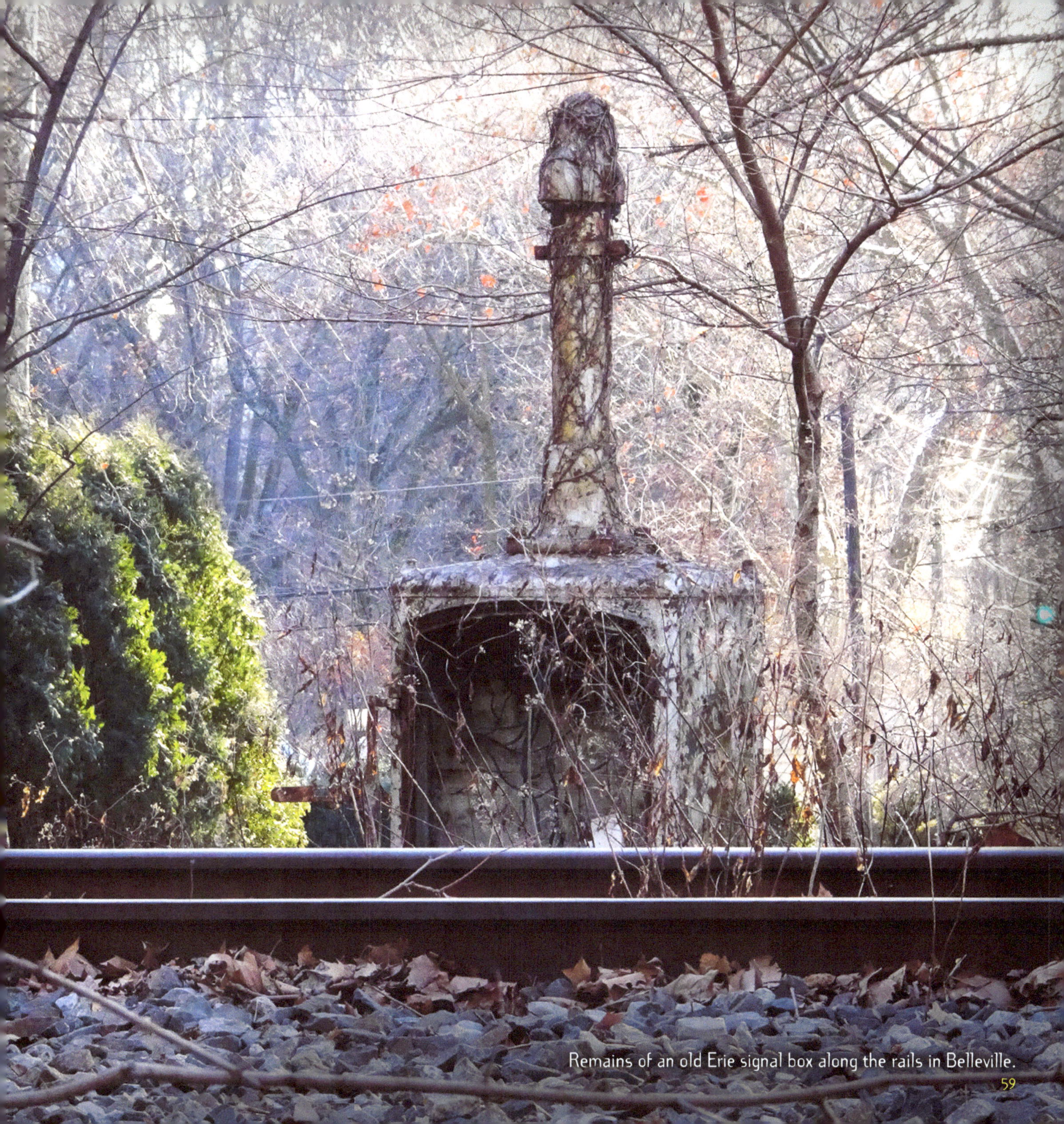

Remains of an old Erie signal box along the rails in Belleville.

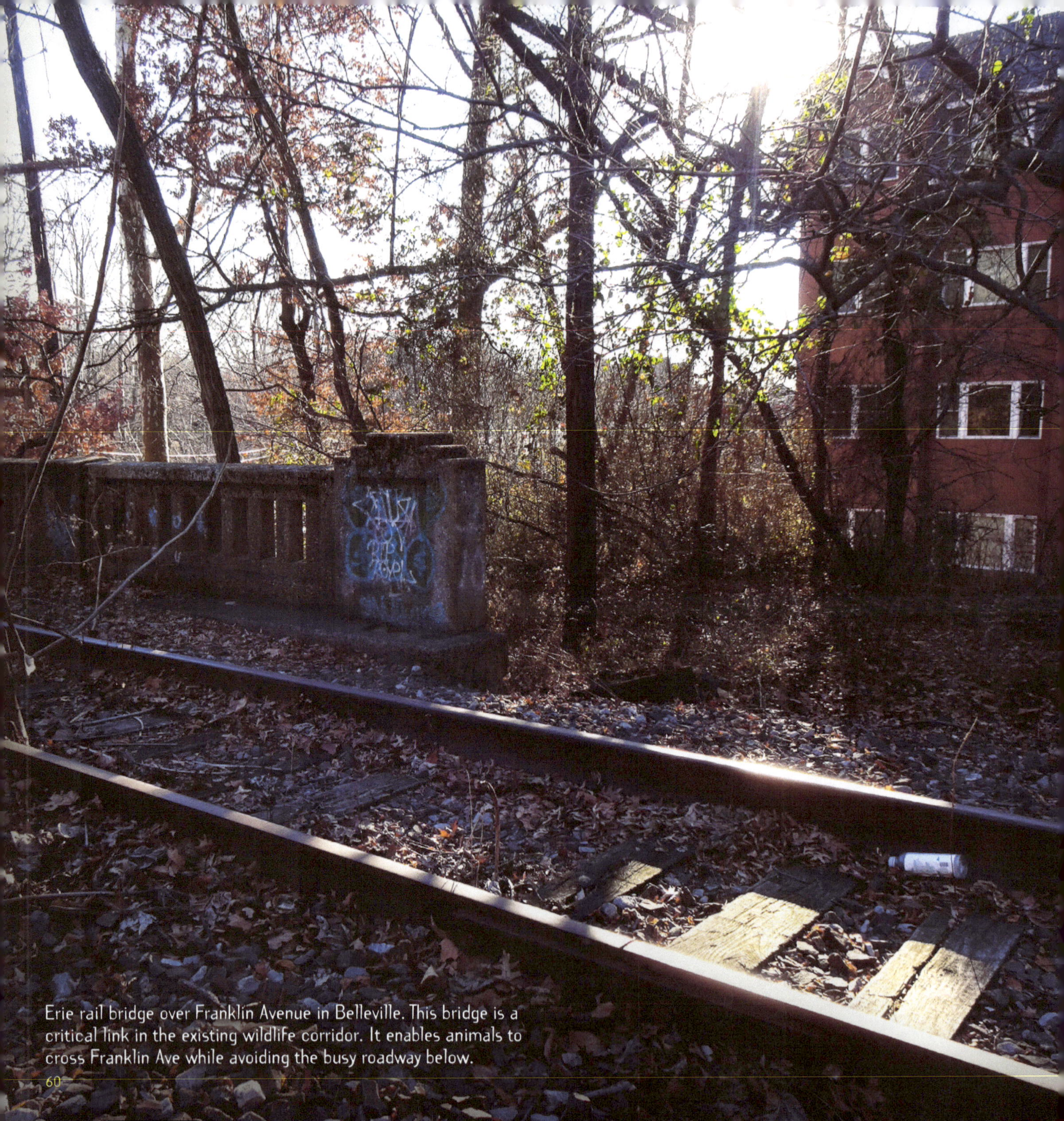

Erie rail bridge over Franklin Avenue in Belleville. This bridge is a critical link in the existing wildlife corridor. It enables animals to cross Franklin Ave while avoiding the busy roadway below.

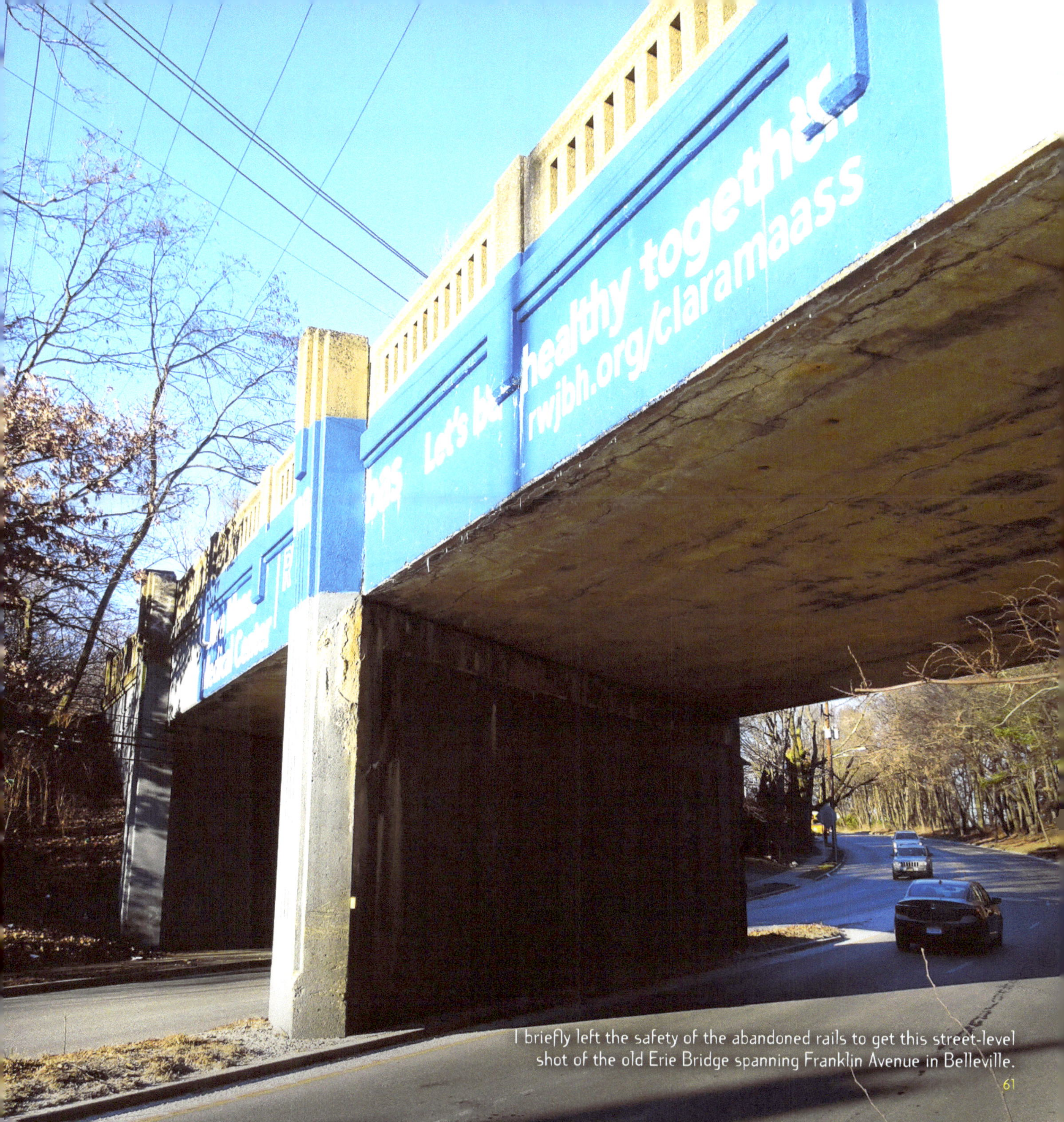

I briefly left the safety of the abandoned rails to get this street-level shot of the old Erie Bridge spanning Franklin Avenue in Belleville.

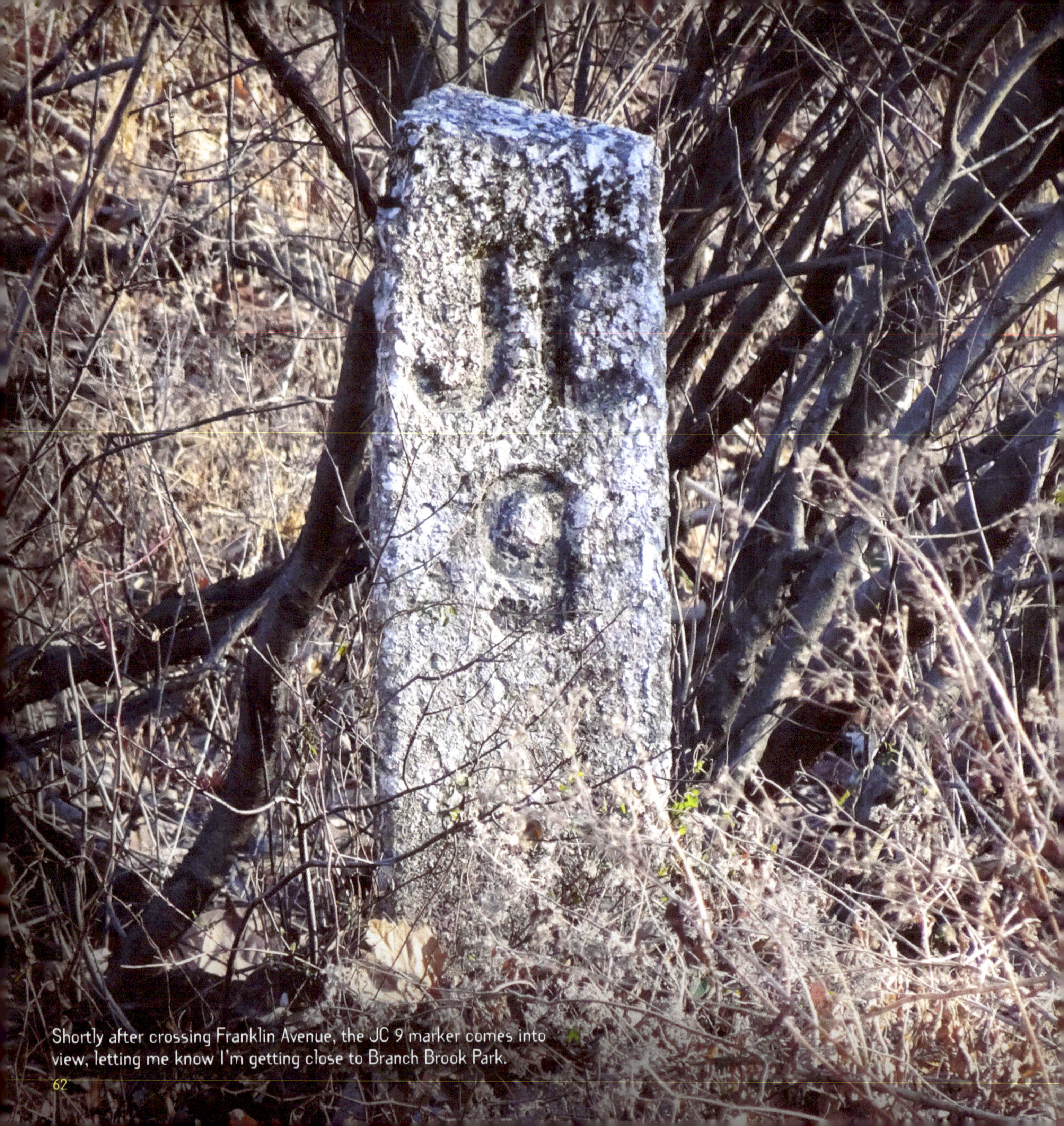

Shortly after crossing Franklin Avenue, the JC 9 marker comes into view, letting me know I'm getting close to Branch Brook Park.

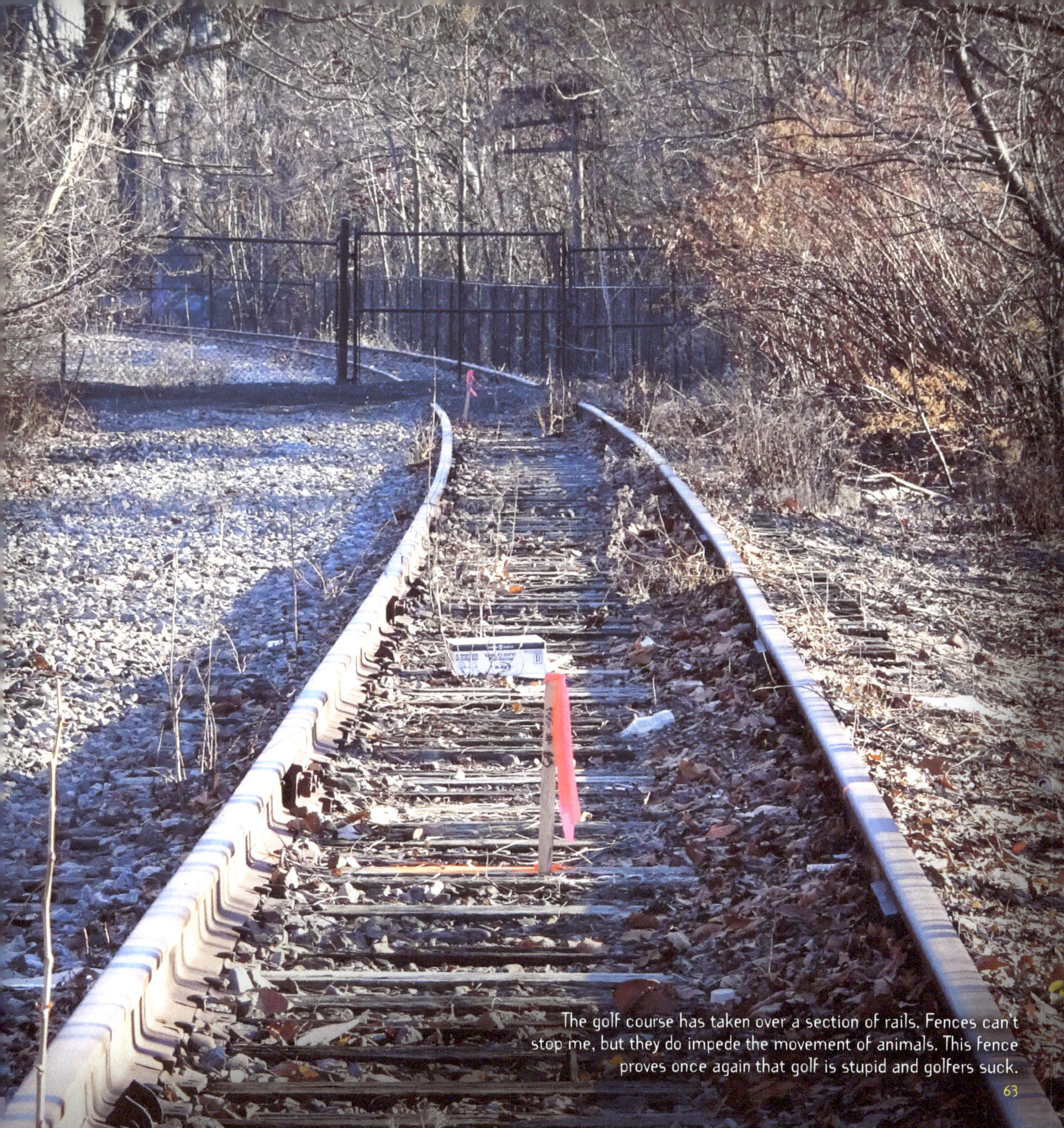

The golf course has taken over a section of rails. Fences can't stop me, but they do impede the movement of animals. This fence proves once again that golf is stupid and golfers suck.

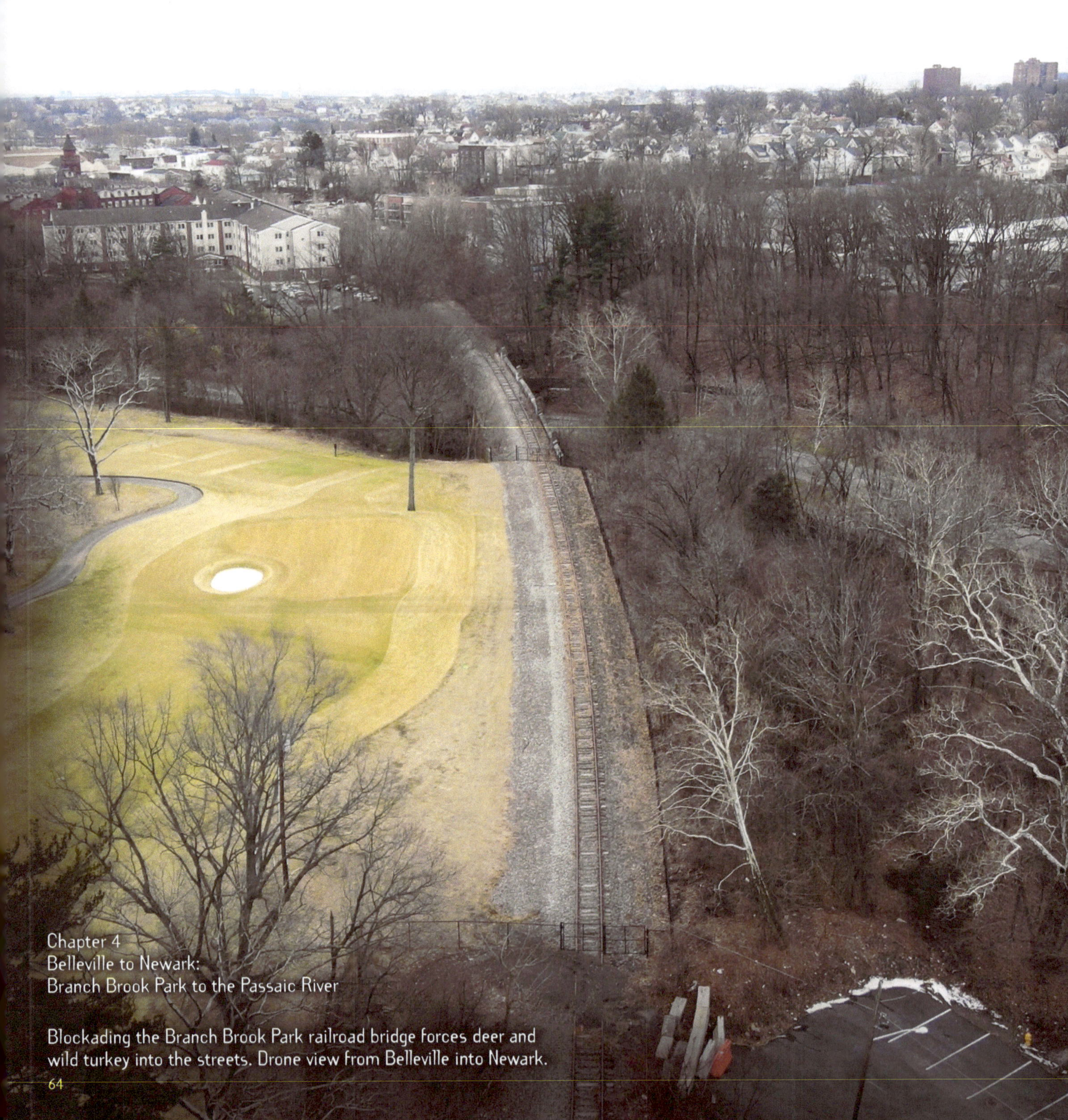

Chapter 4
Belleville to Newark:
Branch Brook Park to the Passaic River

Blockading the Branch Brook Park railroad bridge forces deer and wild turkey into the streets. Drone view from Belleville into Newark.

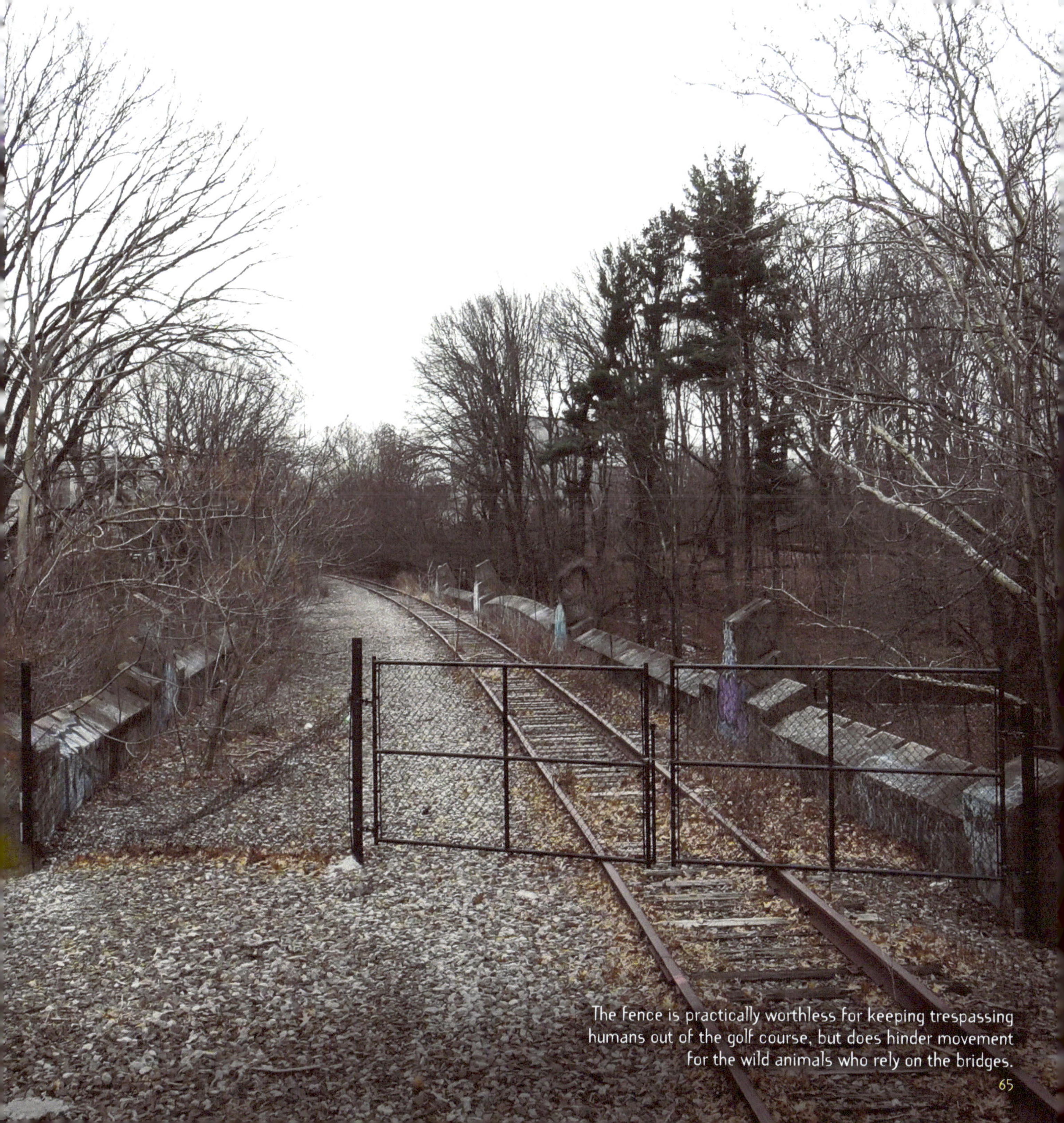

The fence is practically worthless for keeping trespassing humans out of the golf course, but does hinder movement for the wild animals who rely on the bridges.

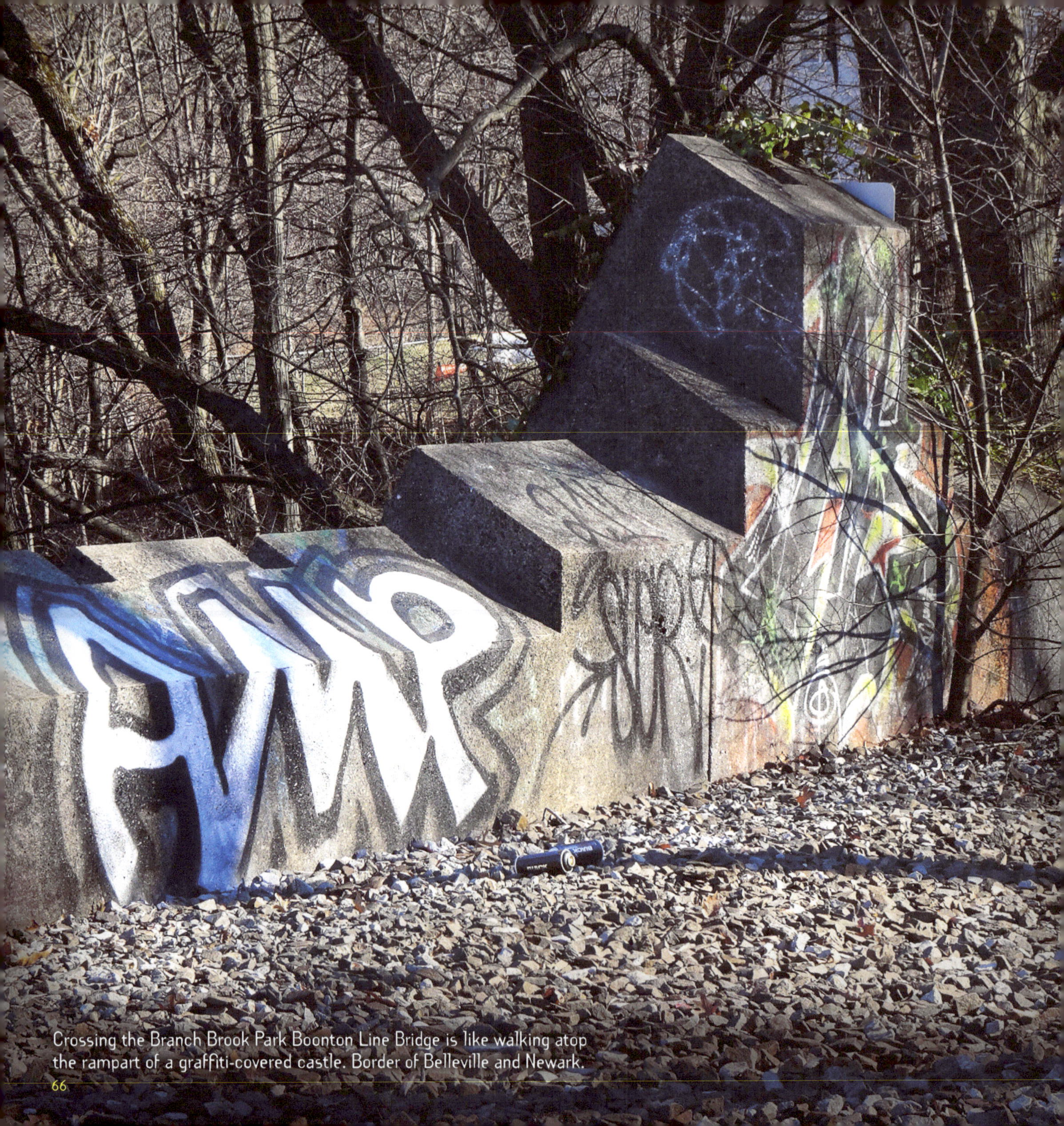

Crossing the Branch Brook Park Boonton Line Bridge is like walking atop the rampart of a graffiti-covered castle. Border of Belleville and Newark.

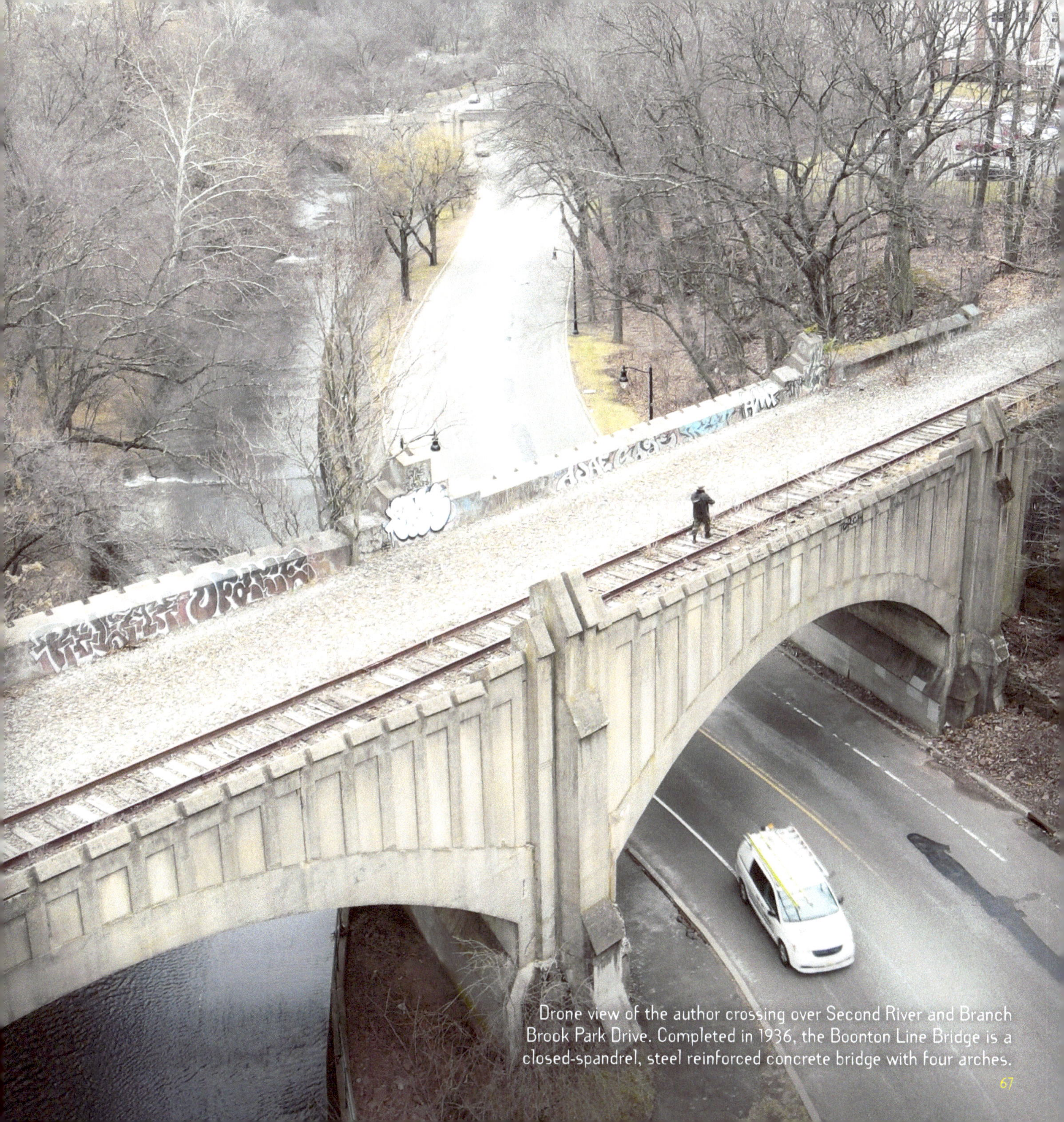

Drone view of the author crossing over Second River and Branch Brook Park Drive. Completed in 1936, the Boonton Line Bridge is a closed-spandrel, steel reinforced concrete bridge with four arches.

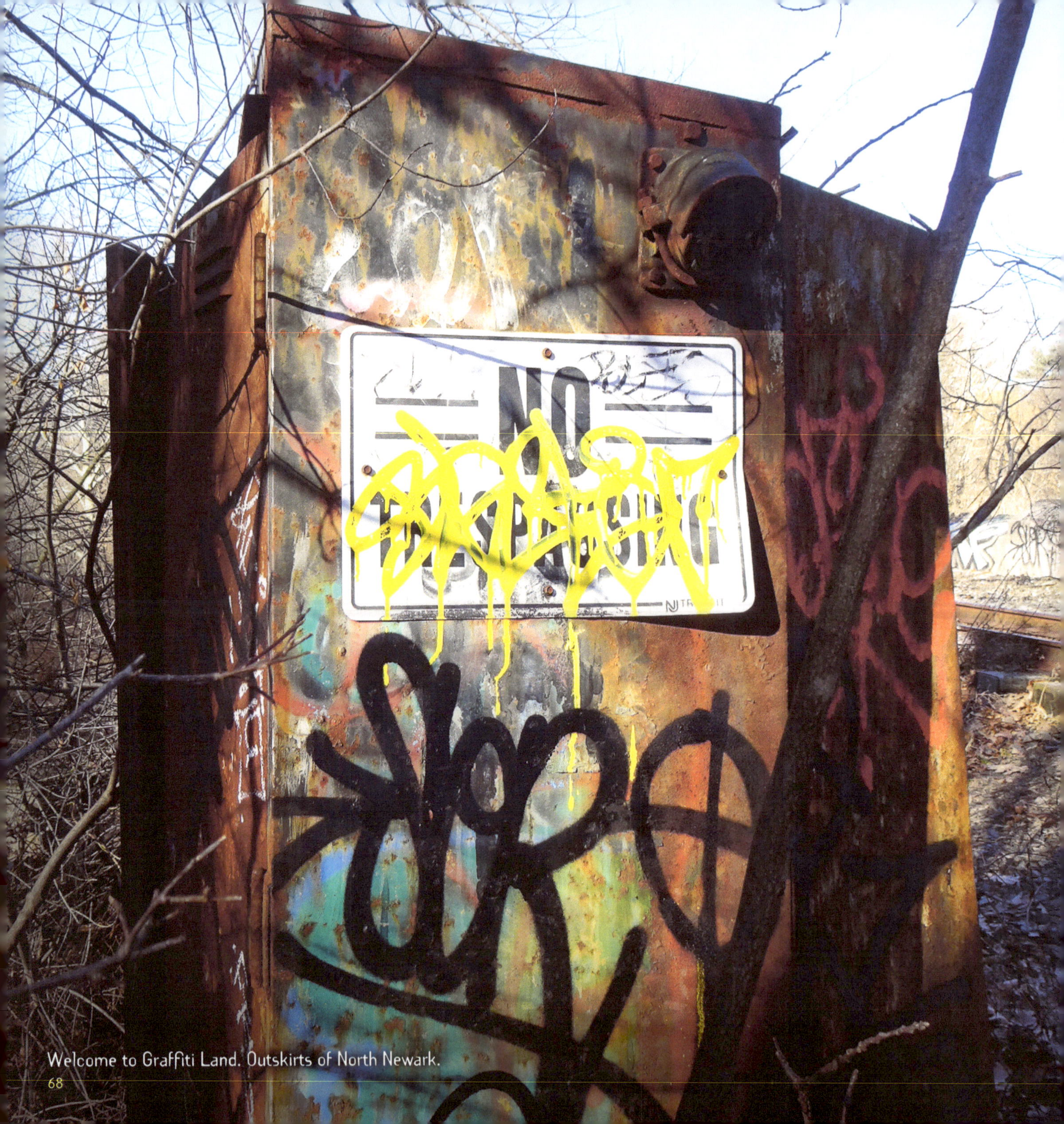

Welcome to Graffiti Land. Outskirts of North Newark.

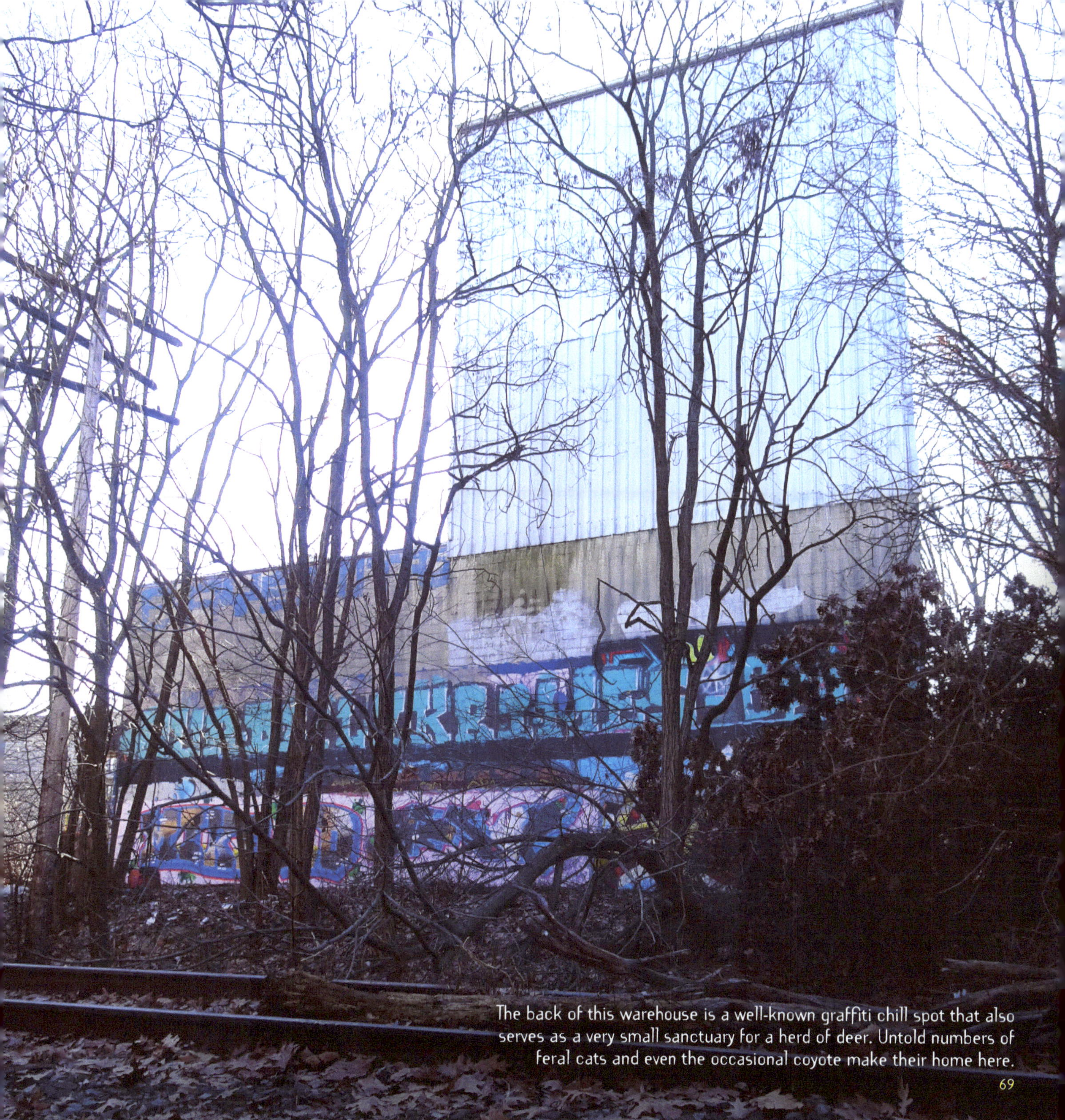

The back of this warehouse is a well-known graffiti chill spot that also serves as a very small sanctuary for a herd of deer. Untold numbers of feral cats and even the occasional coyote make their home here.

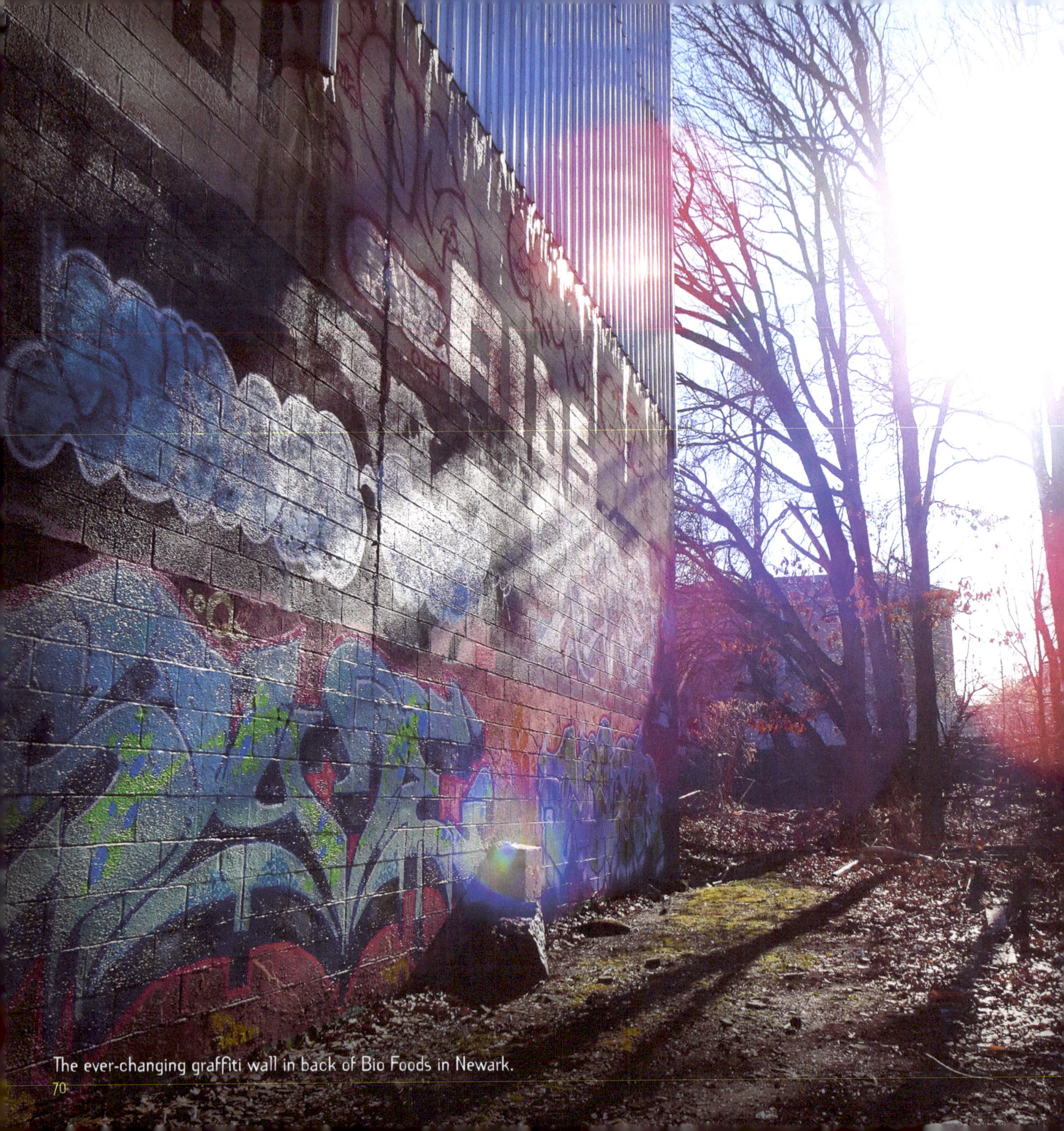

The ever-changing graffiti wall in back of Bio Foods in Newark.

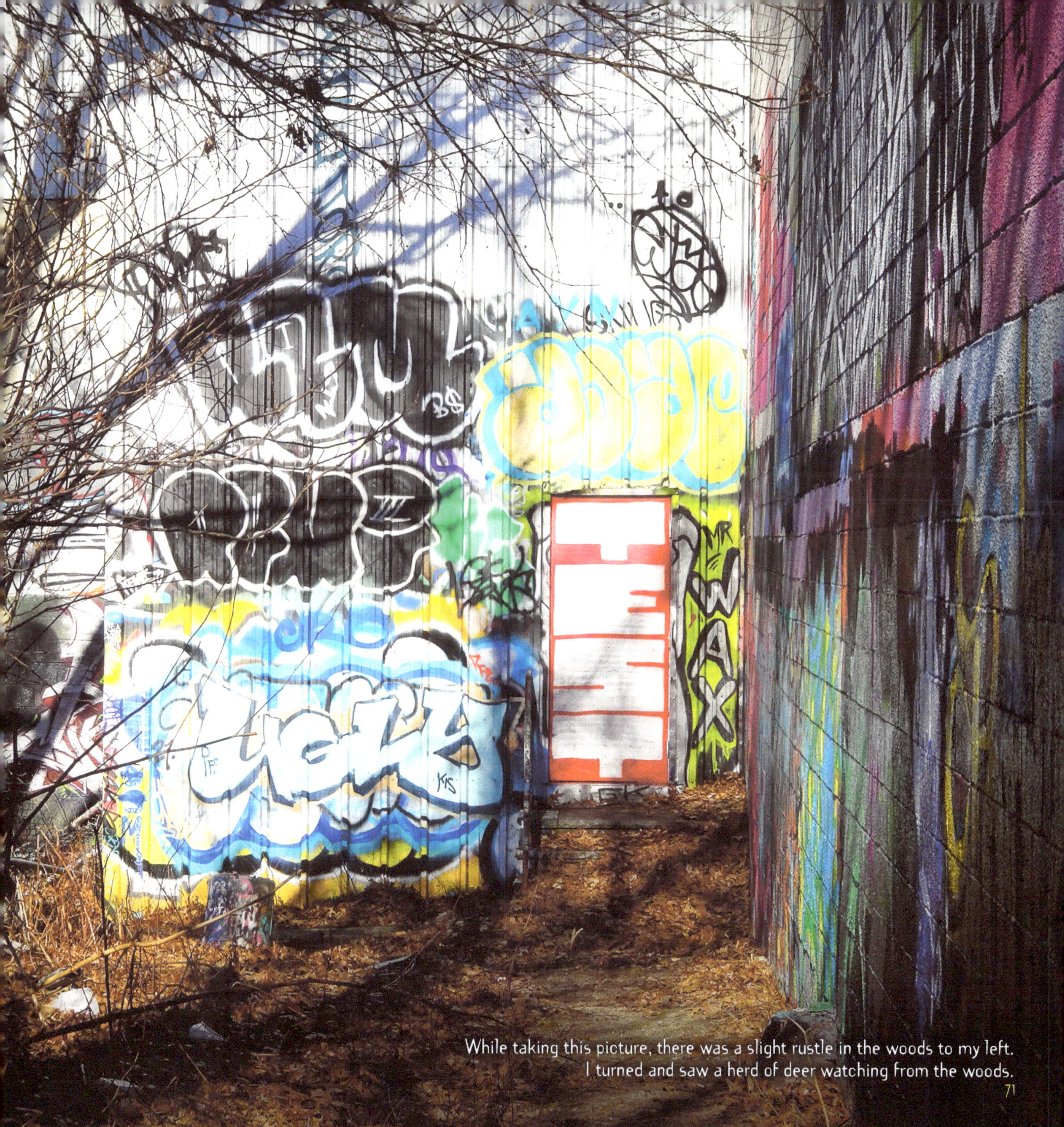

While taking this picture, there was a slight rustle in the woods to my left.
I turned and saw a herd of deer watching from the woods.

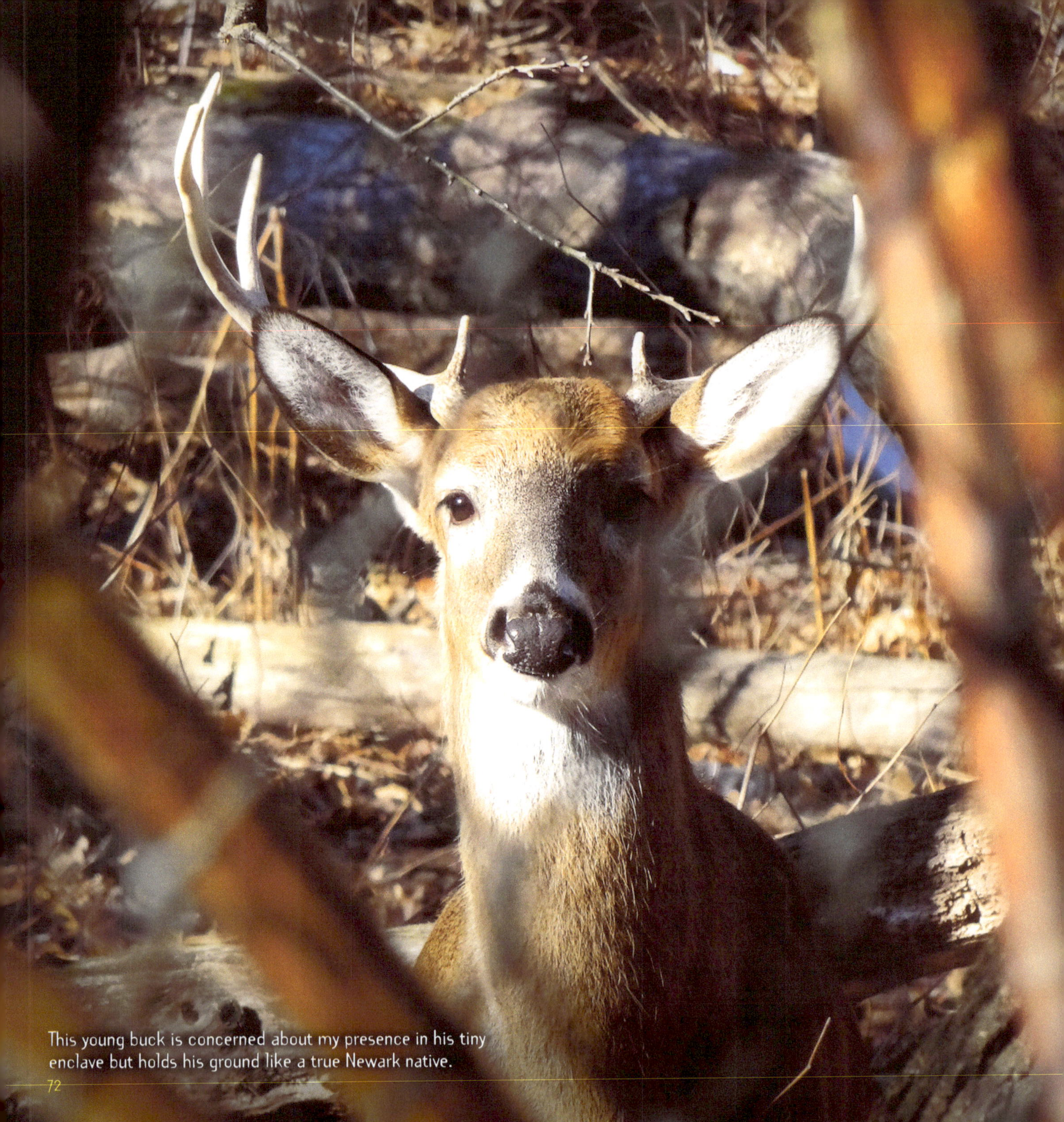

This young buck is concerned about my presence in his tiny enclave but holds his ground like a true Newark native.

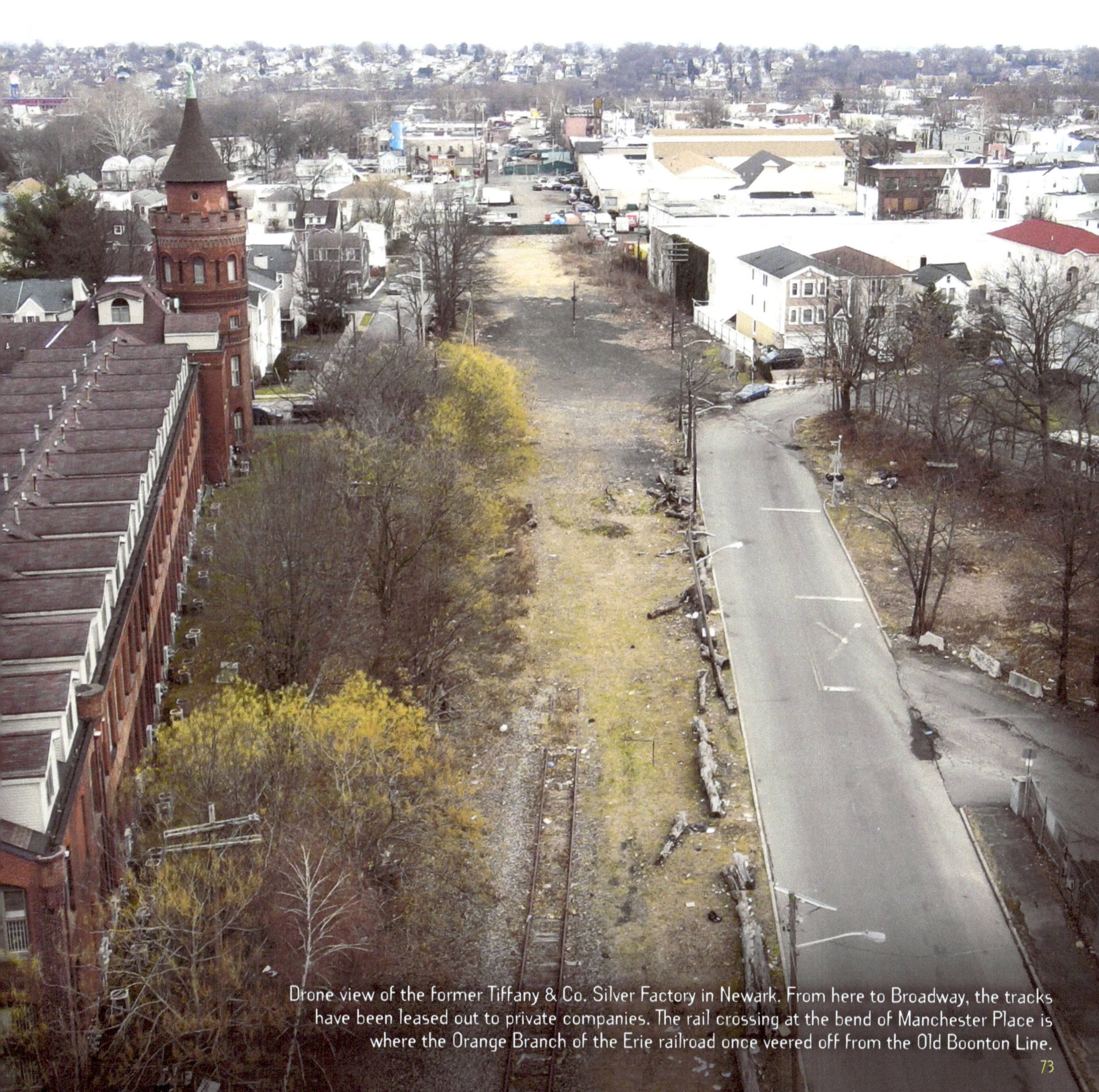

Drone view of the former Tiffany & Co. Silver Factory in Newark. From here to Broadway, the tracks have been leased out to private companies. The rail crossing at the bend of Manchester Place is where the Orange Branch of the Erie railroad once veered off from the Old Boonton Line.

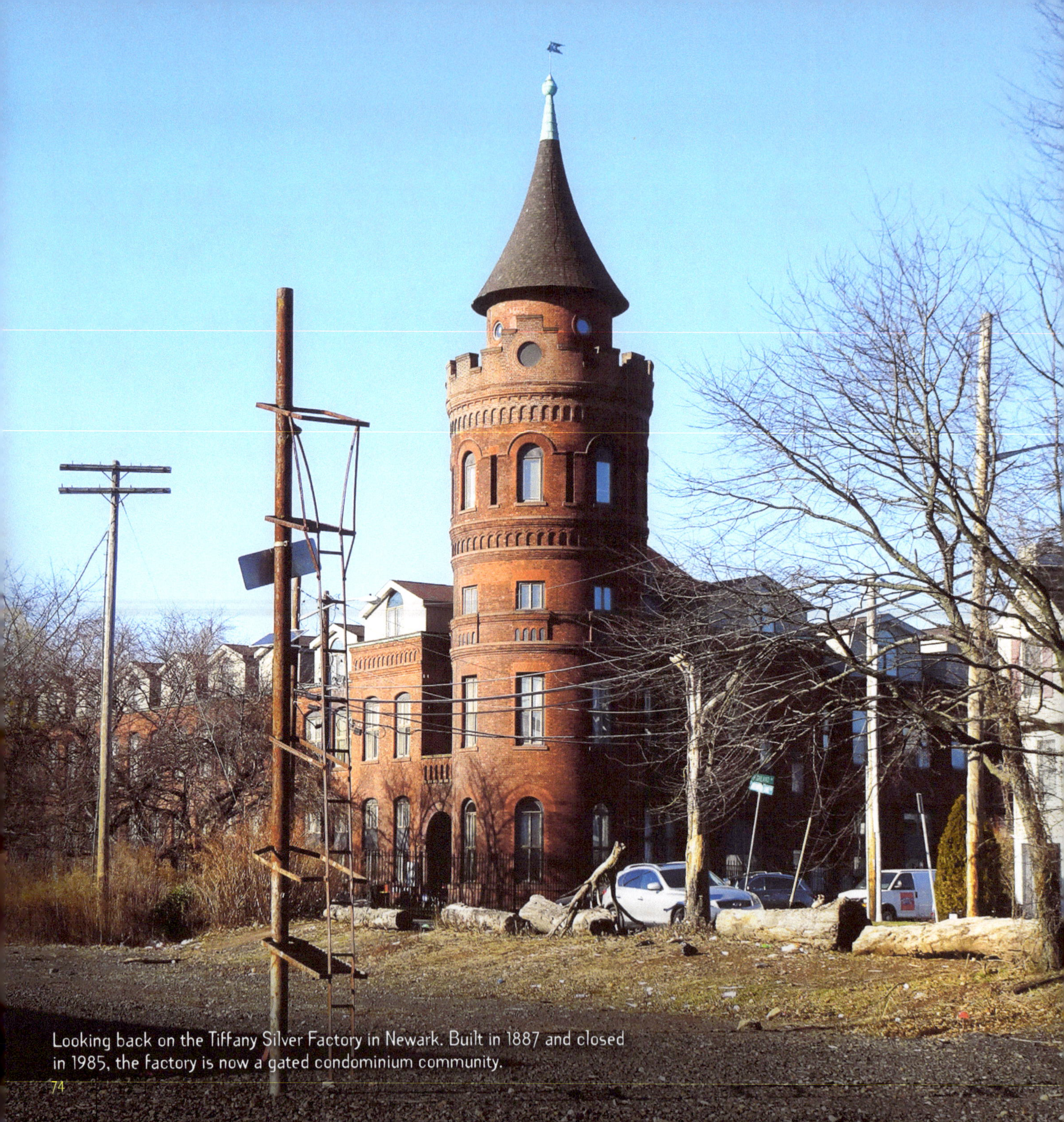

Looking back on the Tiffany Silver Factory in Newark. Built in 1887 and closed in 1985, the factory is now a gated condominium community.

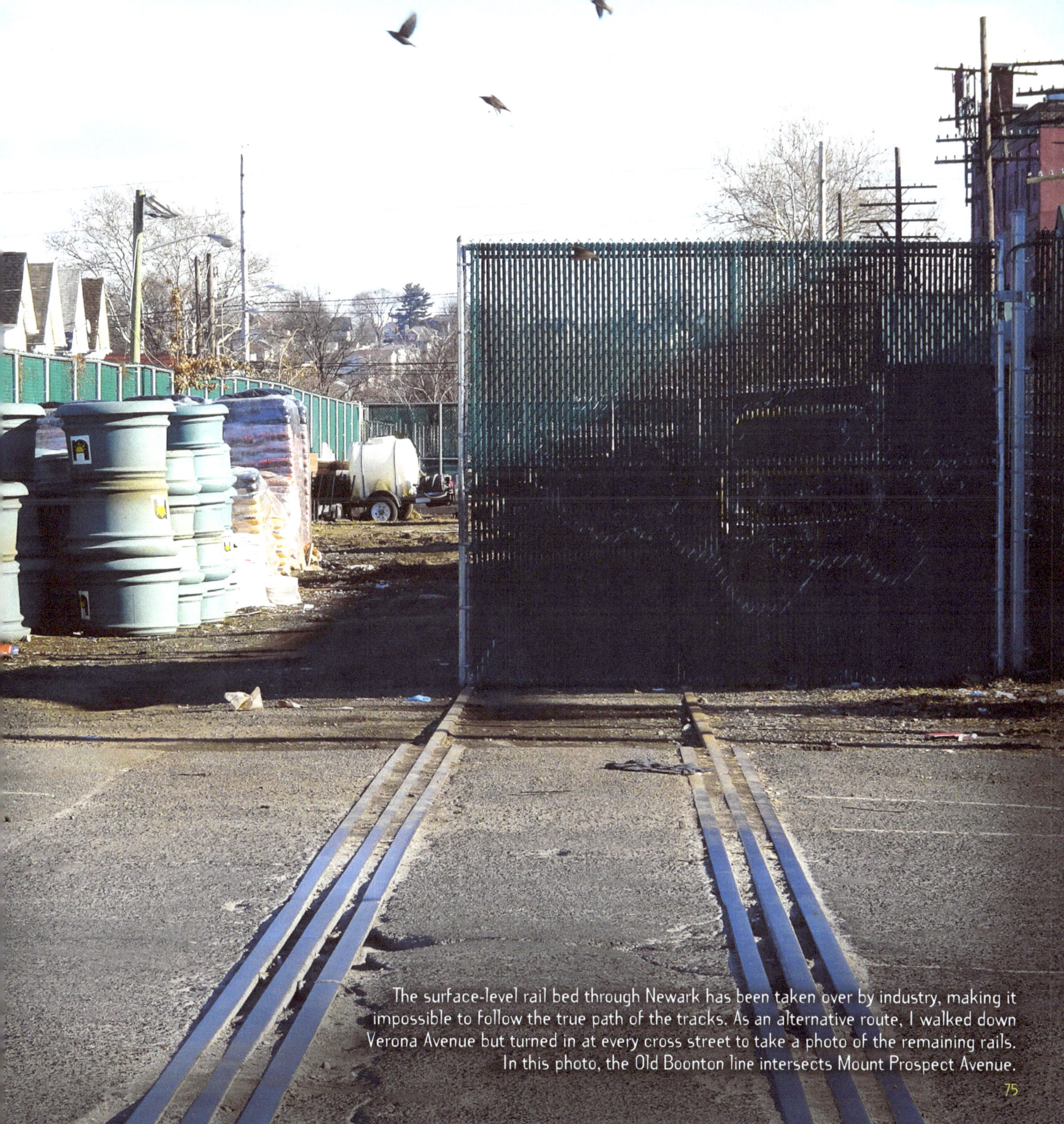

The surface-level rail bed through Newark has been taken over by industry, making it impossible to follow the true path of the tracks. As an alternative route, I walked down Verona Avenue but turned in at every cross street to take a photo of the remaining rails. In this photo, the Old Boonton line intersects Mount Prospect Avenue.

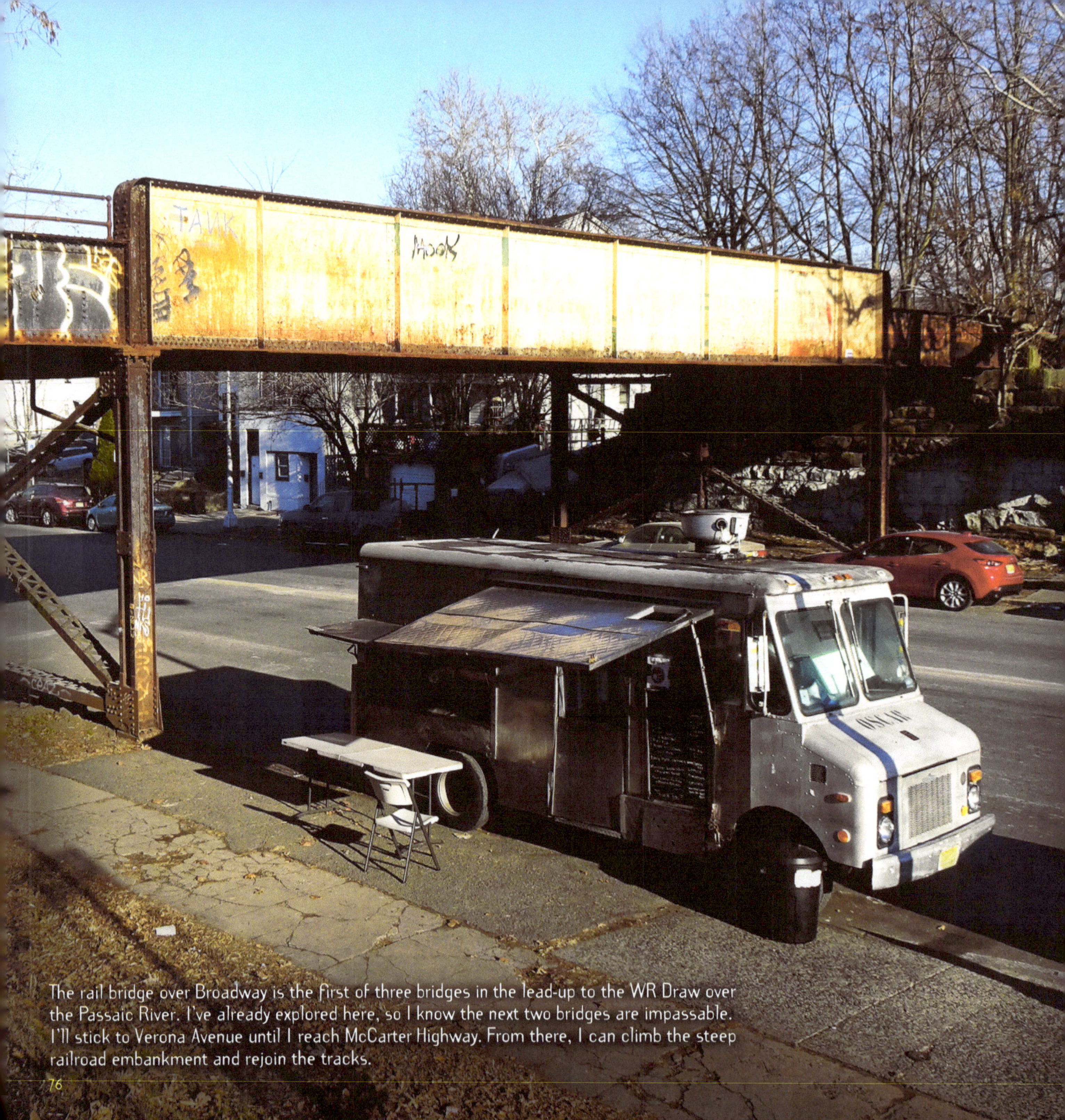

The rail bridge over Broadway is the first of three bridges in the lead-up to the WR Draw over the Passaic River. I've already explored here, so I know the next two bridges are impassable. I'll stick to Verona Avenue until I reach McCarter Highway. From there, I can climb the steep railroad embankment and rejoin the tracks.

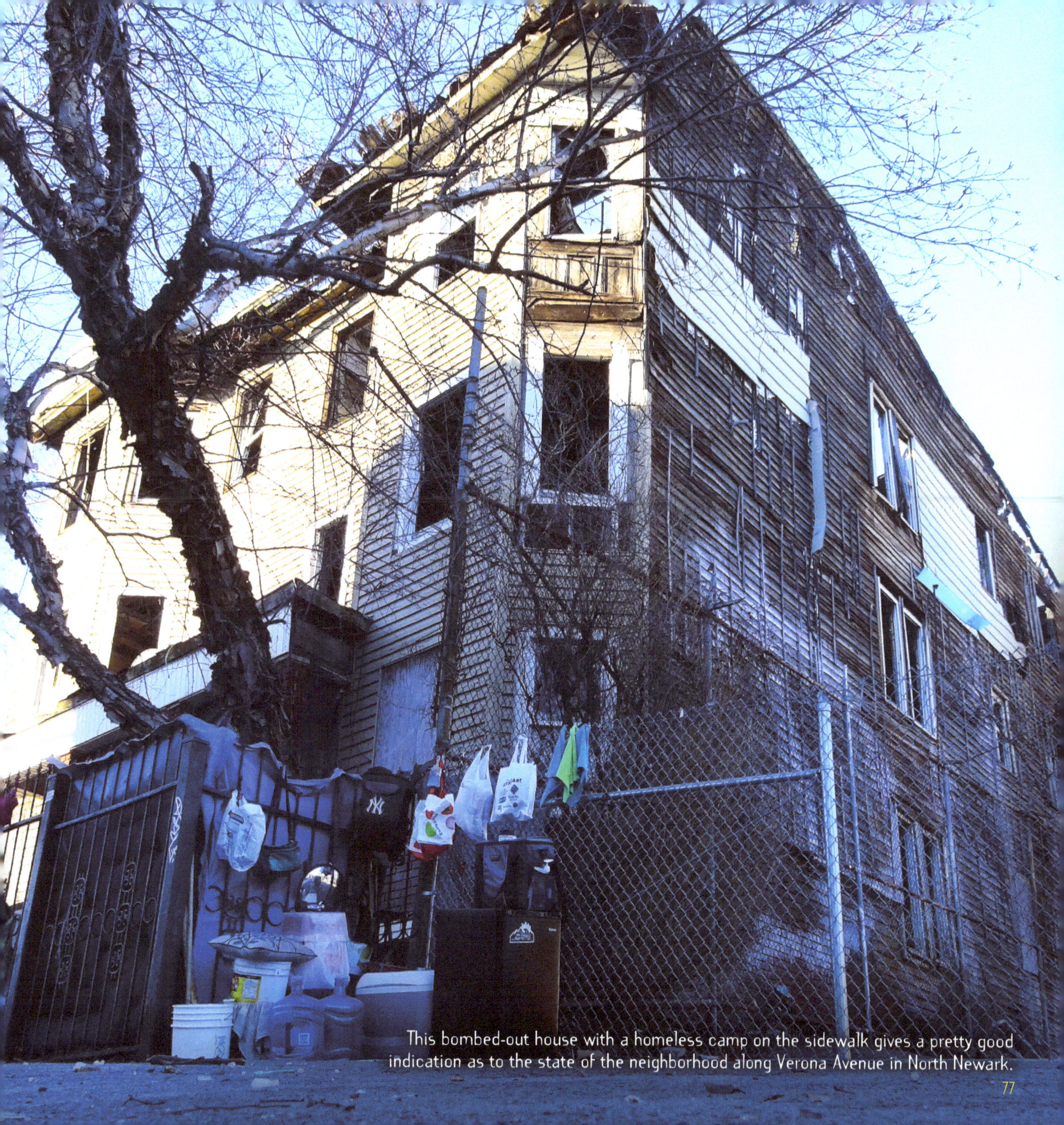

This bombed-out house with a homeless camp on the sidewalk gives a pretty good indication as to the state of the neighborhood along Verona Avenue in North Newark.

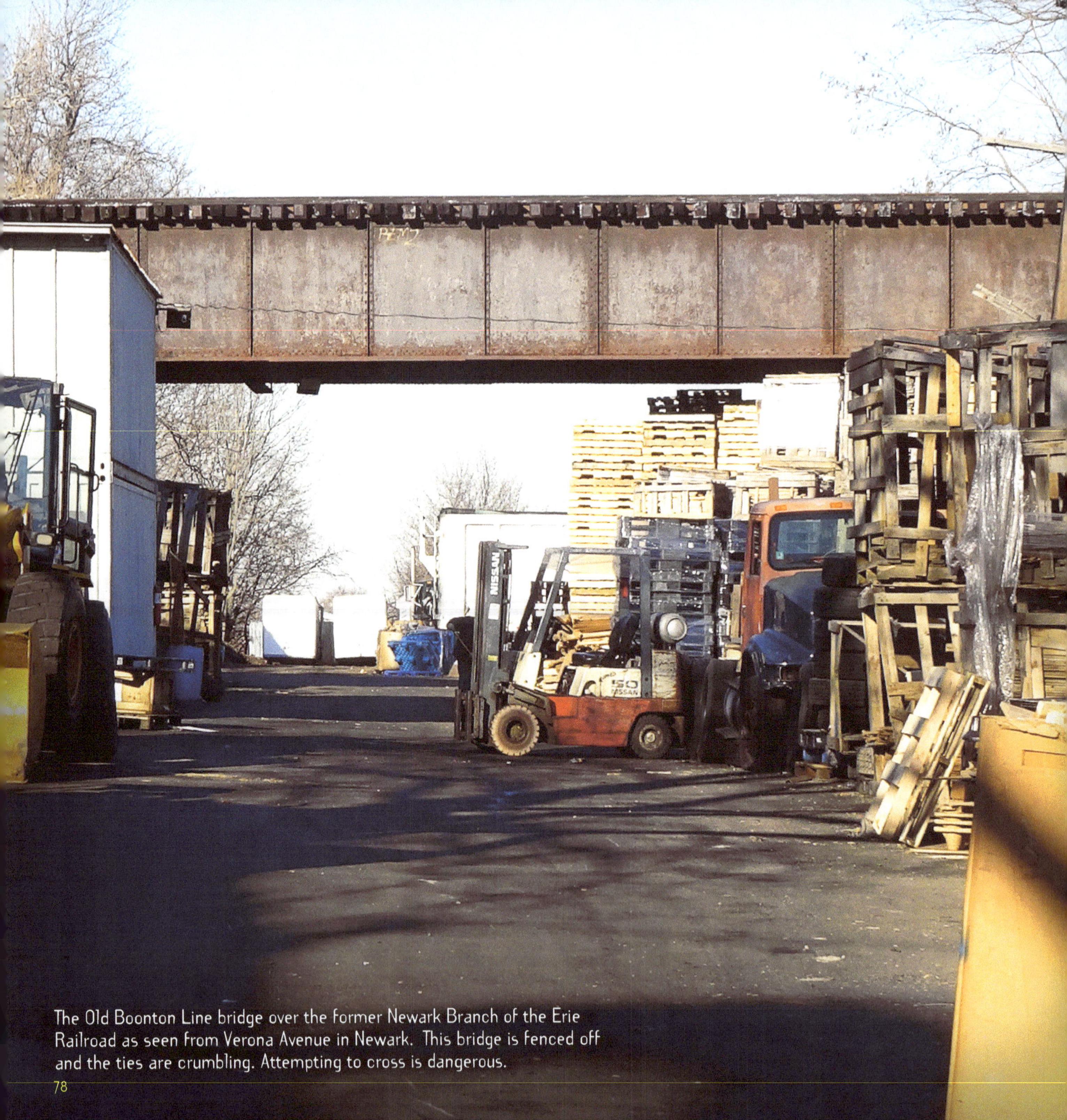

The Old Boonton Line bridge over the former Newark Branch of the Erie Railroad as seen from Verona Avenue in Newark. This bridge is fenced off and the ties are crumbling. Attempting to cross is dangerous.

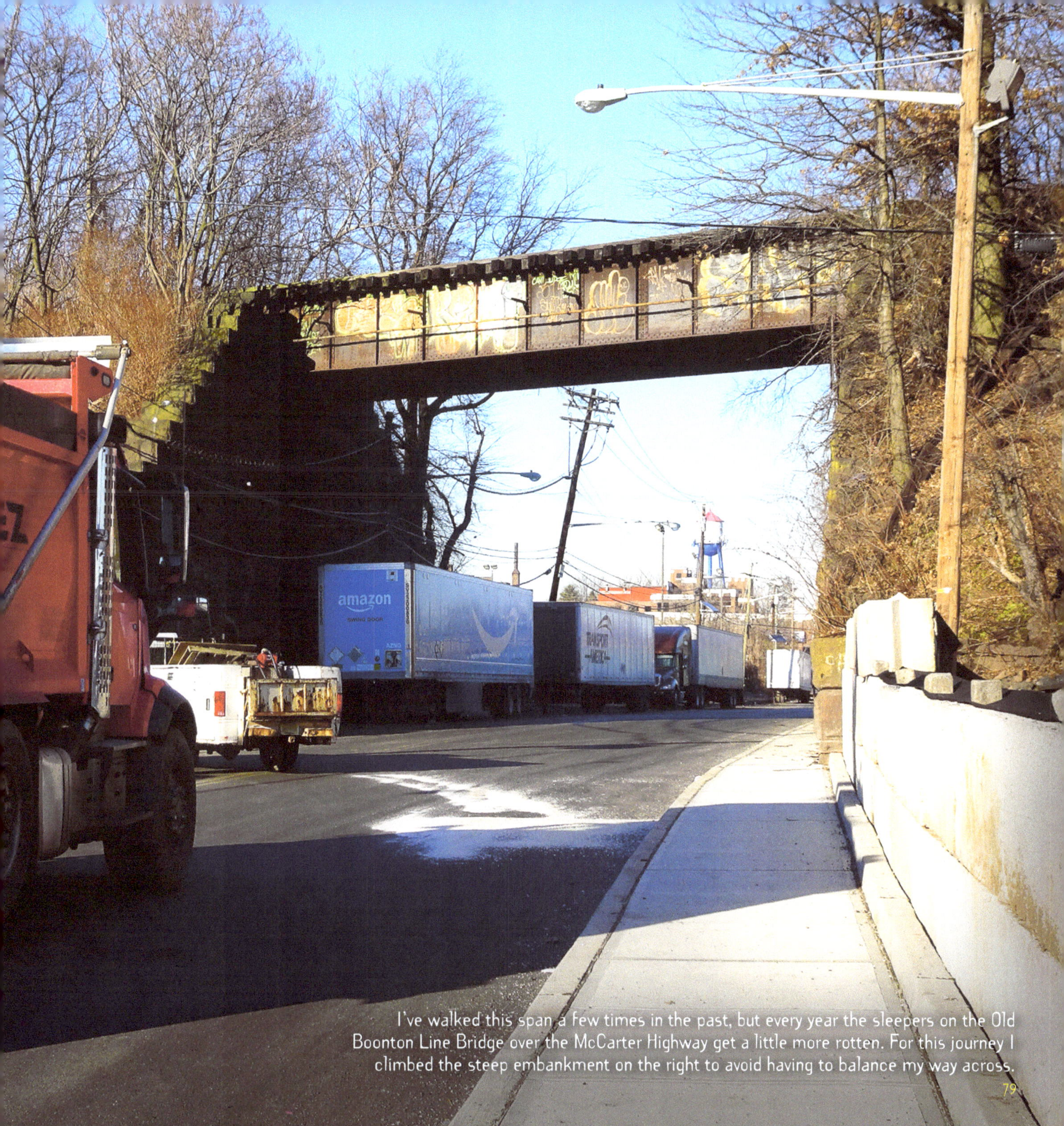

I've walked this span a few times in the past, but every year the sleepers on the Old Boonton Line Bridge over the McCarter Highway get a little more rotten. For this journey I climbed the steep embankment on the right to avoid having to balance my way across.

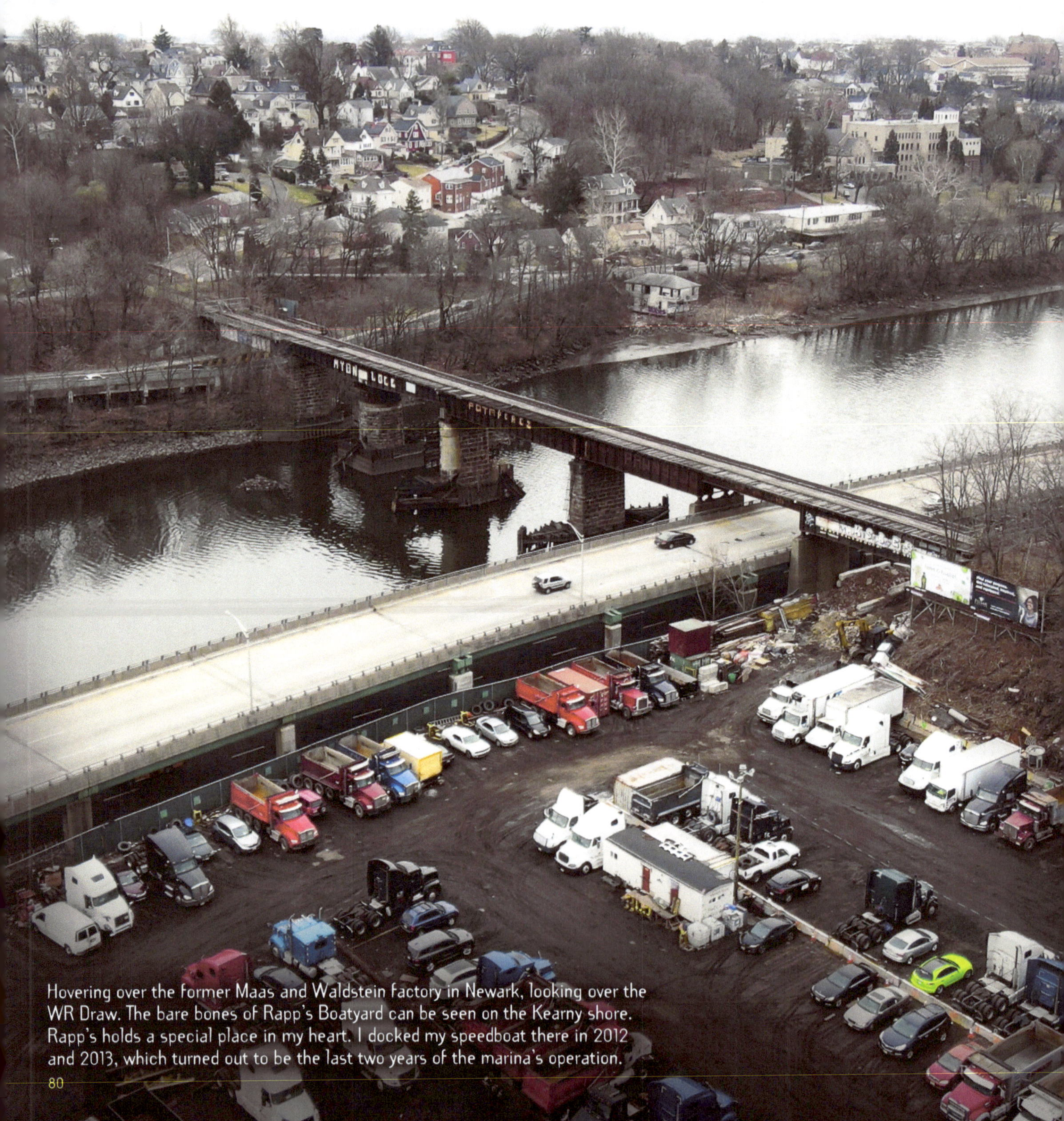

Hovering over the former Maas and Waldstein factory in Newark, looking over the WR Draw. The bare bones of Rapp's Boatyard can be seen on the Kearny shore. Rapp's holds a special place in my heart. I docked my speedboat there in 2012 and 2013, which turned out to be the last two years of the marina's operation.

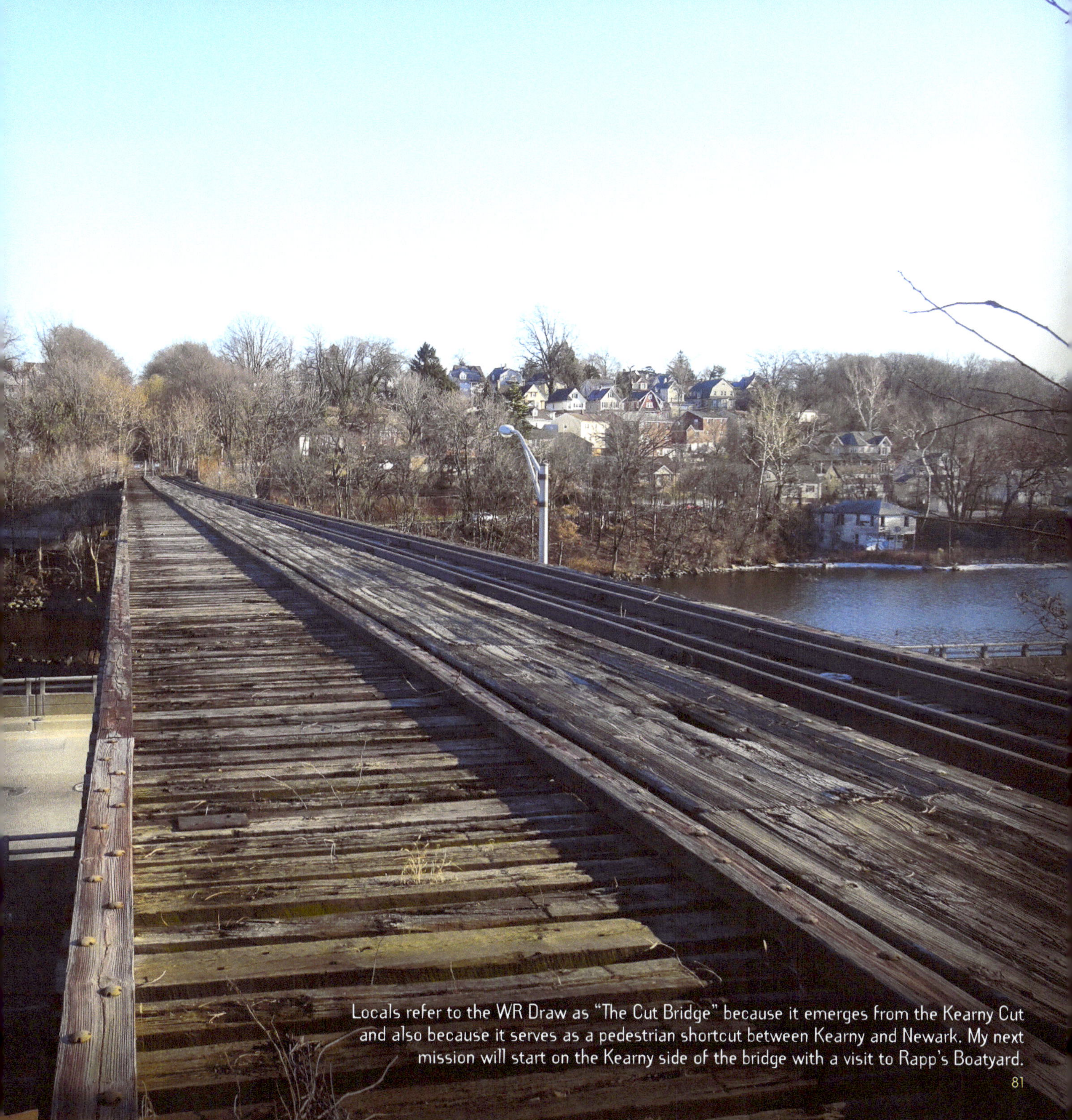

Locals refer to the WR Draw as "The Cut Bridge" because it emerges from the Kearny Cut and also because it serves as a pedestrian shortcut between Kearny and Newark. My next mission will start on the Kearny side of the bridge with a visit to Rapp's Boatyard.

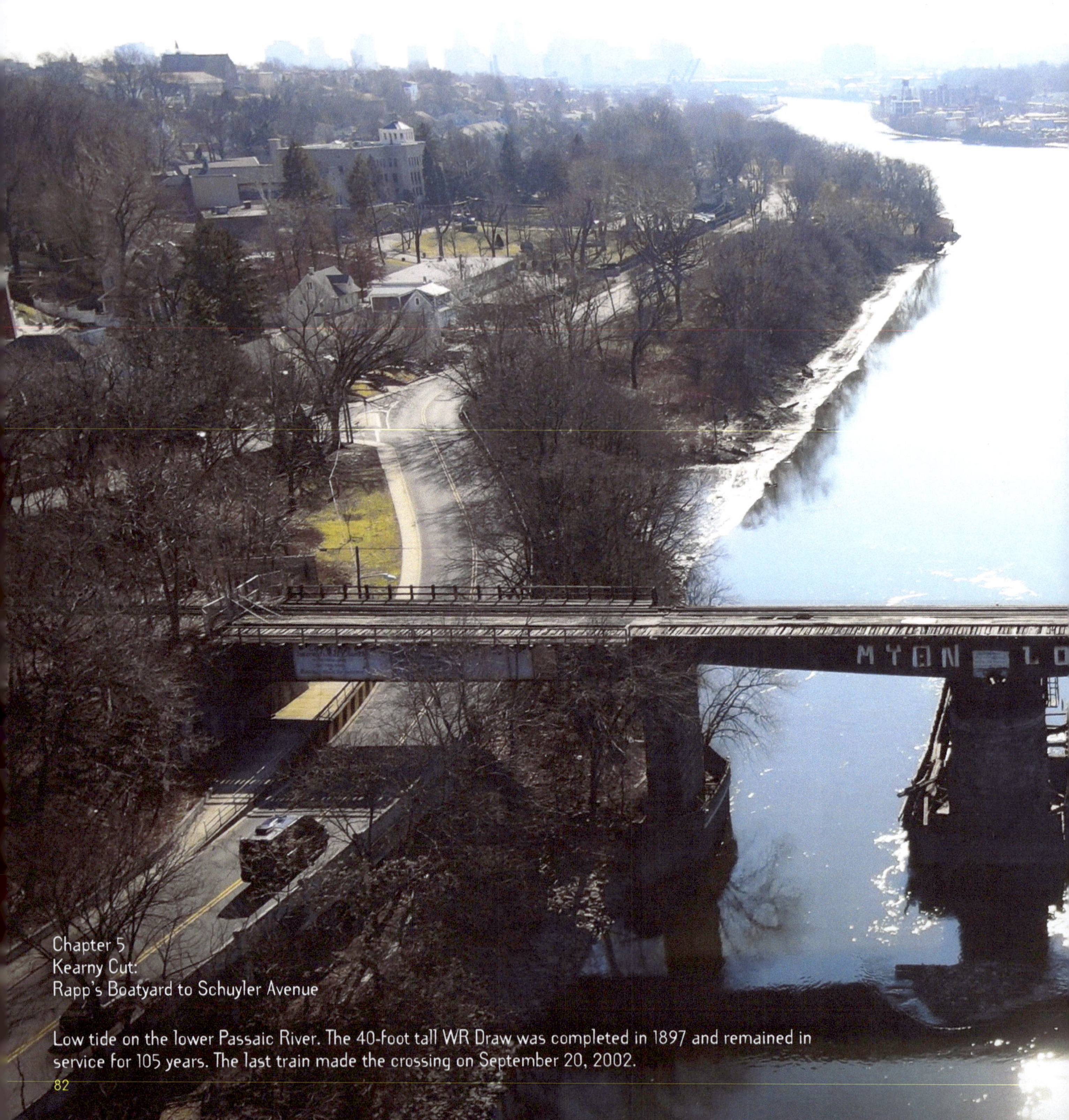

Chapter 5
Kearny Cut:
Rapp's Boatyard to Schuyler Avenue

Low tide on the lower Passaic River. The 40-foot tall WR Draw was completed in 1897 and remained in service for 105 years. The last train made the crossing on September 20, 2002.

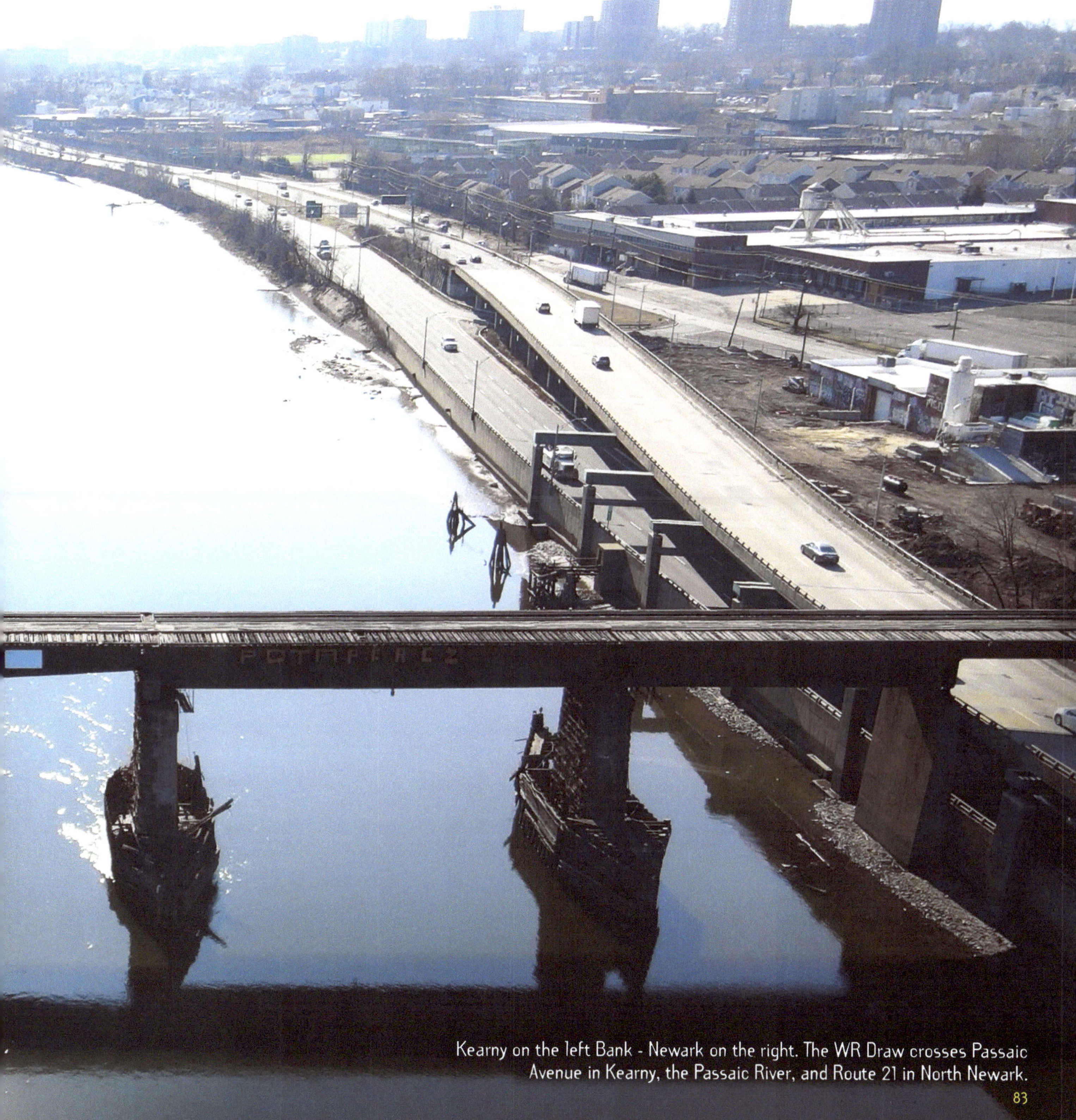

Kearny on the left Bank - Newark on the right. The WR Draw crosses Passaic Avenue in Kearny, the Passaic River, and Route 21 in North Newark.

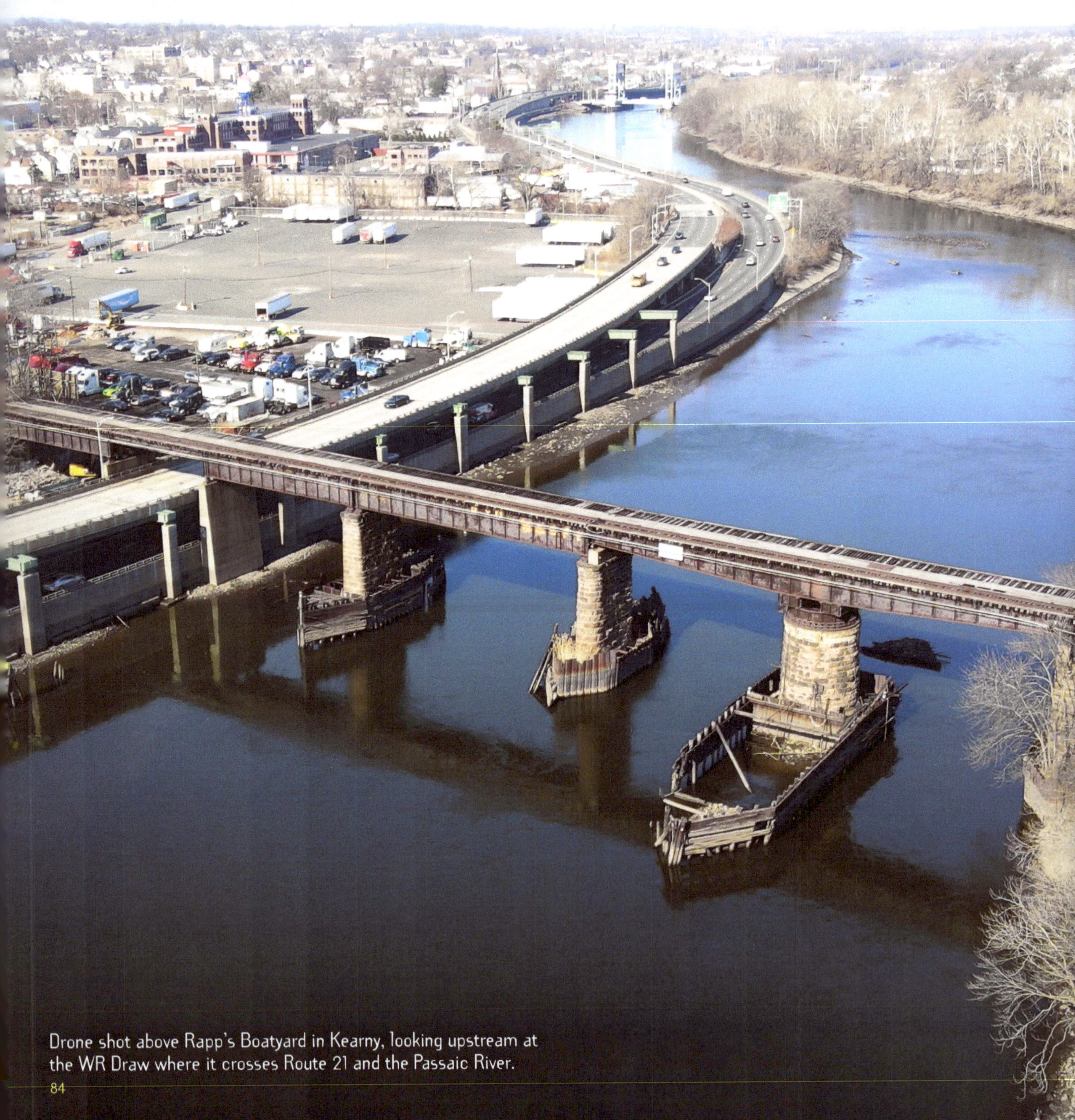

Drone shot above Rapp's Boatyard in Kearny, looking upstream at the WR Draw where it crosses Route 21 and the Passaic River.

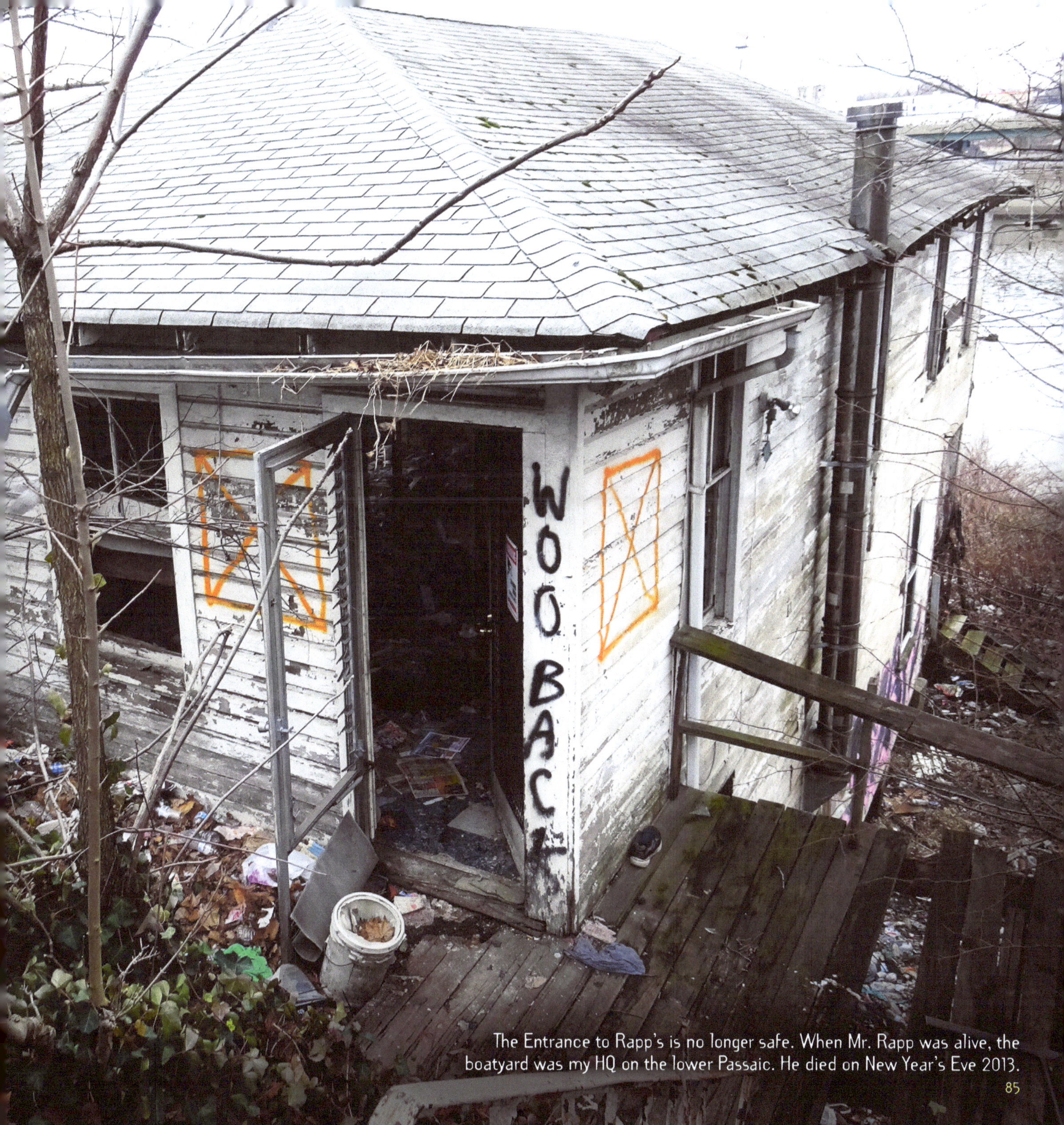

The Entrance to Rapp's is no longer safe. When Mr. Rapp was alive, the boatyard was my HQ on the lower Passaic. He died on New Year's Eve 2013.

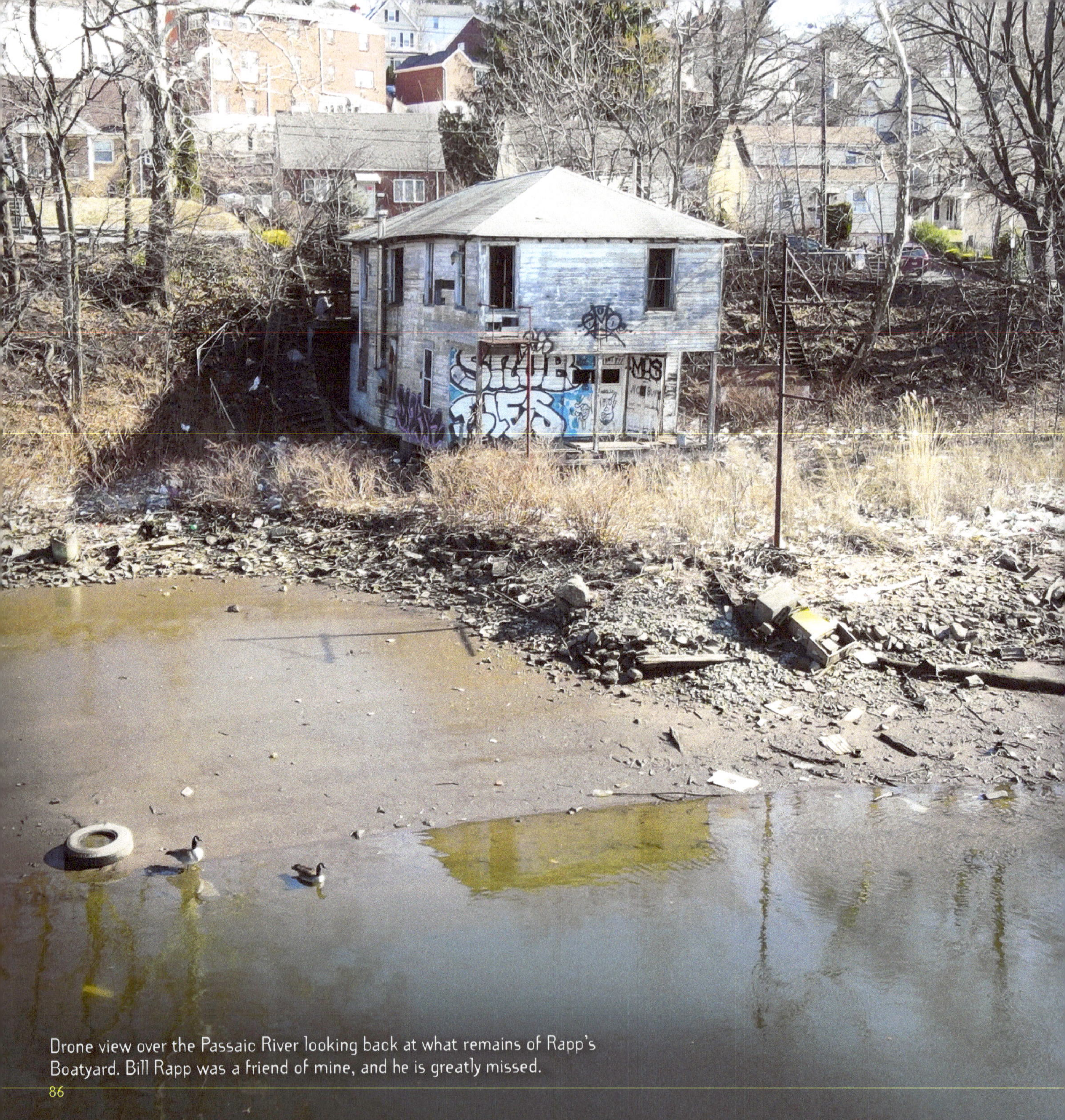

Drone view over the Passaic River looking back at what remains of Rapp's Boatyard. Bill Rapp was a friend of mine, and he is greatly missed.

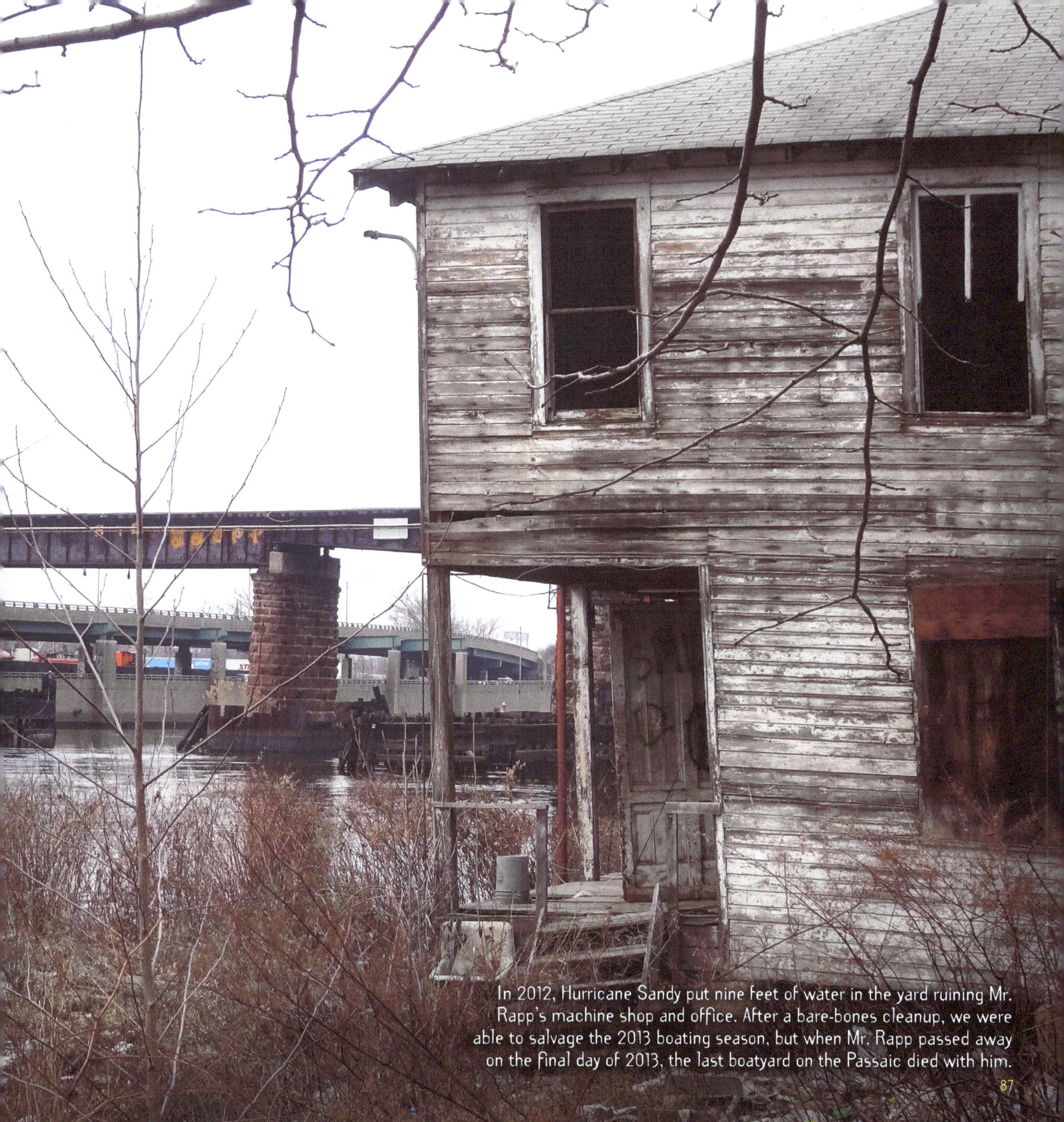

In 2012, Hurricane Sandy put nine feet of water in the yard ruining Mr. Rapp's machine shop and office. After a bare-bones cleanup, we were able to salvage the 2013 boating season, but when Mr. Rapp passed away on the final day of 2013, the last boatyard on the Passaic died with him.

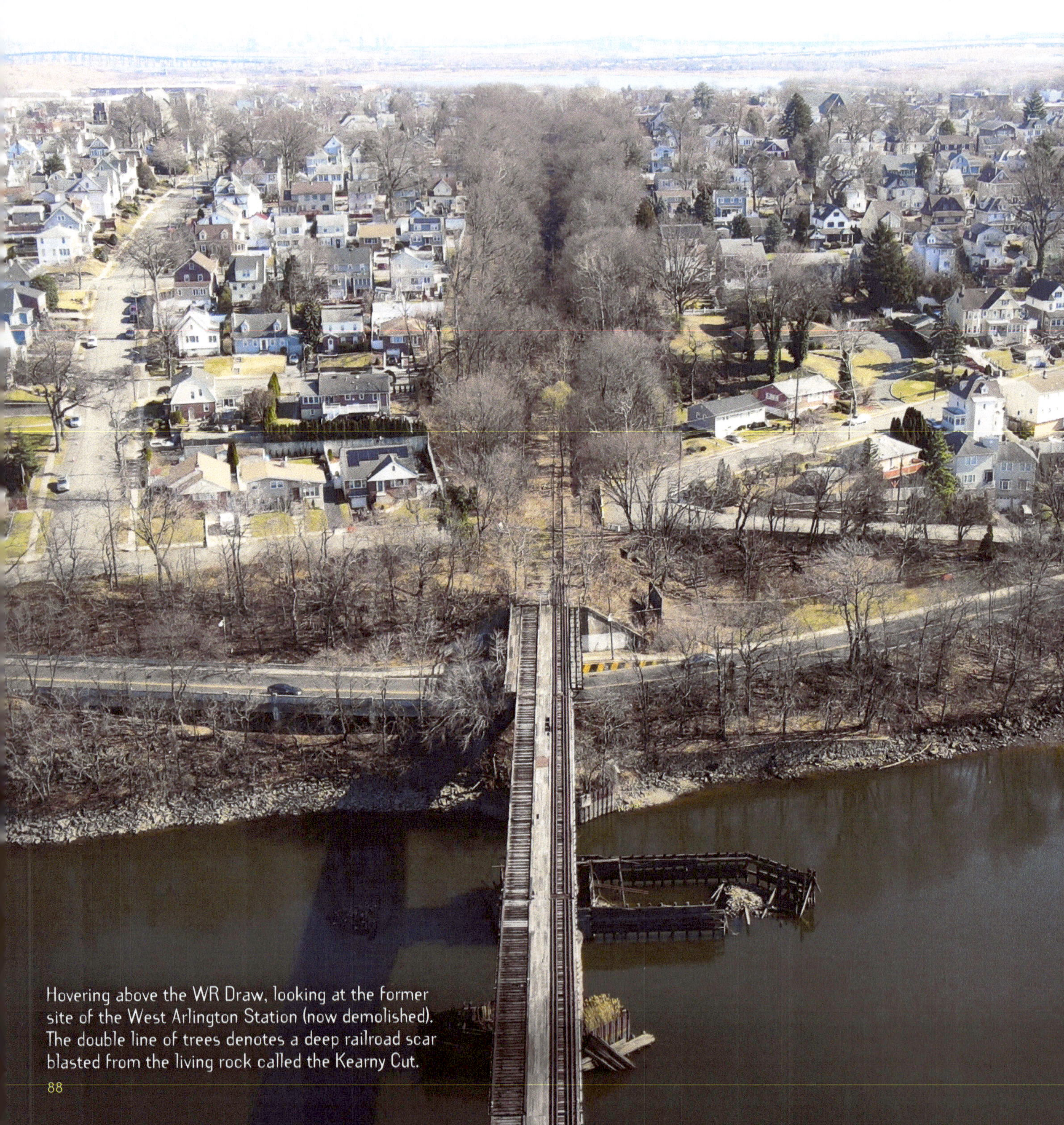

Hovering above the WR Draw, looking at the former site of the West Arlington Station (now demolished). The double line of trees denotes a deep railroad scar blasted from the living rock called the Kearny Cut.

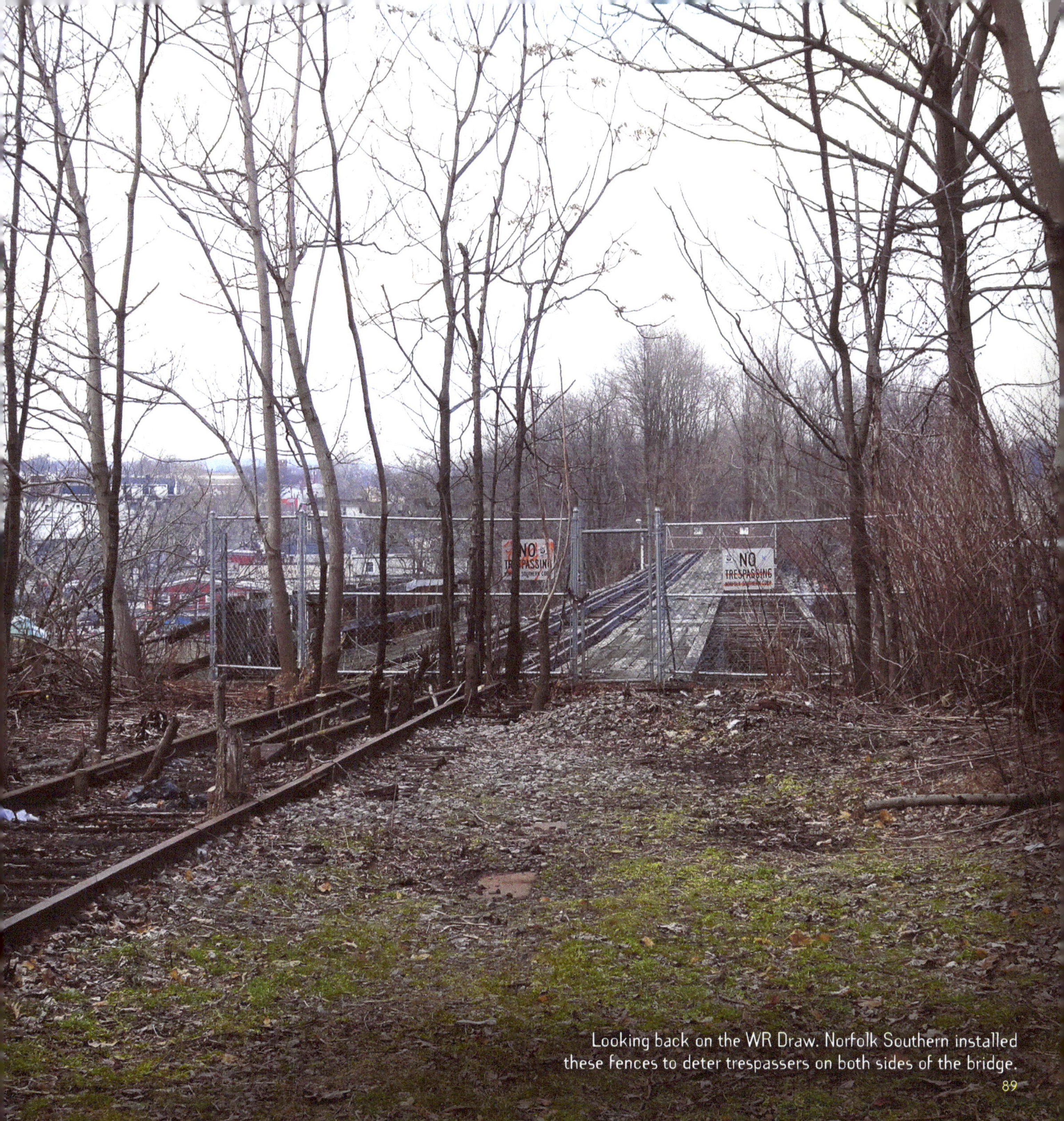

Looking back on the WR Draw. Norfolk Southern installed these fences to deter trespassers on both sides of the bridge.

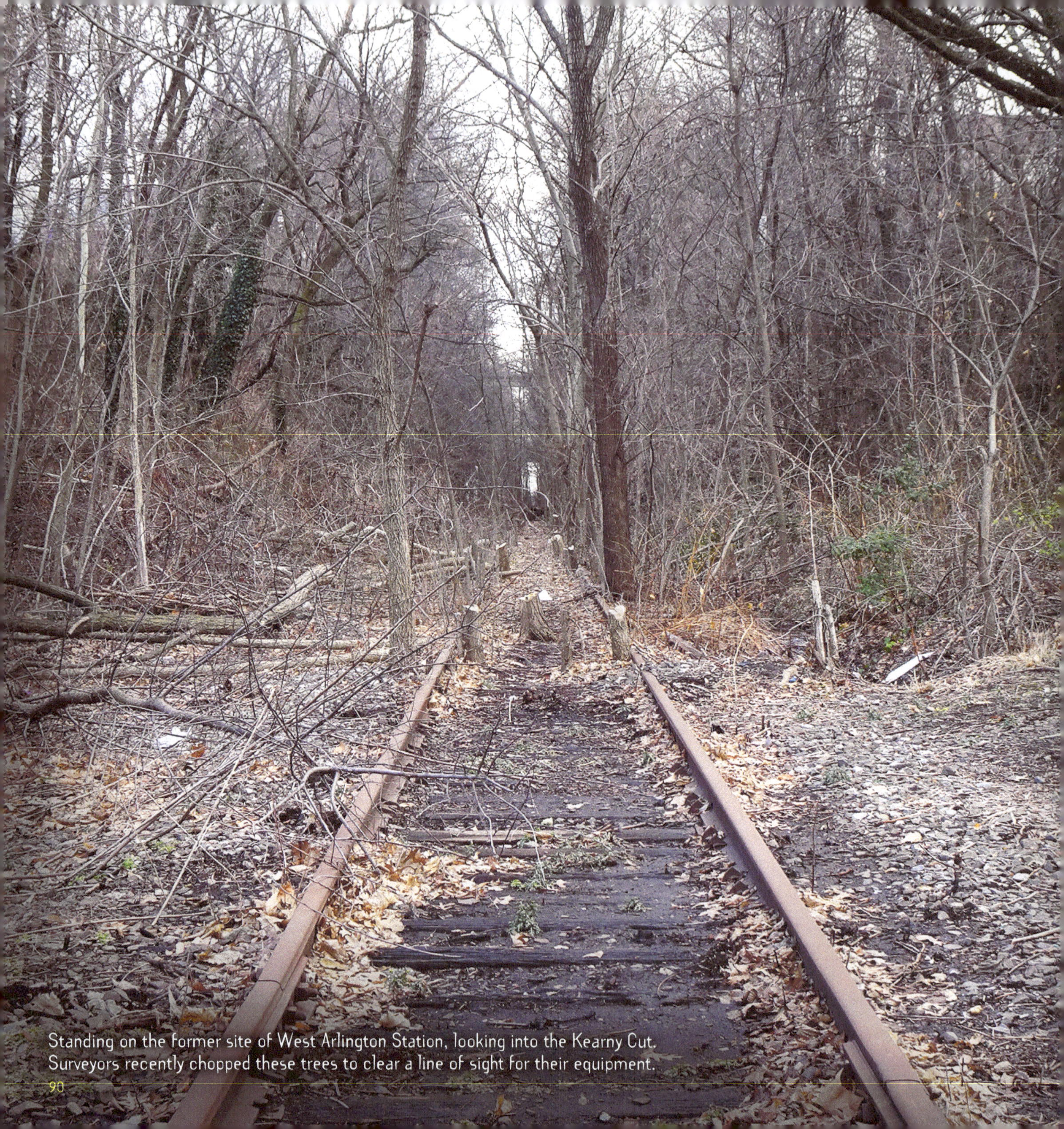

Standing on the former site of West Arlington Station, looking into the Kearny Cut. Surveyors recently chopped these trees to clear a line of sight for their equipment.

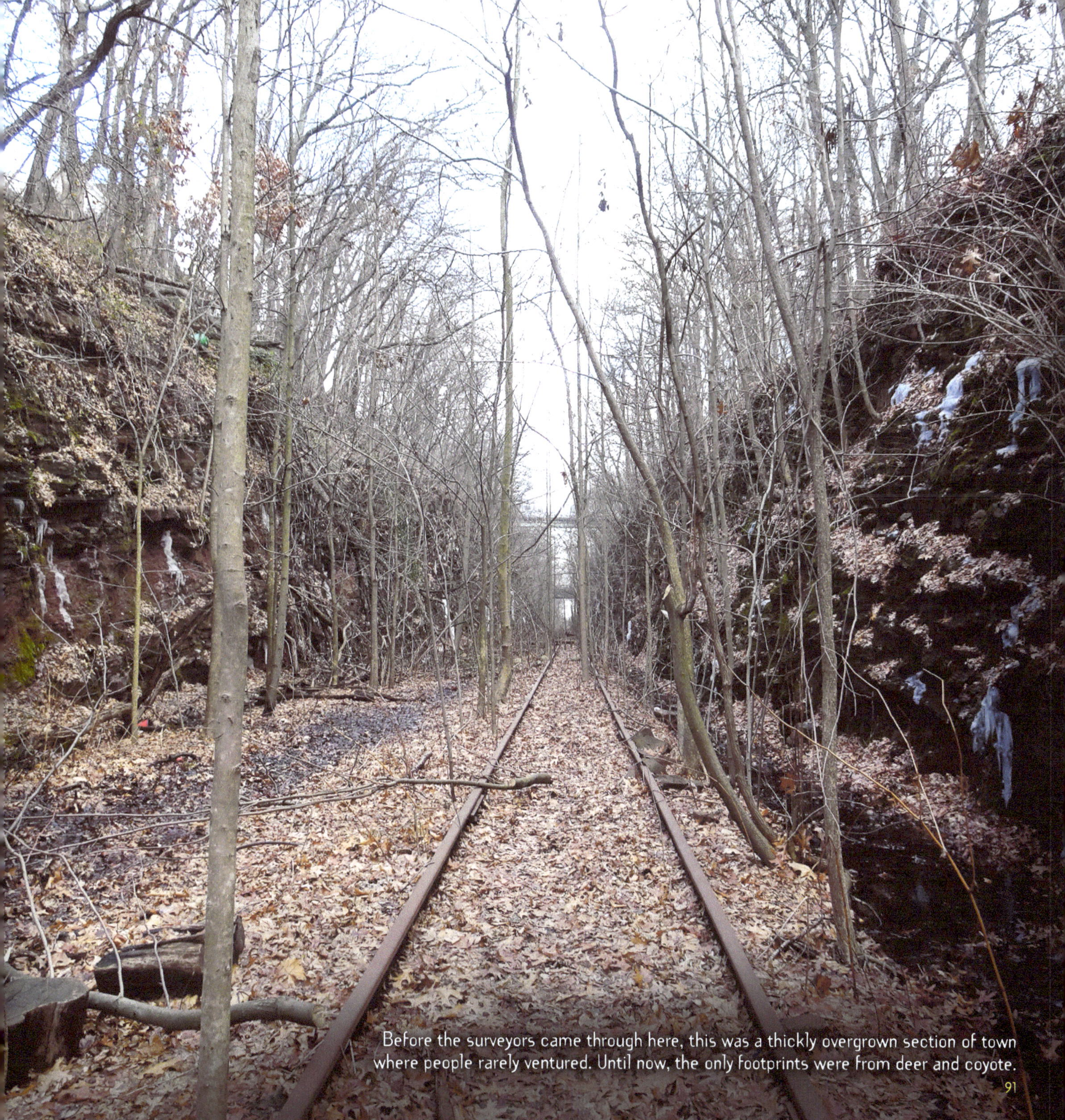

Before the surveyors came through here, this was a thickly overgrown section of town where people rarely ventured. Until now, the only footprints were from deer and coyote.

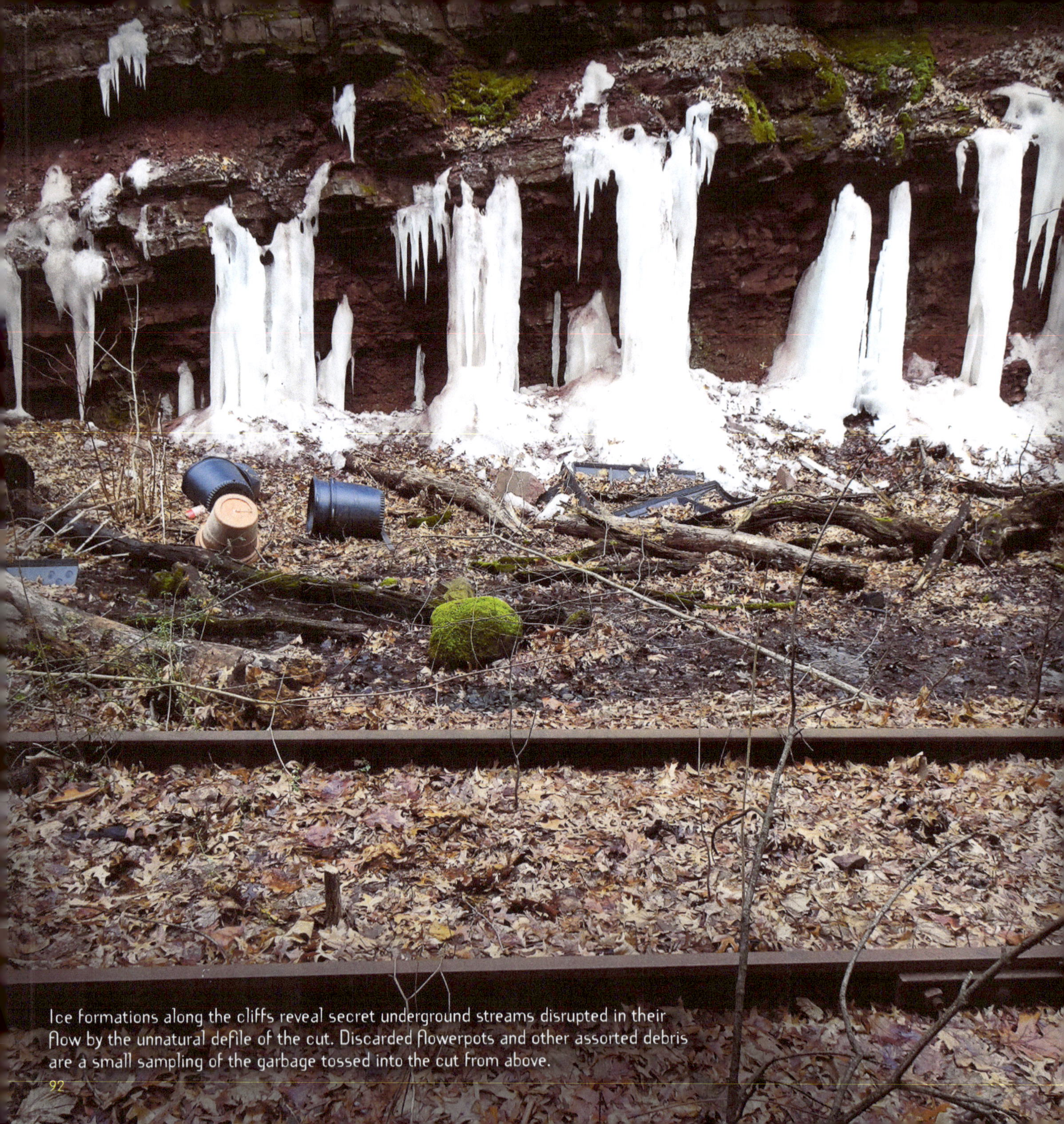

Ice formations along the cliffs reveal secret underground streams disrupted in their flow by the unnatural defile of the cut. Discarded flowerpots and other assorted debris are a small sampling of the garbage tossed into the cut from above.

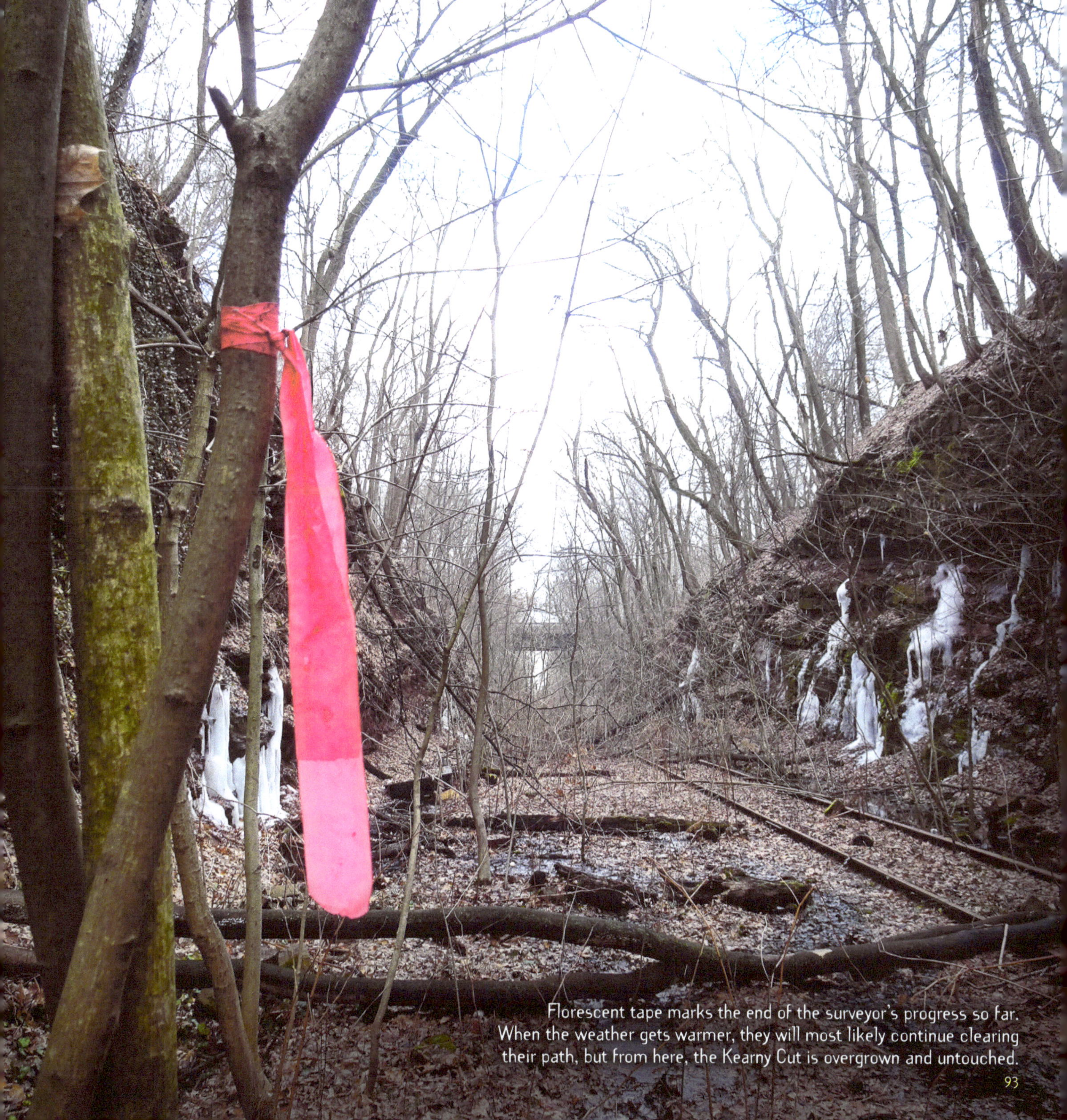

Florescent tape marks the end of the surveyor's progress so far. When the weather gets warmer, they will most likely continue clearing their path, but from here, the Kearny Cut is overgrown and untouched.

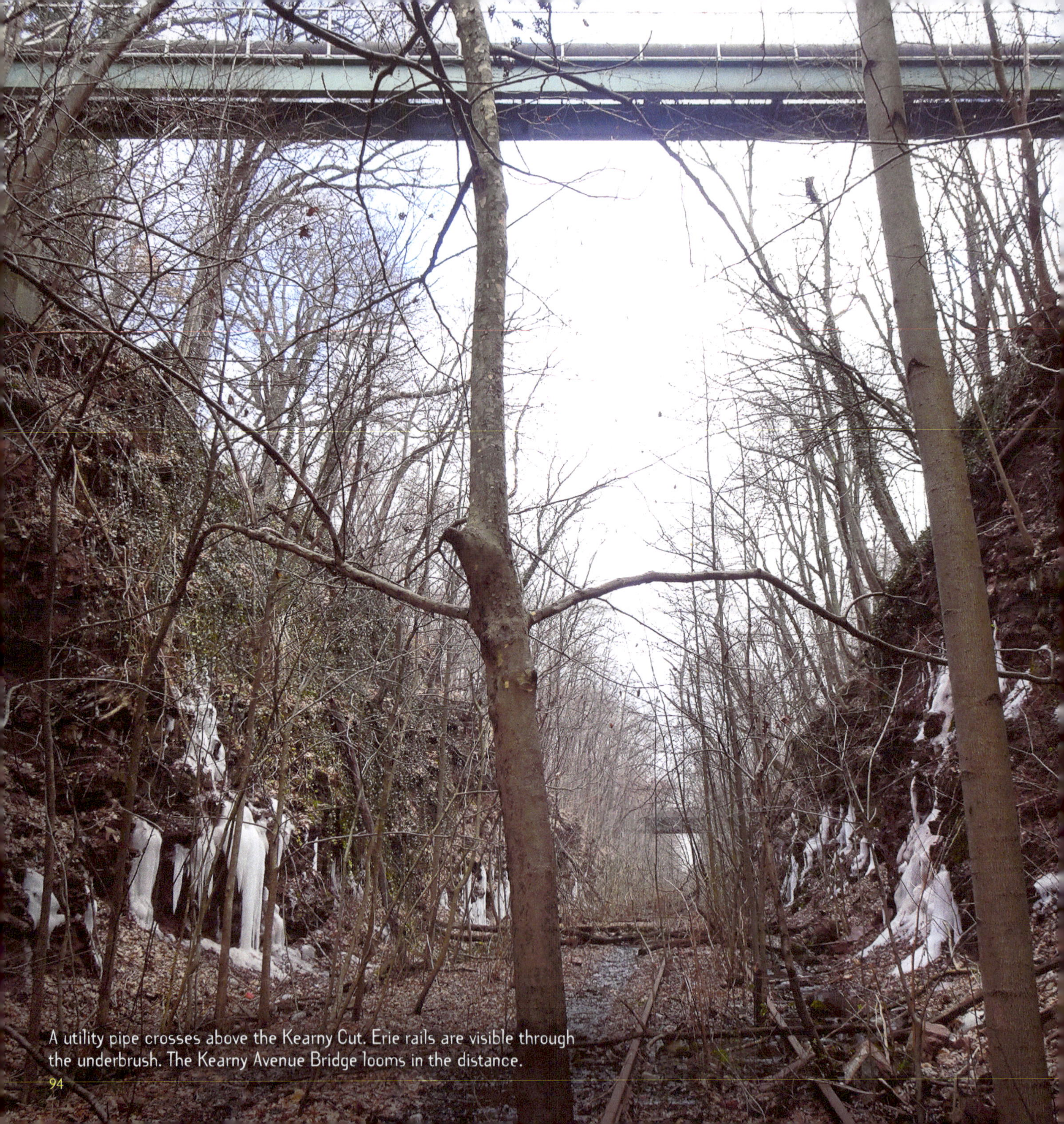

A utility pipe crosses above the Kearny Cut. Erie rails are visible through the underbrush. The Kearny Avenue Bridge looms in the distance.

Approaching the Kearny Avenue Bridge. The green patch up ahead is pachysandra that escaped from the garden above and went native in the swampy soil of the cut. The Chestnut Avenue Bridge can be seen in the distance.

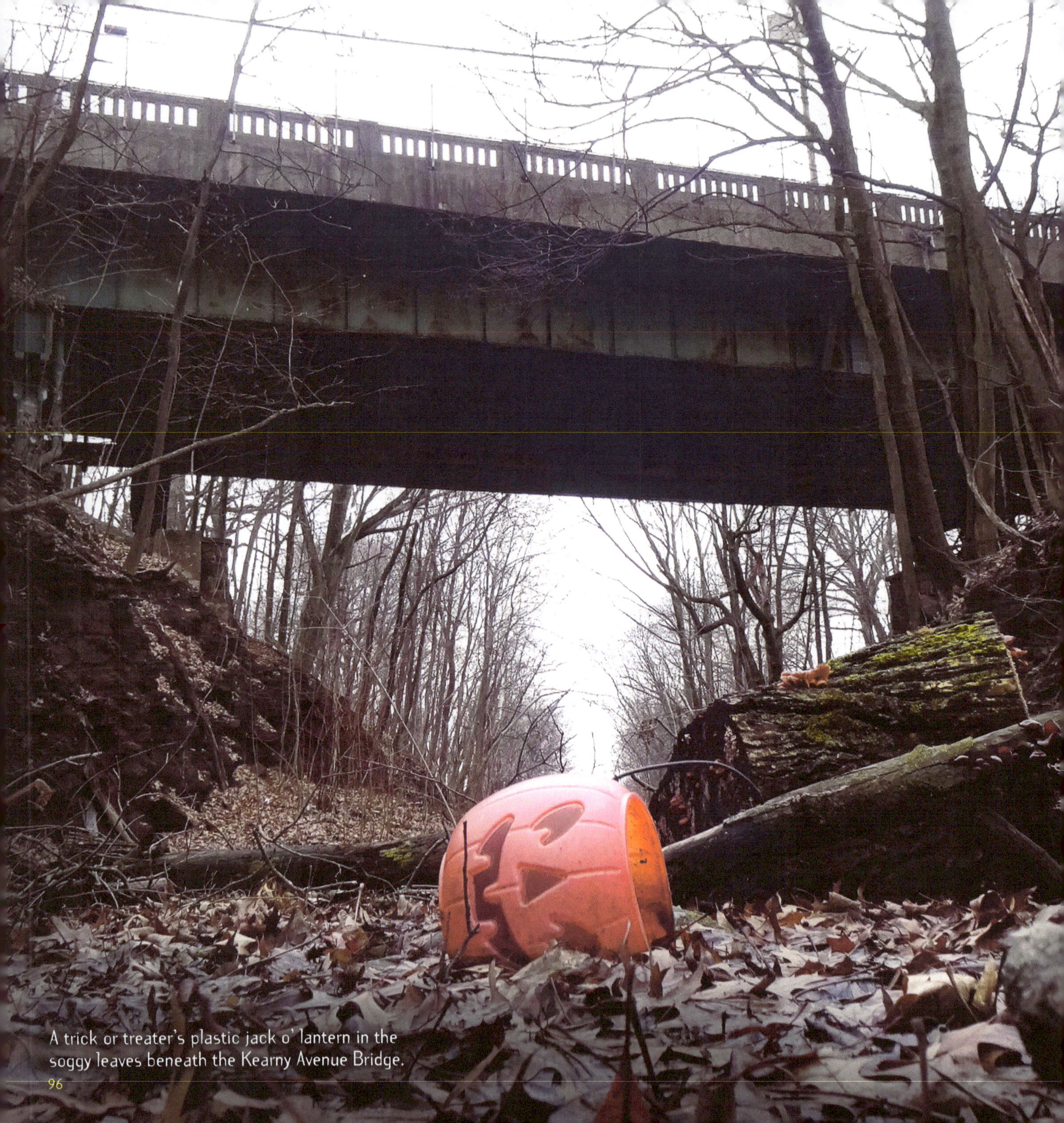

A trick or treater's plastic jack o' lantern in the soggy leaves beneath the Kearny Avenue Bridge.

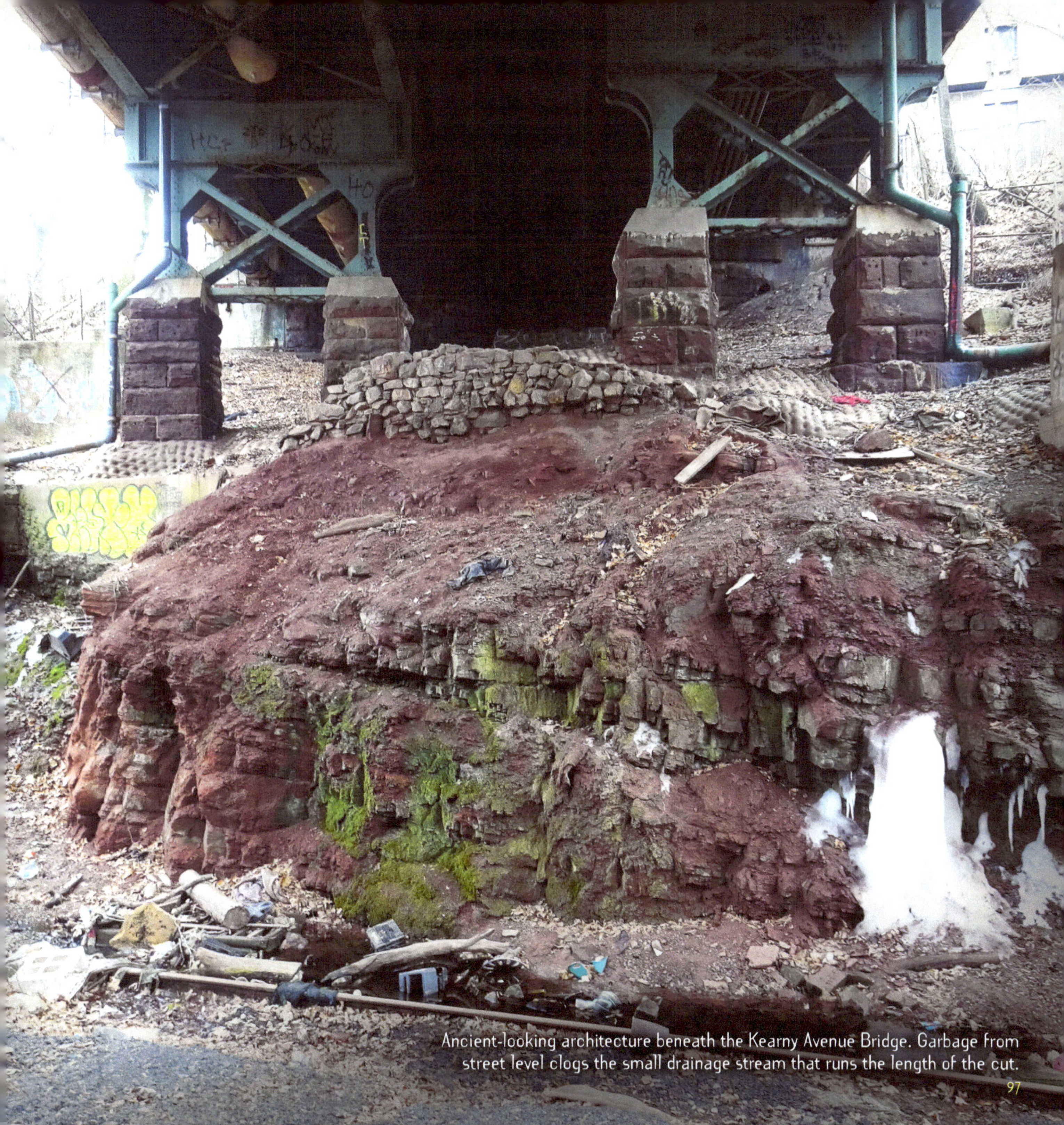

Ancient-looking architecture beneath the Kearny Avenue Bridge. Garbage from street level clogs the small drainage stream that runs the length of the cut.

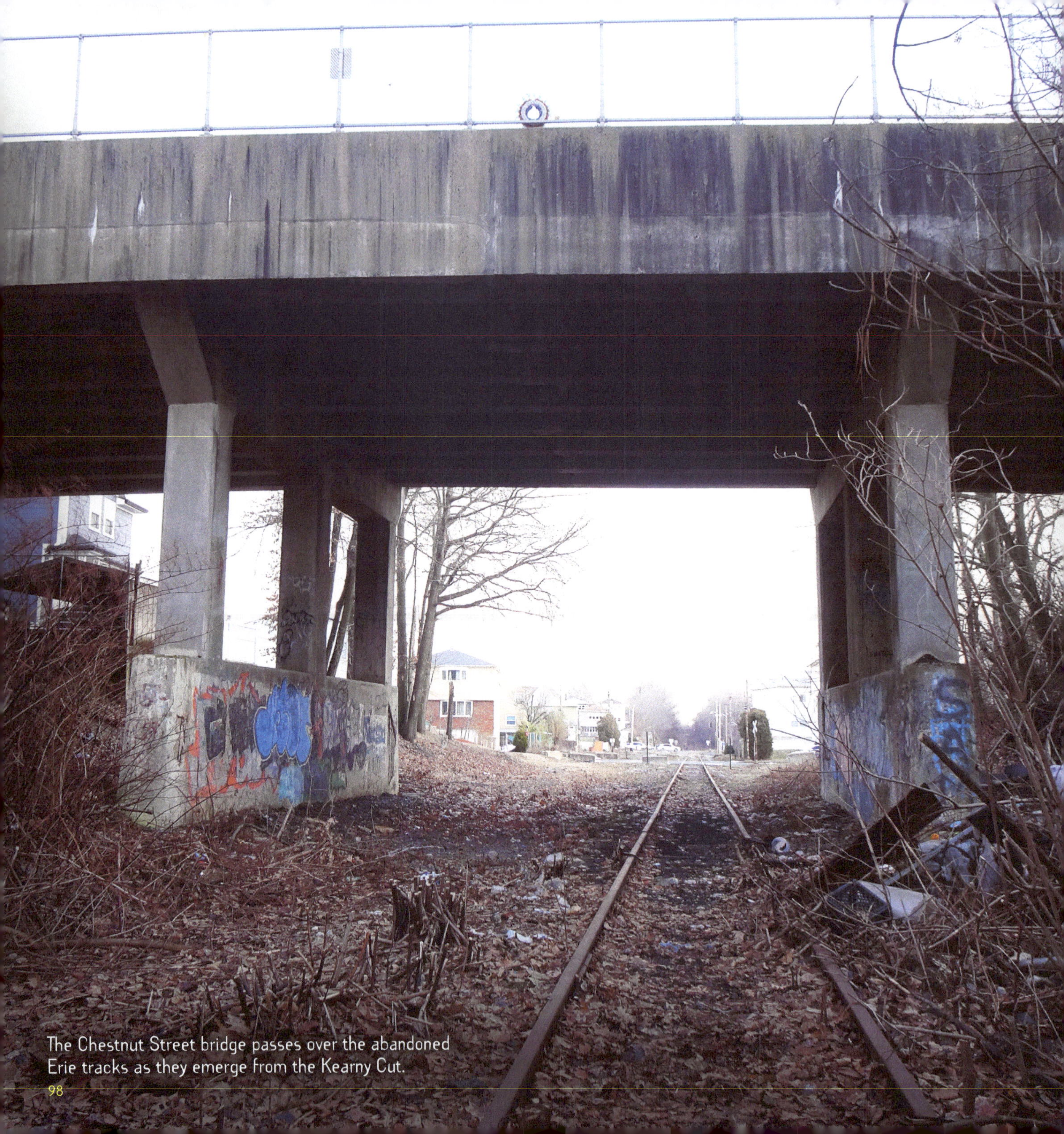
The Chestnut Street bridge passes over the abandoned Erie tracks as they emerge from the Kearny Cut.

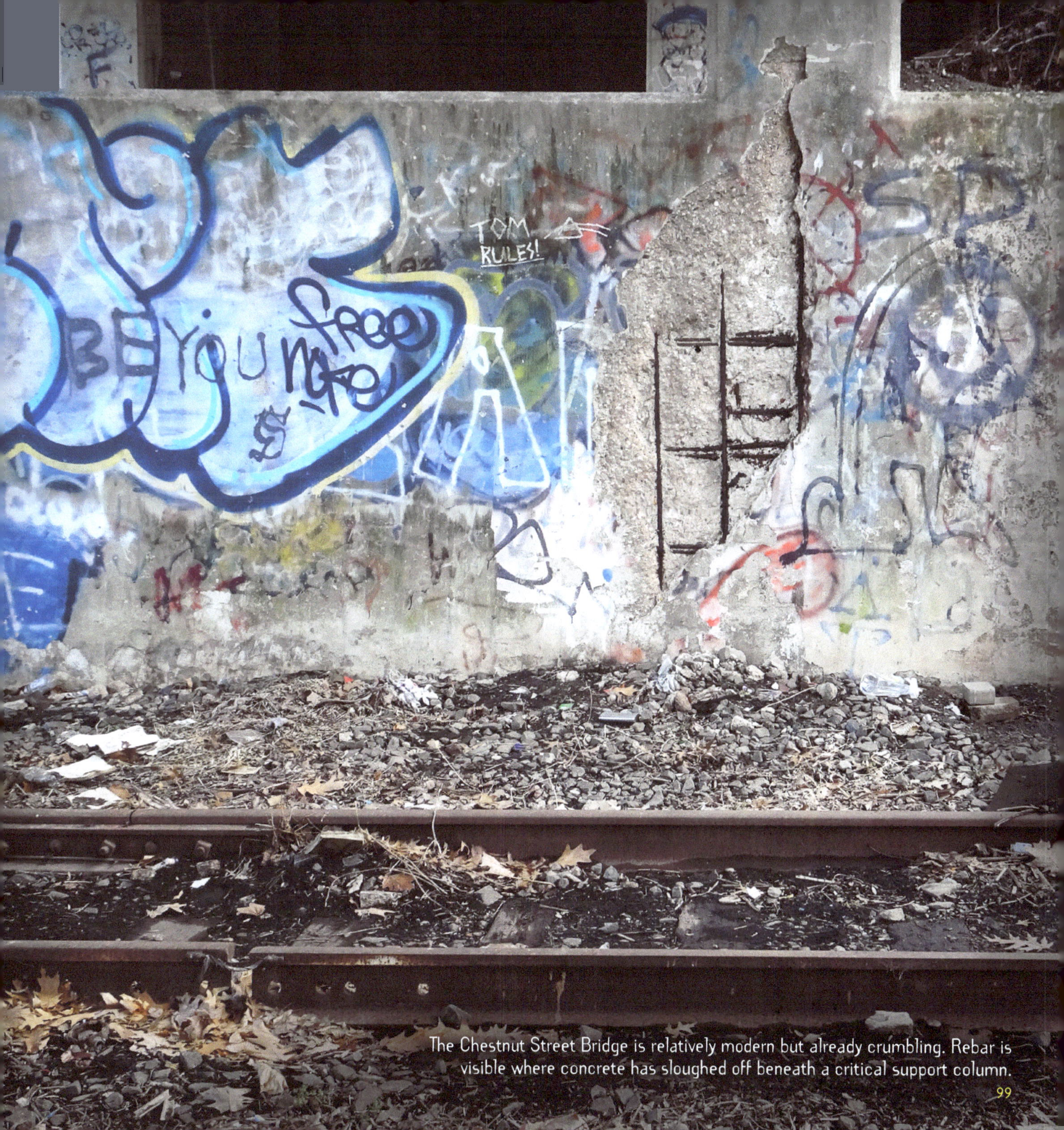

The Chestnut Street Bridge is relatively modern but already crumbling. Rebar is visible where concrete has sloughed off beneath a critical support column.

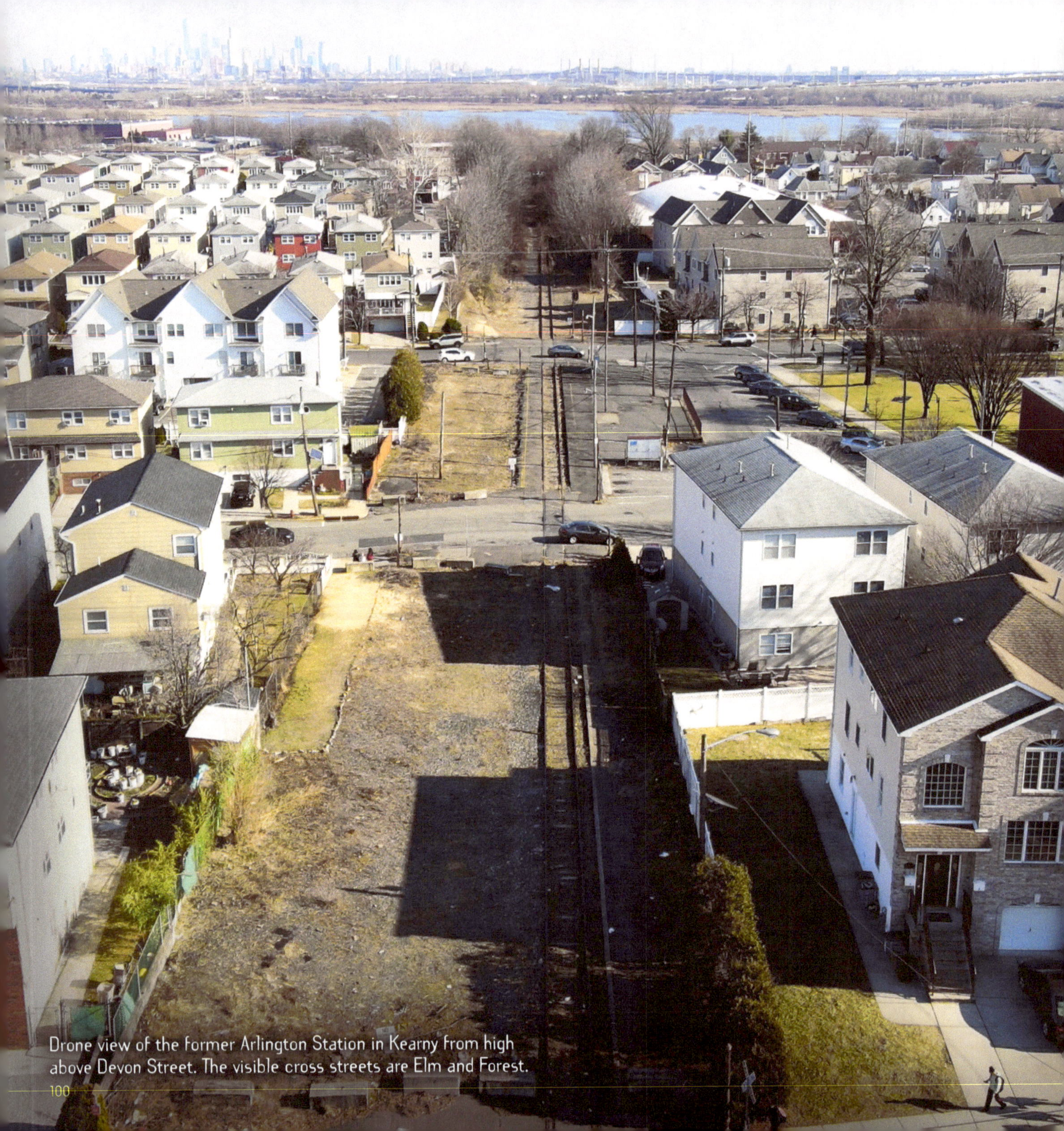

Drone view of the former Arlington Station in Kearny from high above Devon Street. The visible cross streets are Elm and Forest.

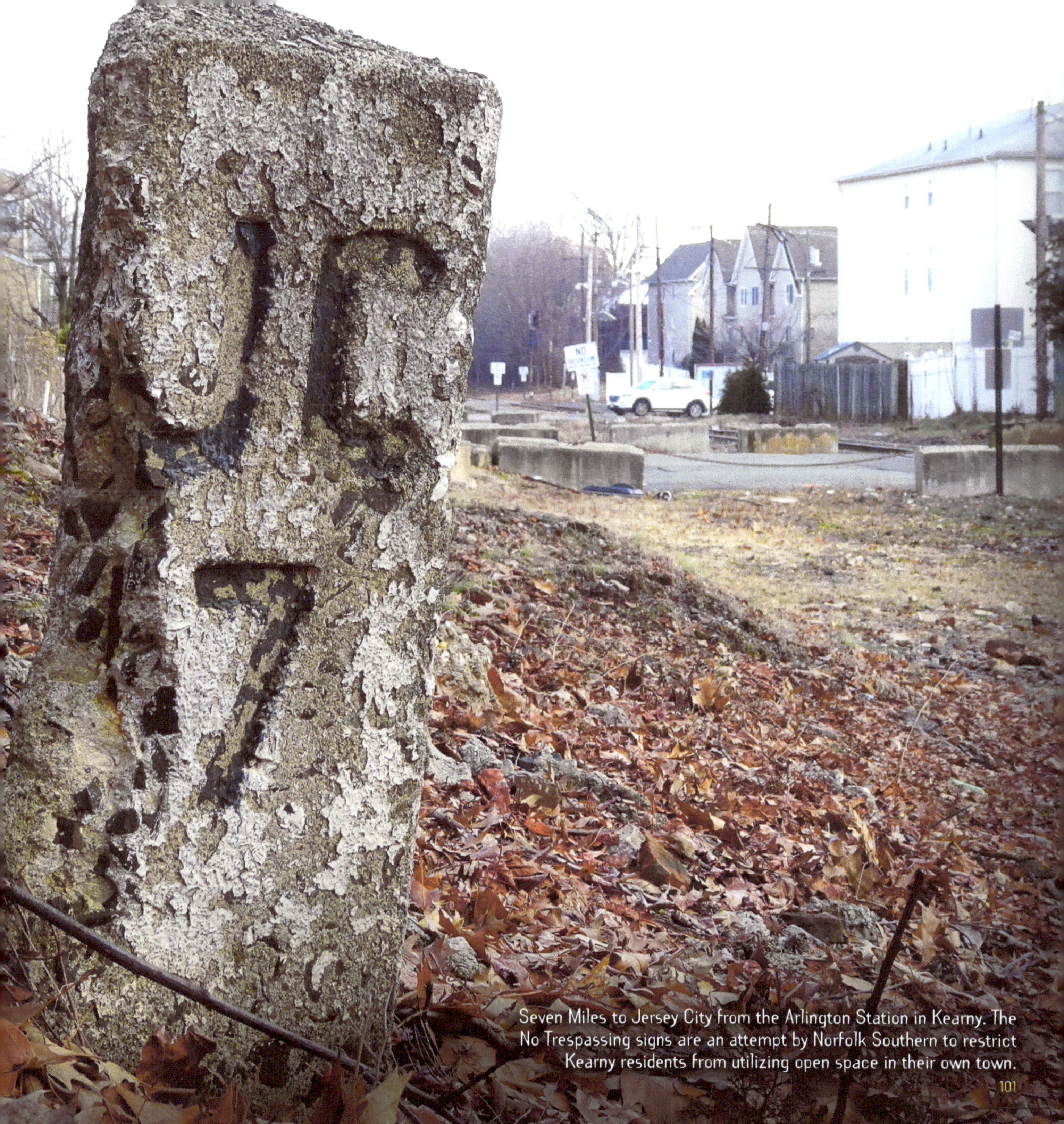

Seven Miles to Jersey City from the Arlington Station in Kearny. The No Trespassing signs are an attempt by Norfolk Southern to restrict Kearny residents from utilizing open space in their own town.

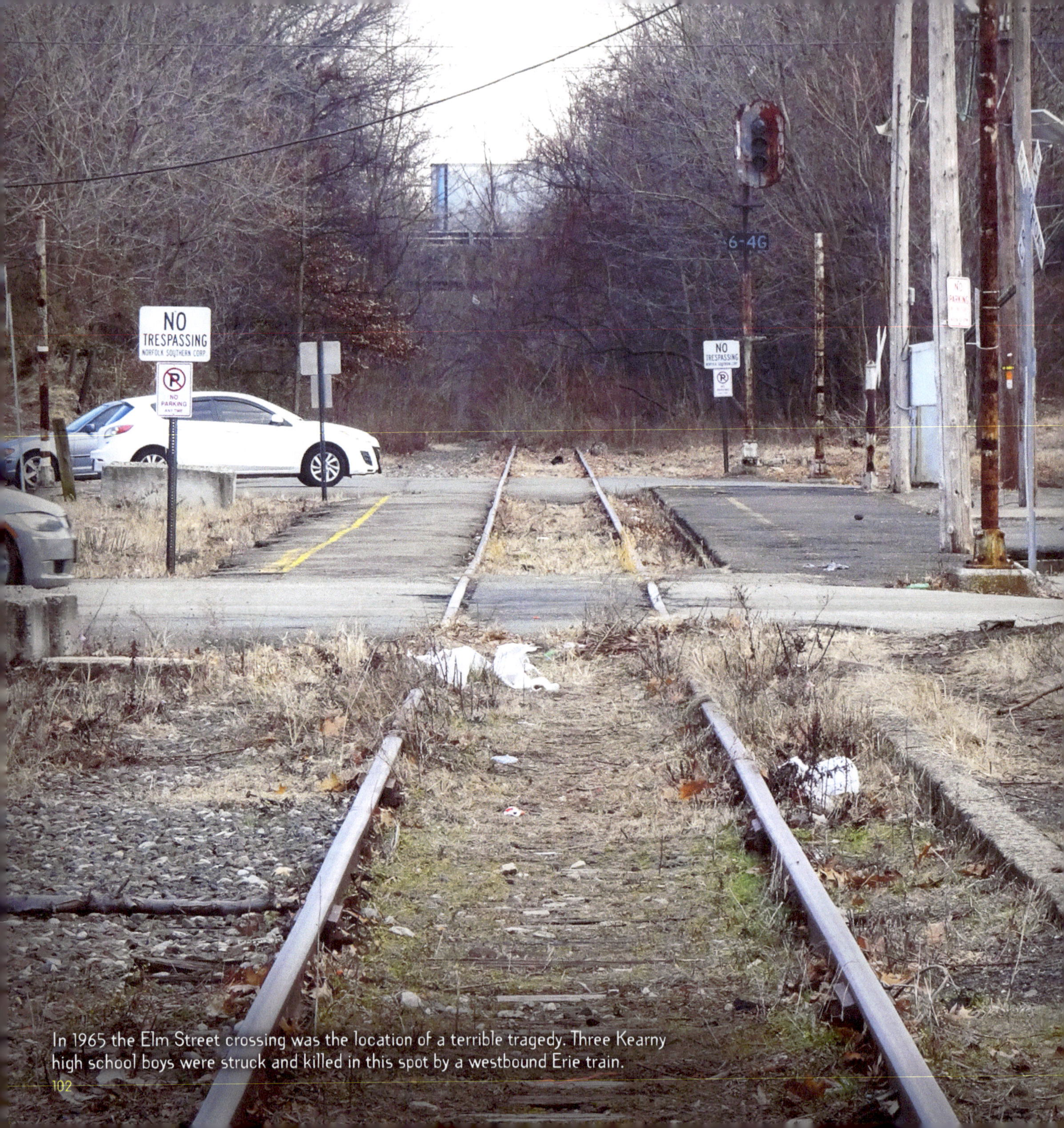

In 1965 the Elm Street crossing was the location of a terrible tragedy. Three Kearny high school boys were struck and killed in this spot by a westbound Erie train.

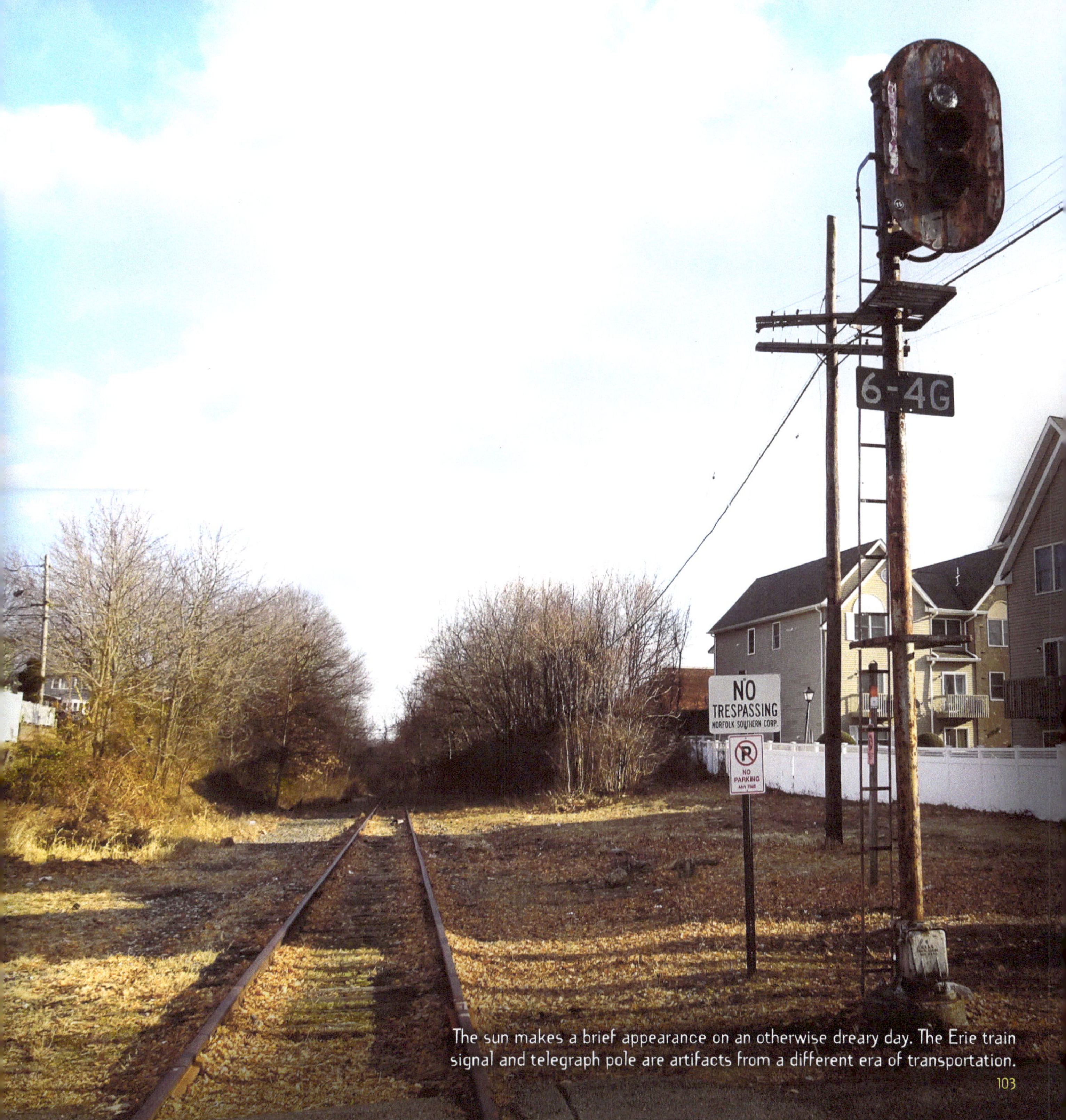

The sun makes a brief appearance on an otherwise dreary day. The Erie train signal and telegraph pole are artifacts from a different era of transportation.

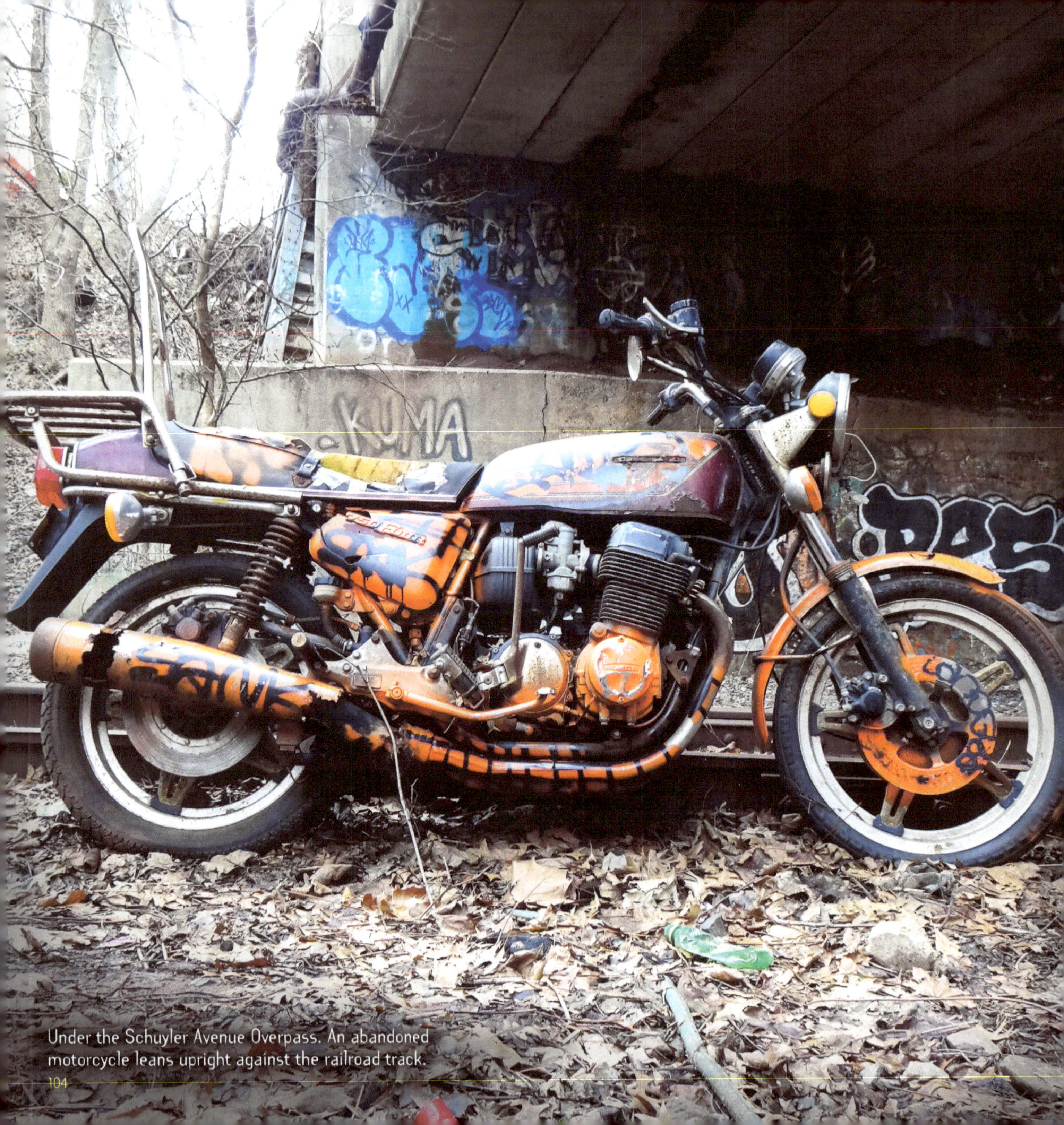

Under the Schuyler Avenue Overpass. An abandoned motorcycle leans upright against the railroad track.

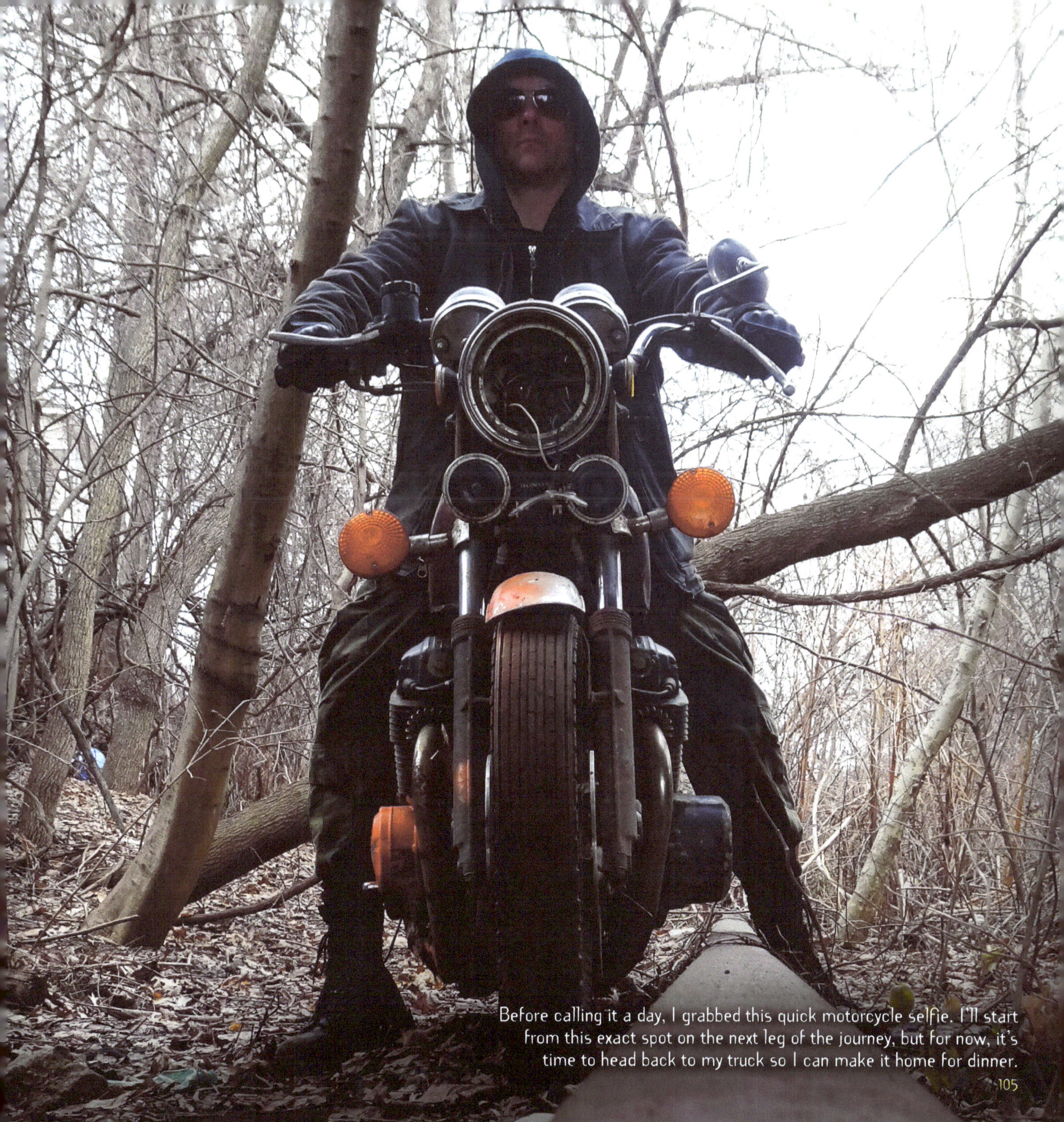

Before calling it a day, I grabbed this quick motorcycle selfie. I'll start from this exact spot on the next leg of the journey, but for now, it's time to head back to my truck so I can make it home for dinner.

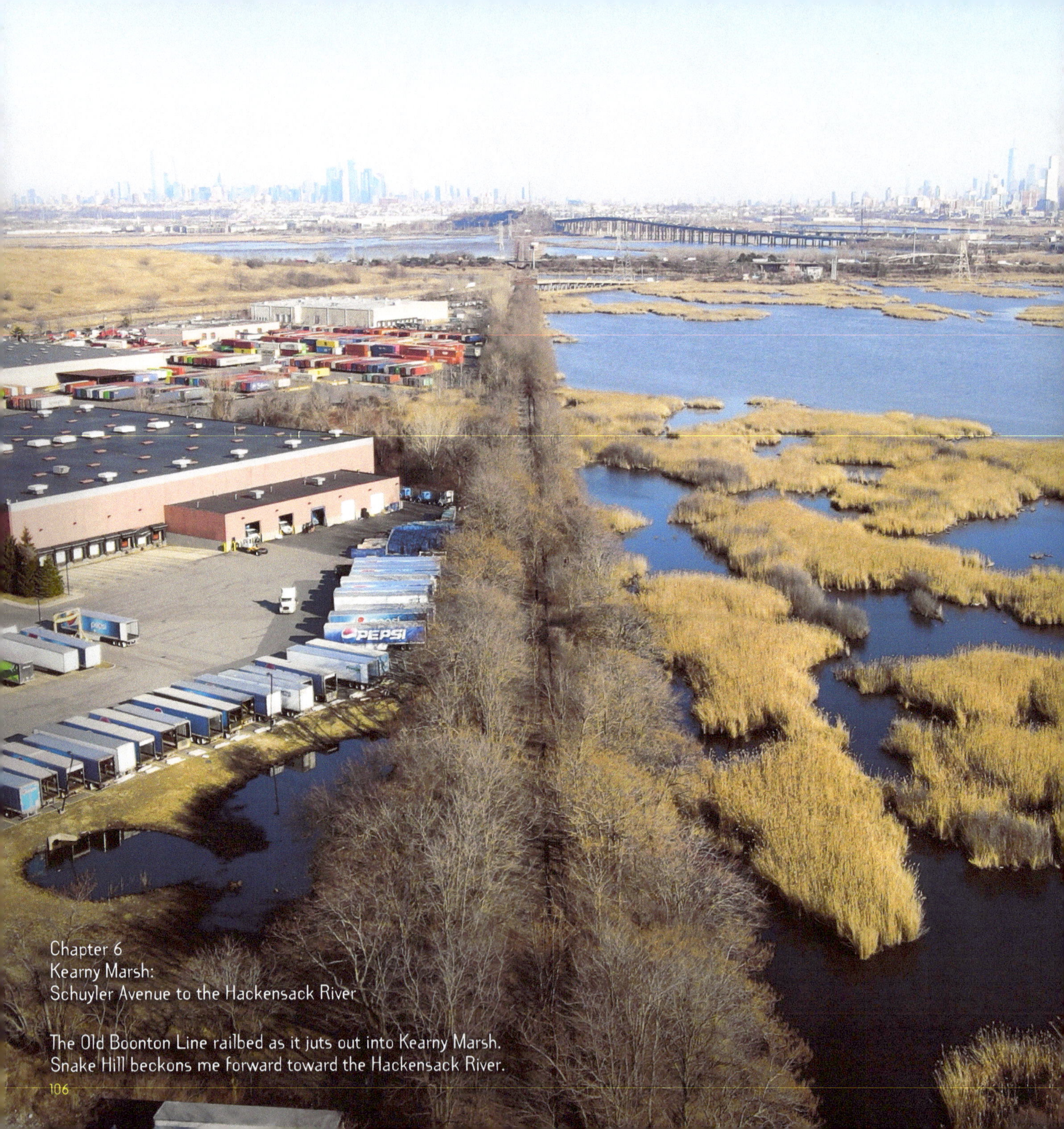

Chapter 6
Kearny Marsh:
Schuyler Avenue to the Hackensack River

The Old Boonton Line railbed as it juts out into Kearny Marsh. Snake Hill beckons me forward toward the Hackensack River.

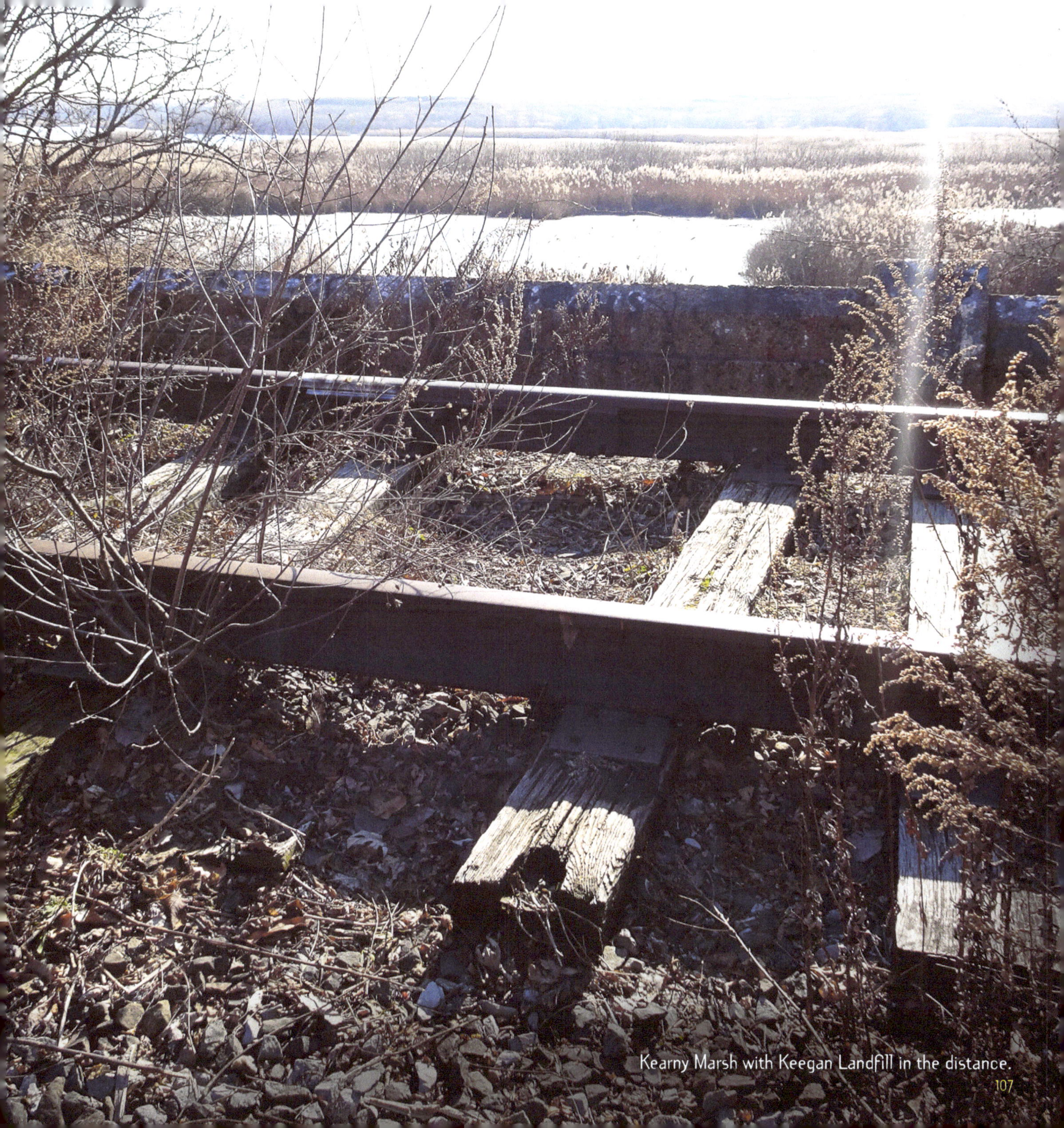

Kearny Marsh with Keegan Landfill in the distance.

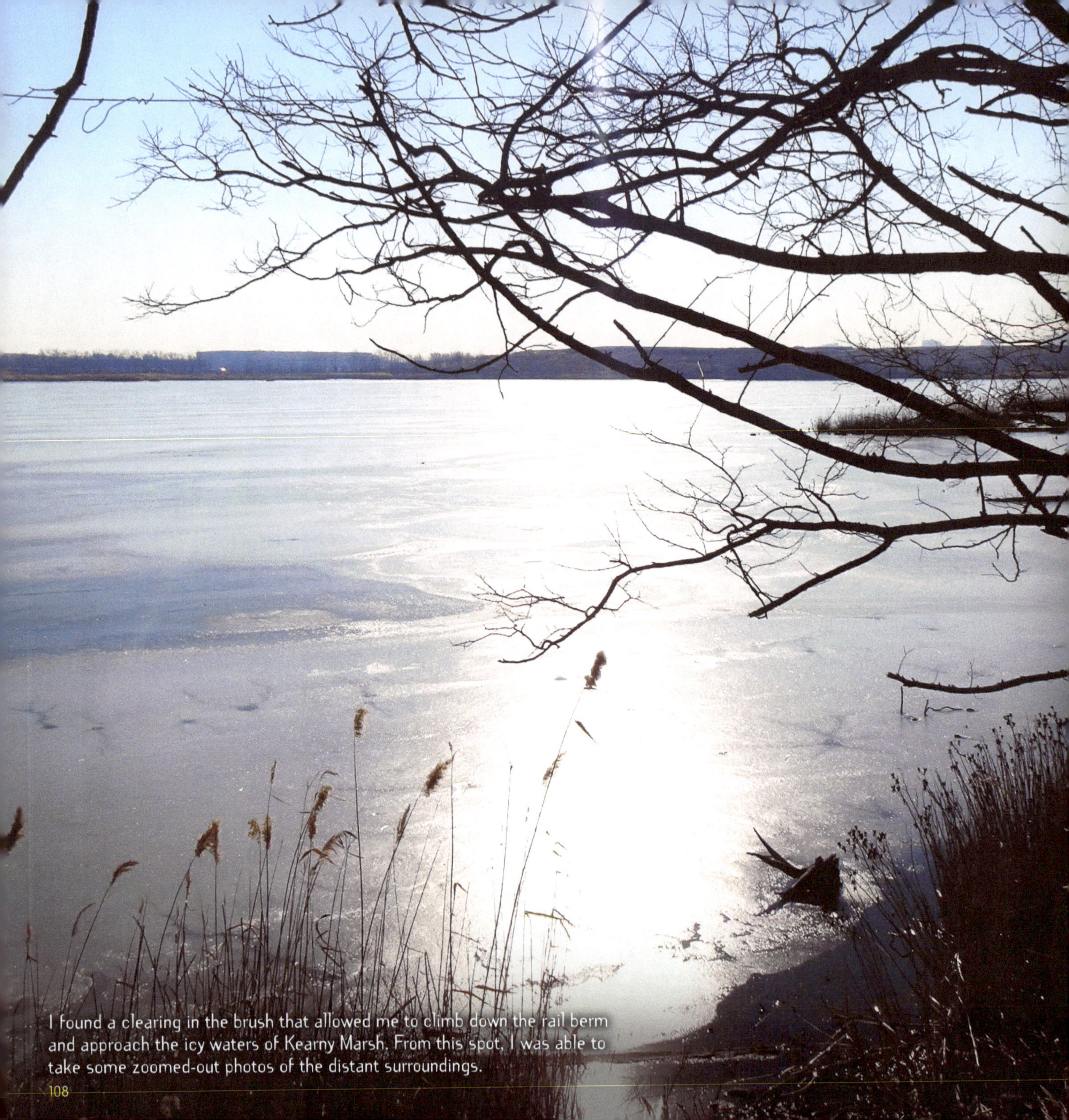

I found a clearing in the brush that allowed me to climb down the rail berm and approach the icy waters of Kearny Marsh. From this spot, I was able to take some zoomed-out photos of the distant surroundings.

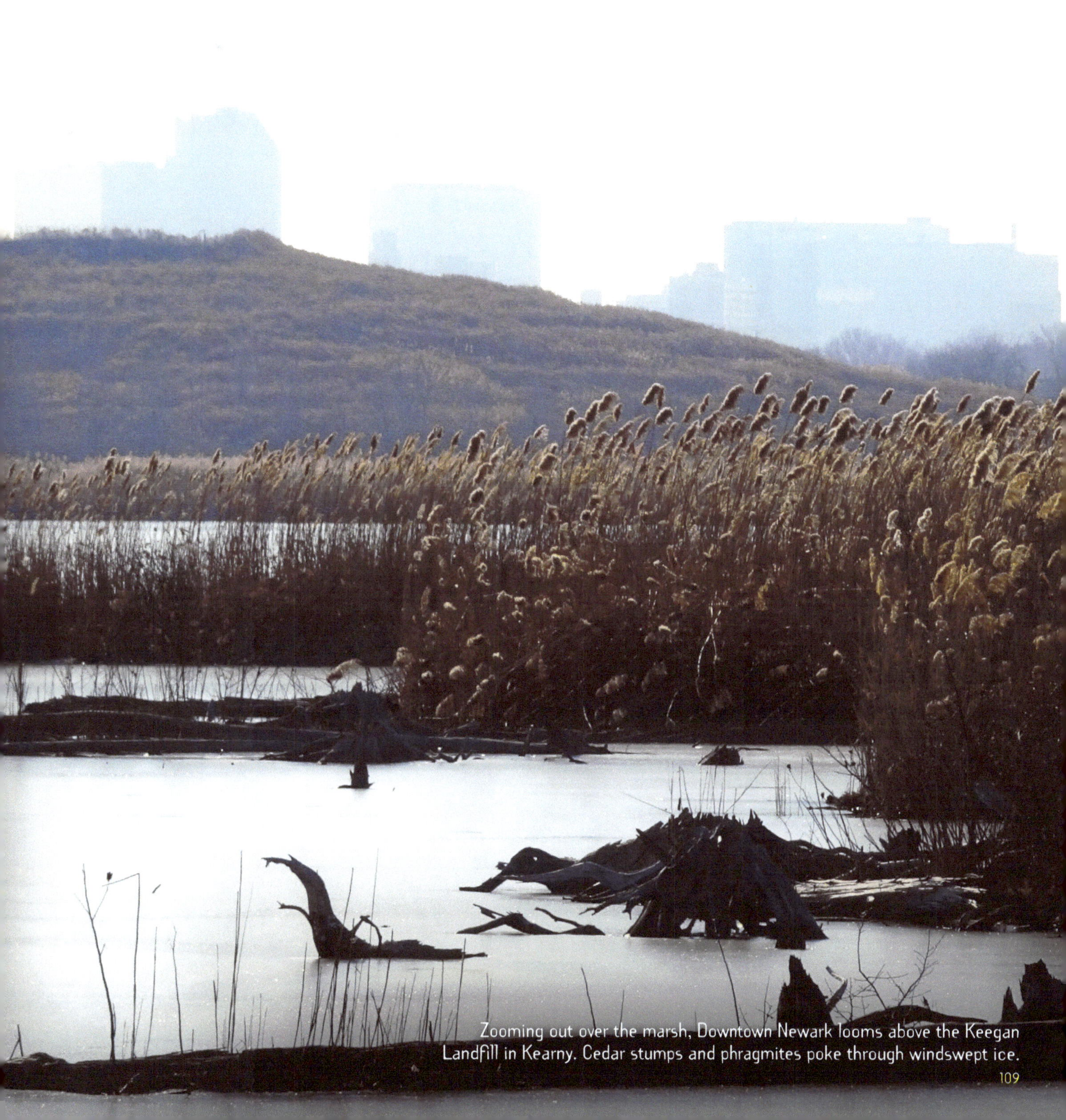

Zooming out over the marsh, Downtown Newark looms above the Keegan Landfill in Kearny. Cedar stumps and phragmites poke through windswept ice.

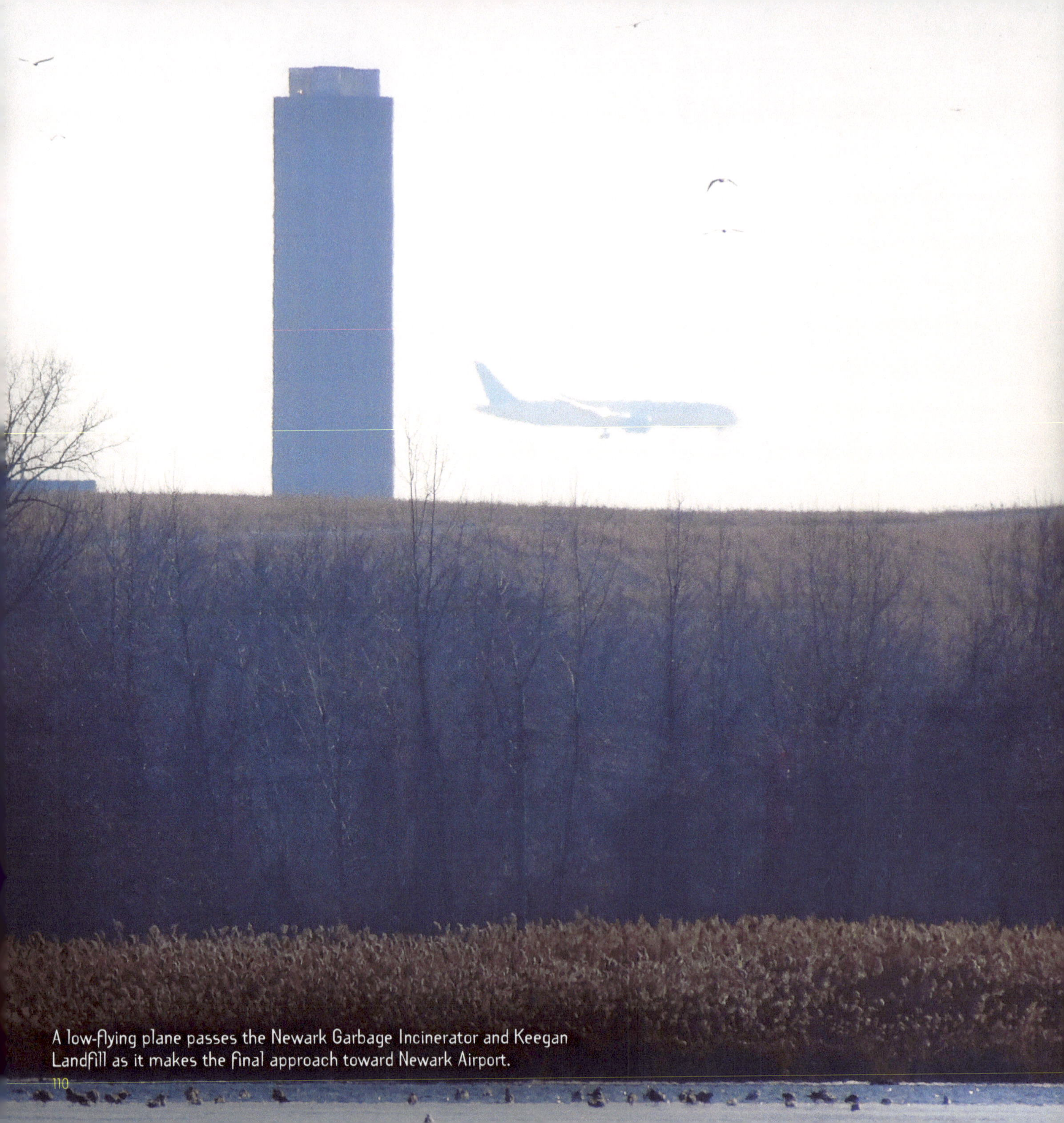

A low-flying plane passes the Newark Garbage Incinerator and Keegan Landfill as it makes the final approach toward Newark Airport.

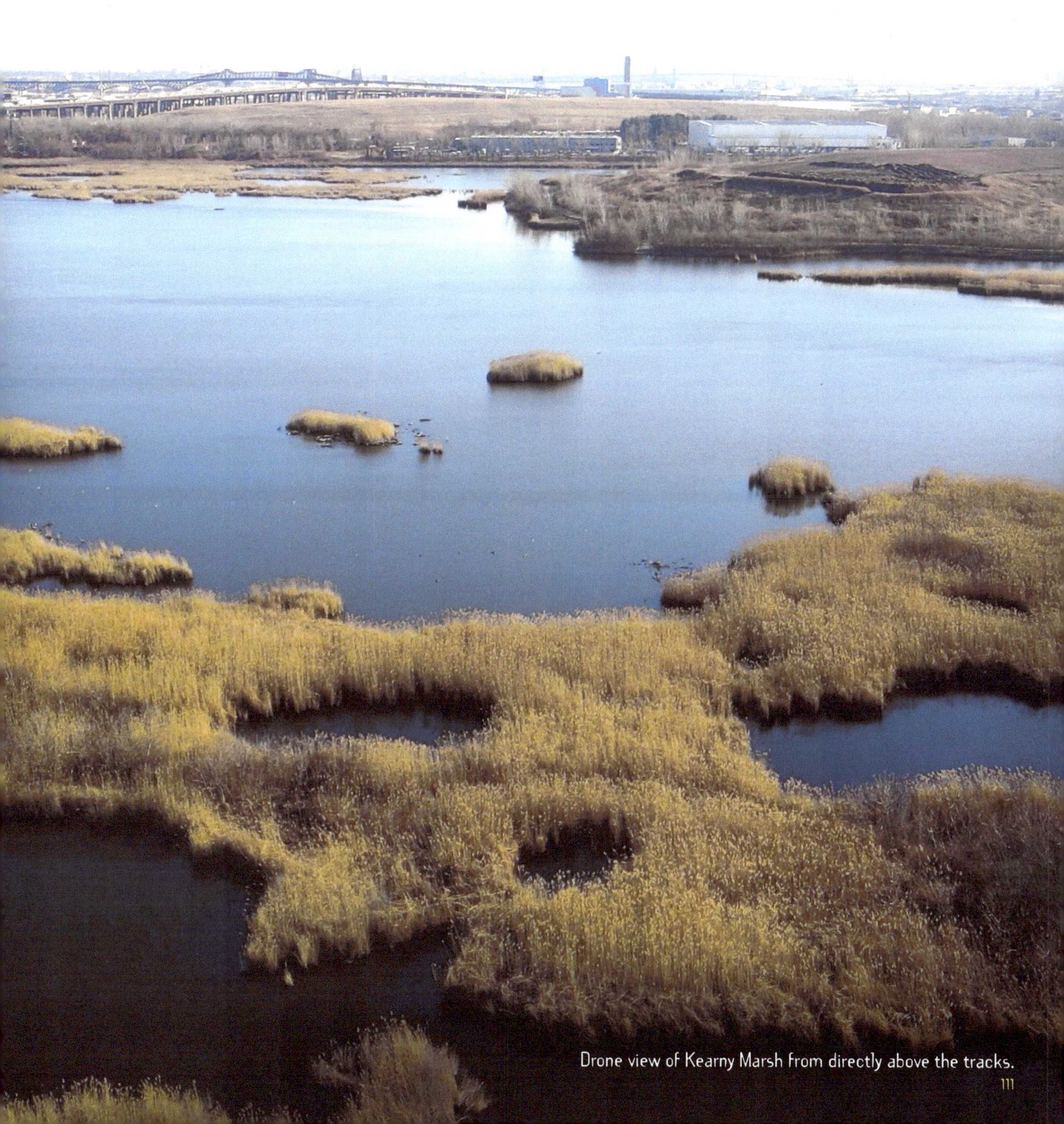

Drone view of Kearny Marsh from directly above the tracks.

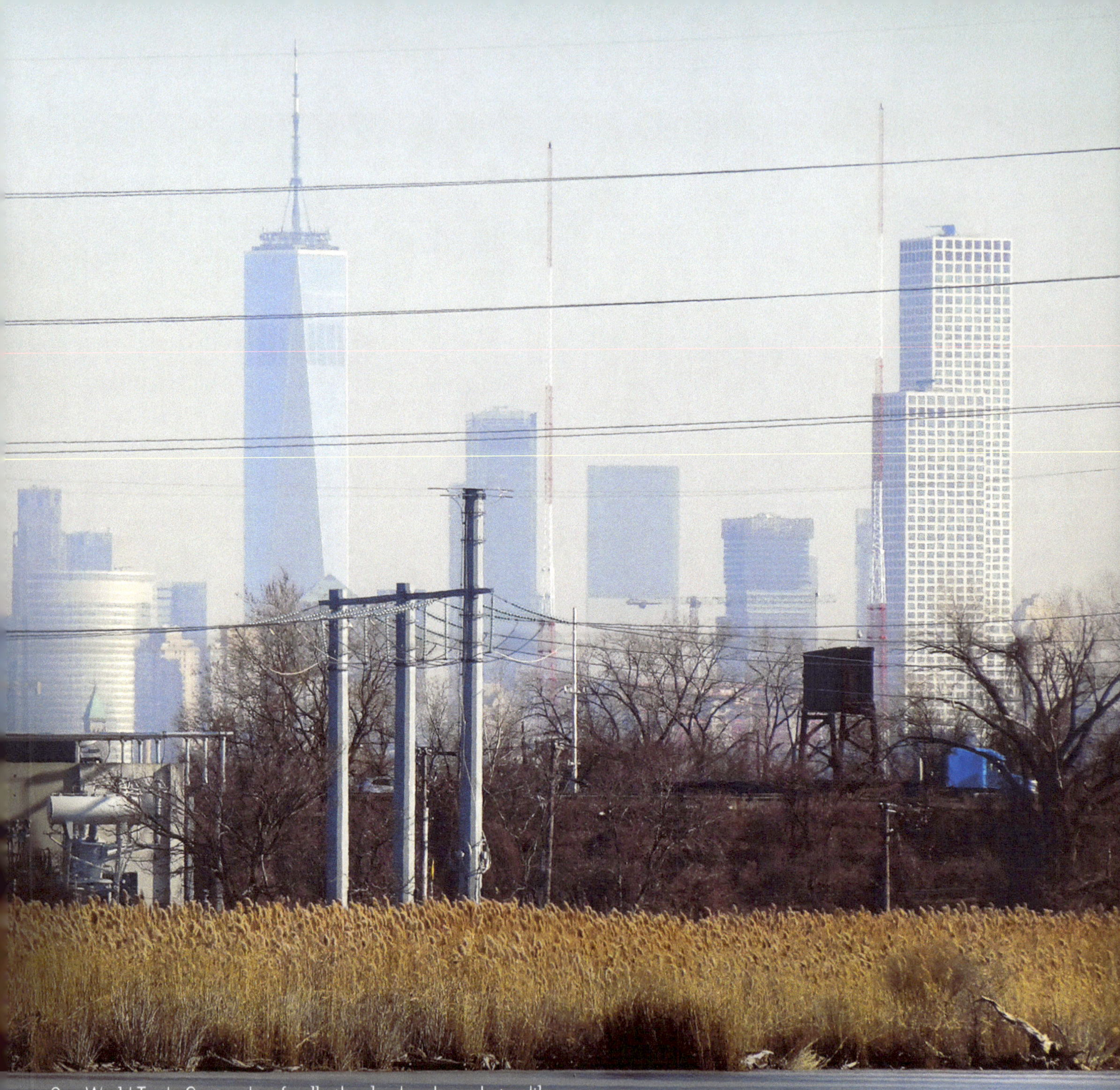

One World Trade Center dwarfs all other landmarks as I steadily make progress along the rails.

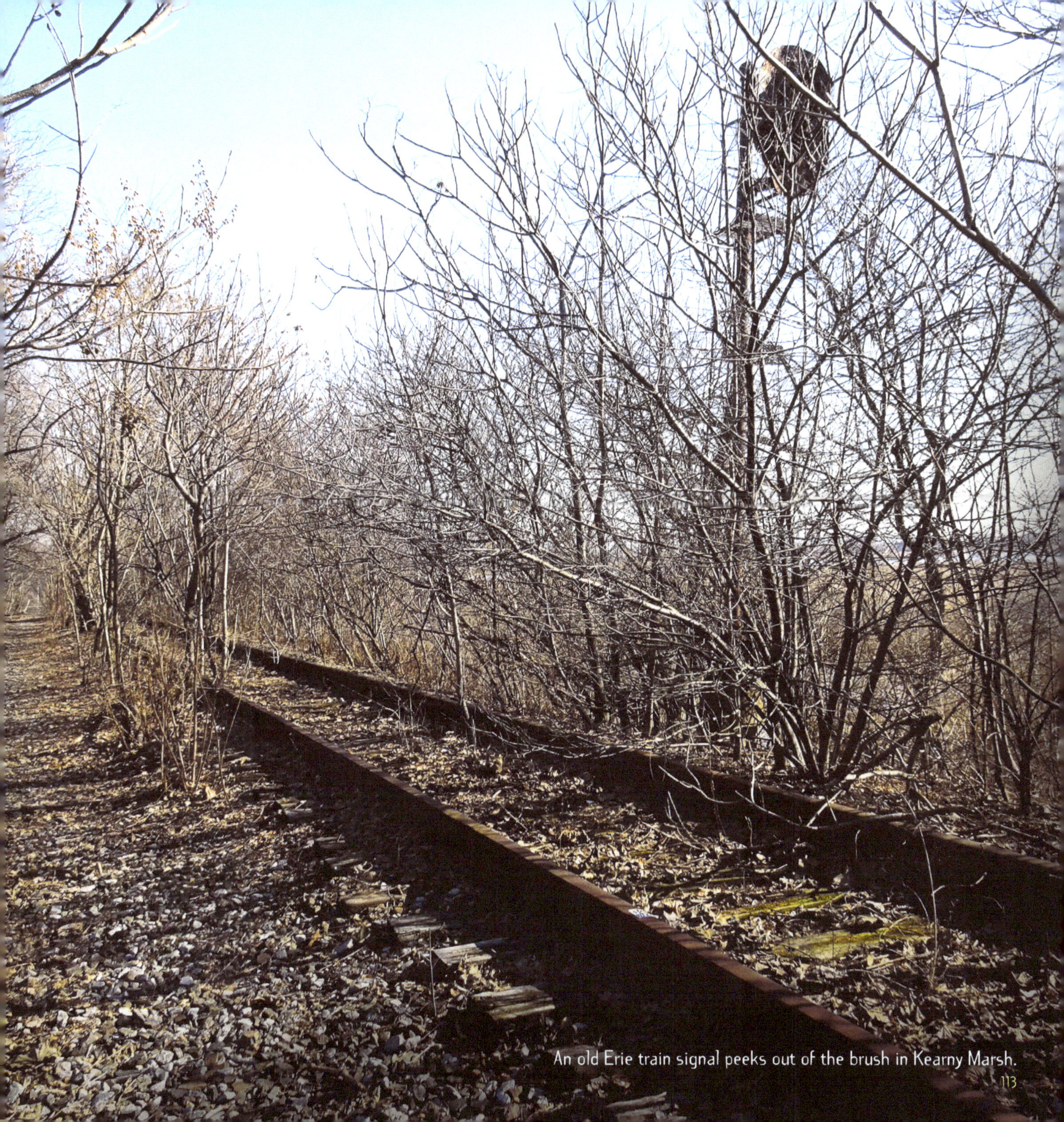

An old Erie train signal peeks out of the brush in Kearny Marsh.

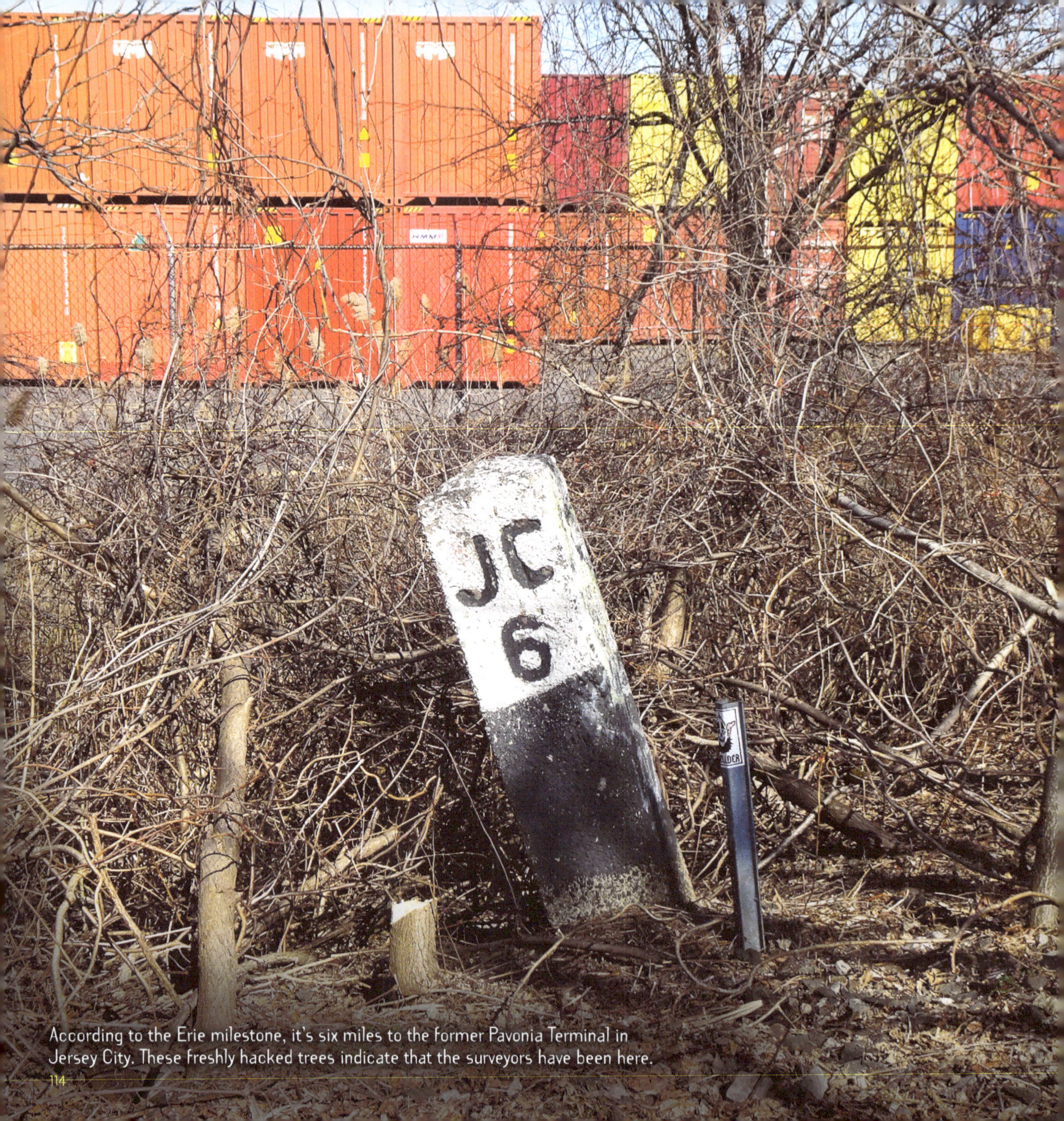

According to the Erie milestone, it's six miles to the former Pavonia Terminal in Jersey City. These freshly hacked trees indicate that the surveyors have been here.

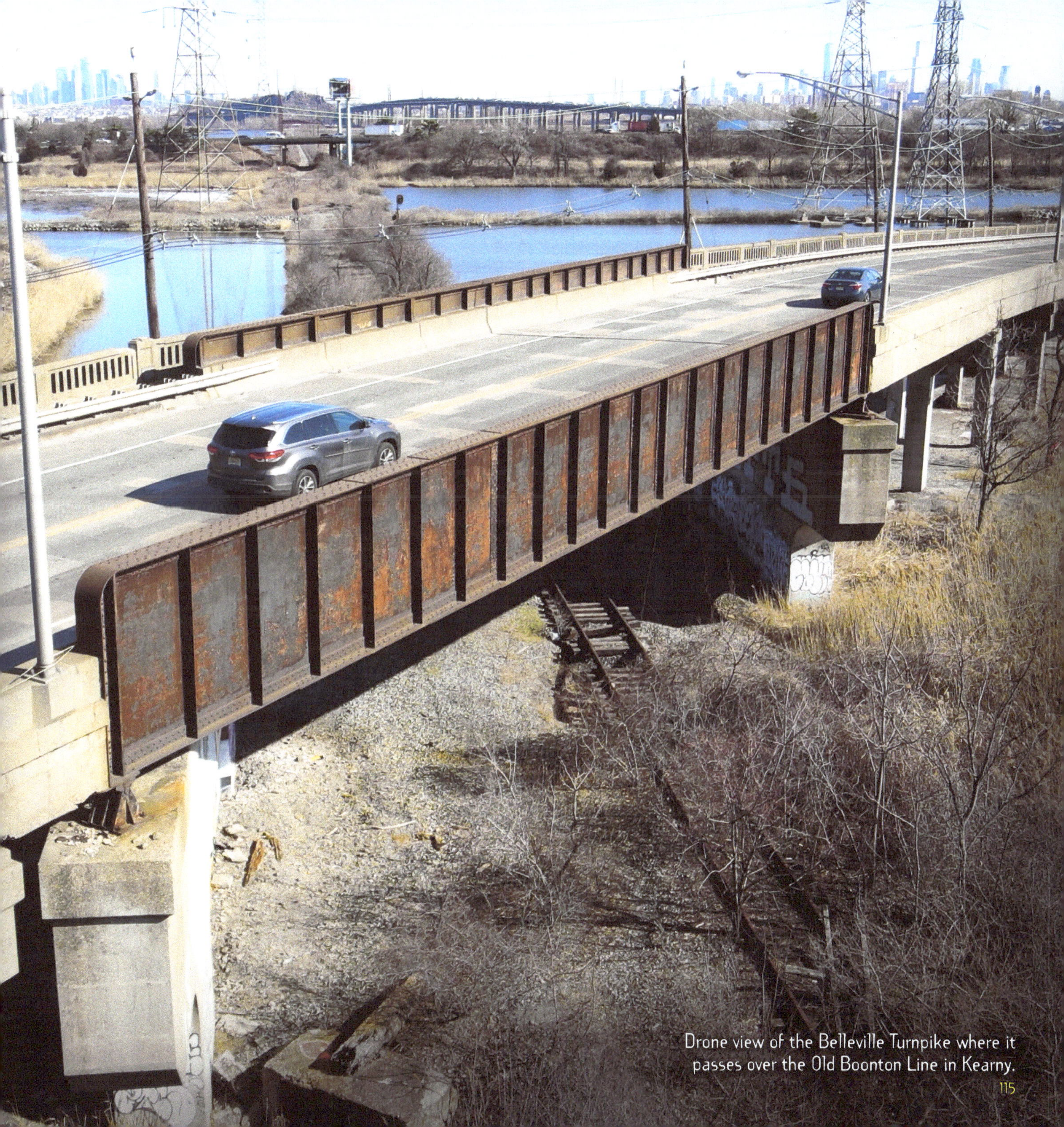

Drone view of the Belleville Turnpike where it passes over the Old Boonton Line in Kearny.

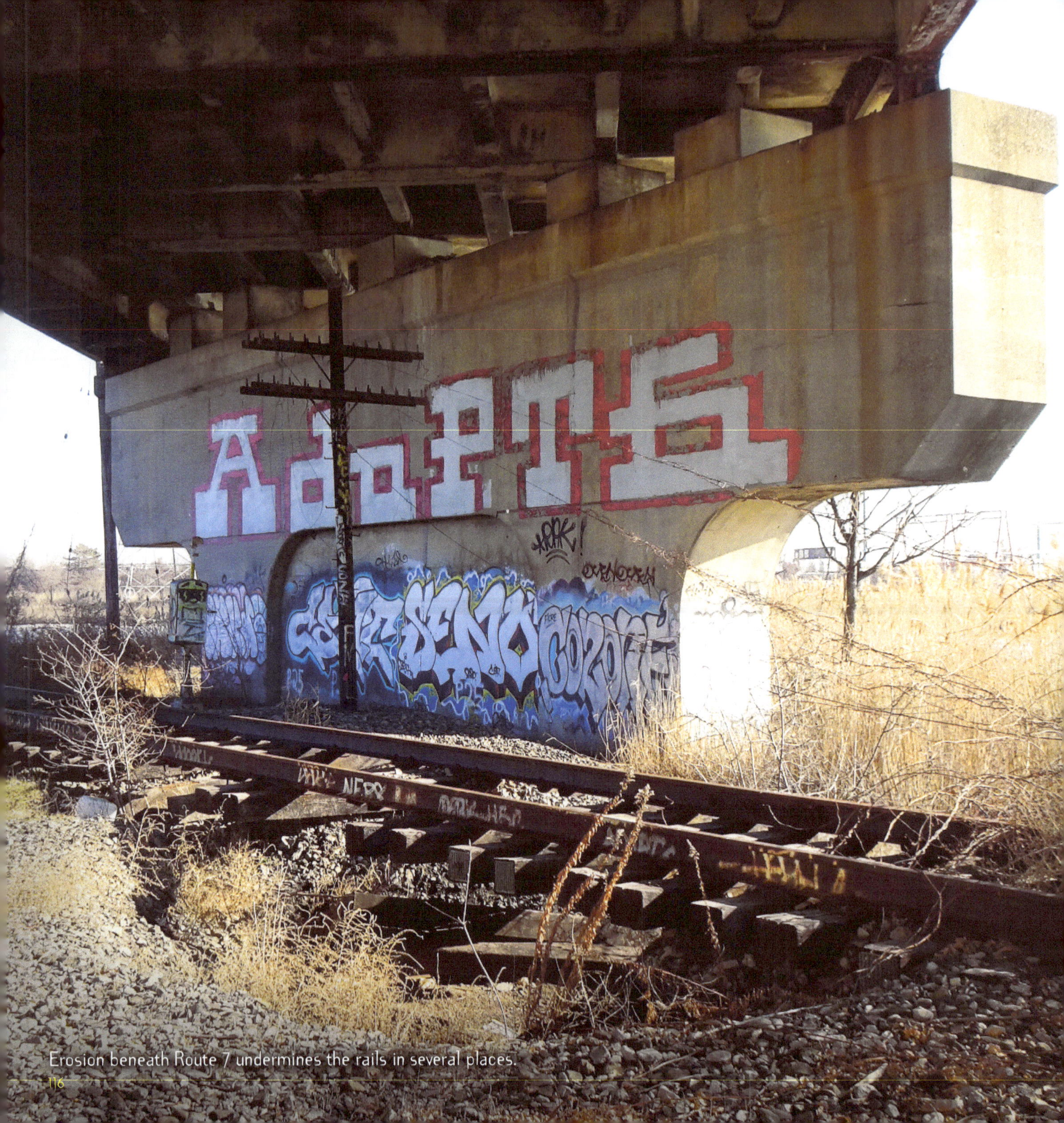

Erosion beneath Route 7 undermines the rails in several places.

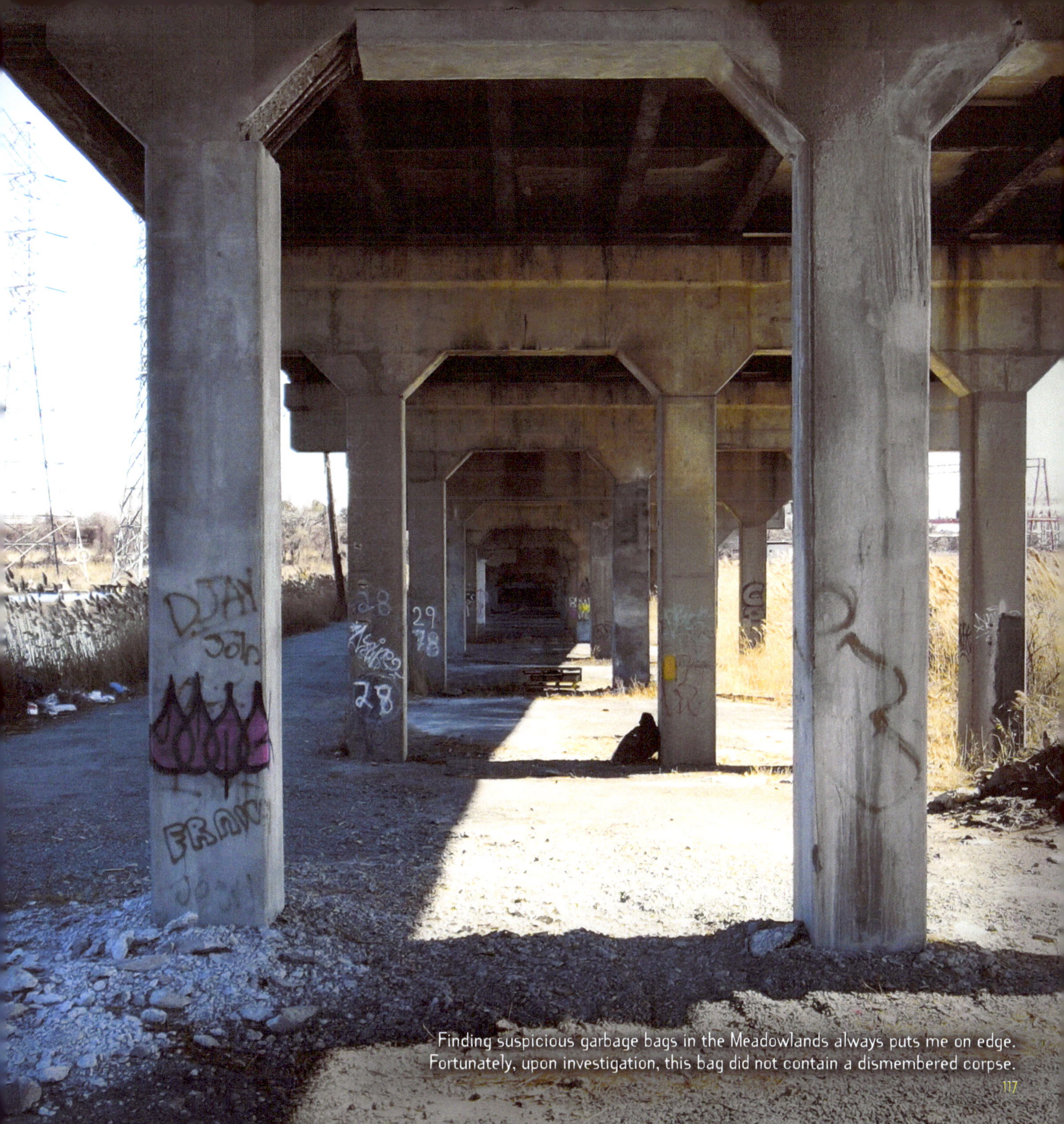

Finding suspicious garbage bags in the Meadowlands always puts me on edge. Fortunately, upon investigation, this bag did not contain a dismembered corpse.

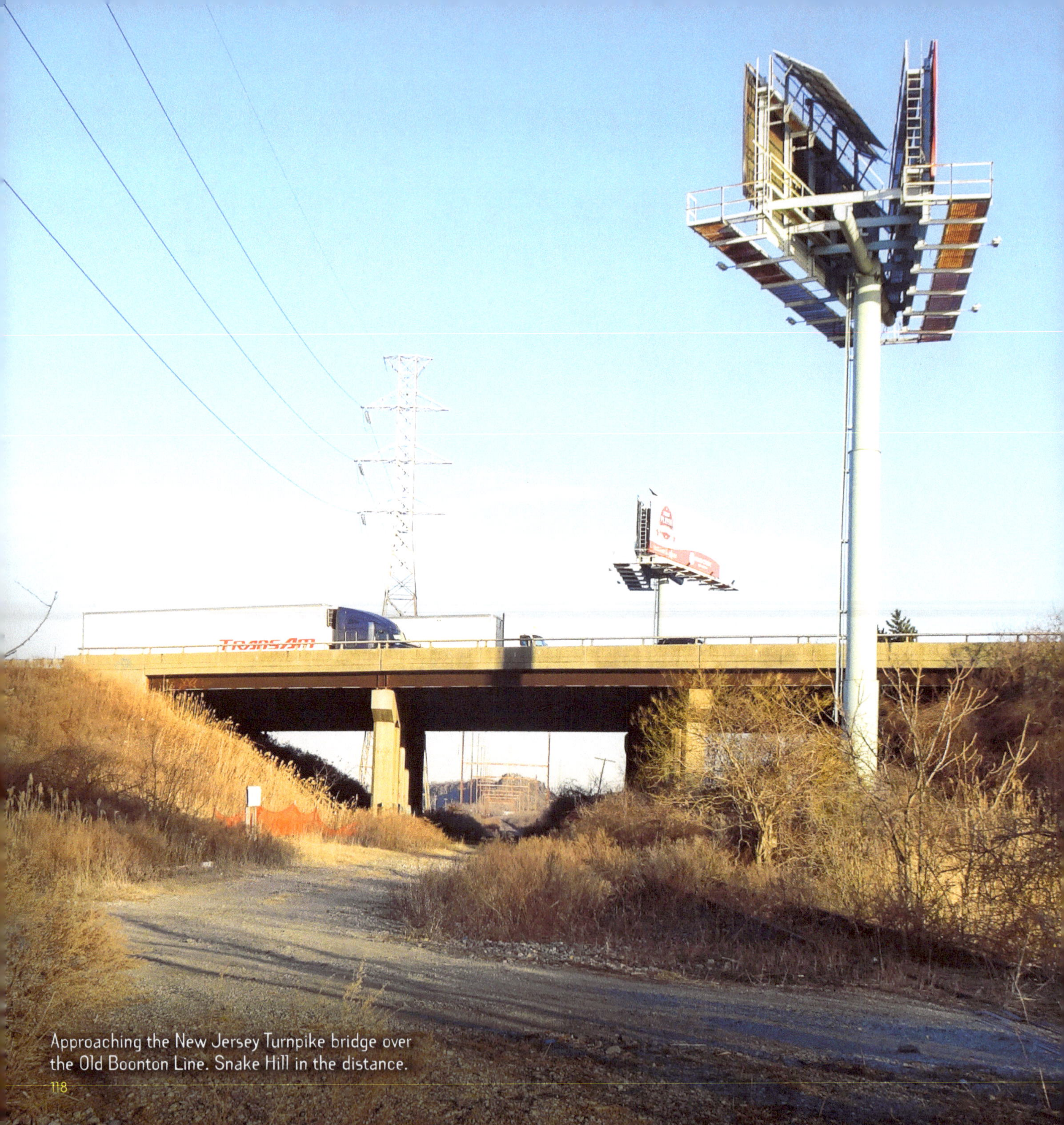

Approaching the New Jersey Turnpike bridge over the Old Boonton Line. Snake Hill in the distance.

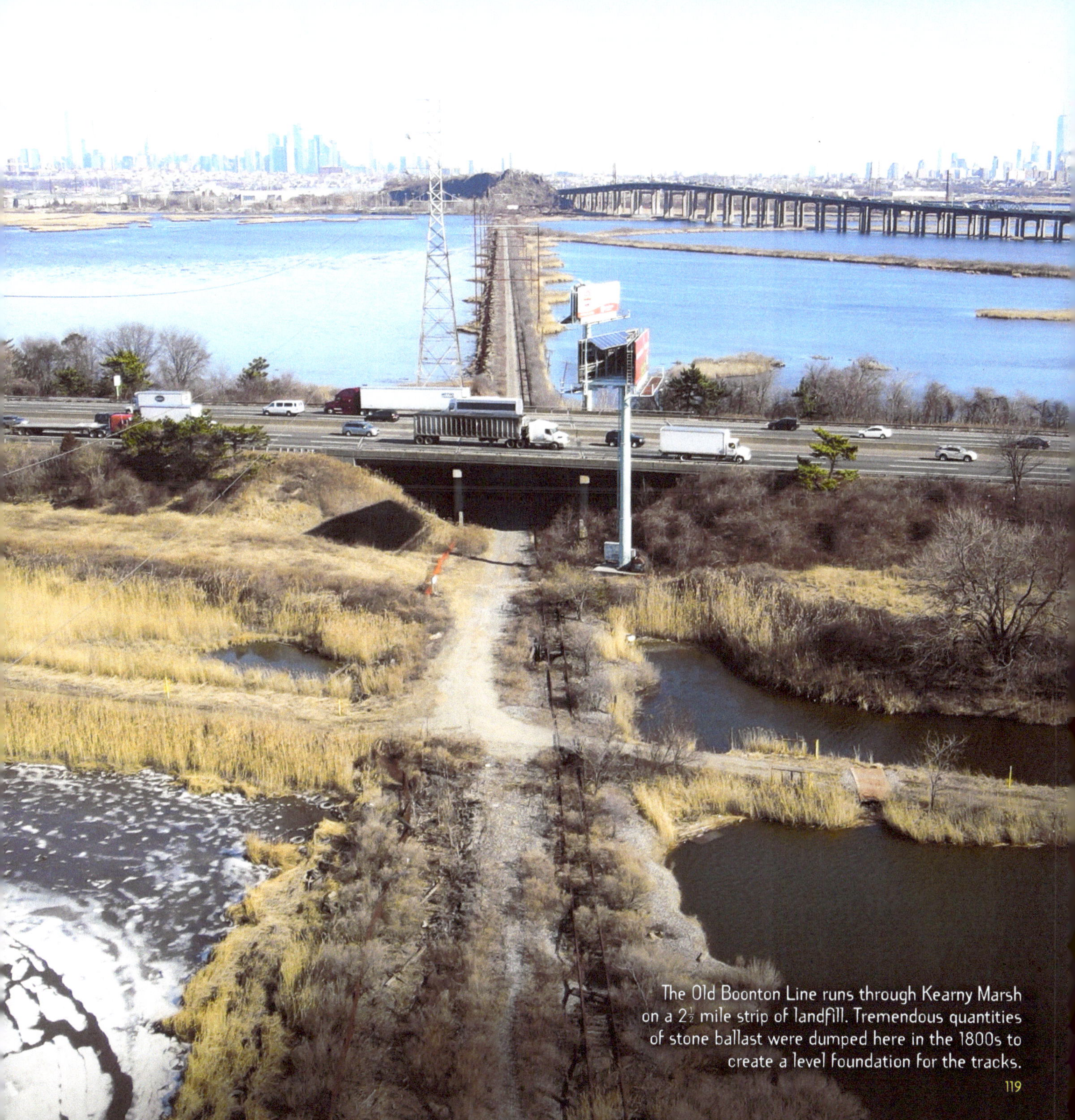

The Old Boonton Line runs through Kearny Marsh on a $2\frac{1}{2}$ mile strip of landfill. Tremendous quantities of stone ballast were dumped here in the 1800s to create a level foundation for the tracks.

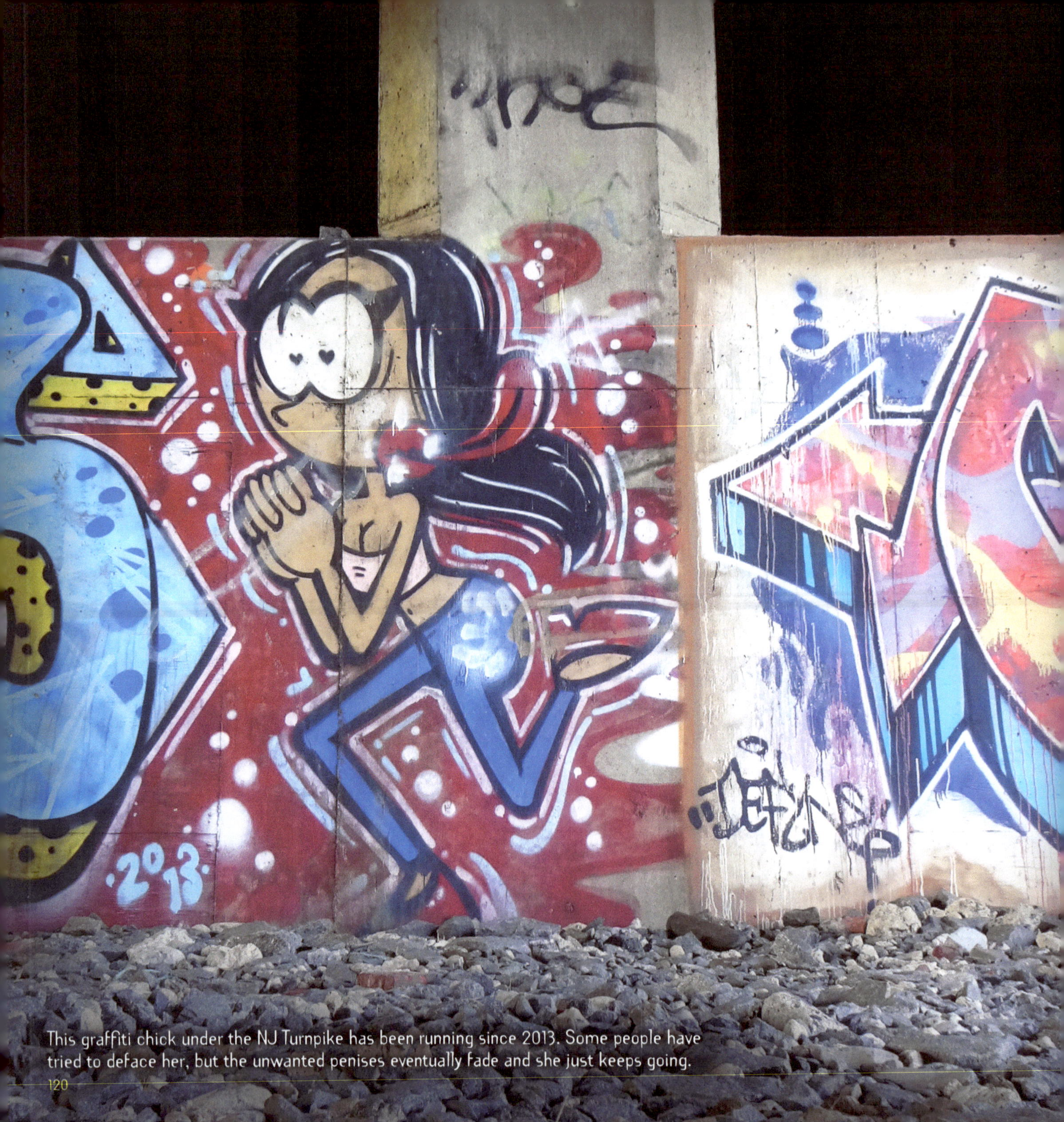

This graffiti chick under the NJ Turnpike has been running since 2013. Some people have tried to deface her, but the unwanted penises eventually fade and she just keeps going.

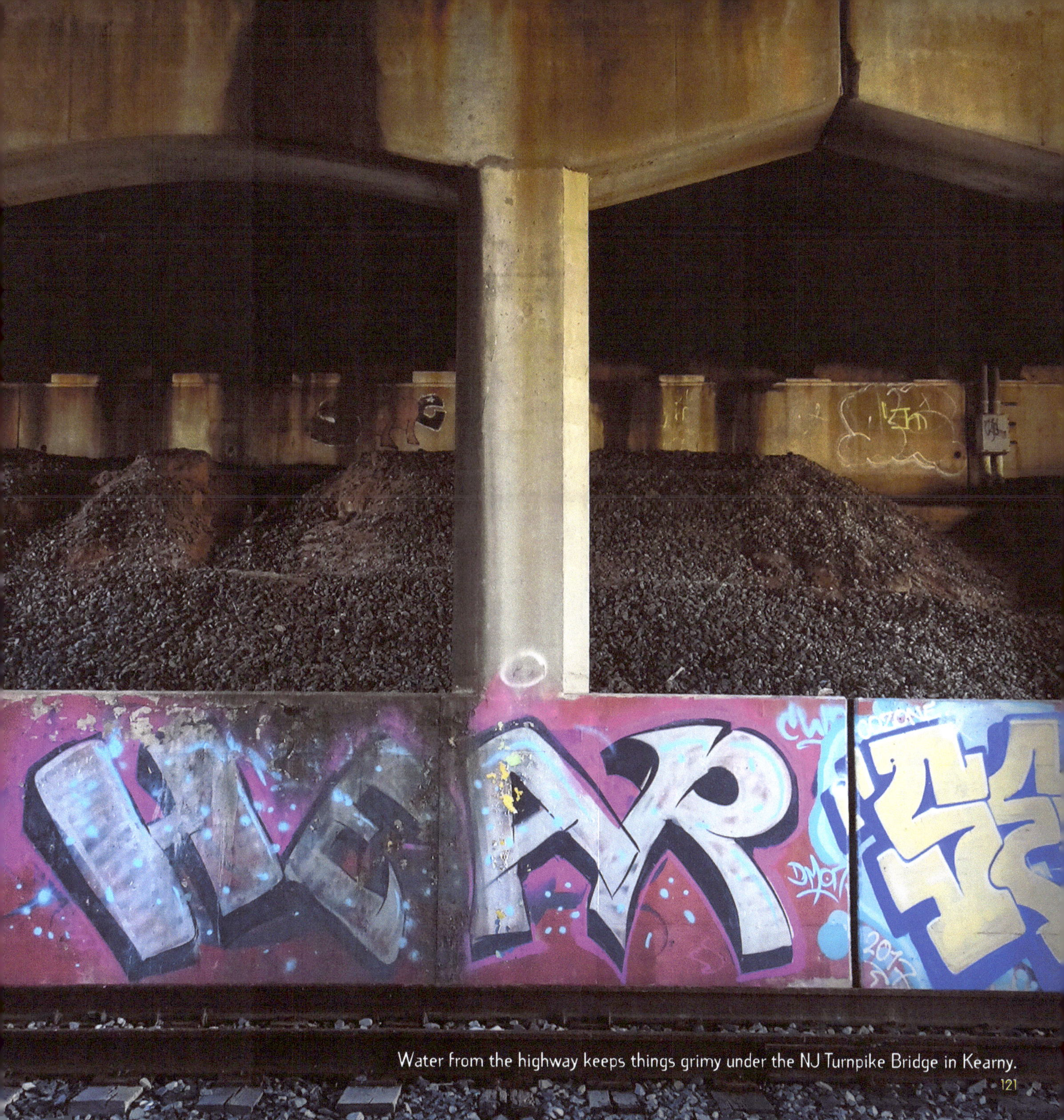

Water from the highway keeps things grimy under the NJ Turnpike Bridge in Kearny.

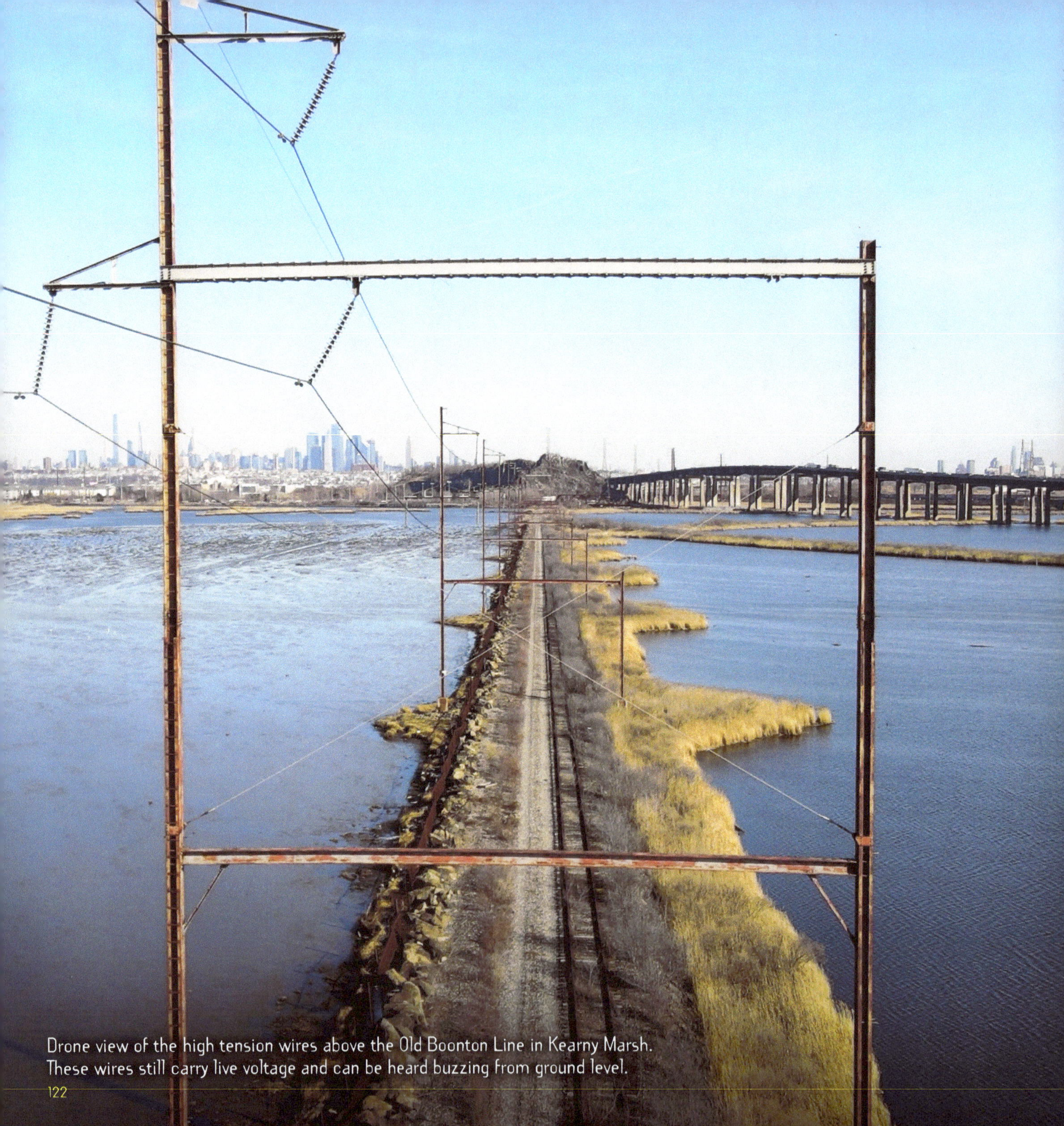

Drone view of the high tension wires above the Old Boonton Line in Kearny Marsh.
These wires still carry live voltage and can be heard buzzing from ground level.

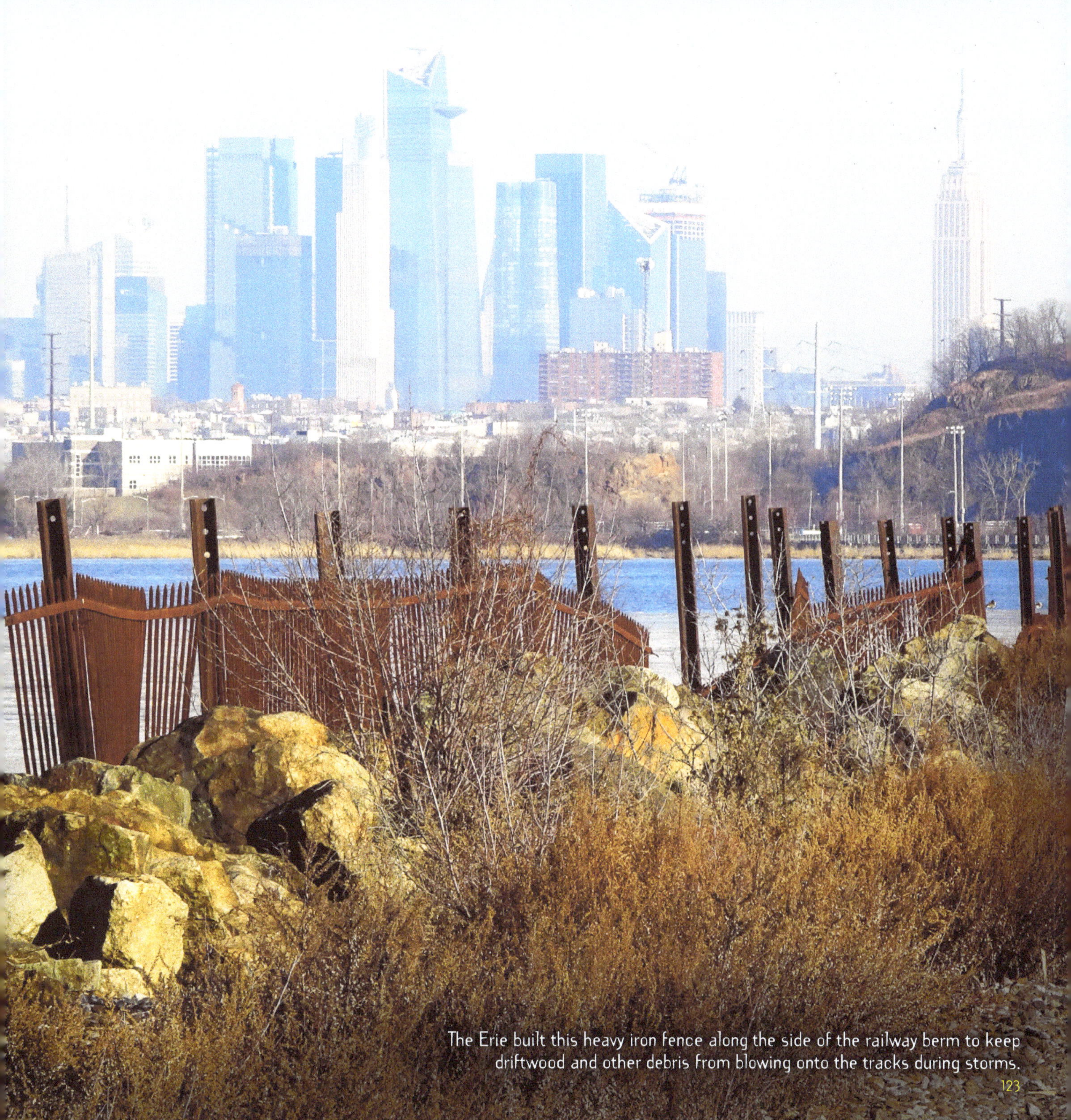
The Erie built this heavy iron fence along the side of the railway berm to keep driftwood and other debris from blowing onto the tracks during storms.

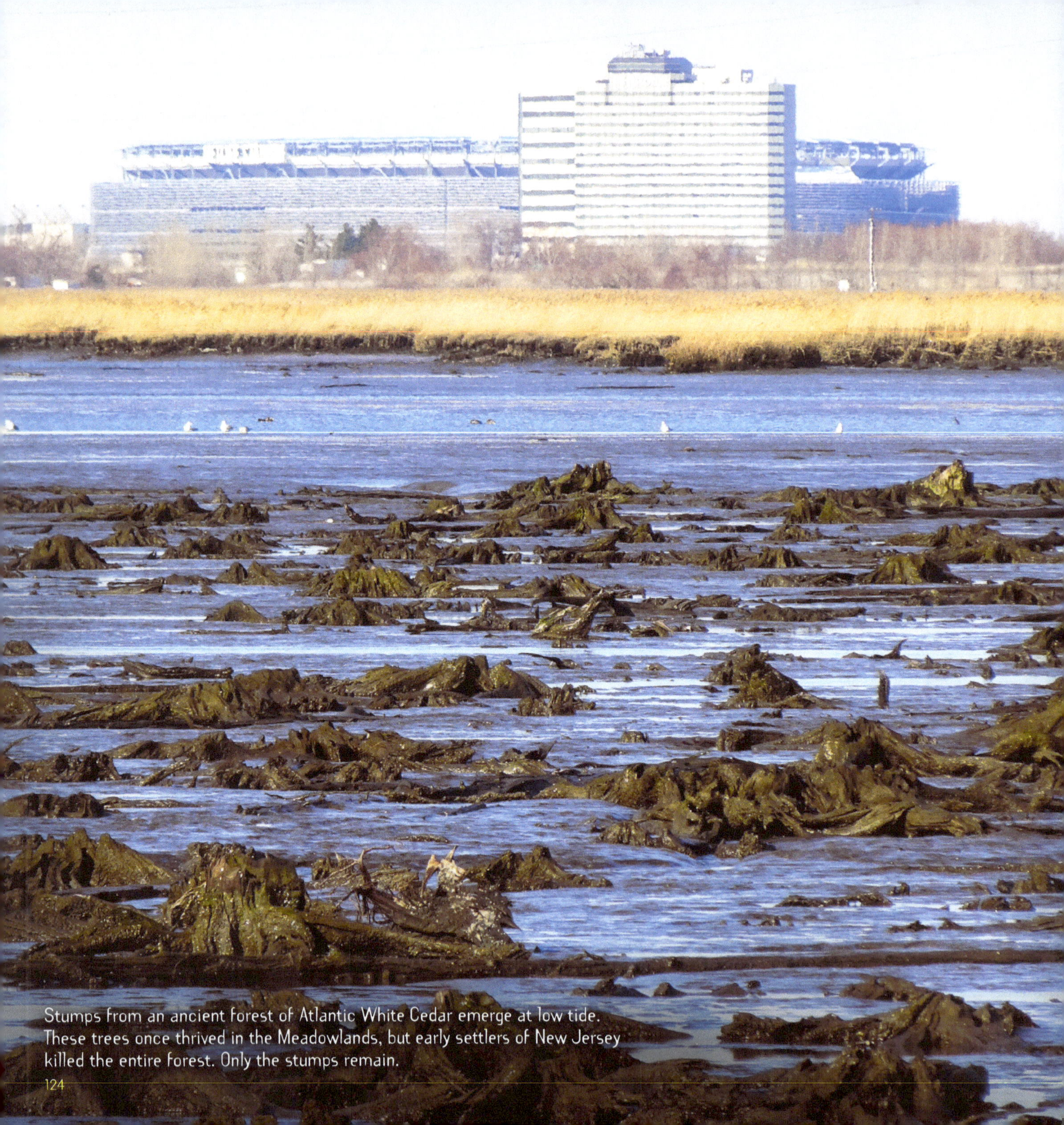

Stumps from an ancient forest of Atlantic White Cedar emerge at low tide. These trees once thrived in the Meadowlands, but early settlers of New Jersey killed the entire forest. Only the stumps remain.

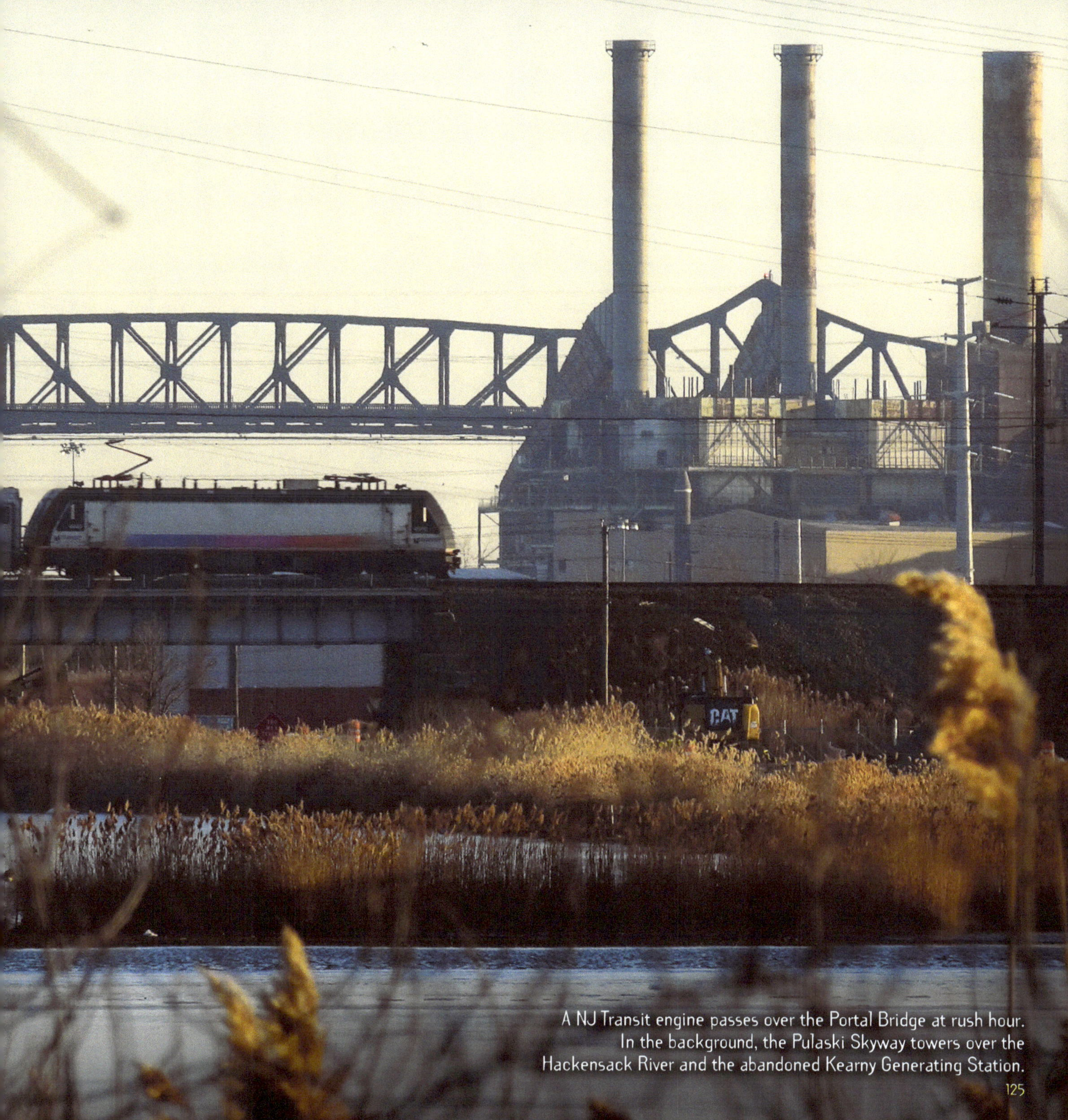

A NJ Transit engine passes over the Portal Bridge at rush hour. In the background, the Pulaski Skyway towers over the Hackensack River and the abandoned Kearny Generating Station.

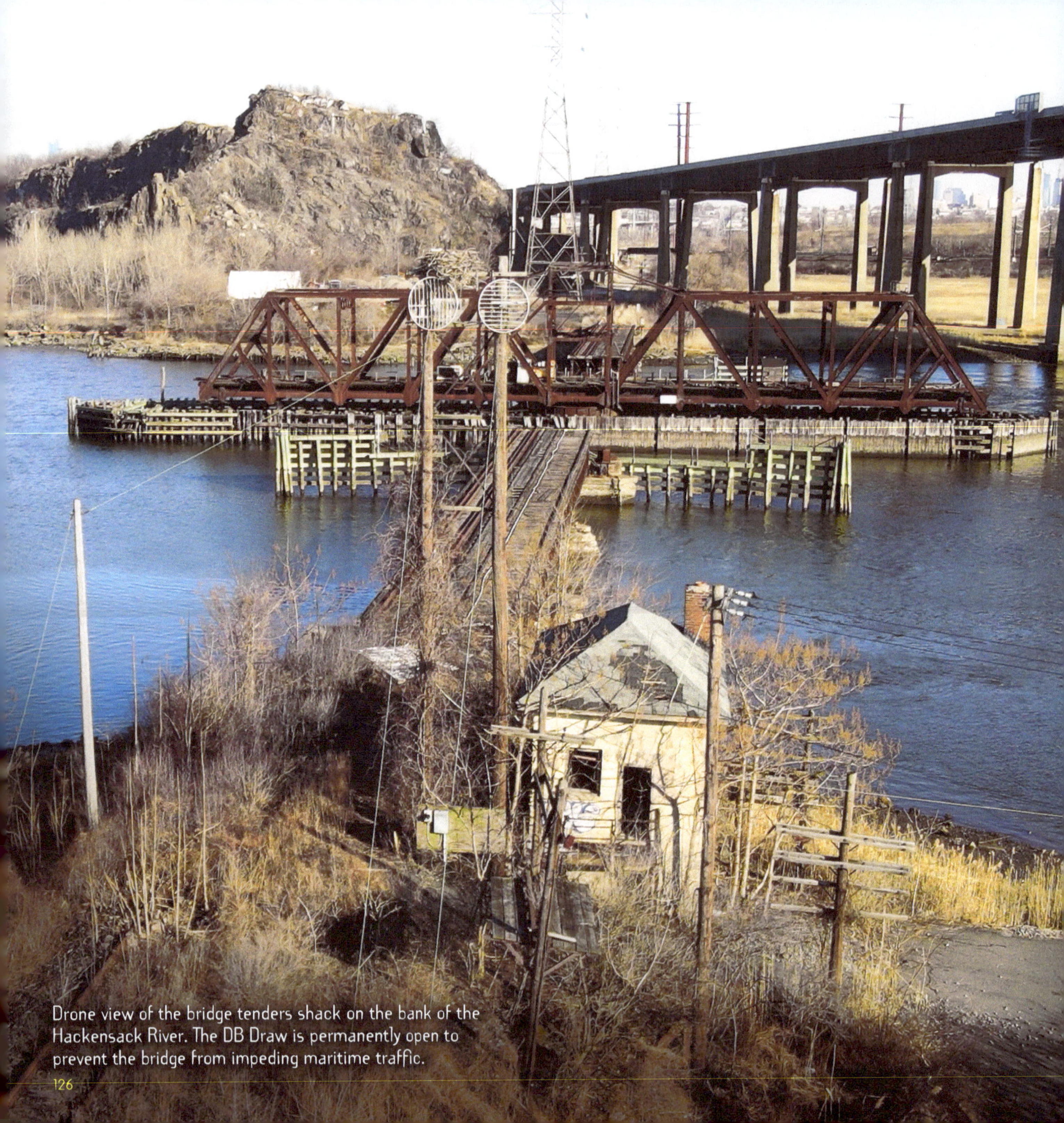

Drone view of the bridge tenders shack on the bank of the Hackensack River. The DB Draw is permanently open to prevent the bridge from impeding maritime traffic.

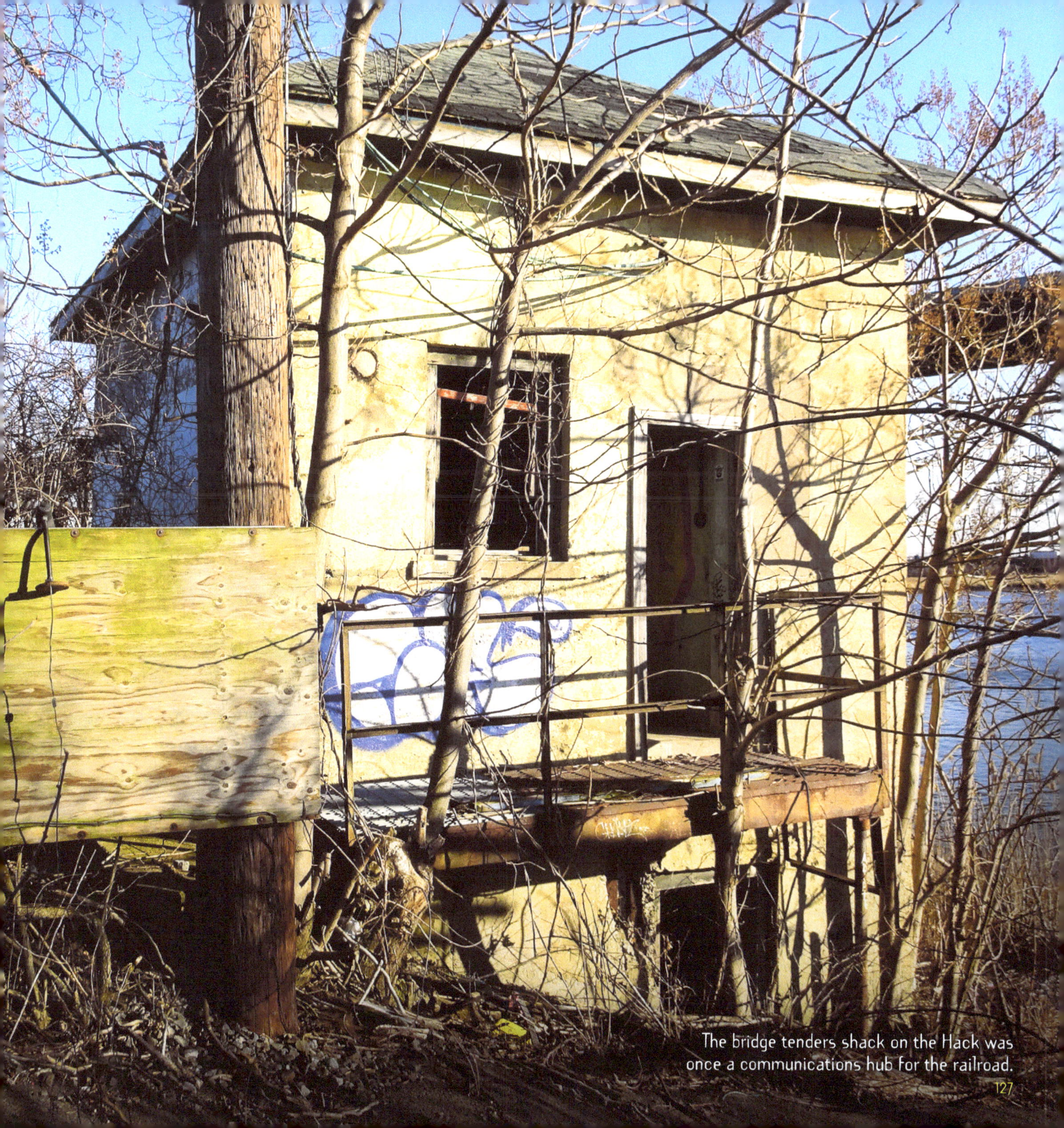

The bridge tenders shack on the Hack was once a communications hub for the railroad.

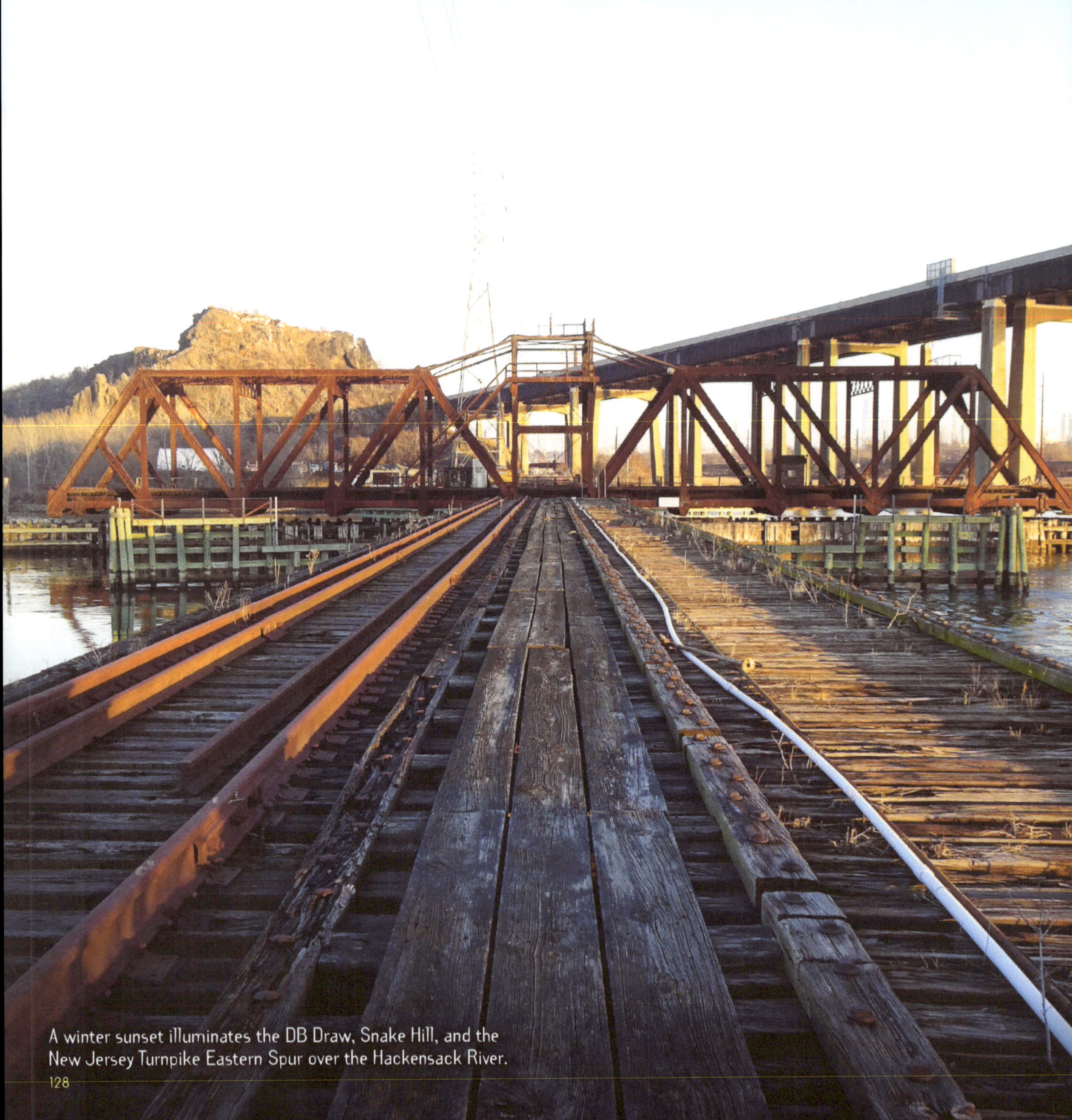

A winter sunset illuminates the DB Draw, Snake Hill, and the New Jersey Turnpike Eastern Spur over the Hackensack River.

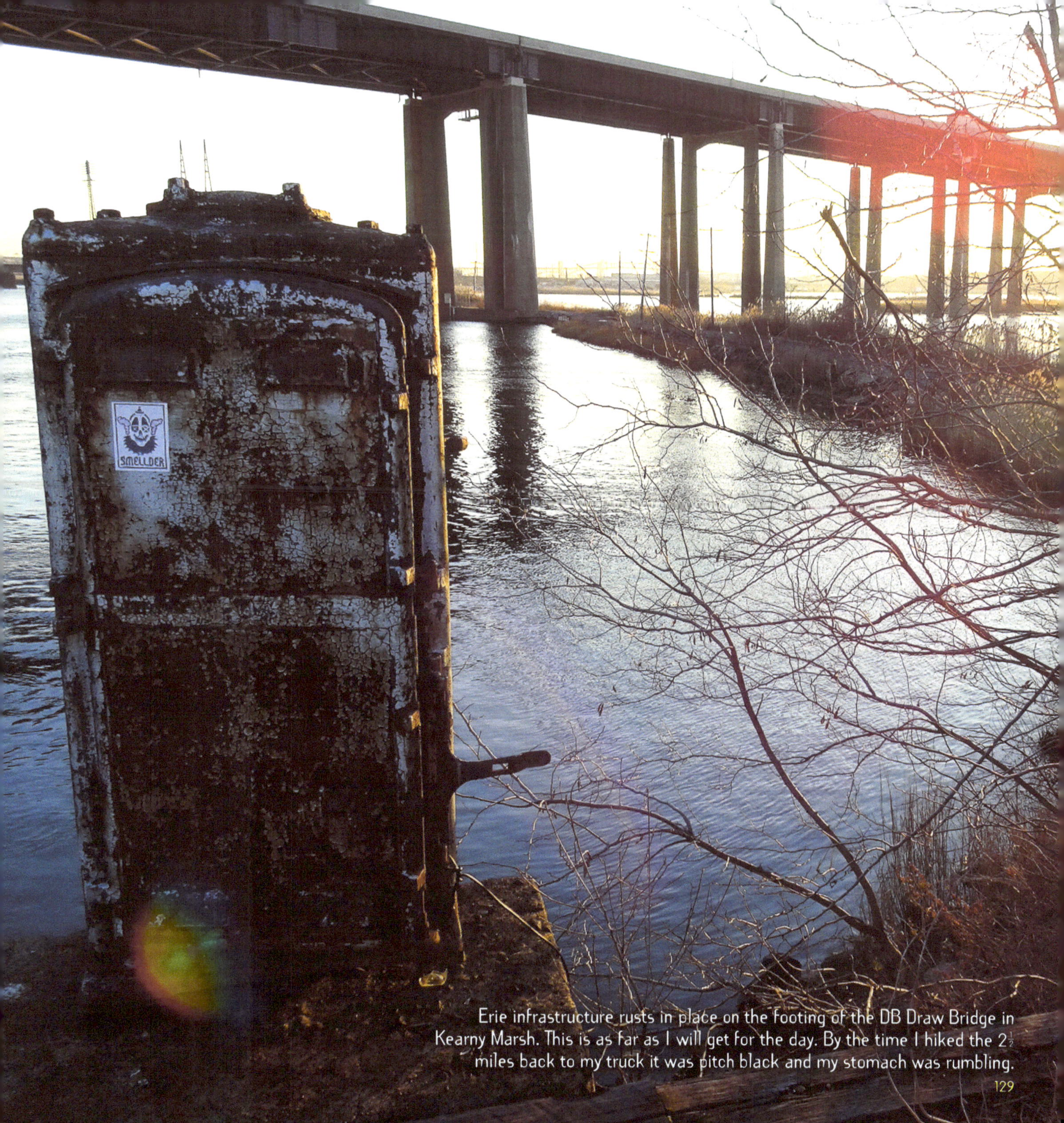

Erie infrastructure rusts in place on the footing of the DB Draw Bridge in Kearny Marsh. This is as far as I will get for the day. By the time I hiked the 2½ miles back to my truck it was pitch black and my stomach was rumbling.

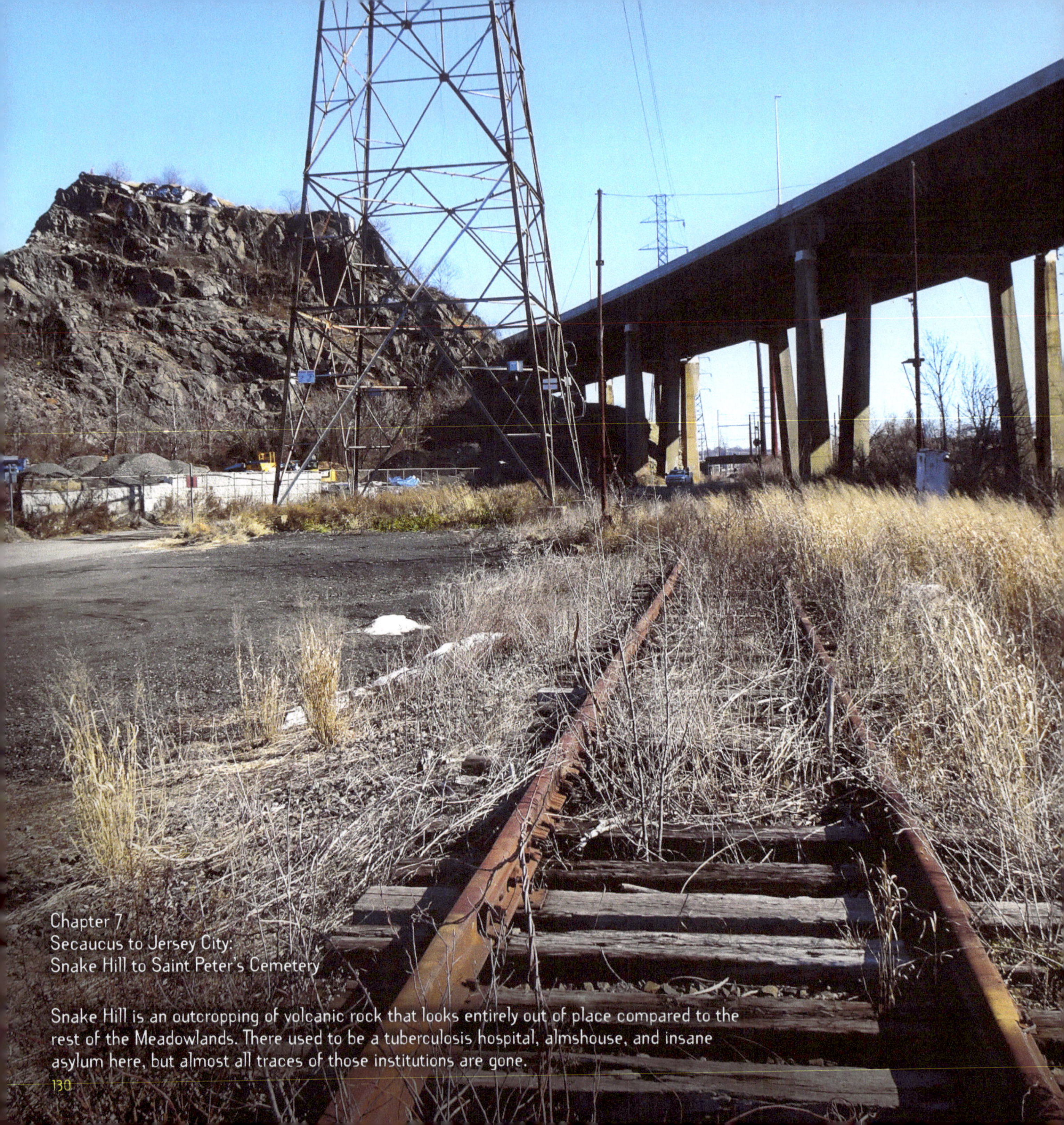

Chapter 7
Secaucus to Jersey City:
Snake Hill to Saint Peter's Cemetery

Snake Hill is an outcropping of volcanic rock that looks entirely out of place compared to the rest of the Meadowlands. There used to be a tuberculosis hospital, almshouse, and insane asylum here, but almost all traces of those institutions are gone.

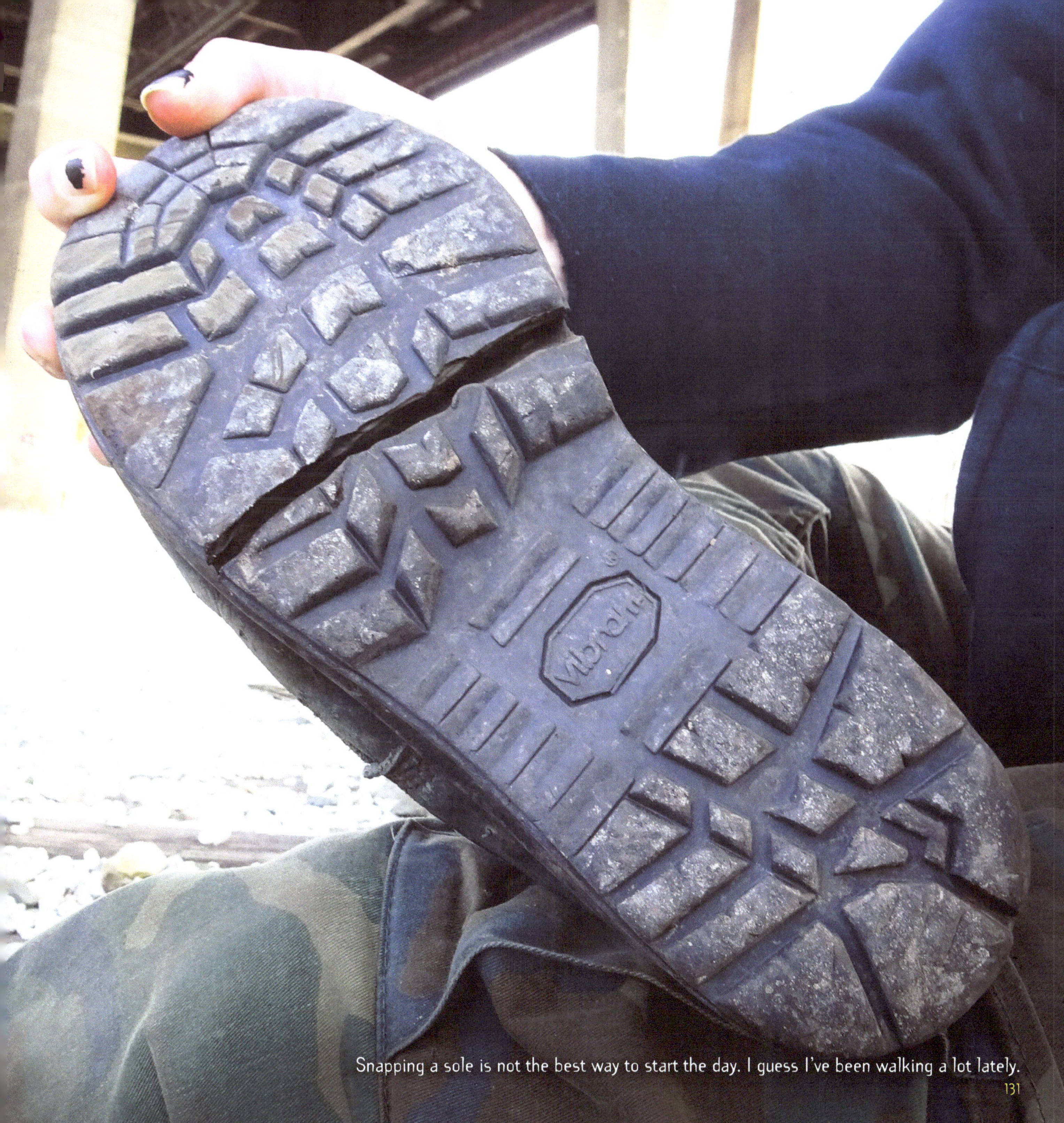

Snapping a sole is not the best way to start the day. I guess I've been walking a lot lately.

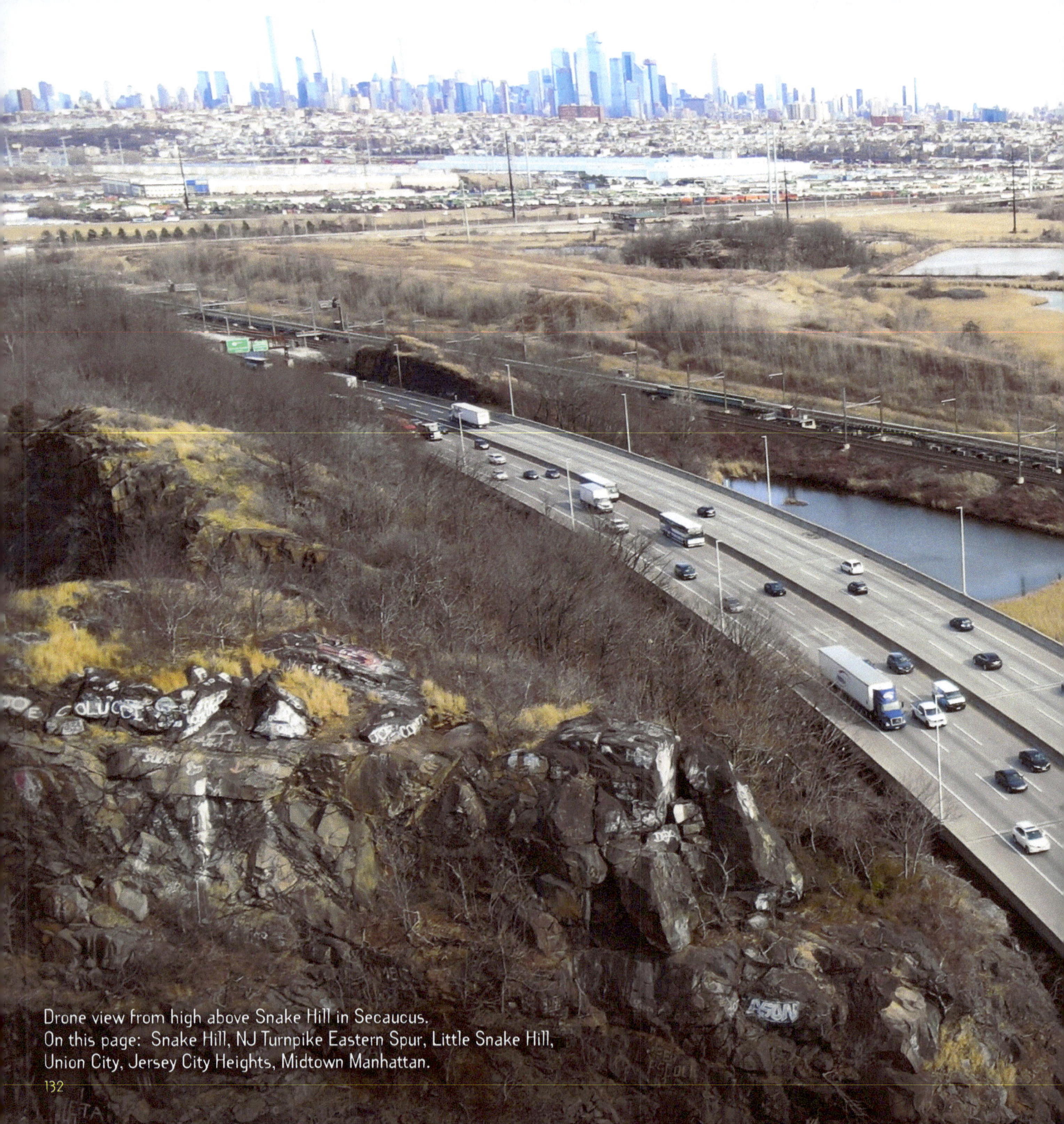

Drone view from high above Snake Hill in Secaucus.
On this page: Snake Hill, NJ Turnpike Eastern Spur, Little Snake Hill, Union City, Jersey City Heights, Midtown Manhattan.

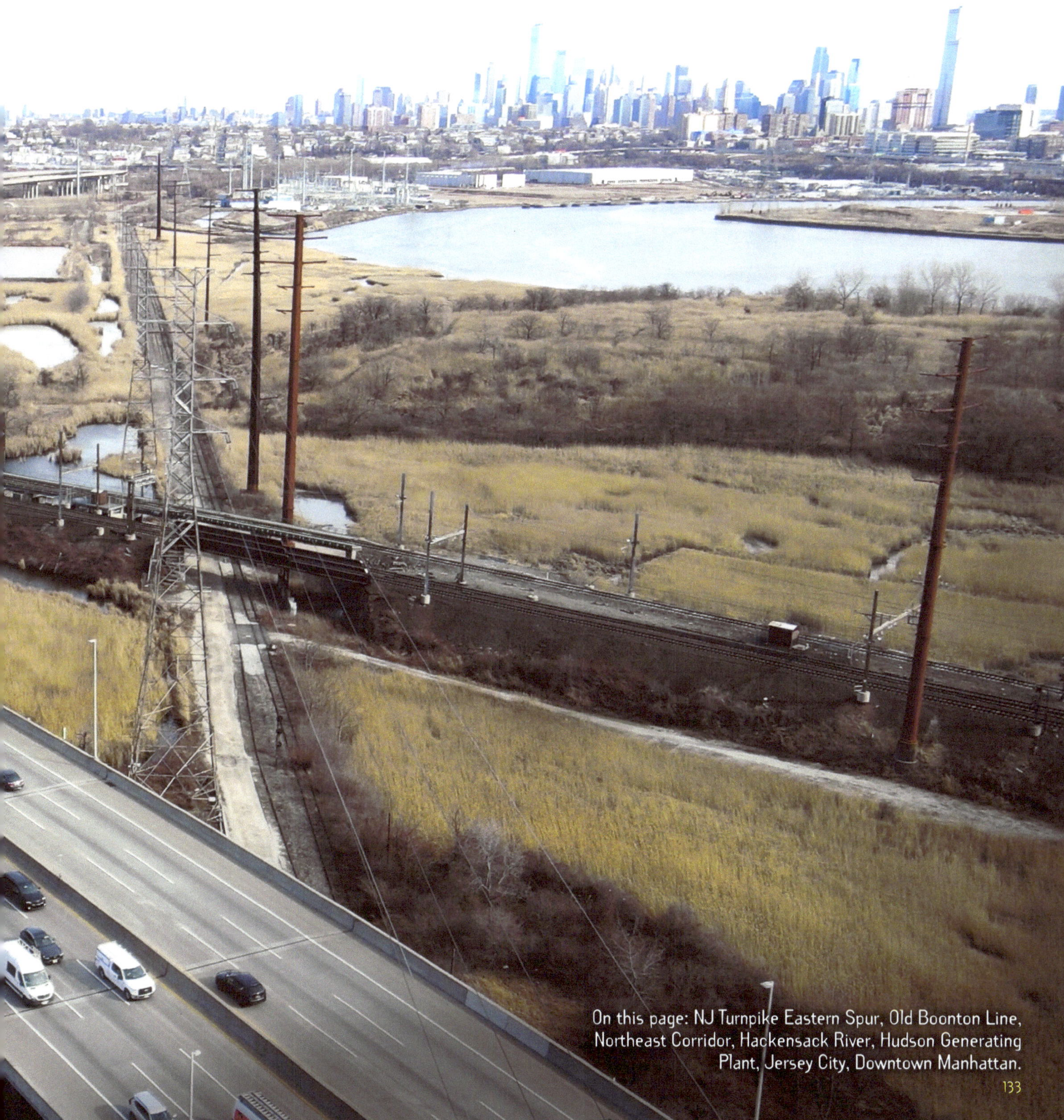

On this page: NJ Turnpike Eastern Spur, Old Boonton Line, Northeast Corridor, Hackensack River, Hudson Generating Plant, Jersey City, Downtown Manhattan.

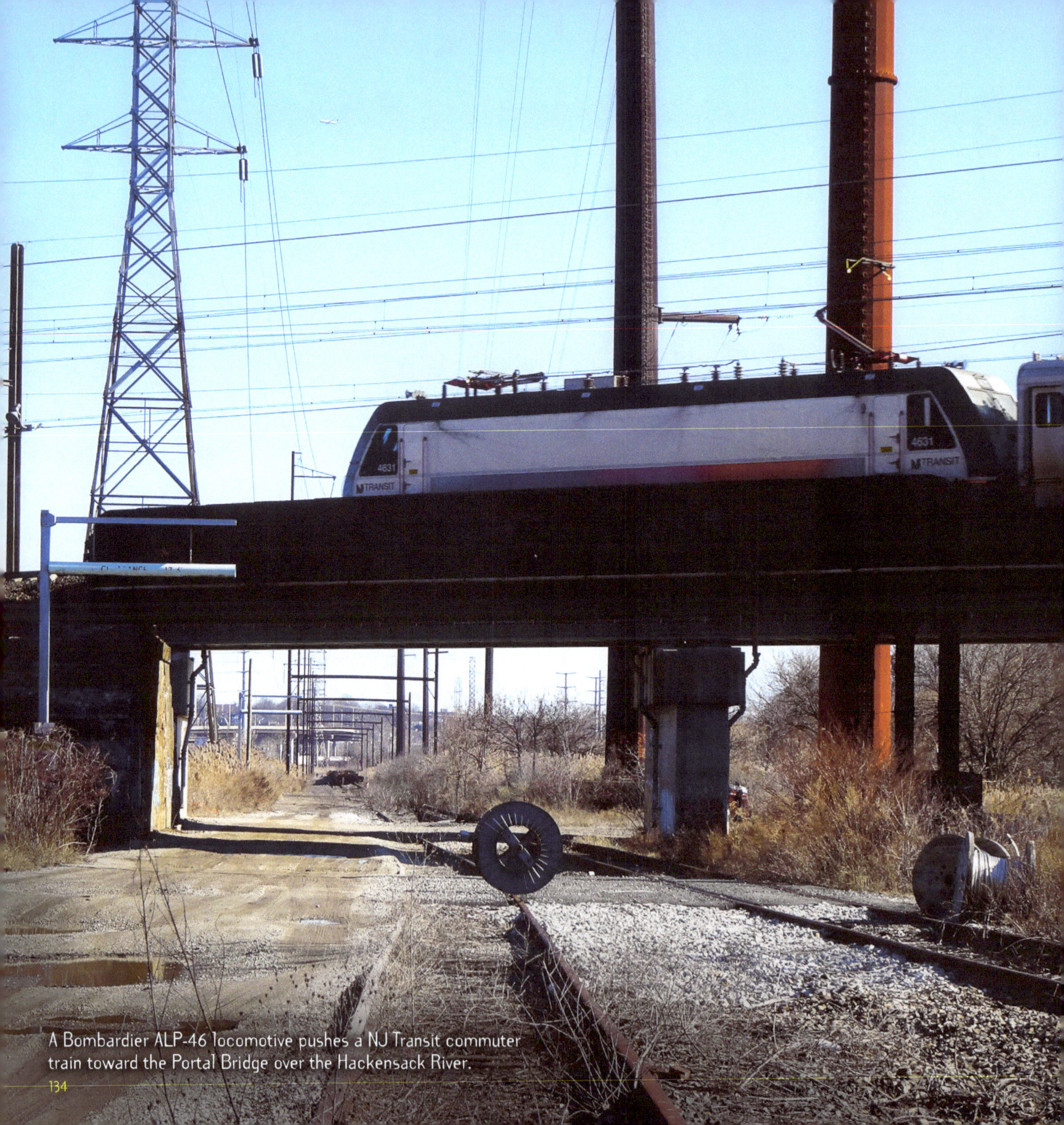

A Bombardier ALP-46 locomotive pushes a NJ Transit commuter train toward the Portal Bridge over the Hackensack River.

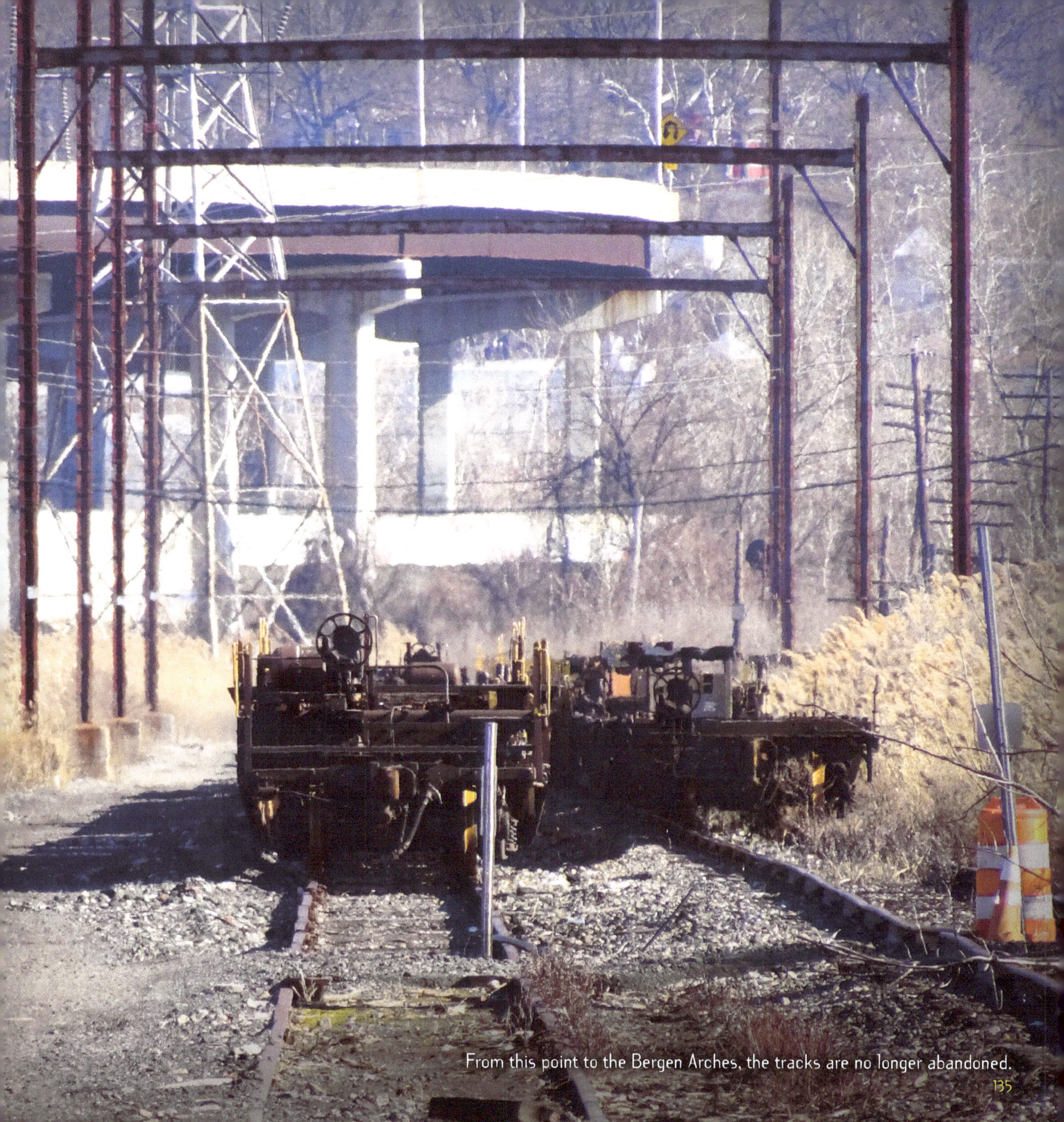

From this point to the Bergen Arches, the tracks are no longer abandoned.

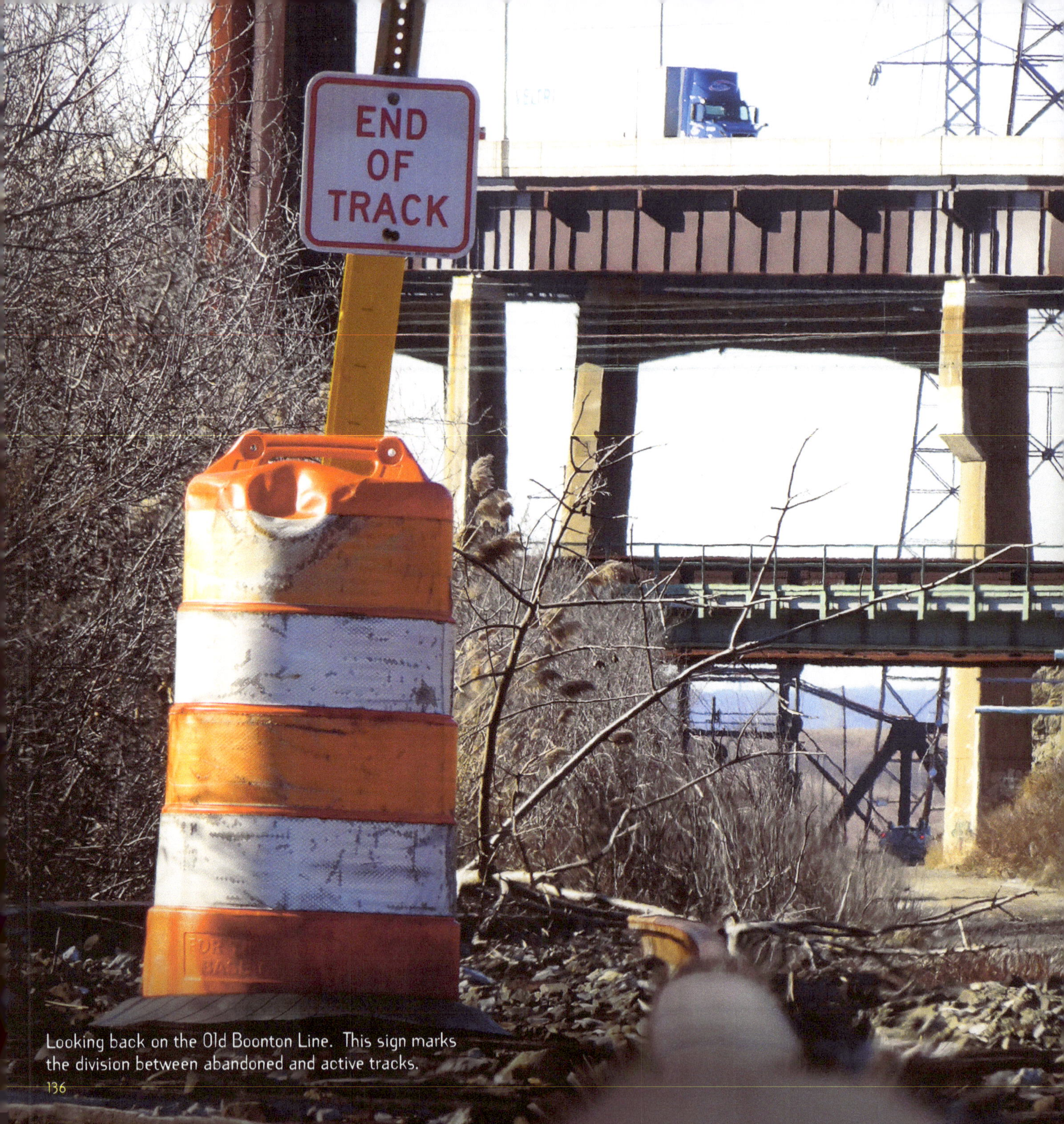

Looking back on the Old Boonton Line. This sign marks the division between abandoned and active tracks.

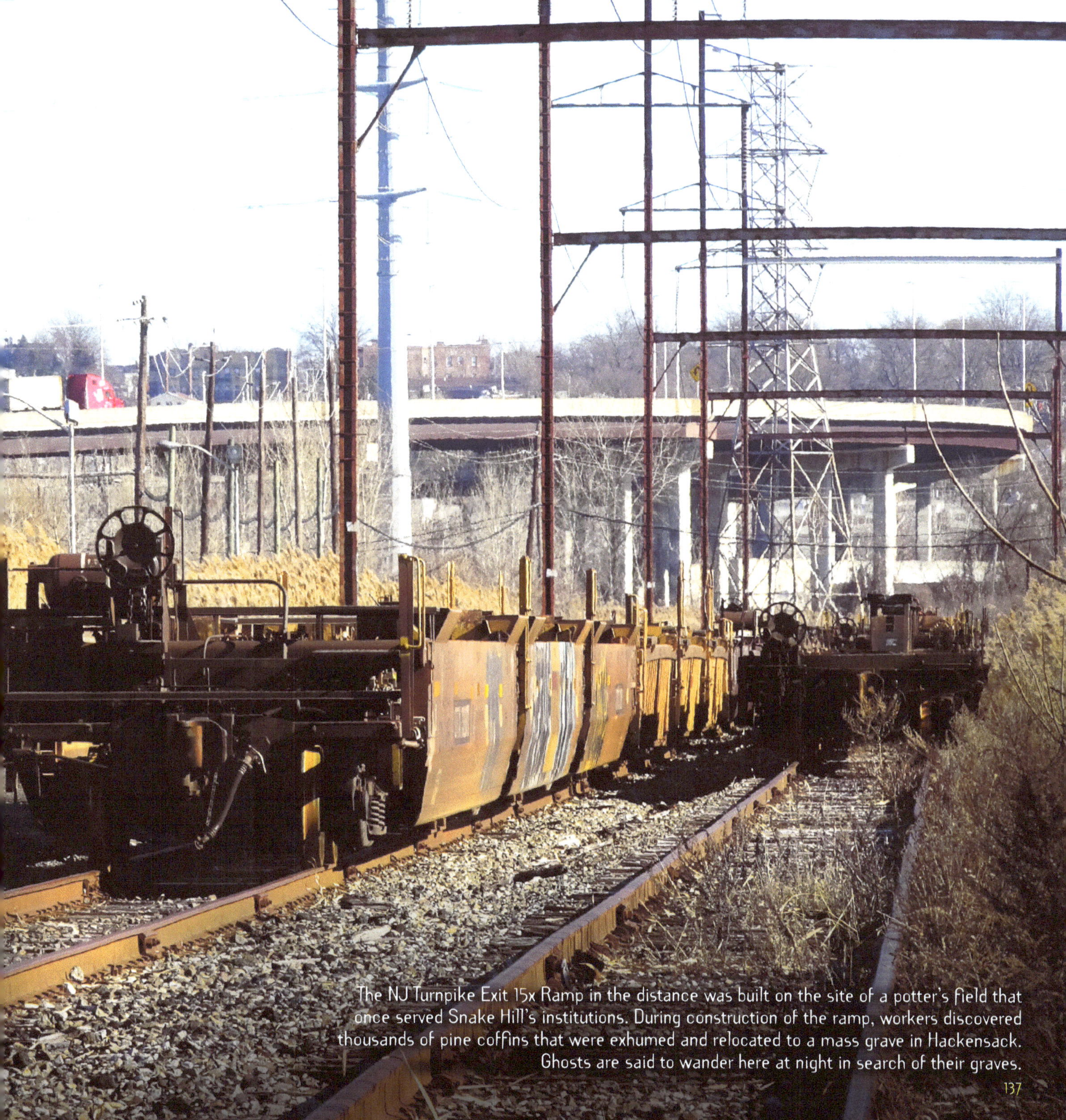

The NJ Turnpike Exit 15x Ramp in the distance was built on the site of a potter's field that once served Snake Hill's institutions. During construction of the ramp, workers discovered thousands of pine coffins that were exhumed and relocated to a mass grave in Hackensack. Ghosts are said to wander here at night in search of their graves.

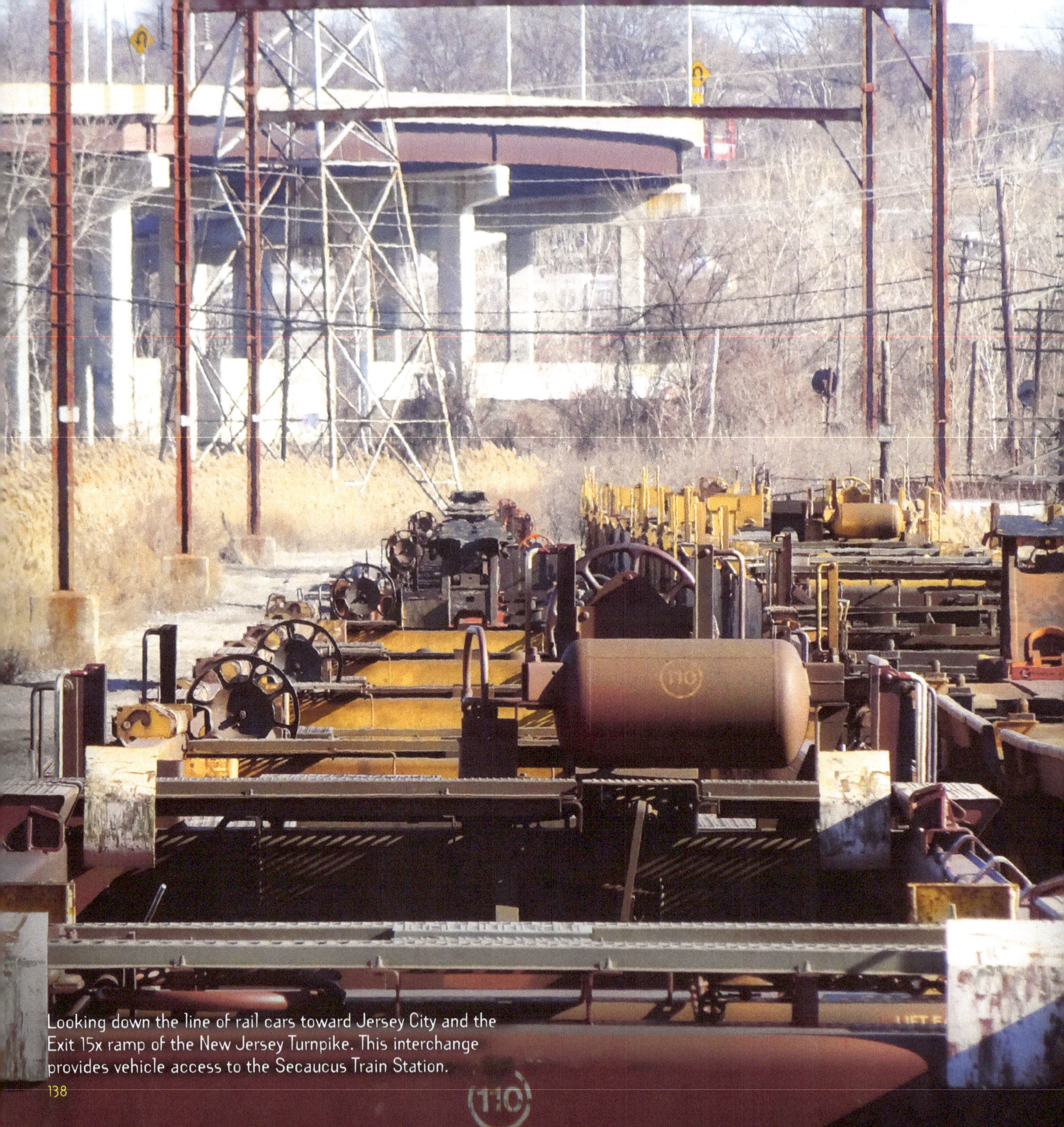

Looking down the line of rail cars toward Jersey City and the Exit 15x ramp of the New Jersey Turnpike. This interchange provides vehicle access to the Secaucus Train Station.

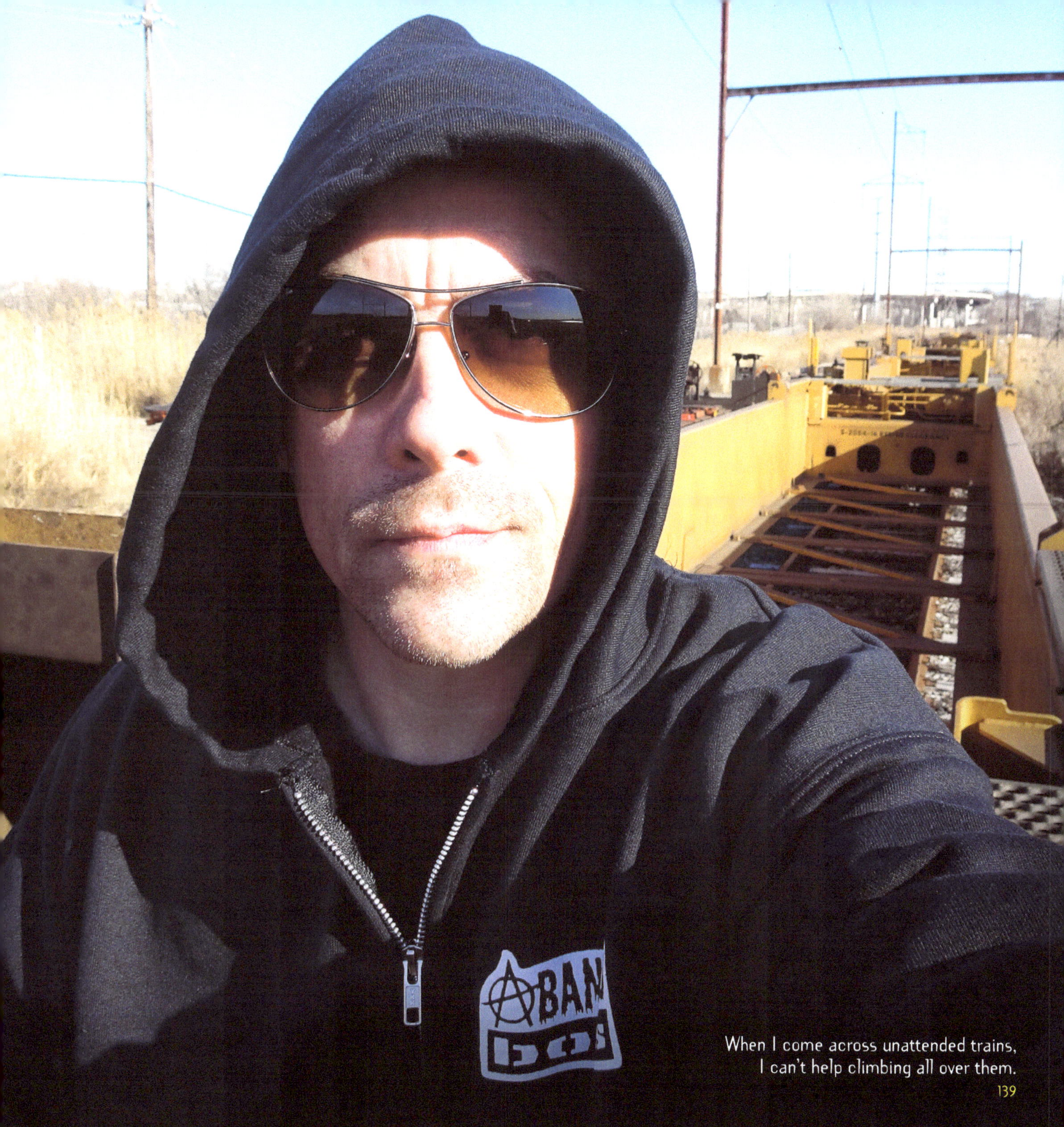

When I come across unattended trains,
I can't help climbing all over them.

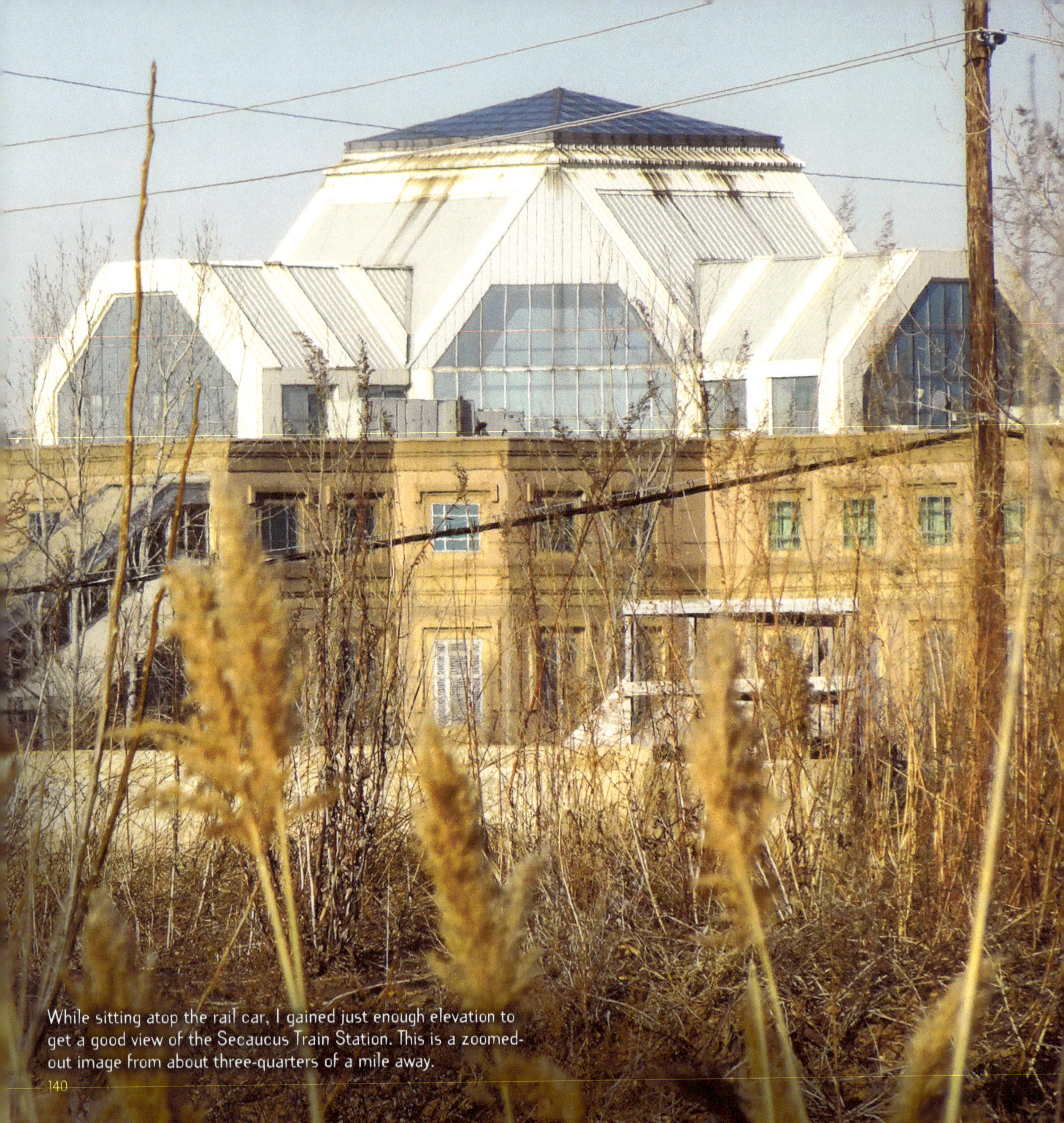

While sitting atop the rail car, I gained just enough elevation to get a good view of the Secaucus Train Station. This is a zoomed-out image from about three-quarters of a mile away.

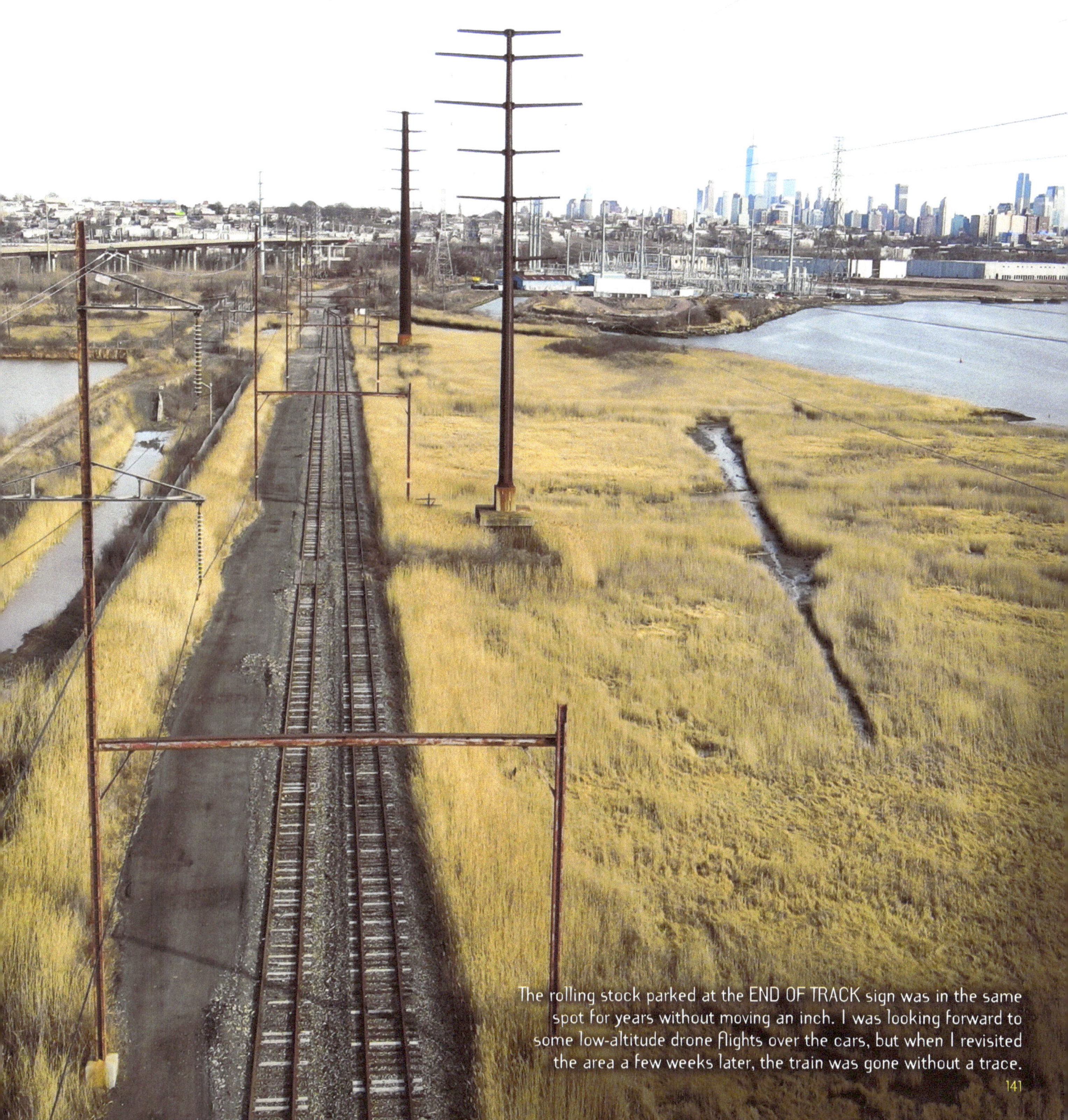

The rolling stock parked at the END OF TRACK sign was in the same spot for years without moving an inch. I was looking forward to some low-altitude drone flights over the cars, but when I revisited the area a few weeks later, the train was gone without a trace.

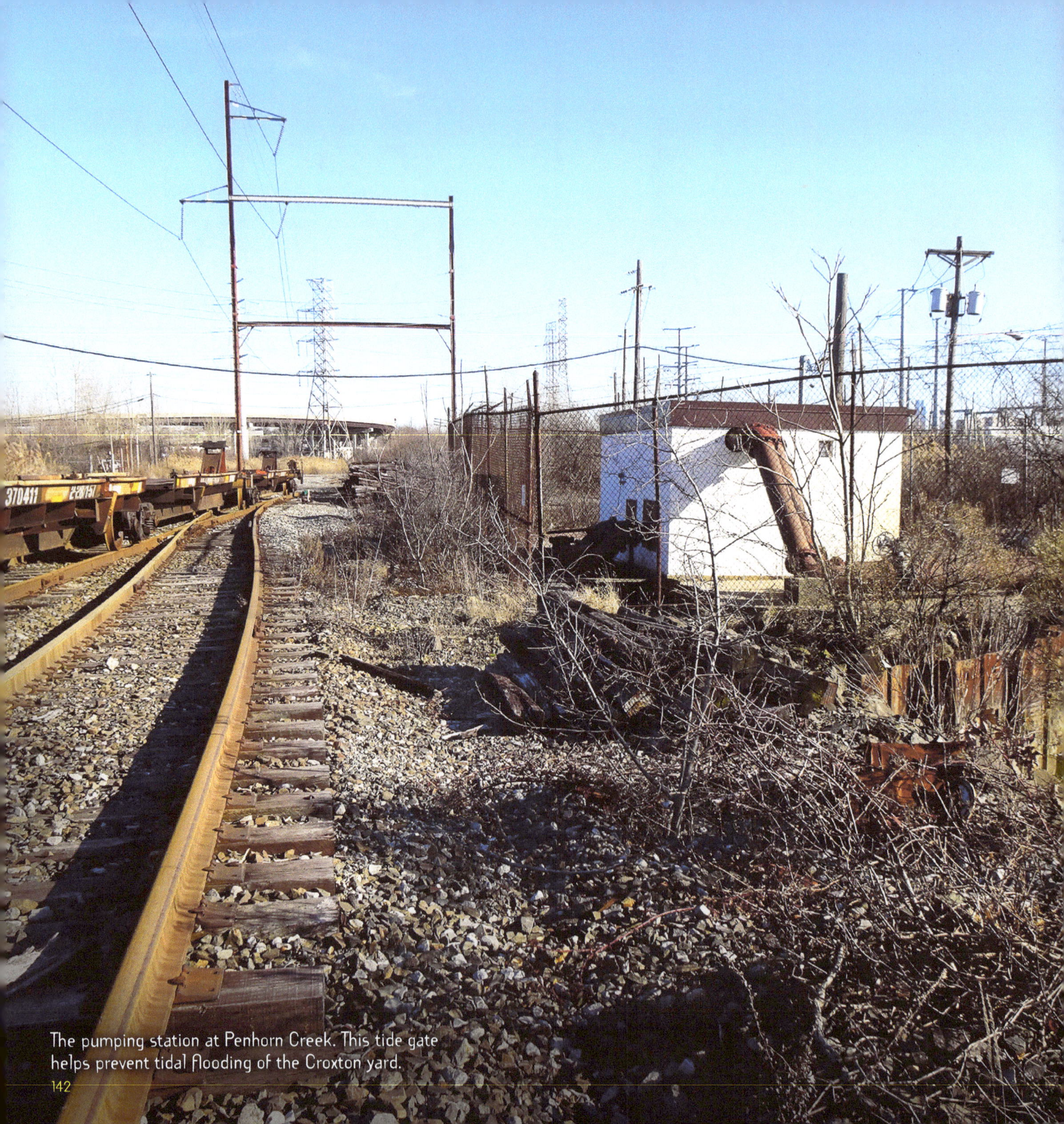

The pumping station at Penhorn Creek. This tide gate helps prevent tidal flooding of the Croxton yard.

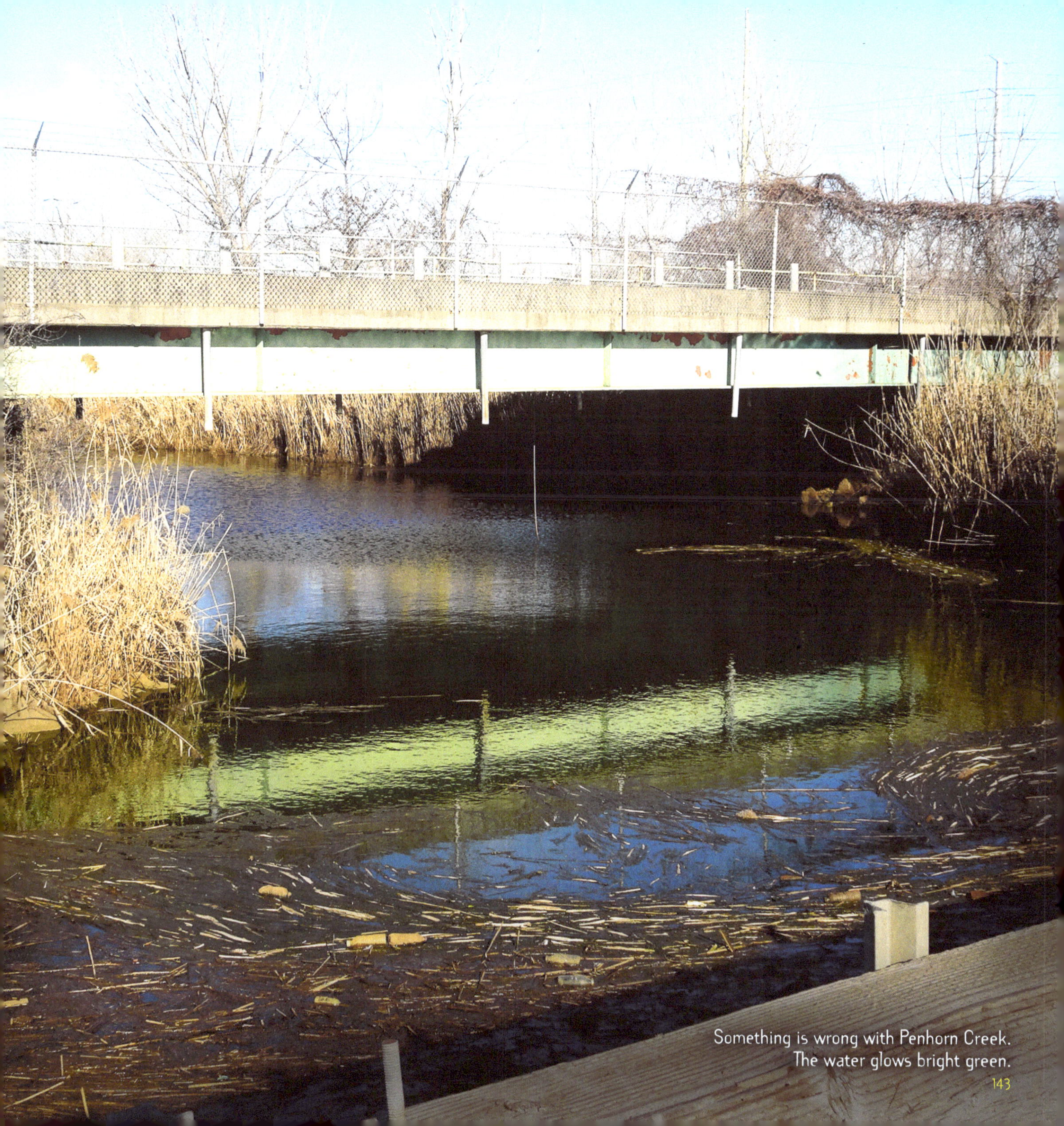

Something is wrong with Penhorn Creek.
The water glows bright green.

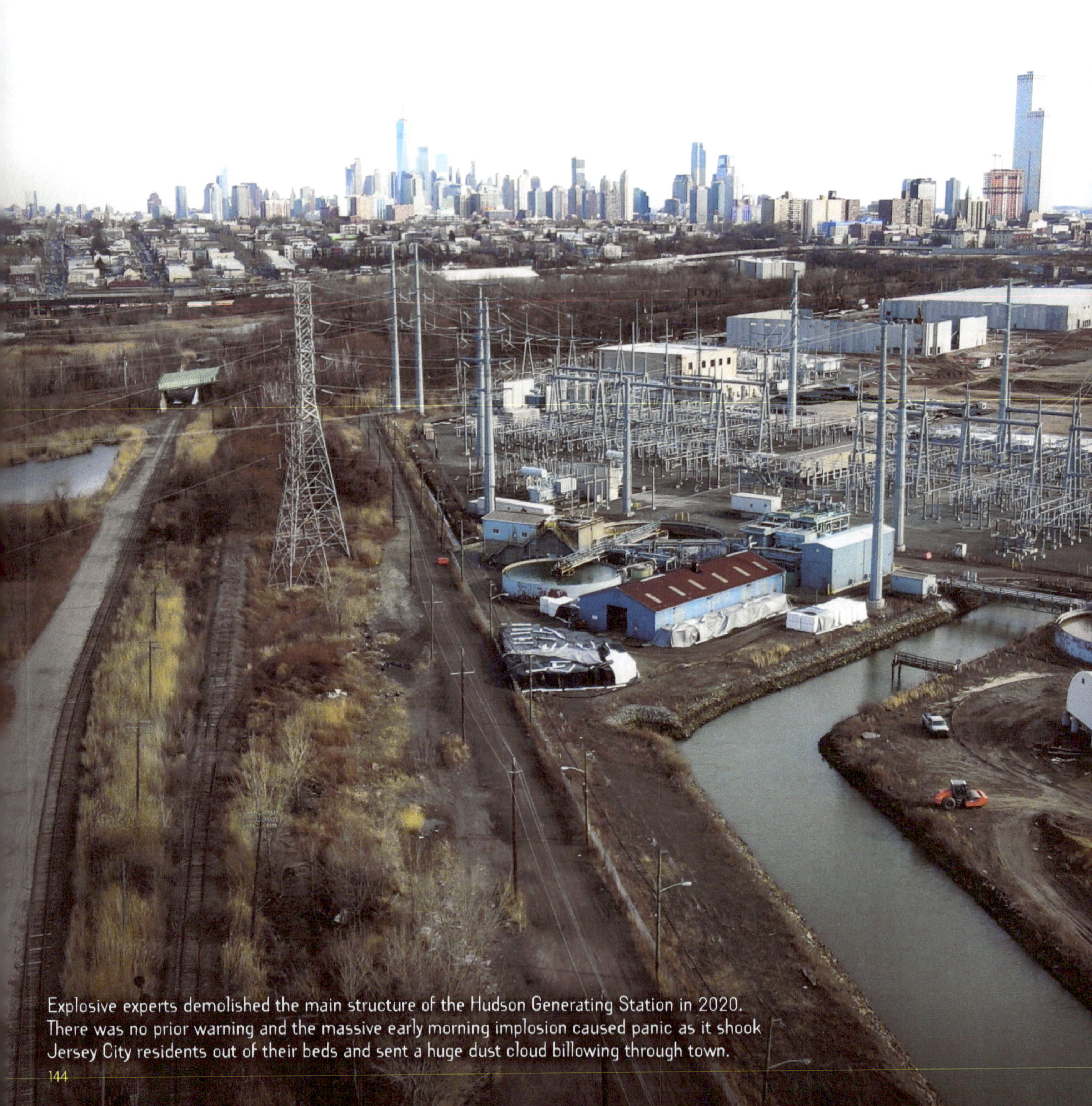

Explosive experts demolished the main structure of the Hudson Generating Station in 2020. There was no prior warning and the massive early morning implosion caused panic as it shook Jersey City residents out of their beds and sent a huge dust cloud billowing through town.

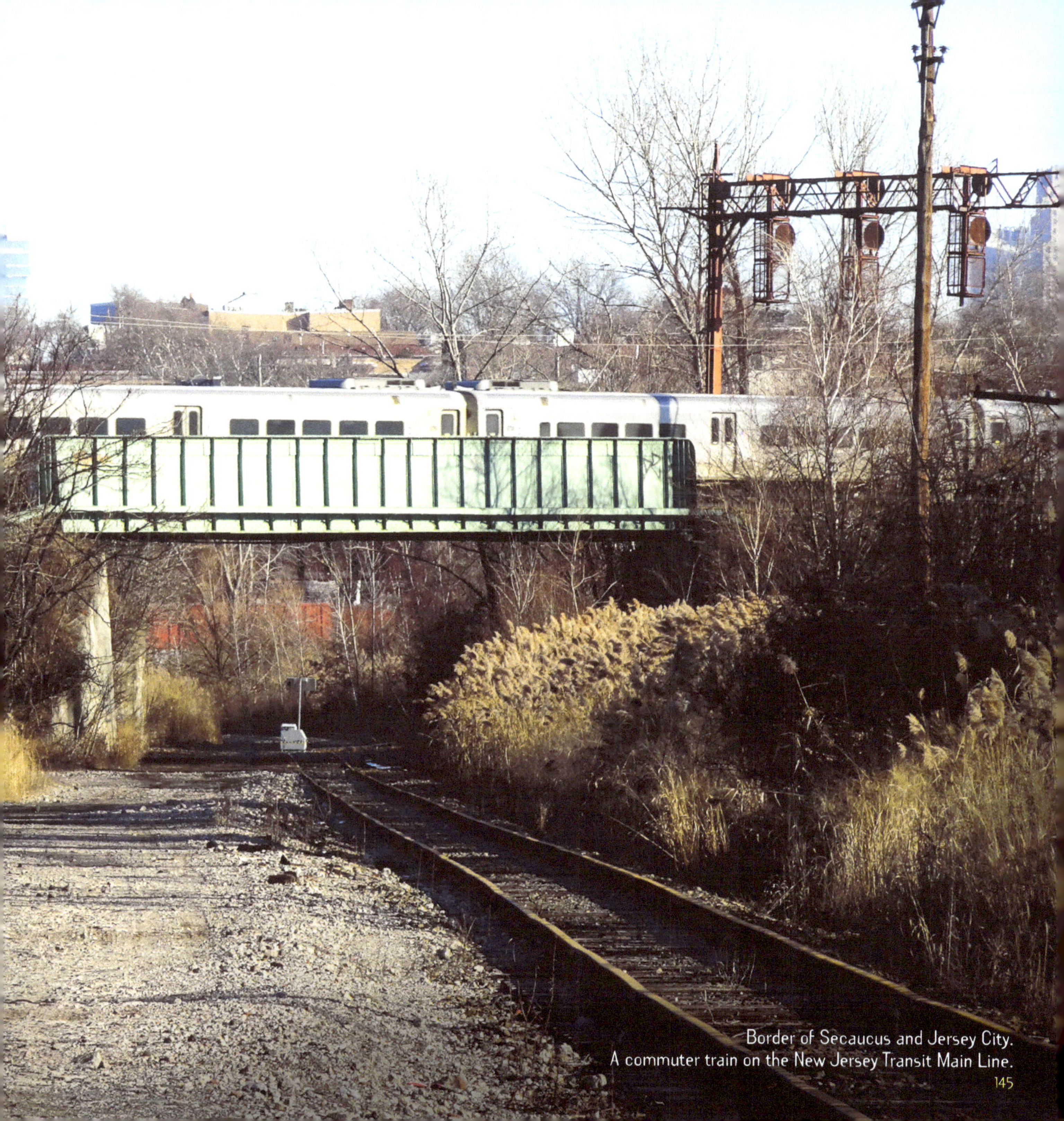

Border of Secaucus and Jersey City.
A commuter train on the New Jersey Transit Main Line.

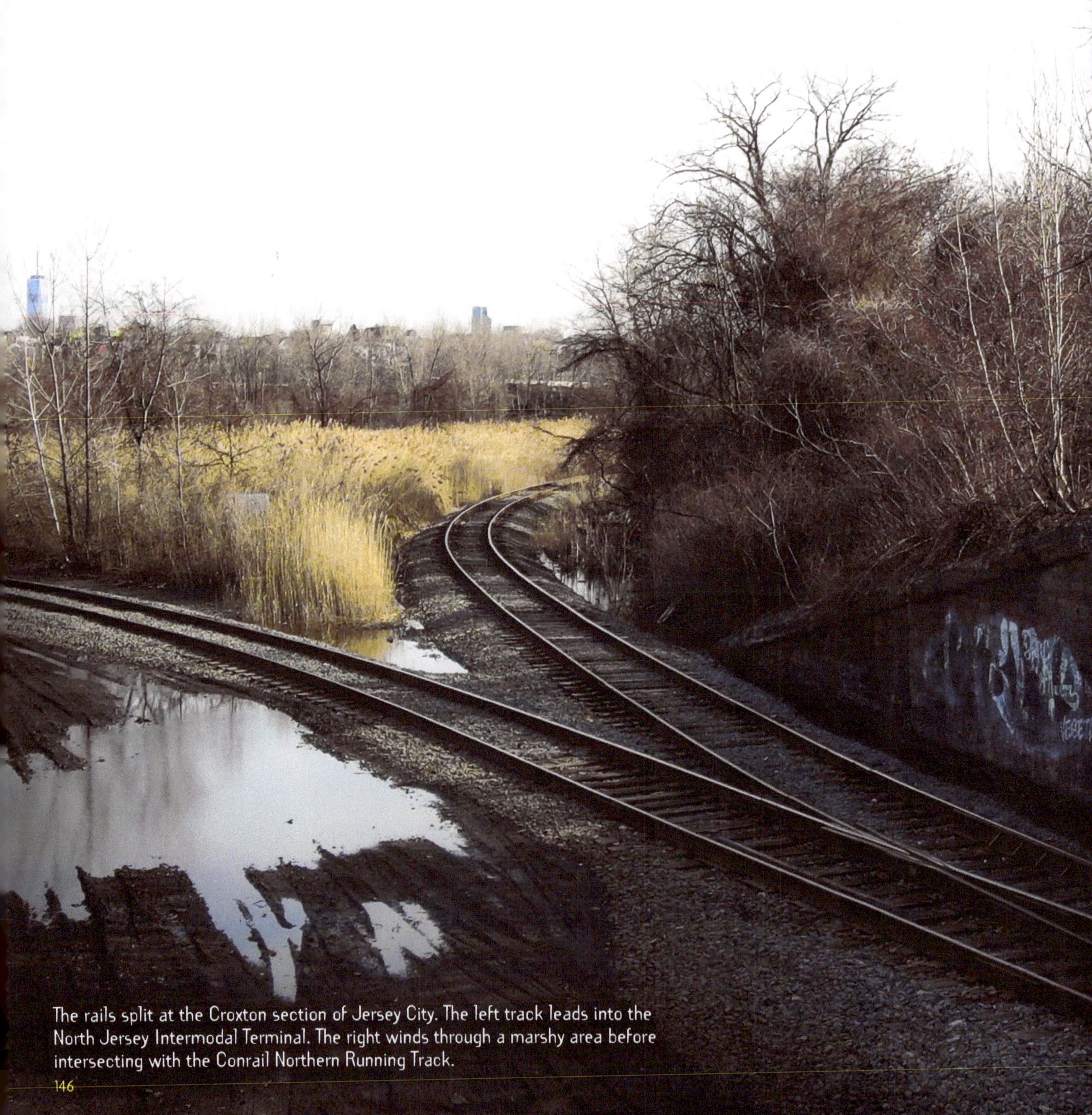

The rails split at the Croxton section of Jersey City. The left track leads into the North Jersey Intermodal Terminal. The right winds through a marshy area before intersecting with the Conrail Northern Running Track.

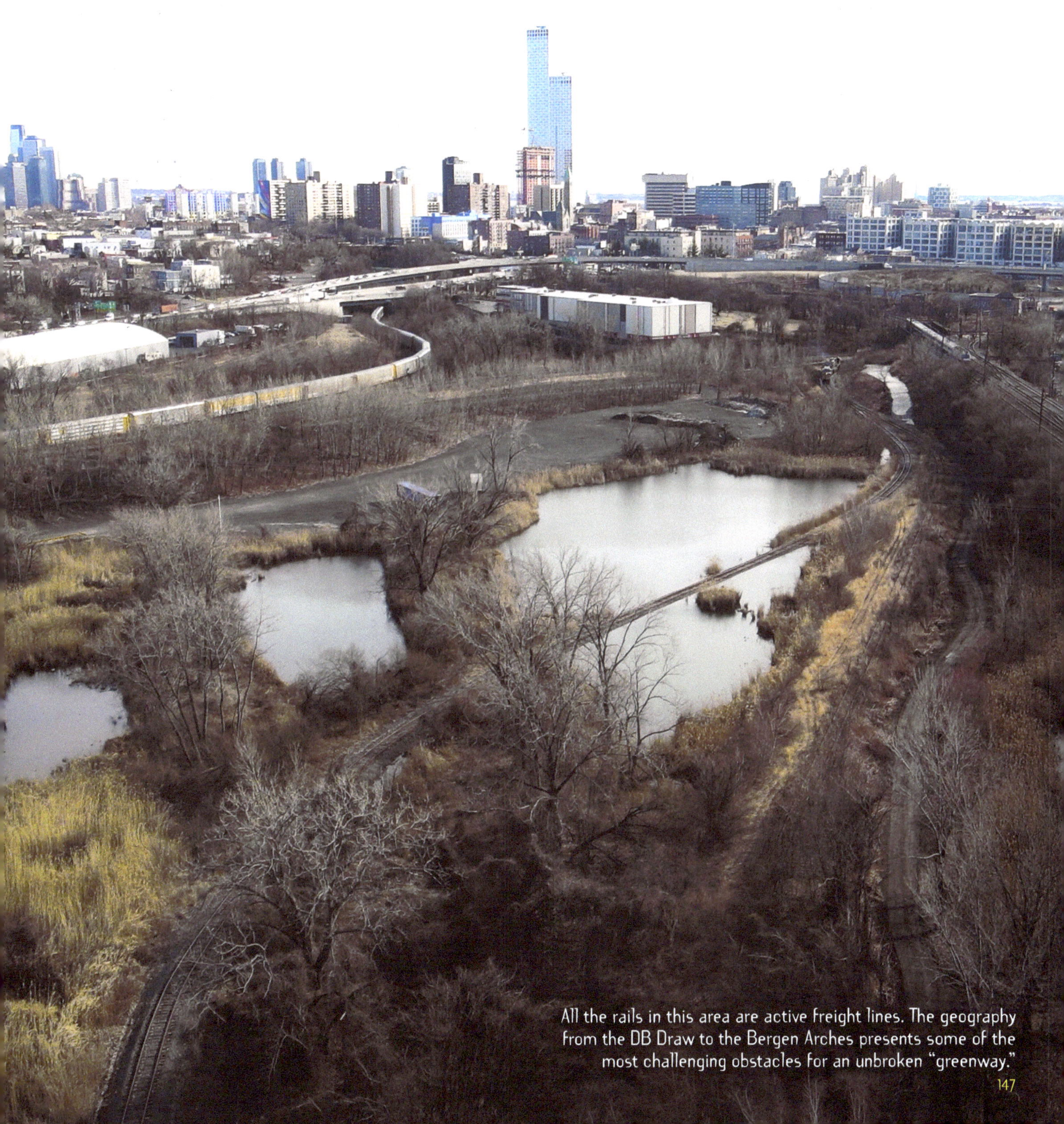

All the rails in this area are active freight lines. The geography from the DB Draw to the Bergen Arches presents some of the most challenging obstacles for an unbroken "greenway."

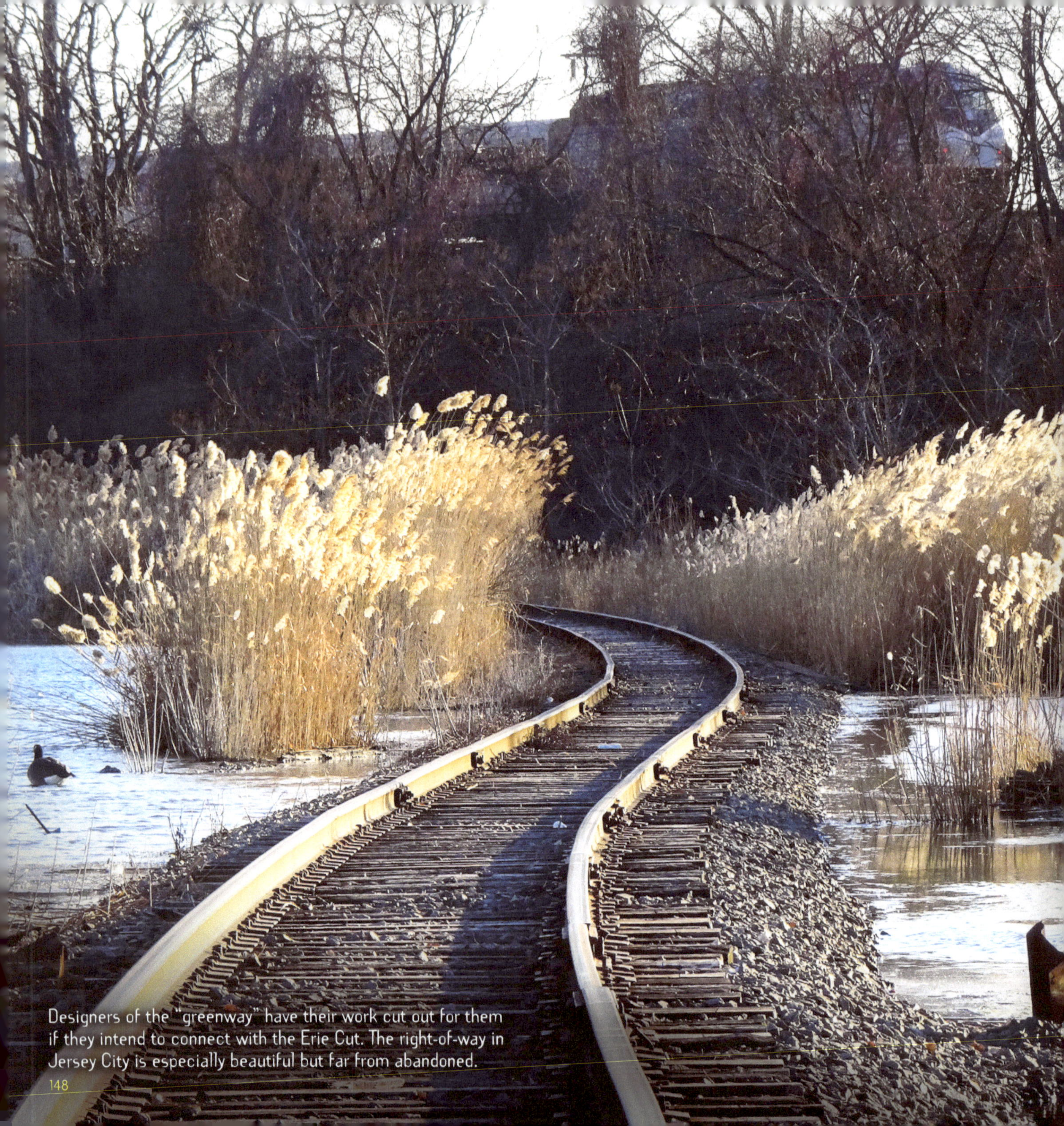

Designers of the "greenway" have their work cut out for them if they intend to connect with the Erie Cut. The right-of-way in Jersey City is especially beautiful but far from abandoned.

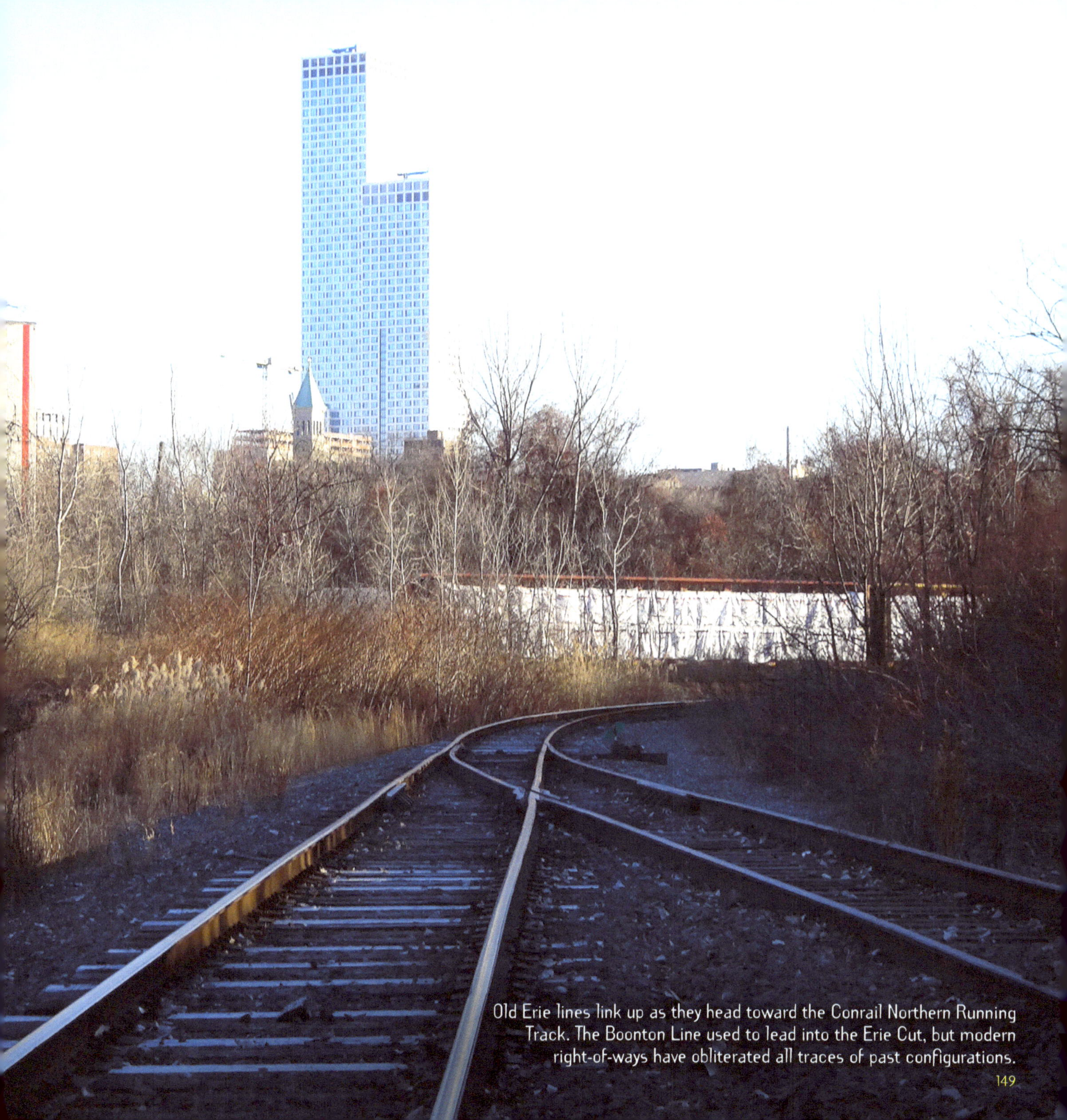

Old Erie lines link up as they head toward the Conrail Northern Running Track. The Boonton Line used to lead into the Erie Cut, but modern right-of-ways have obliterated all traces of past configurations.

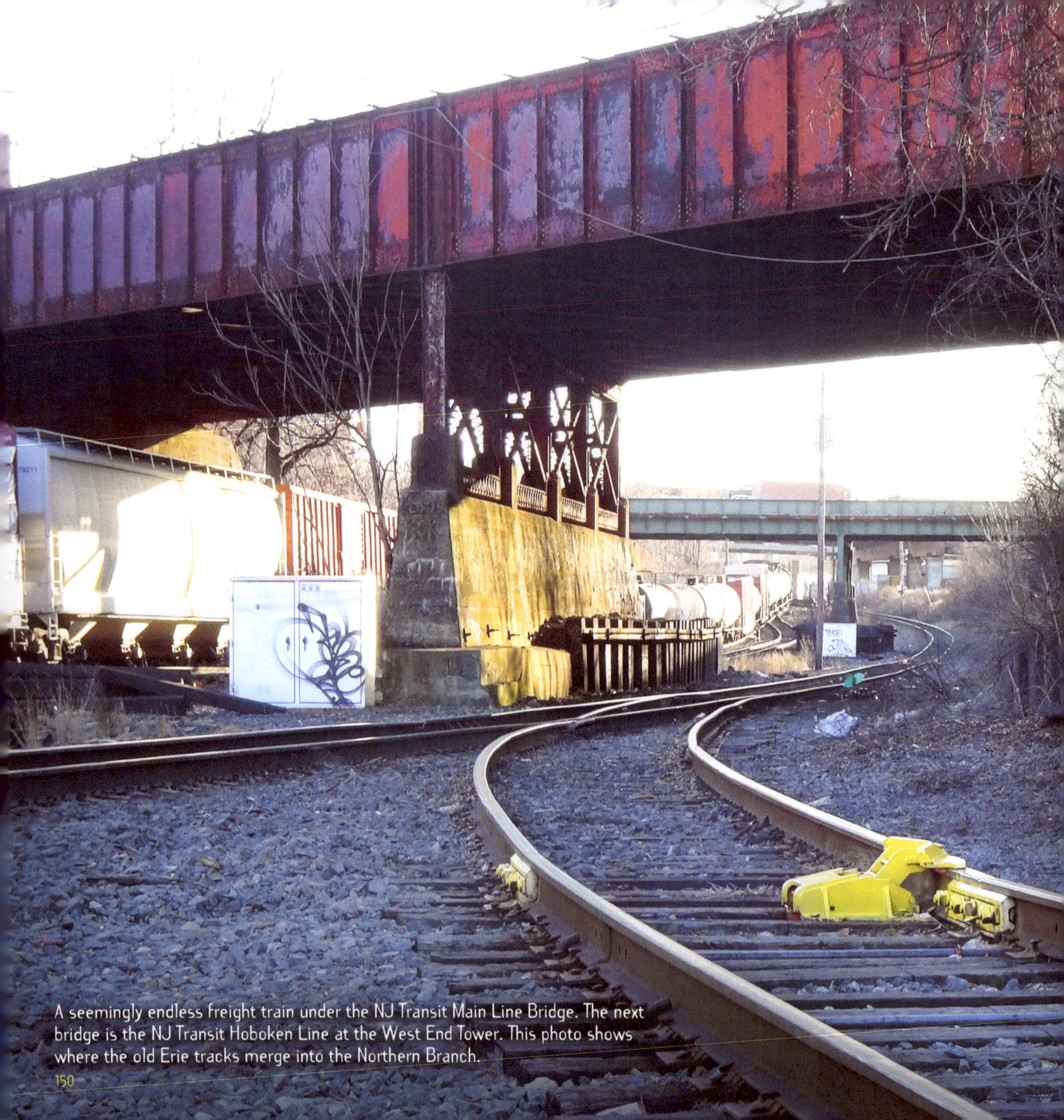

A seemingly endless freight train under the NJ Transit Main Line Bridge. The next bridge is the NJ Transit Hoboken Line at the West End Tower. This photo shows where the old Erie tracks merge into the Northern Branch.

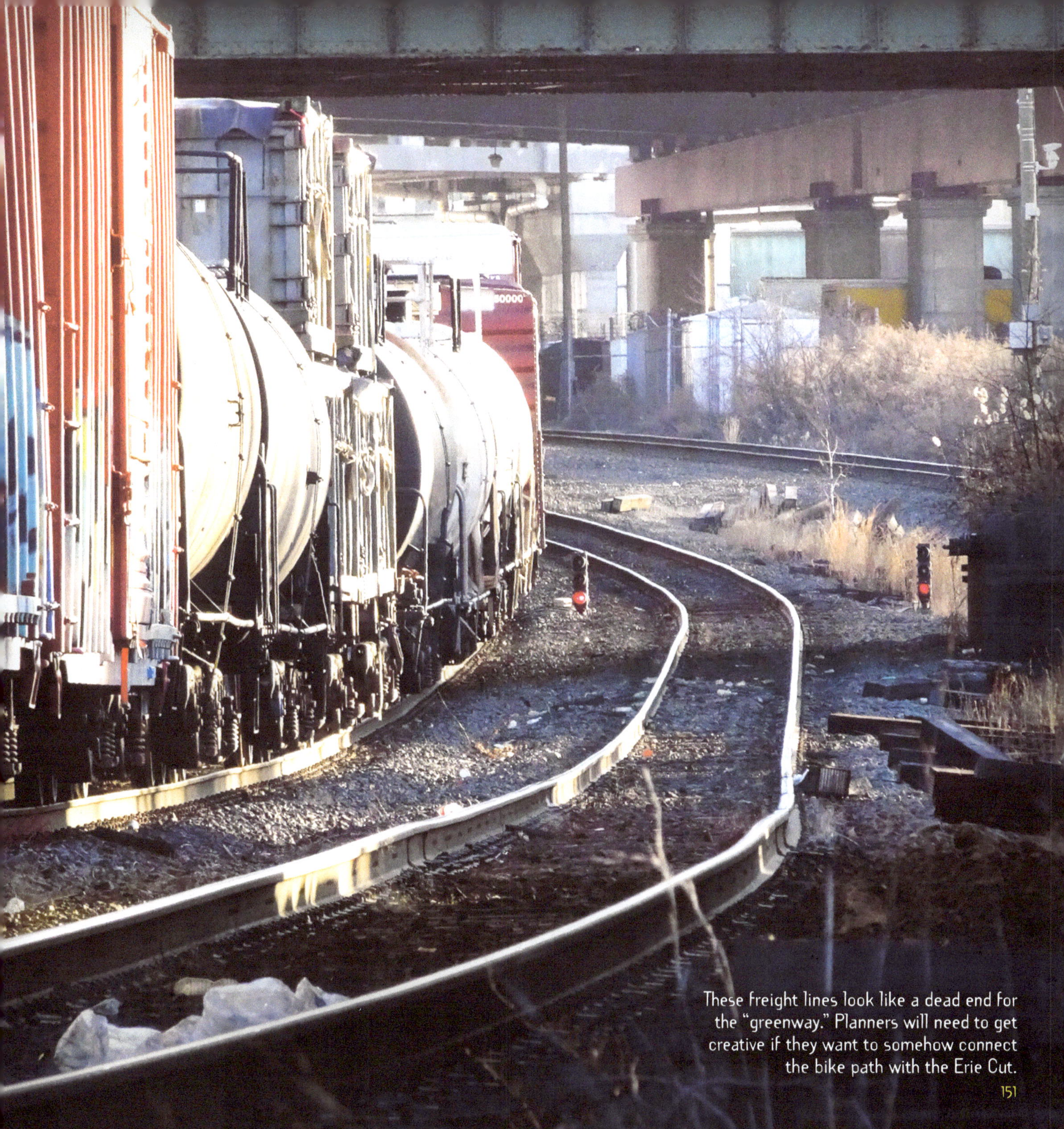

These freight lines look like a dead end for the "greenway." Planners will need to get creative if they want to somehow connect the bike path with the Erie Cut.

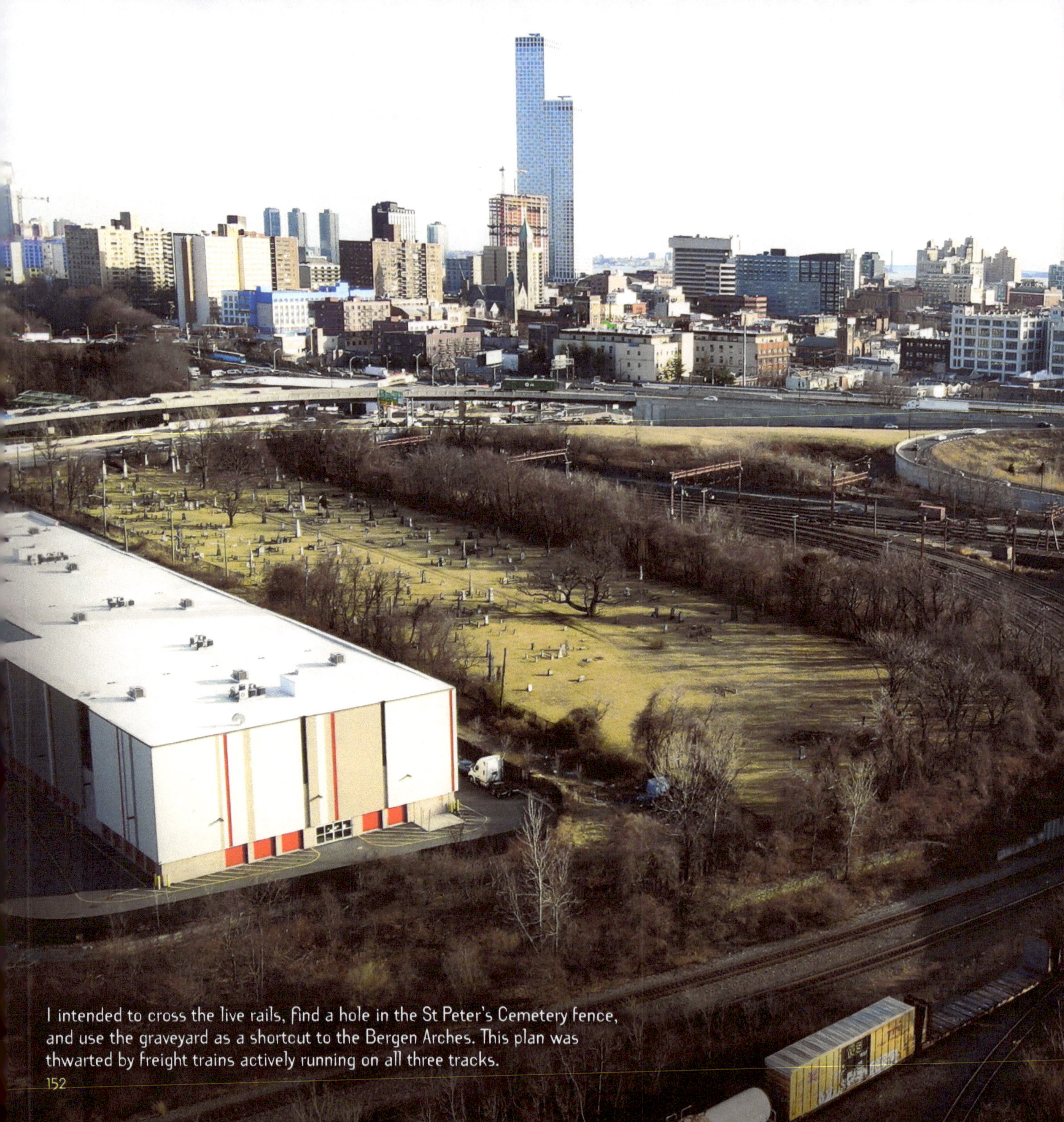

I intended to cross the live rails, find a hole in the St Peter's Cemetery fence, and use the graveyard as a shortcut to the Bergen Arches. This plan was thwarted by freight trains actively running on all three tracks.

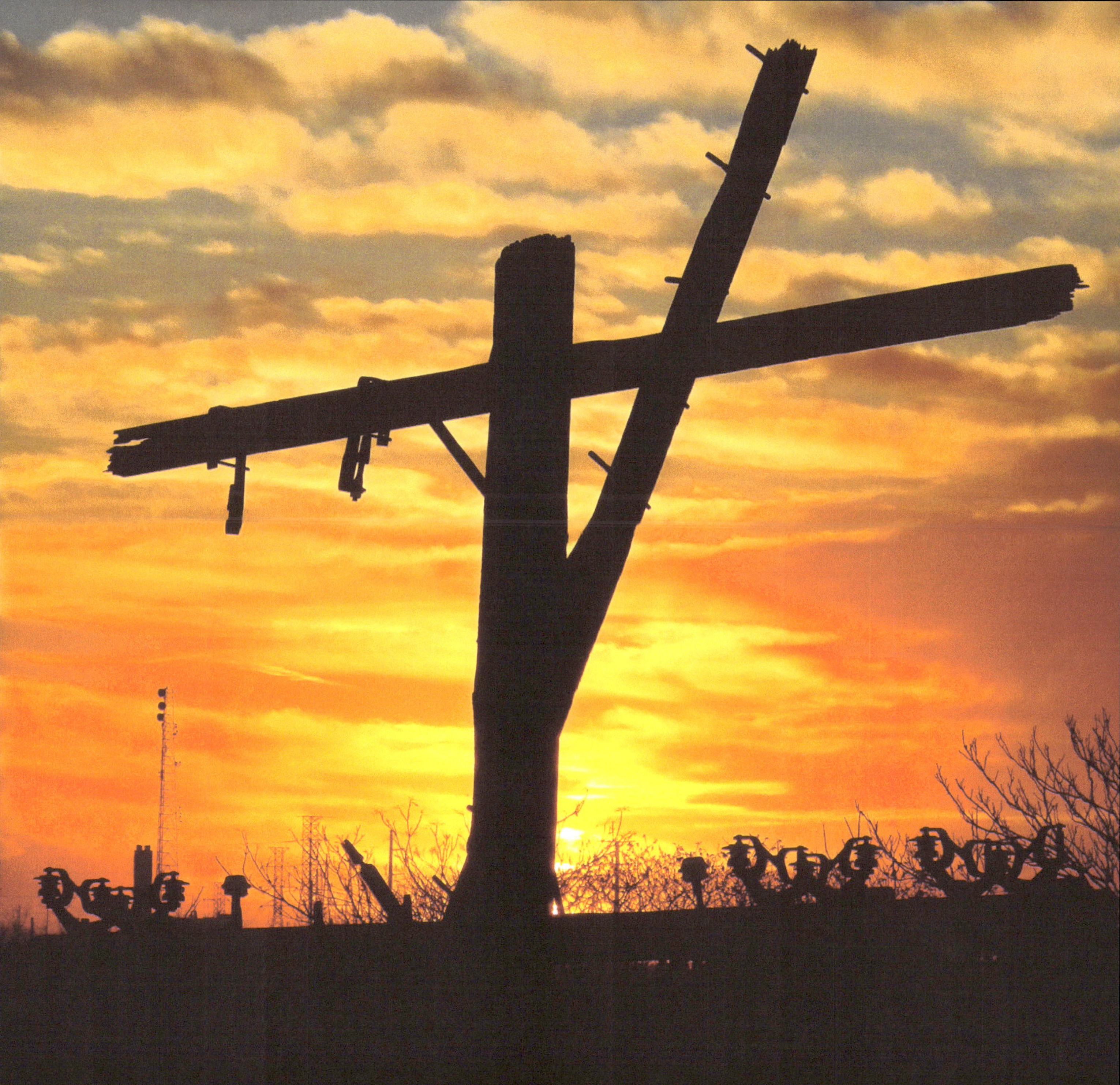

I was so engrossed with this area that I didn't realize the sun was going down. Walking back to Snake Hill in the dark was worth it just to witness this fiery sunset over the Meadowlands.

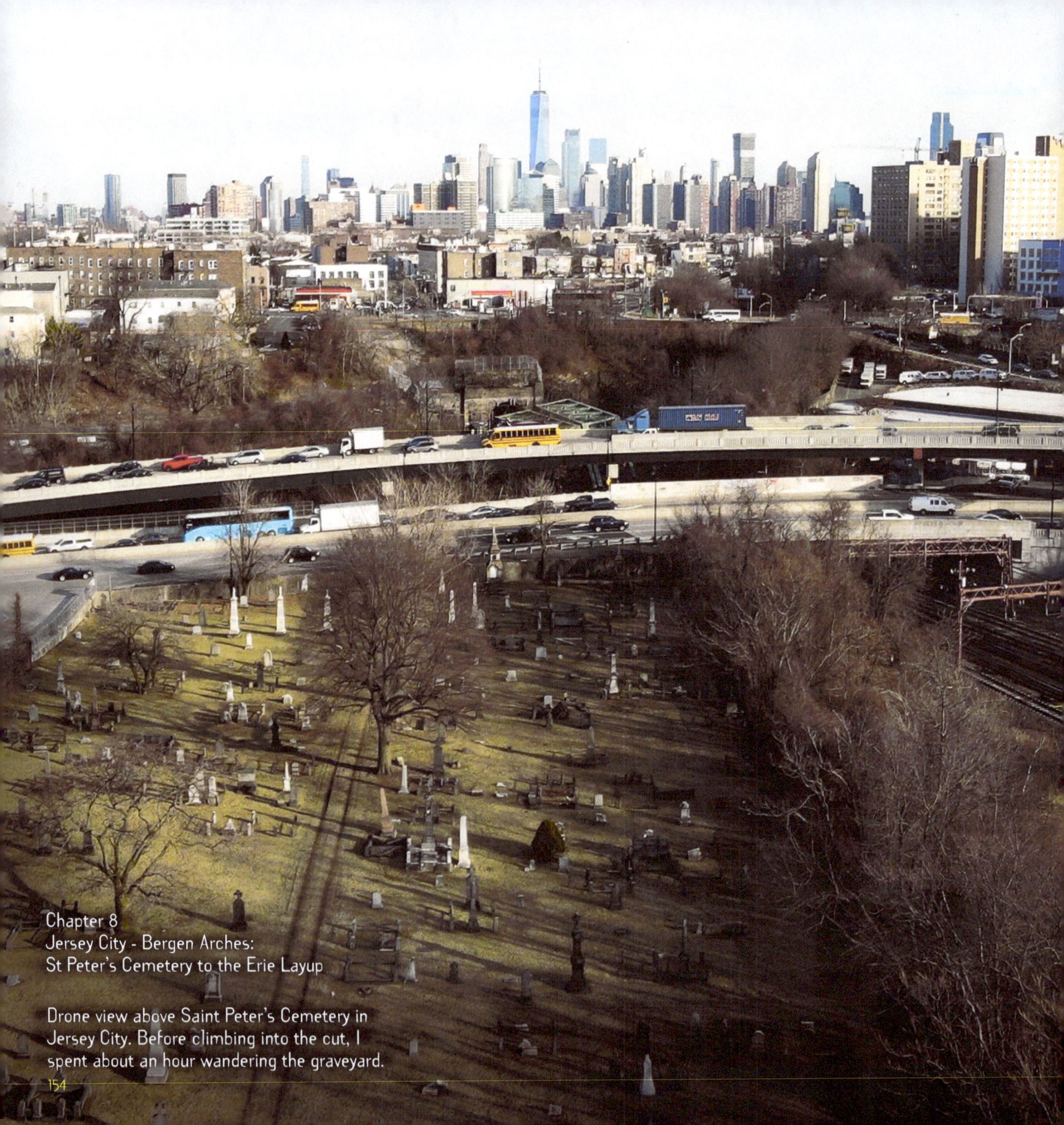

Chapter 8
Jersey City - Bergen Arches:
St Peter's Cemetery to the Erie Layup

Drone view above Saint Peter's Cemetery in Jersey City. Before climbing into the cut, I spent about an hour wandering the graveyard.

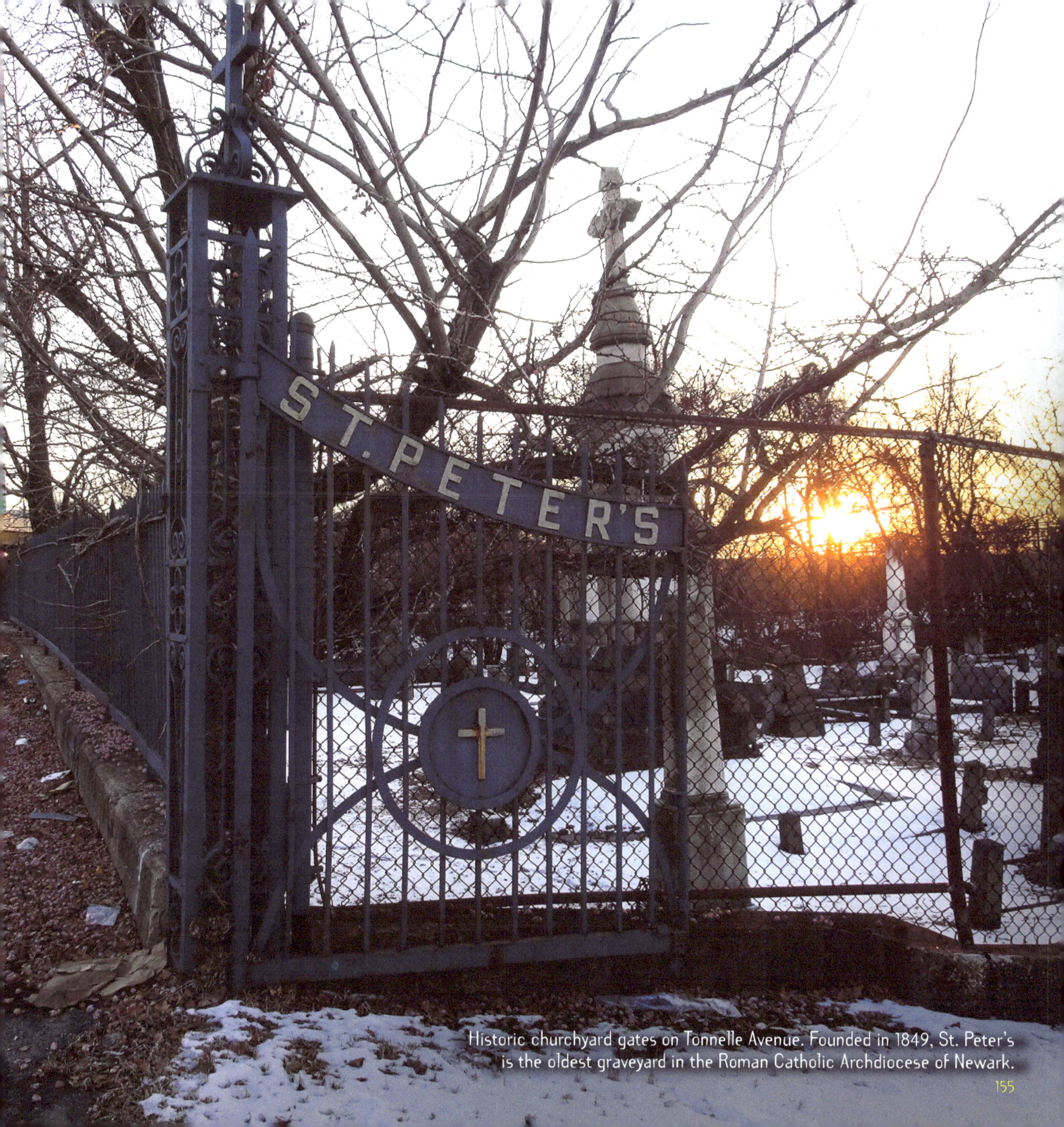

Historic churchyard gates on Tonnelle Avenue. Founded in 1849, St. Peter's is the oldest graveyard in the Roman Catholic Archdiocese of Newark.

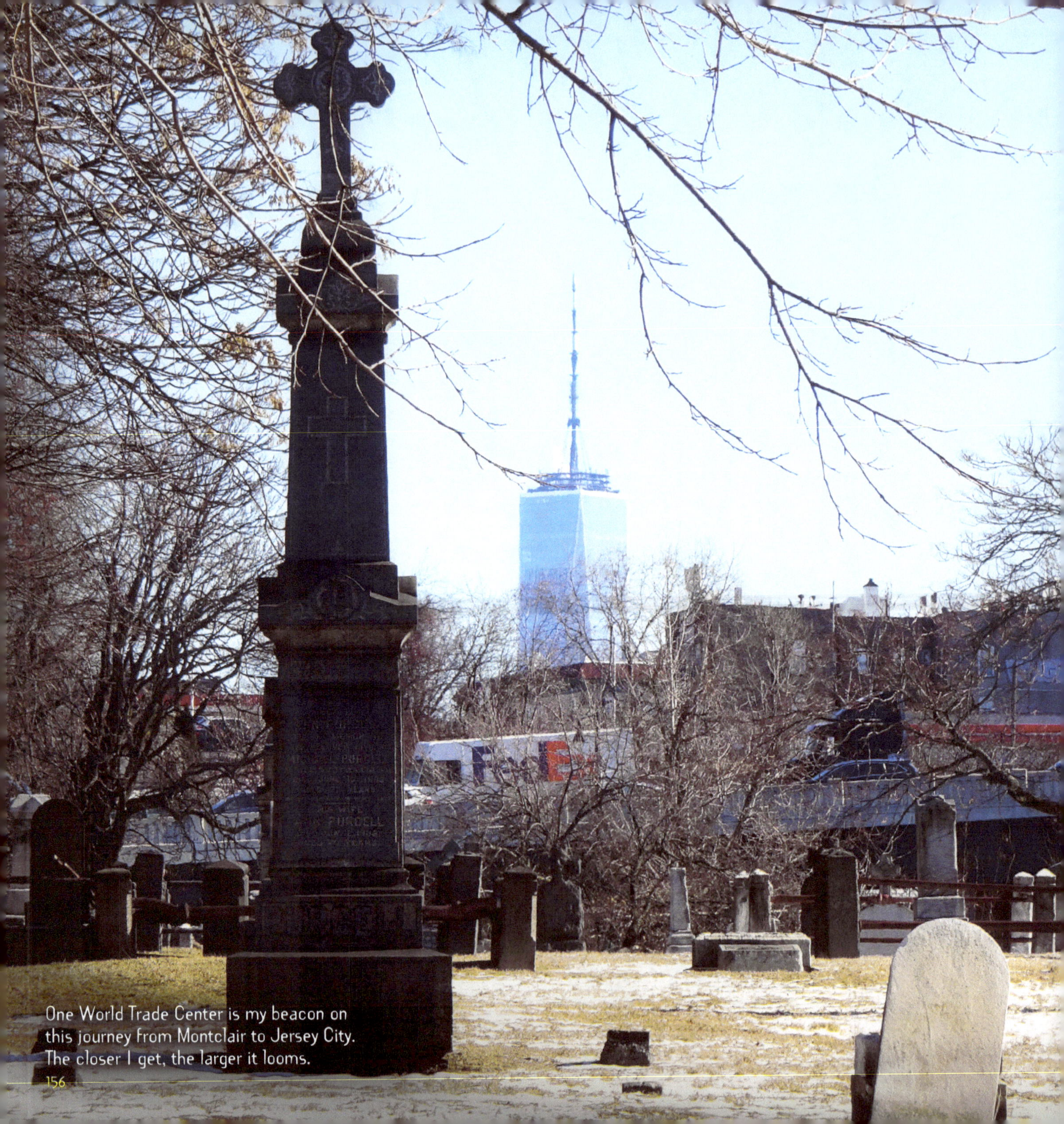

One World Trade Center is my beacon on this journey from Montclair to Jersey City. The closer I get, the larger it looms.

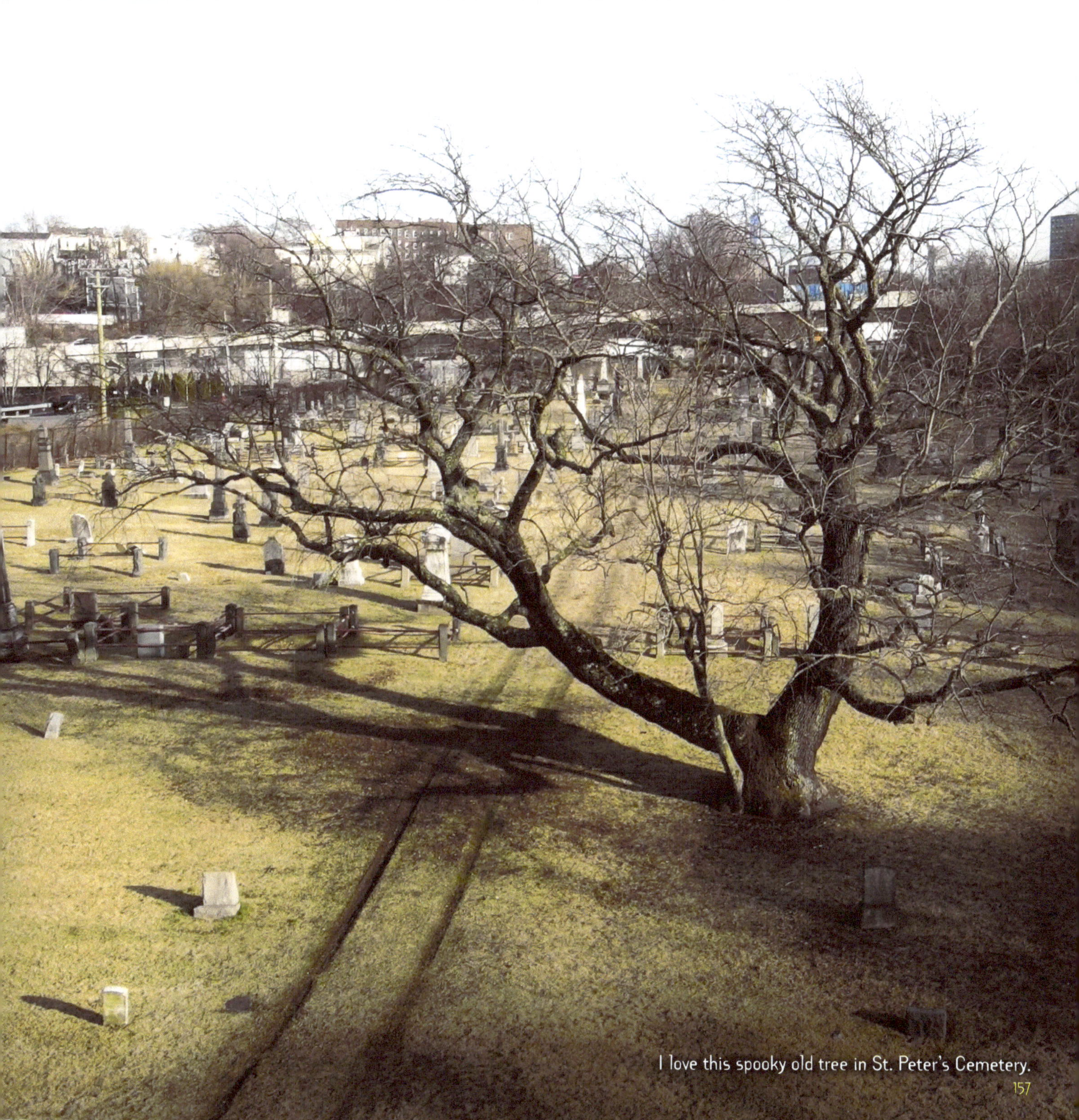

I love this spooky old tree in St. Peter's Cemetery.

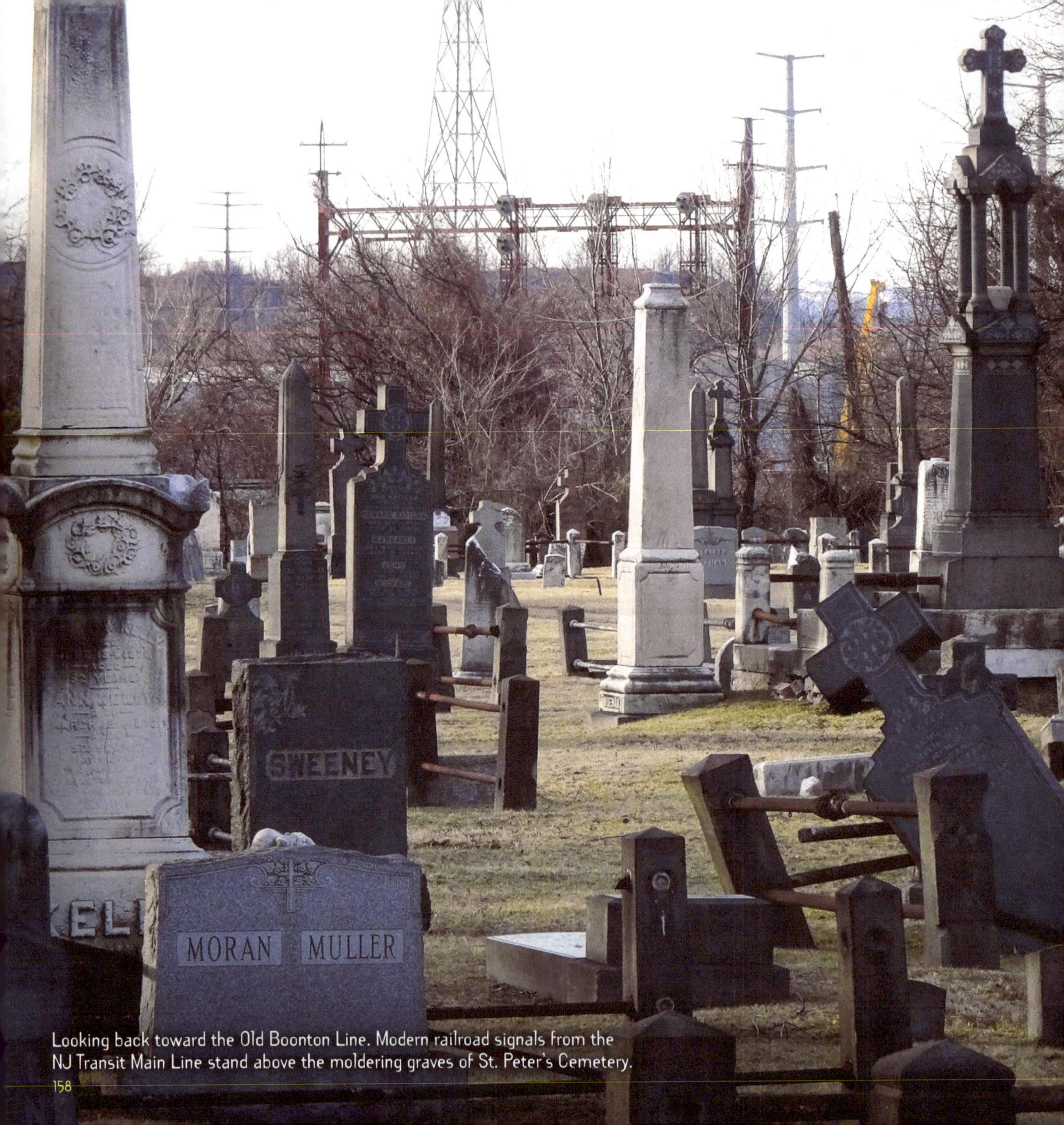

Looking back toward the Old Boonton Line. Modern railroad signals from the NJ Transit Main Line stand above the moldering graves of St. Peter's Cemetery.

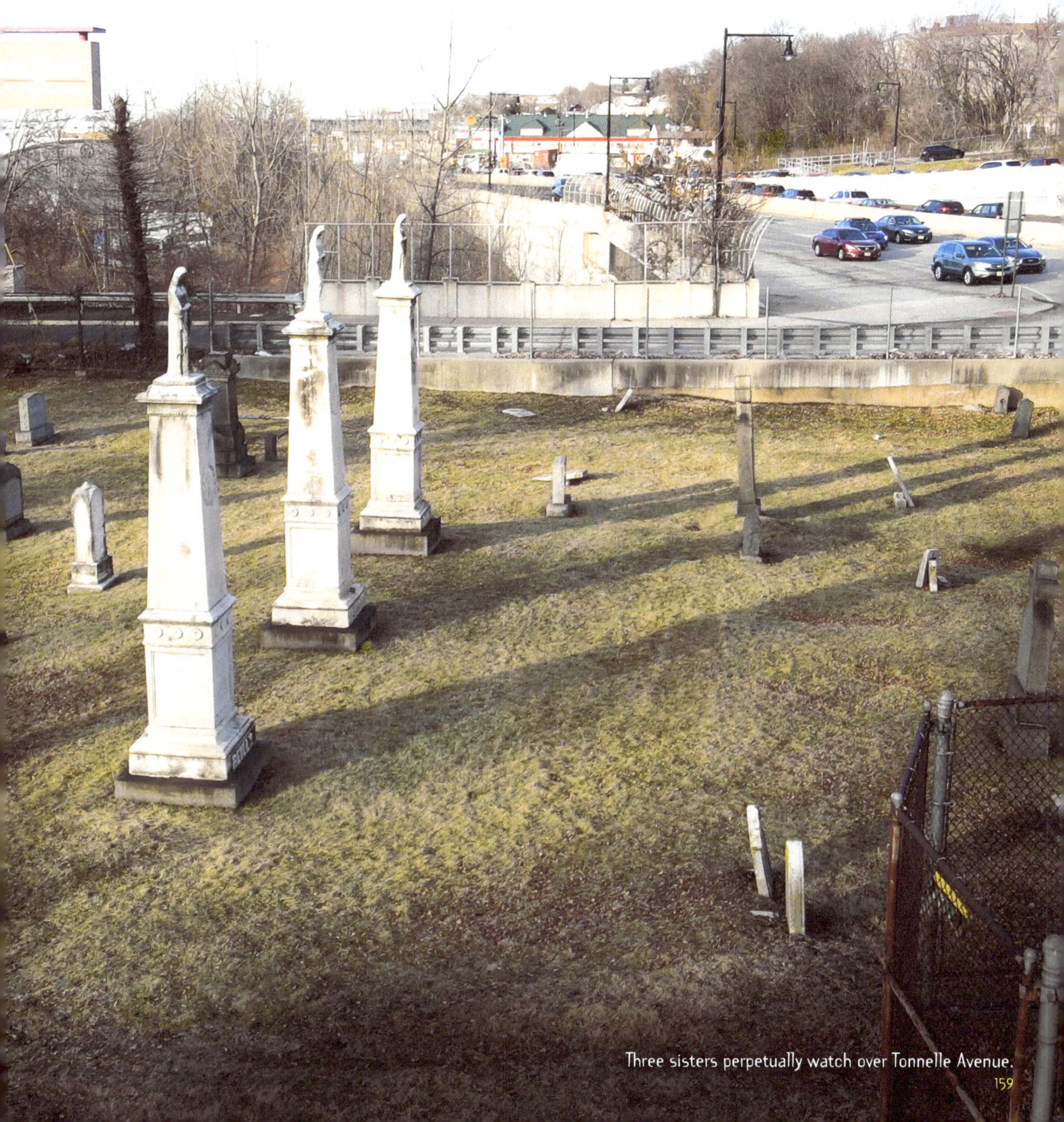

Three sisters perpetually watch over Tonnelle Avenue.

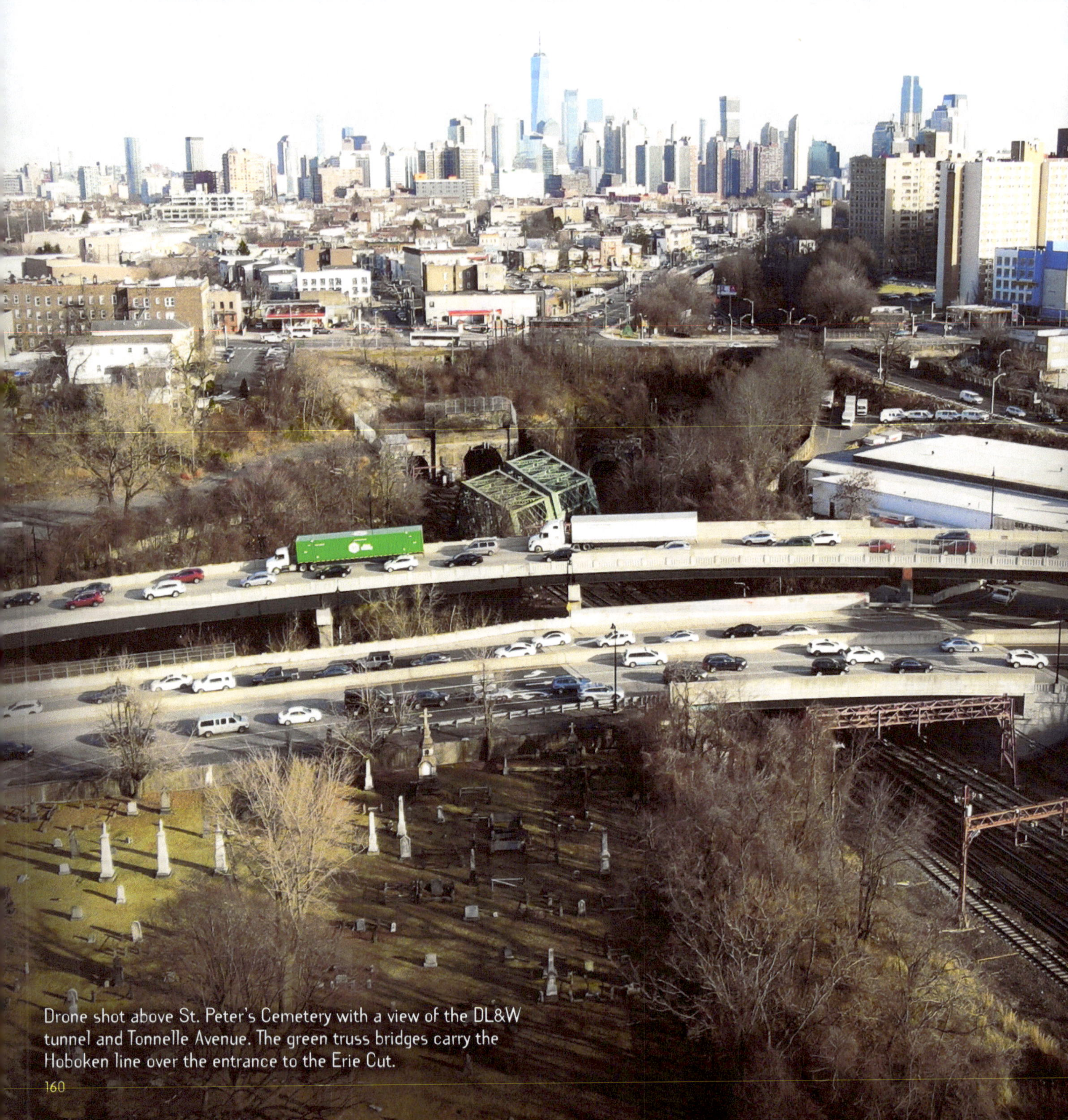

Drone shot above St. Peter's Cemetery with a view of the DL&W tunnel and Tonnelle Avenue. The green truss bridges carry the Hoboken line over the entrance to the Erie Cut.

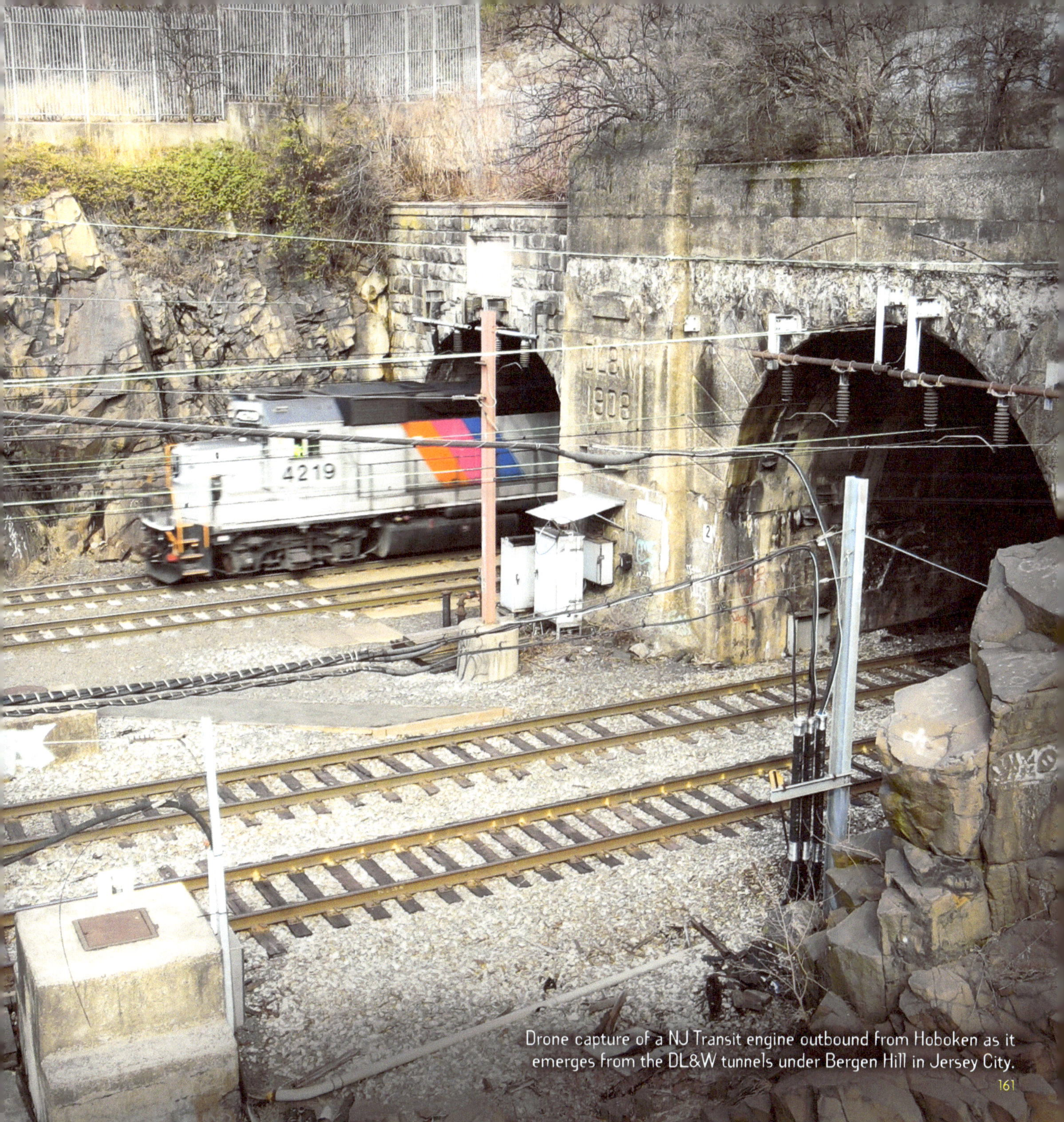

Drone capture of a NJ Transit engine outbound from Hoboken as it emerges from the DL&W tunnels under Bergen Hill in Jersey City.

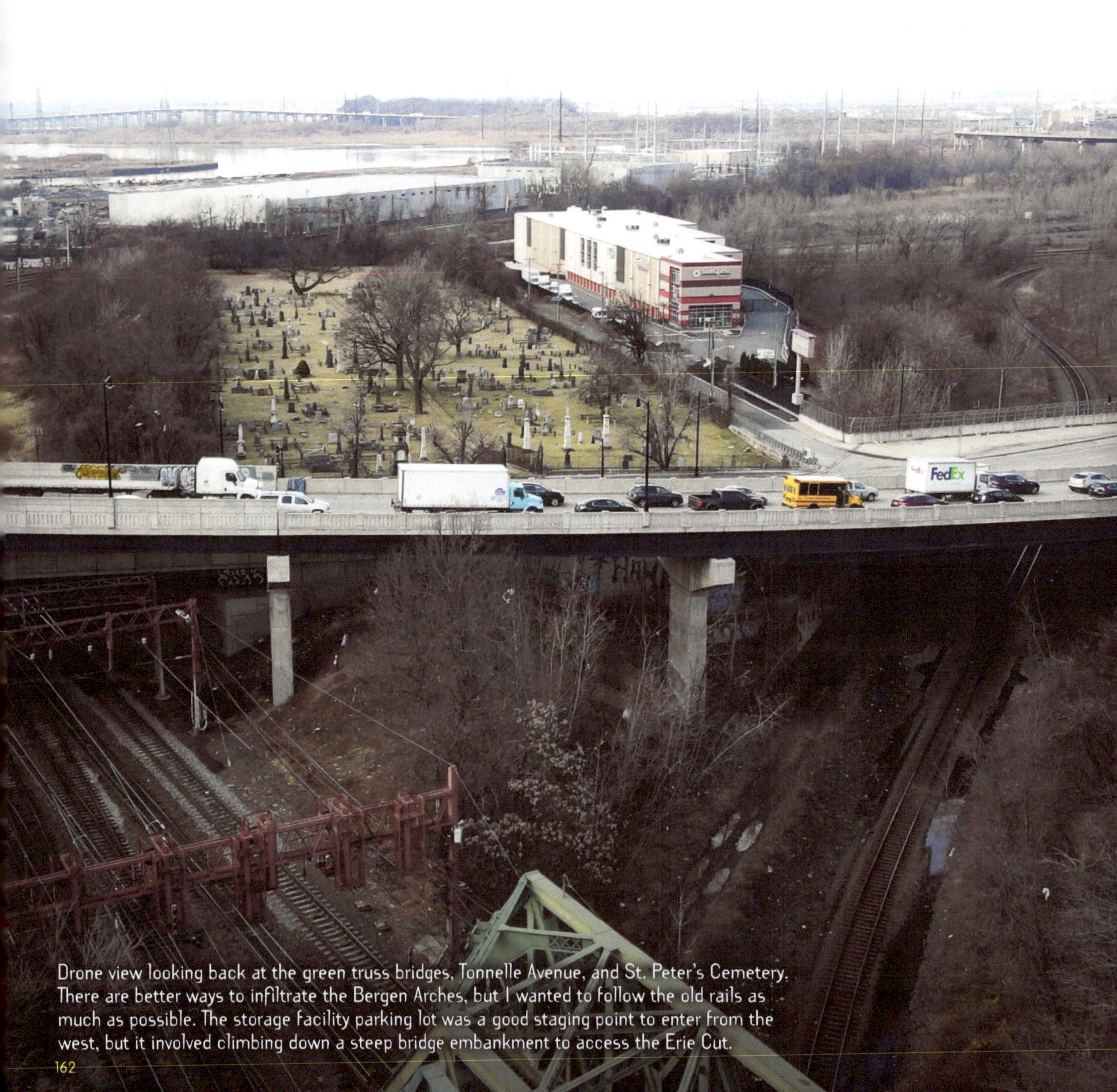

Drone view looking back at the green truss bridges, Tonnelle Avenue, and St. Peter's Cemetery. There are better ways to infiltrate the Bergen Arches, but I wanted to follow the old rails as much as possible. The storage facility parking lot was a good staging point to enter from the west, but it involved climbing down a steep bridge embankment to access the Erie Cut.

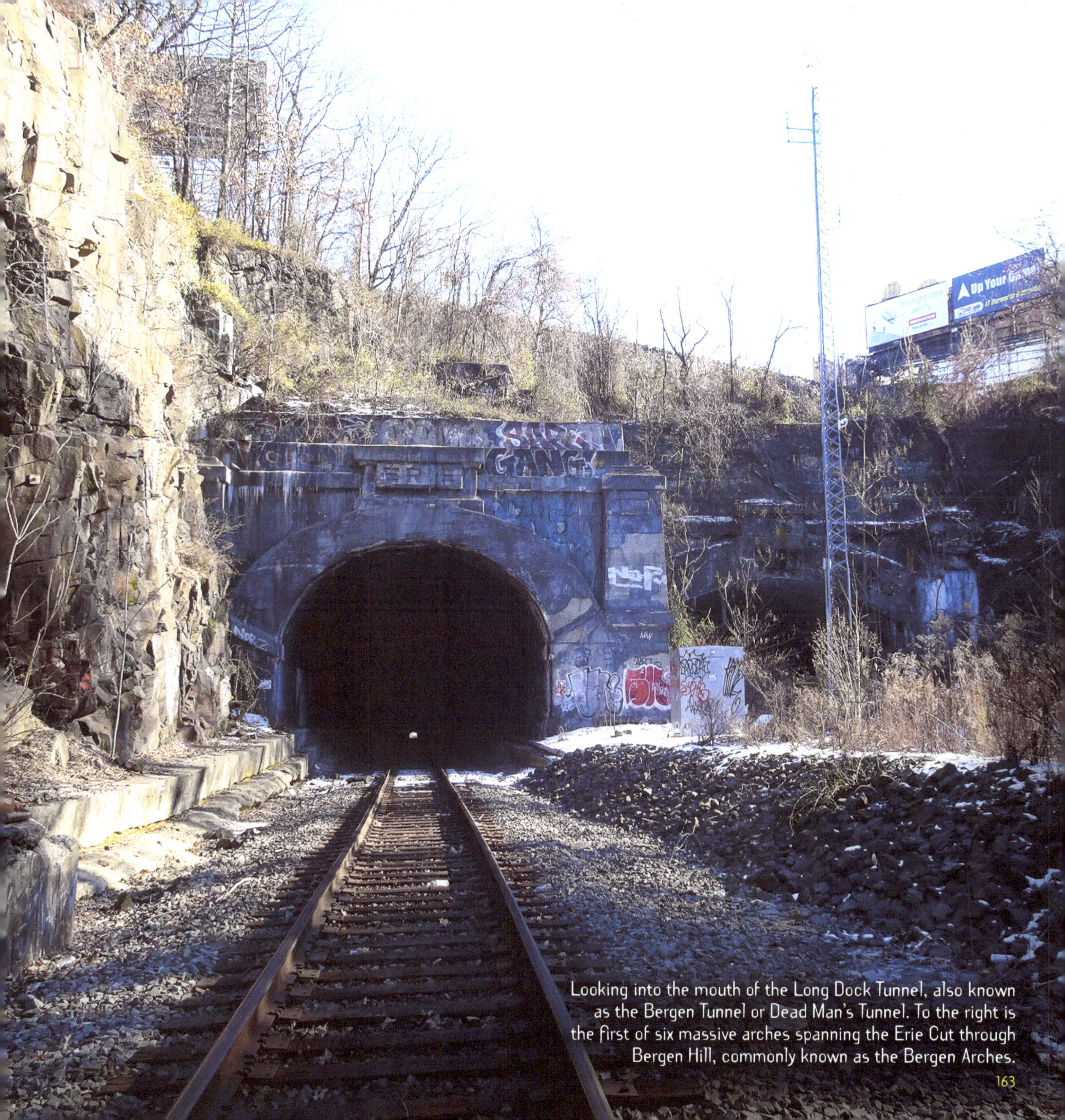

Looking into the mouth of the Long Dock Tunnel, also known as the Bergen Tunnel or Dead Man's Tunnel. To the right is the first of six massive arches spanning the Erie Cut through Bergen Hill, commonly known as the Bergen Arches.

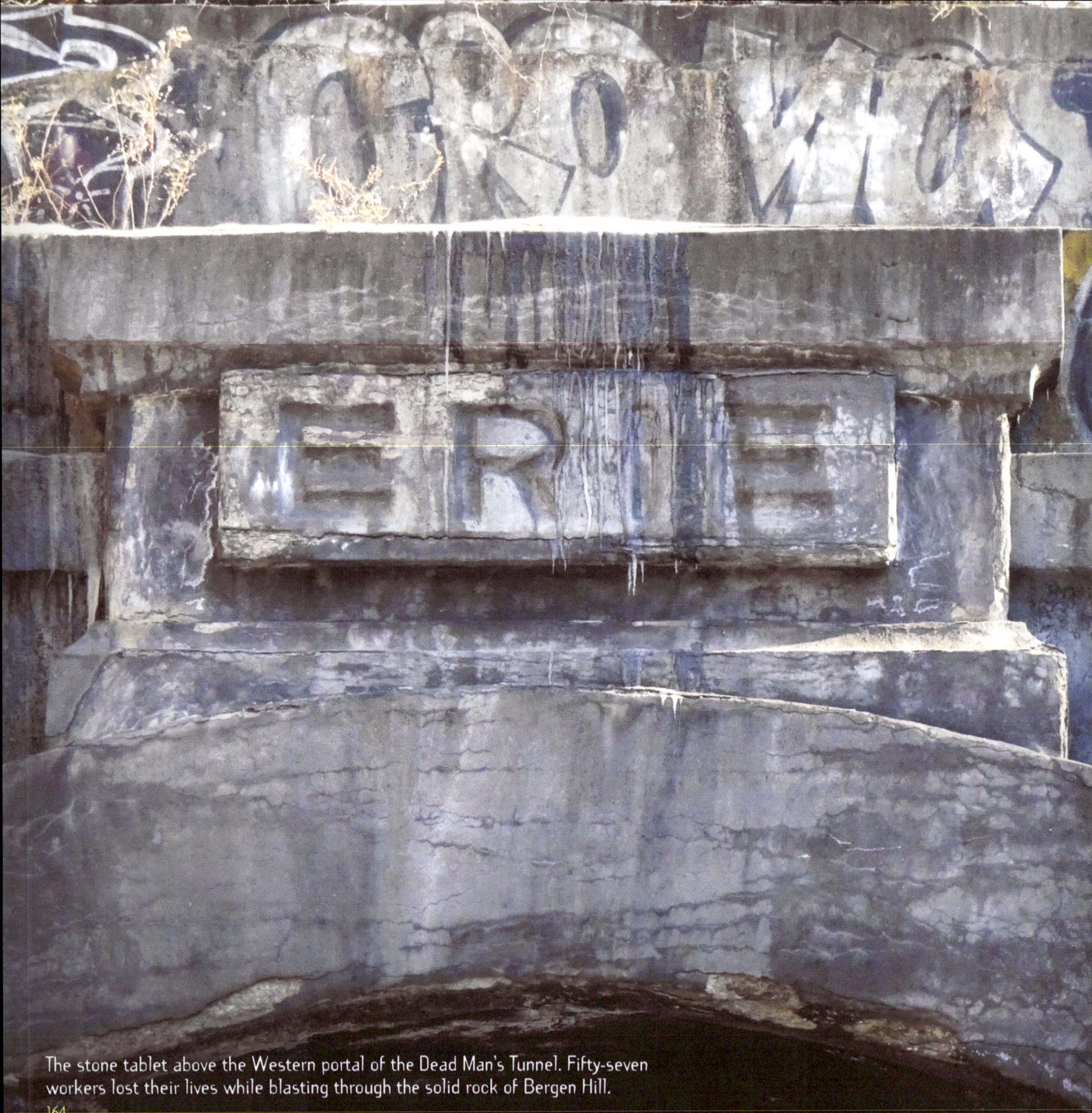

The stone tablet above the Western portal of the Dead Man's Tunnel. Fifty-seven workers lost their lives while blasting through the solid rock of Bergen Hill.

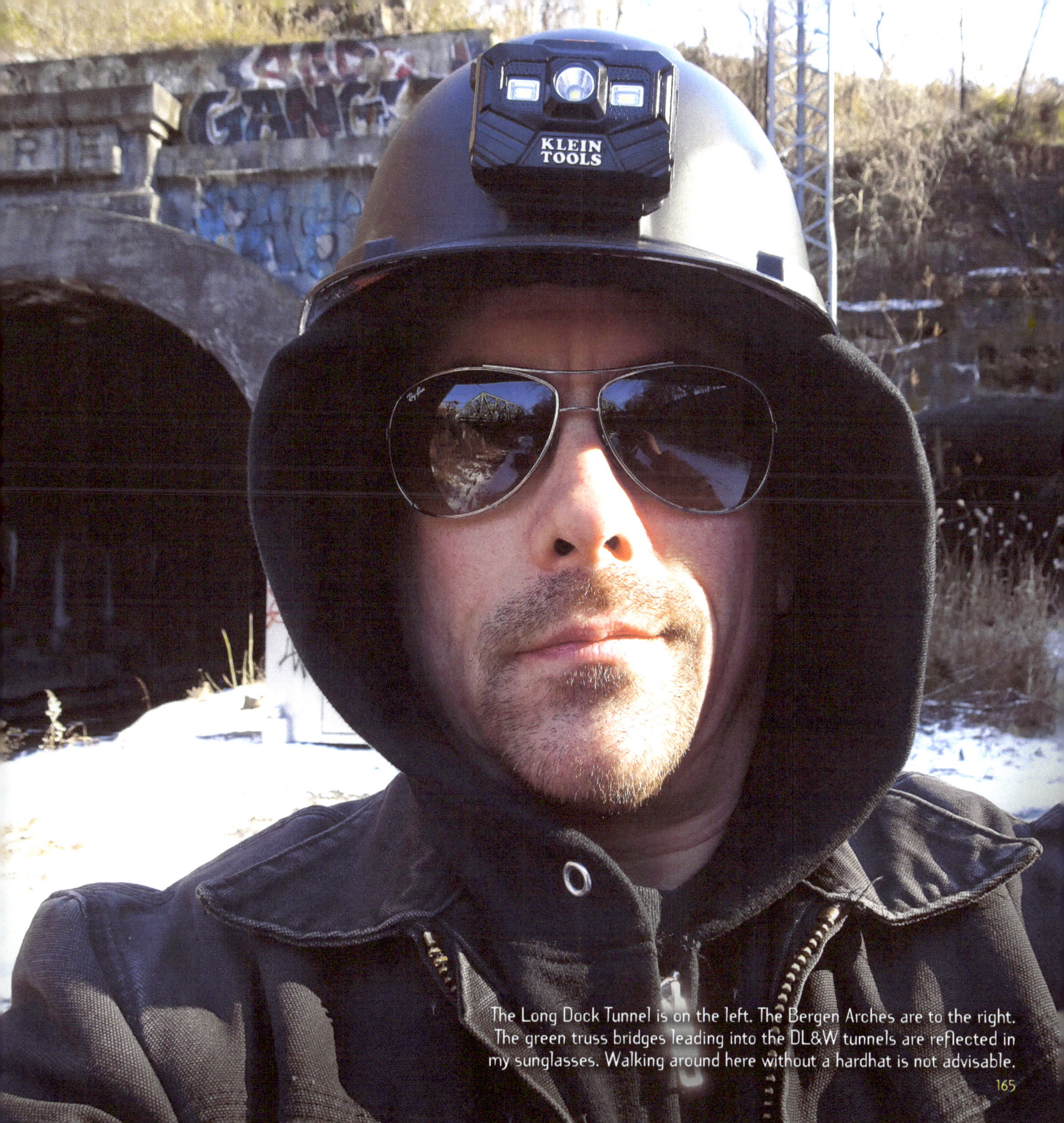

The Long Dock Tunnel is on the left. The Bergen Arches are to the right. The green truss bridges leading into the DL&W tunnels are reflected in my sunglasses. Walking around here without a hardhat is not advisable.

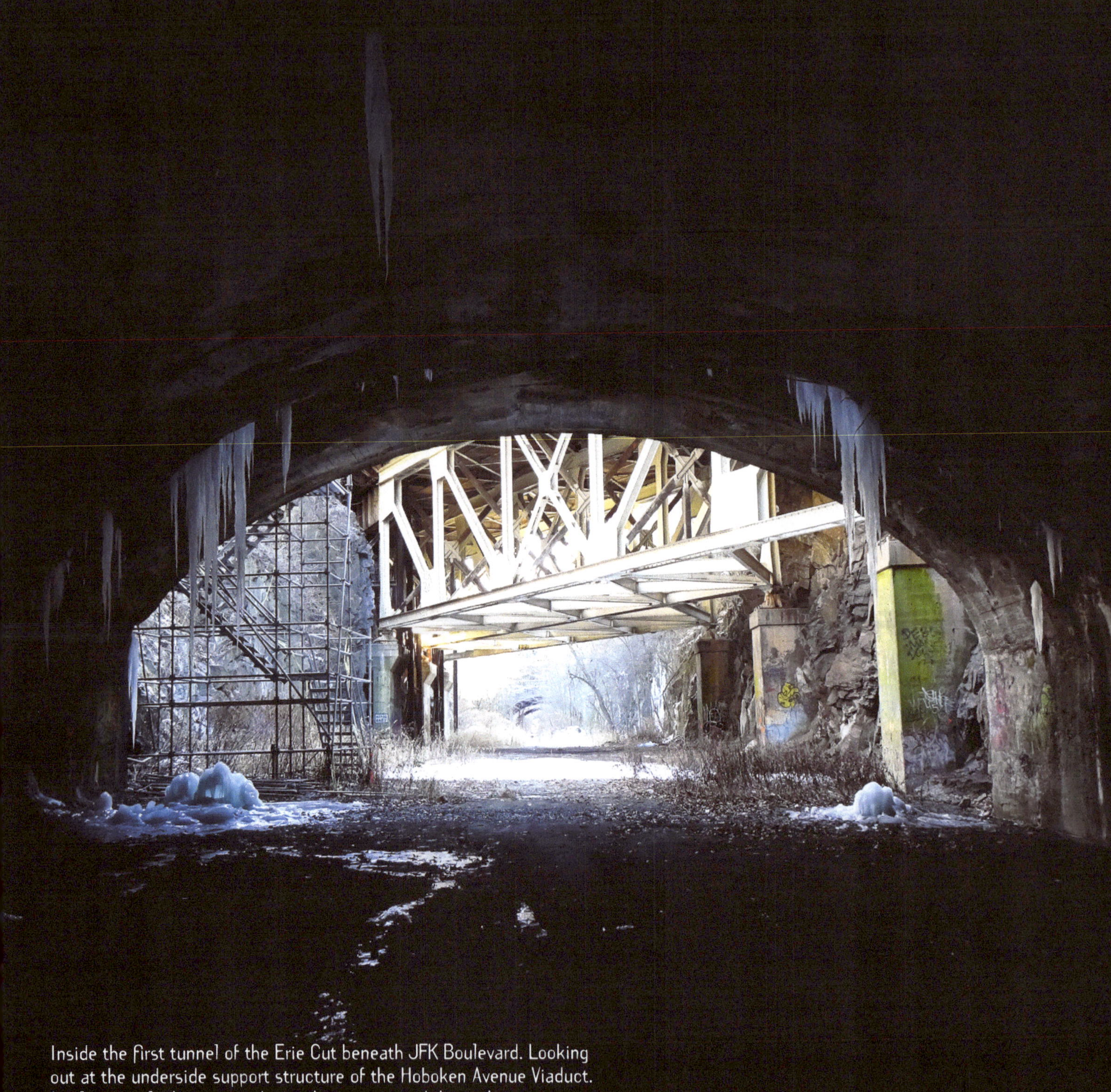

Inside the first tunnel of the Erie Cut beneath JFK Boulevard. Looking out at the underside support structure of the Hoboken Avenue Viaduct. Icicles reveal where groundwater has penetrated the arch.

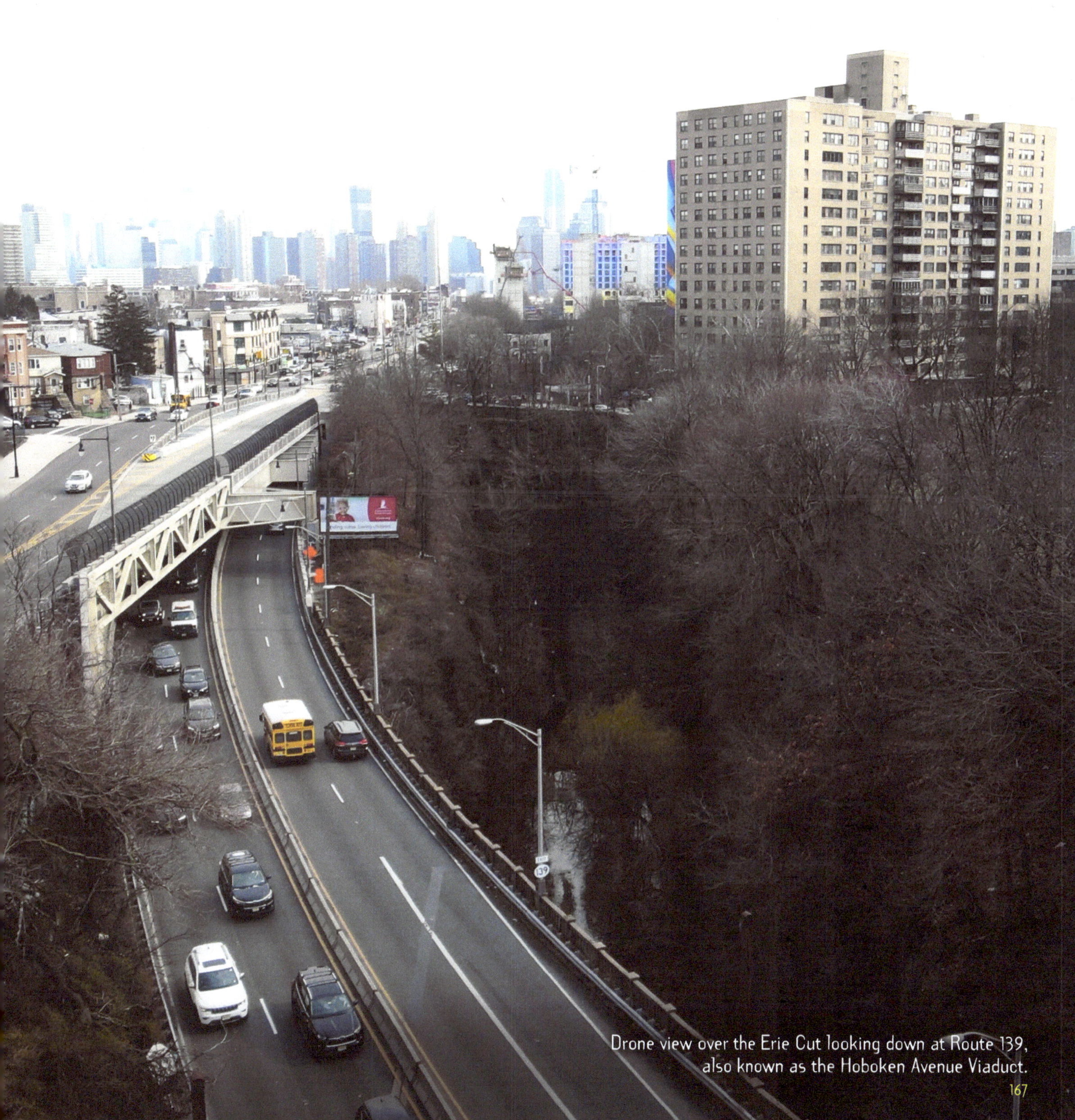

Drone view over the Erie Cut looking down at Route 139, also known as the Hoboken Avenue Viaduct.

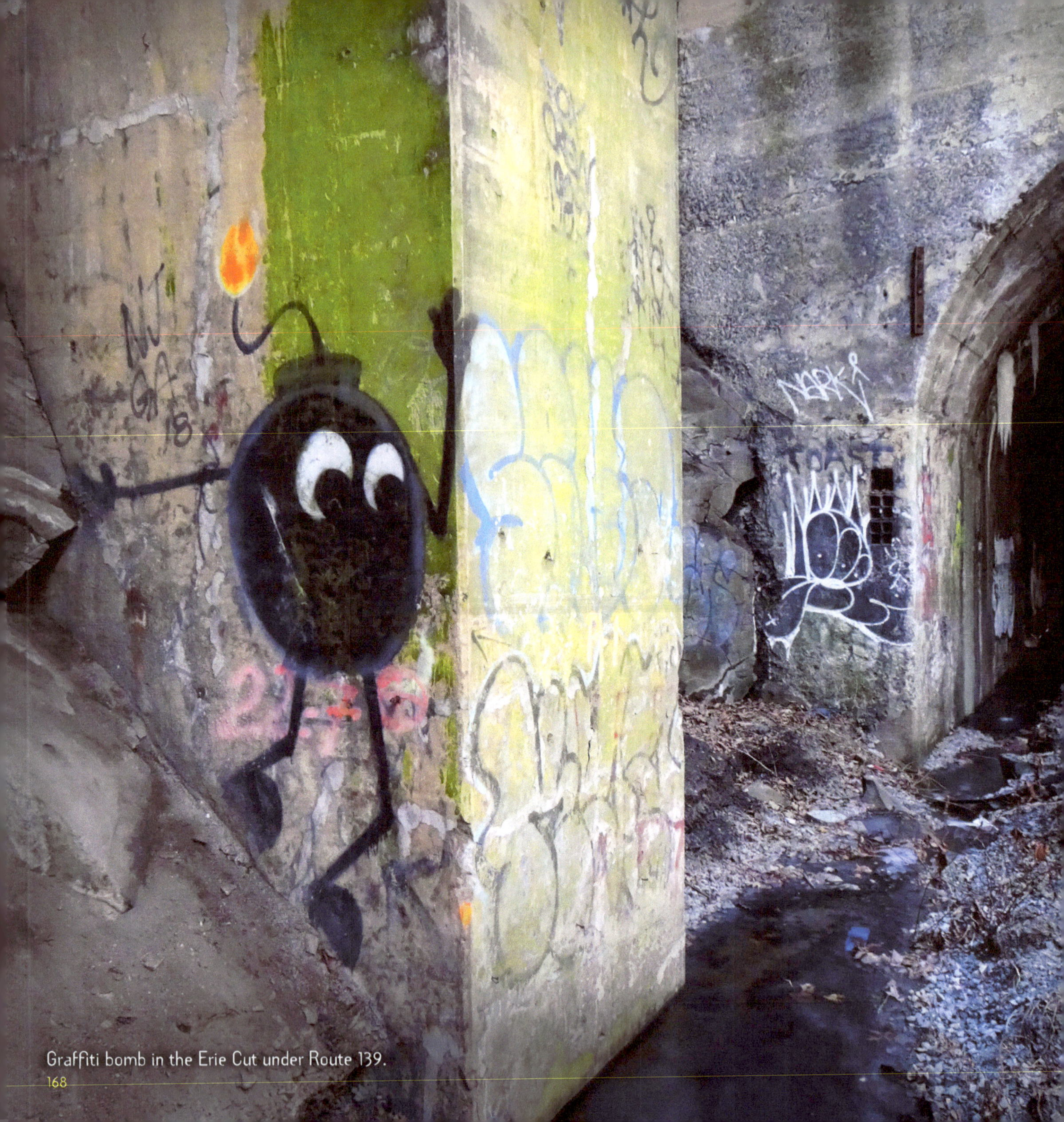

Graffiti bomb in the Erie Cut under Route 139.

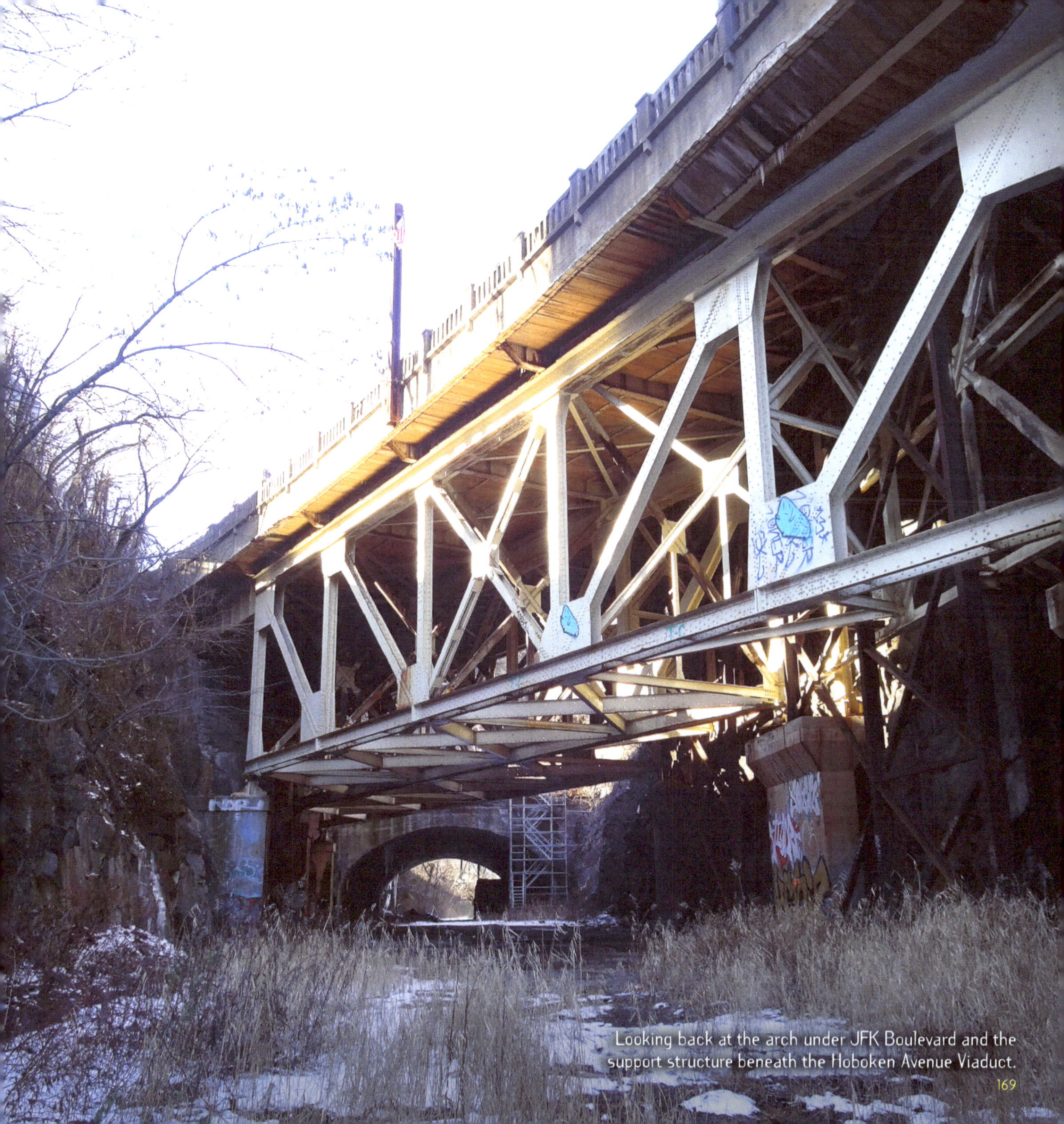

Looking back at the arch under JFK Boulevard and the support structure beneath the Hoboken Avenue Viaduct.

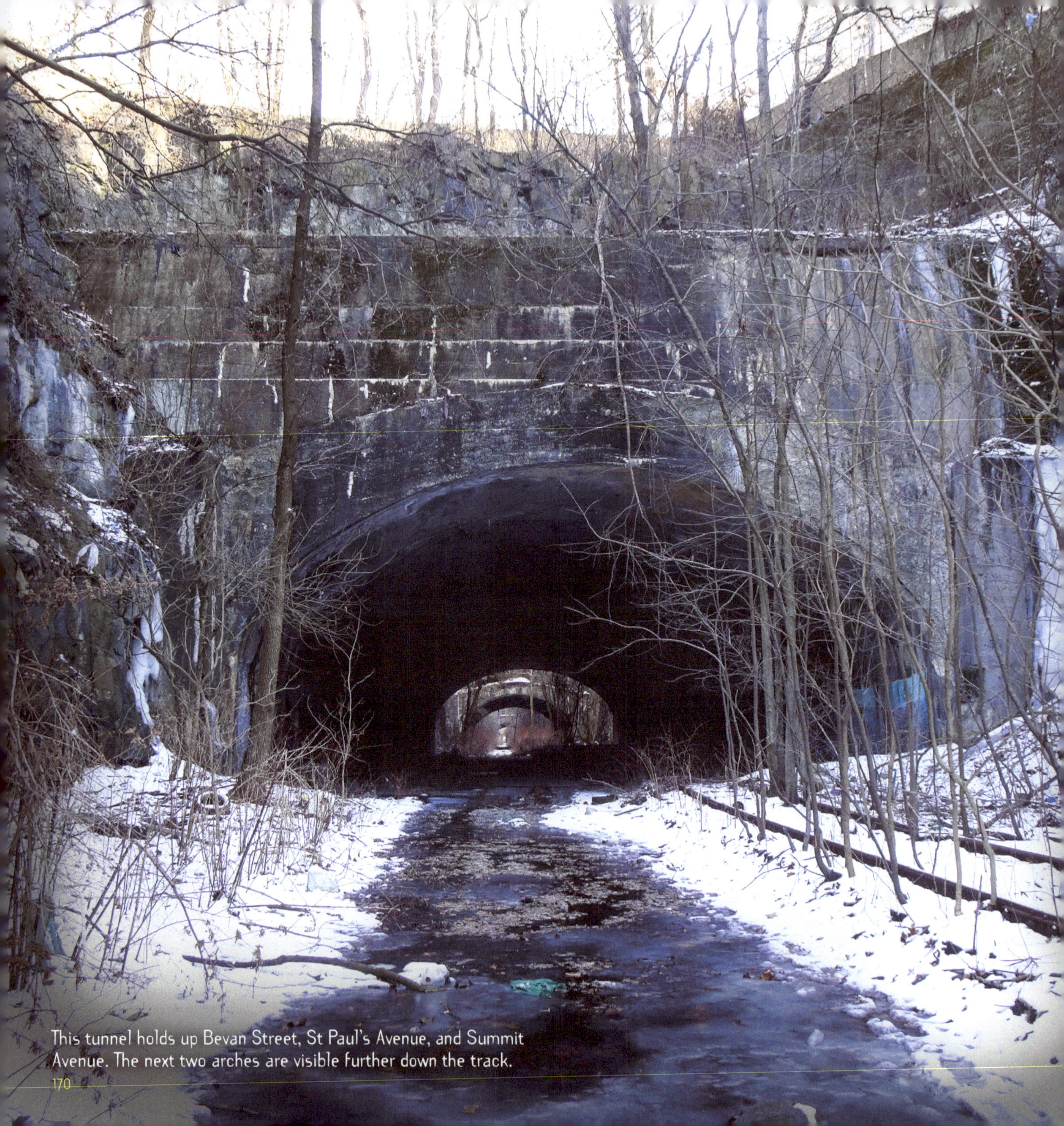

This tunnel holds up Bevan Street, St Paul's Avenue, and Summit Avenue. The next two arches are visible further down the track.

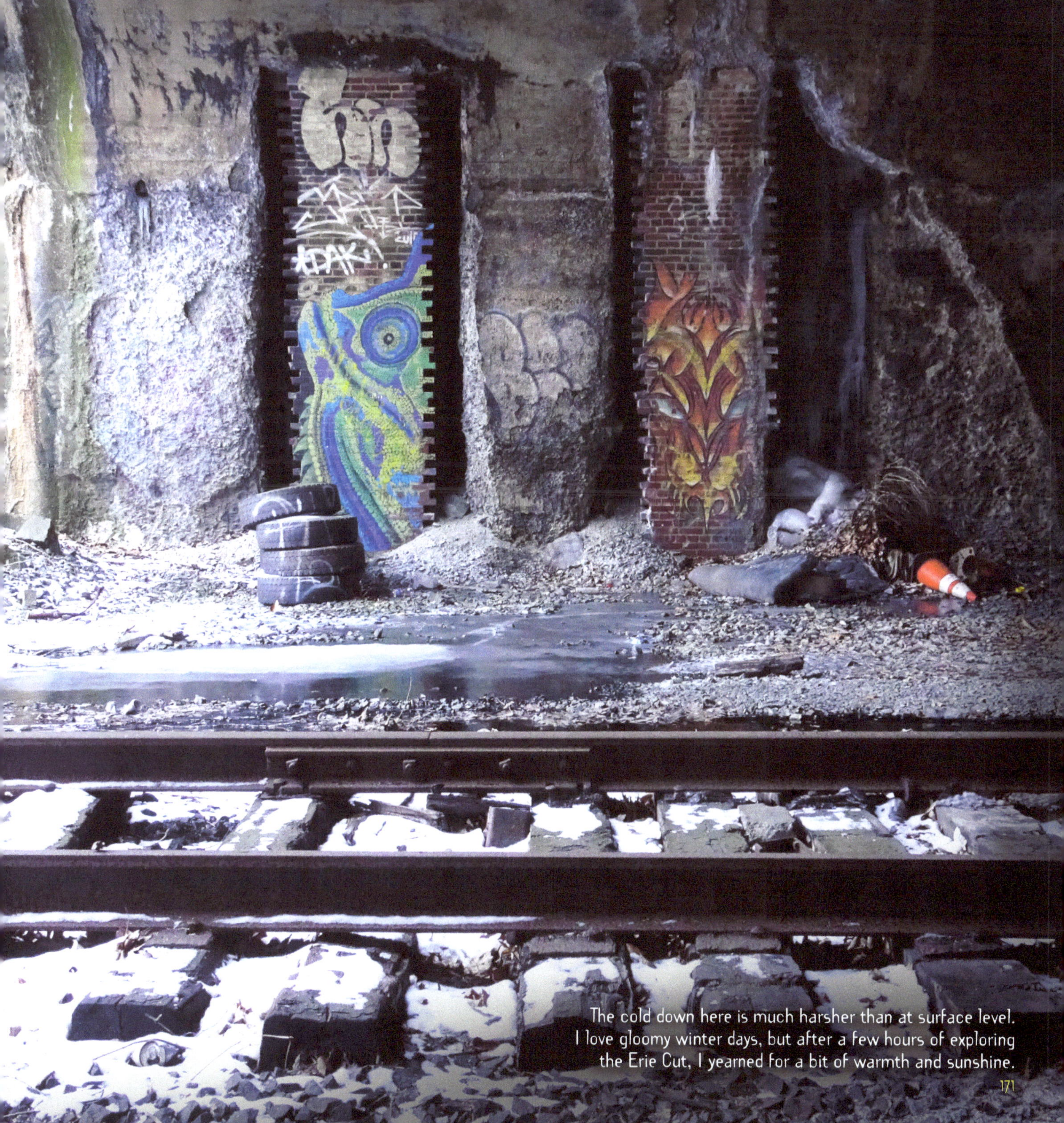

The cold down here is much harsher than at surface level. I love gloomy winter days, but after a few hours of exploring the Erie Cut, I yearned for a bit of warmth and sunshine.

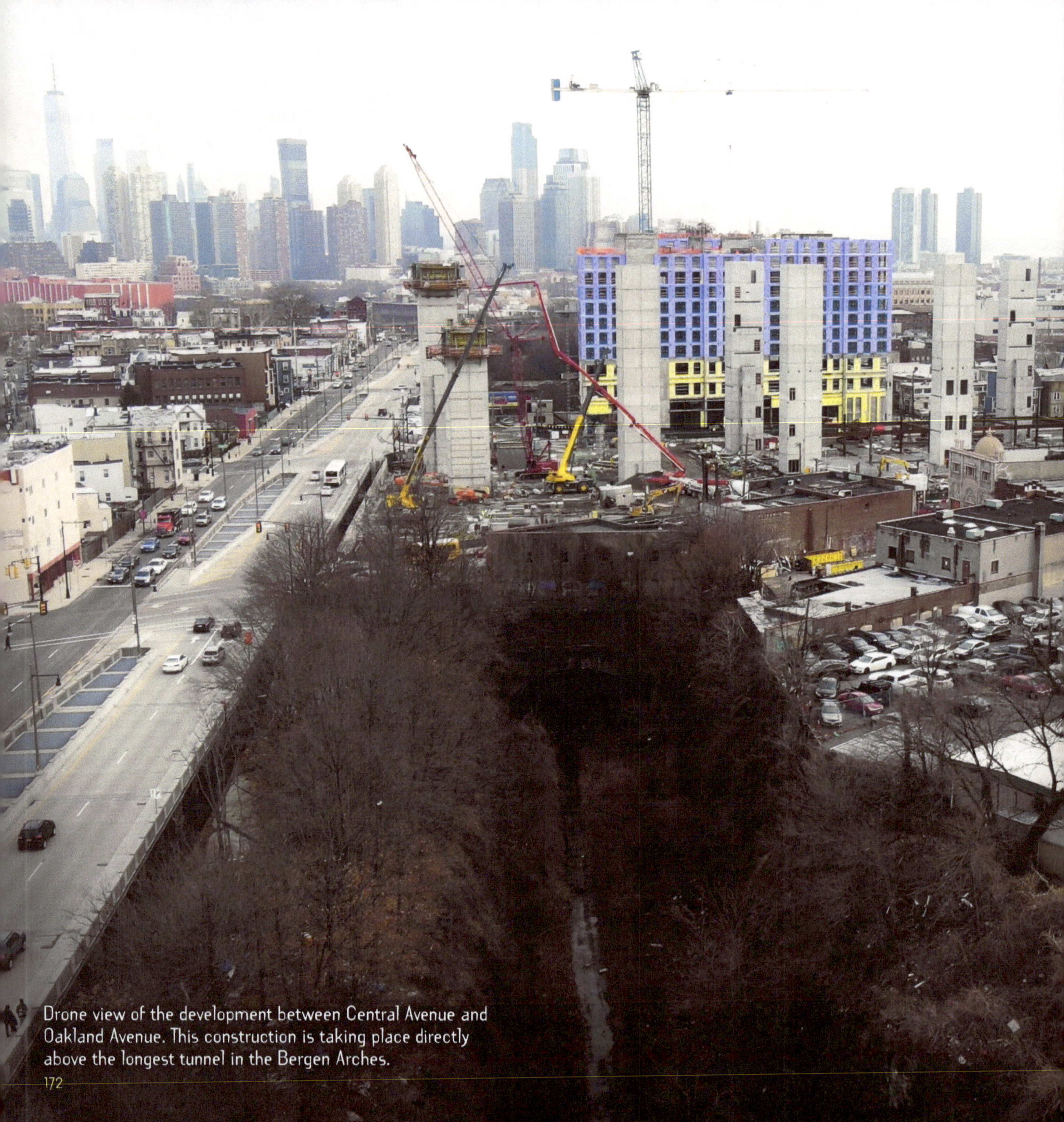

Drone view of the development between Central Avenue and Oakland Avenue. This construction is taking place directly above the longest tunnel in the Bergen Arches.

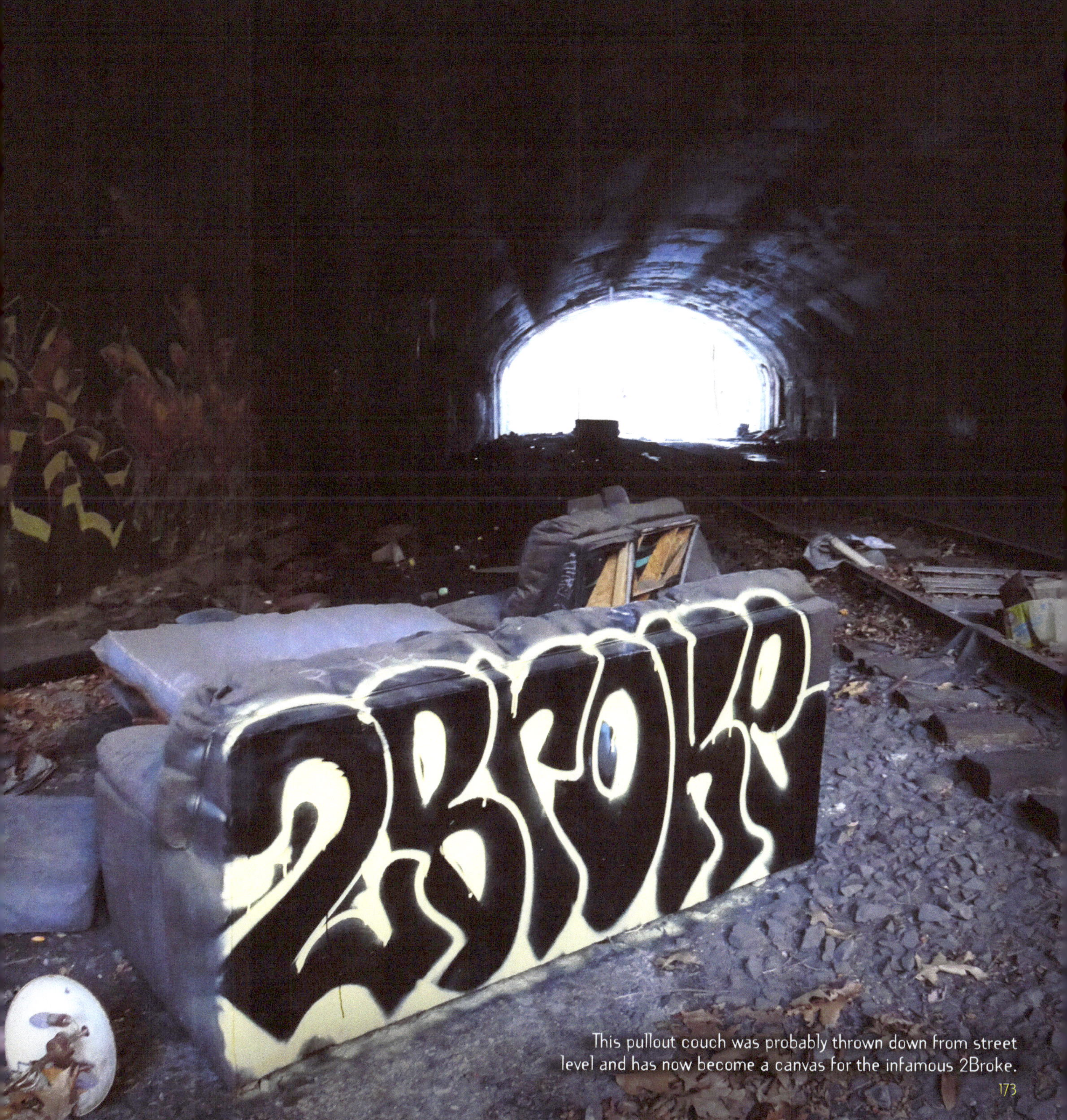

This pullout couch was probably thrown down from street level and has now become a canvas for the infamous 2Broke.

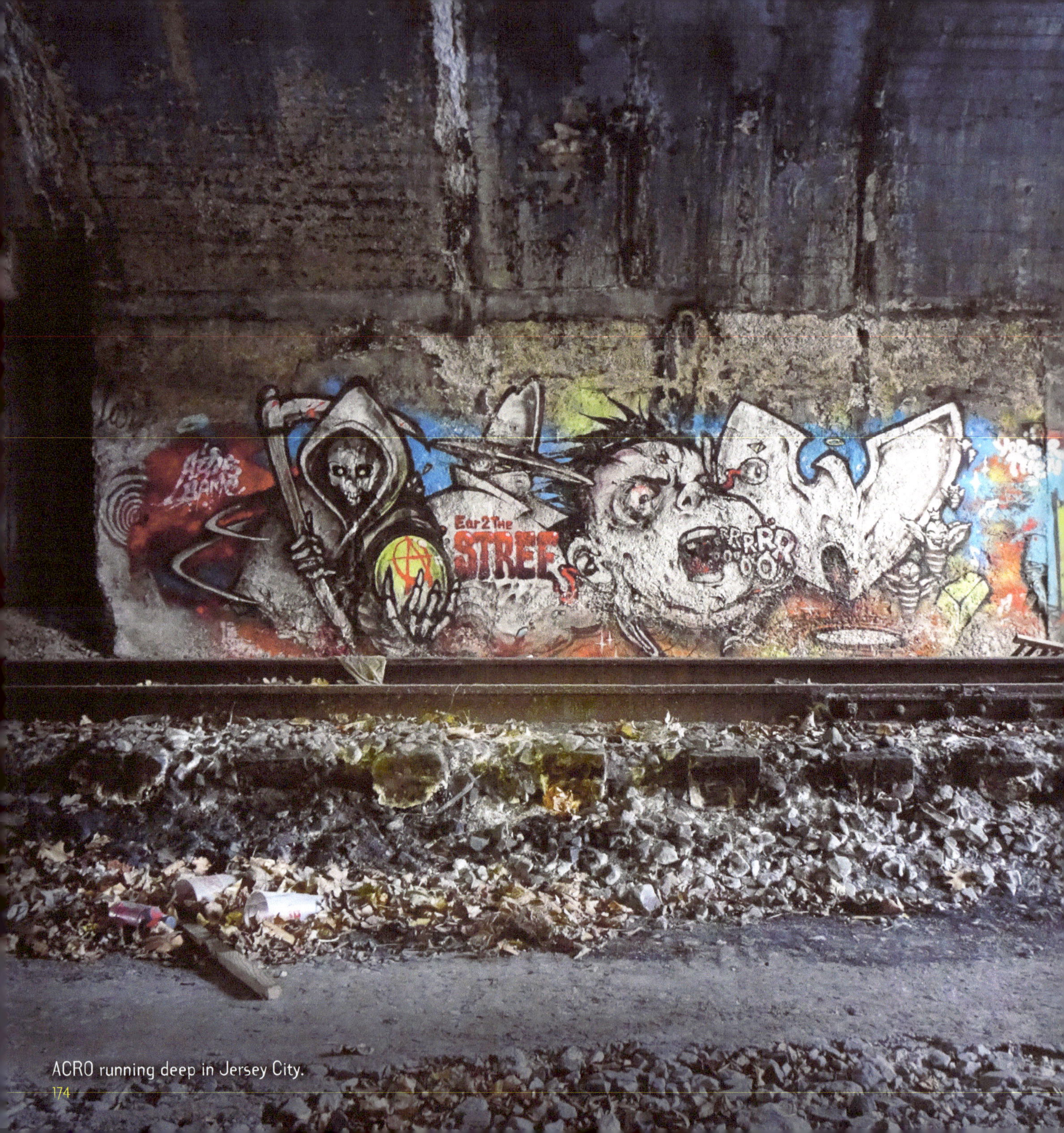

ACRO running deep in Jersey City.

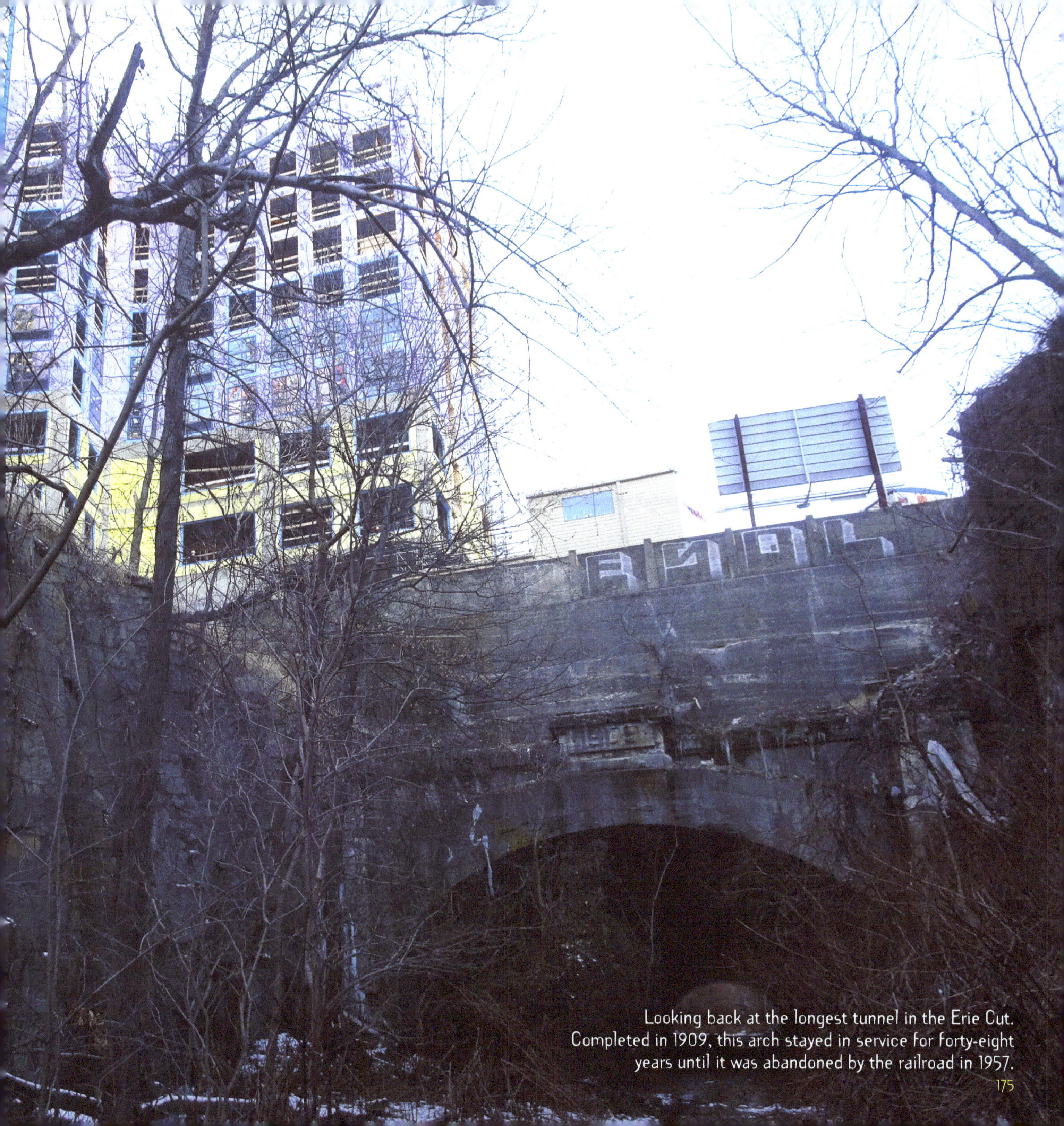

Looking back at the longest tunnel in the Erie Cut. Completed in 1909, this arch stayed in service for forty-eight years until it was abandoned by the railroad in 1957.

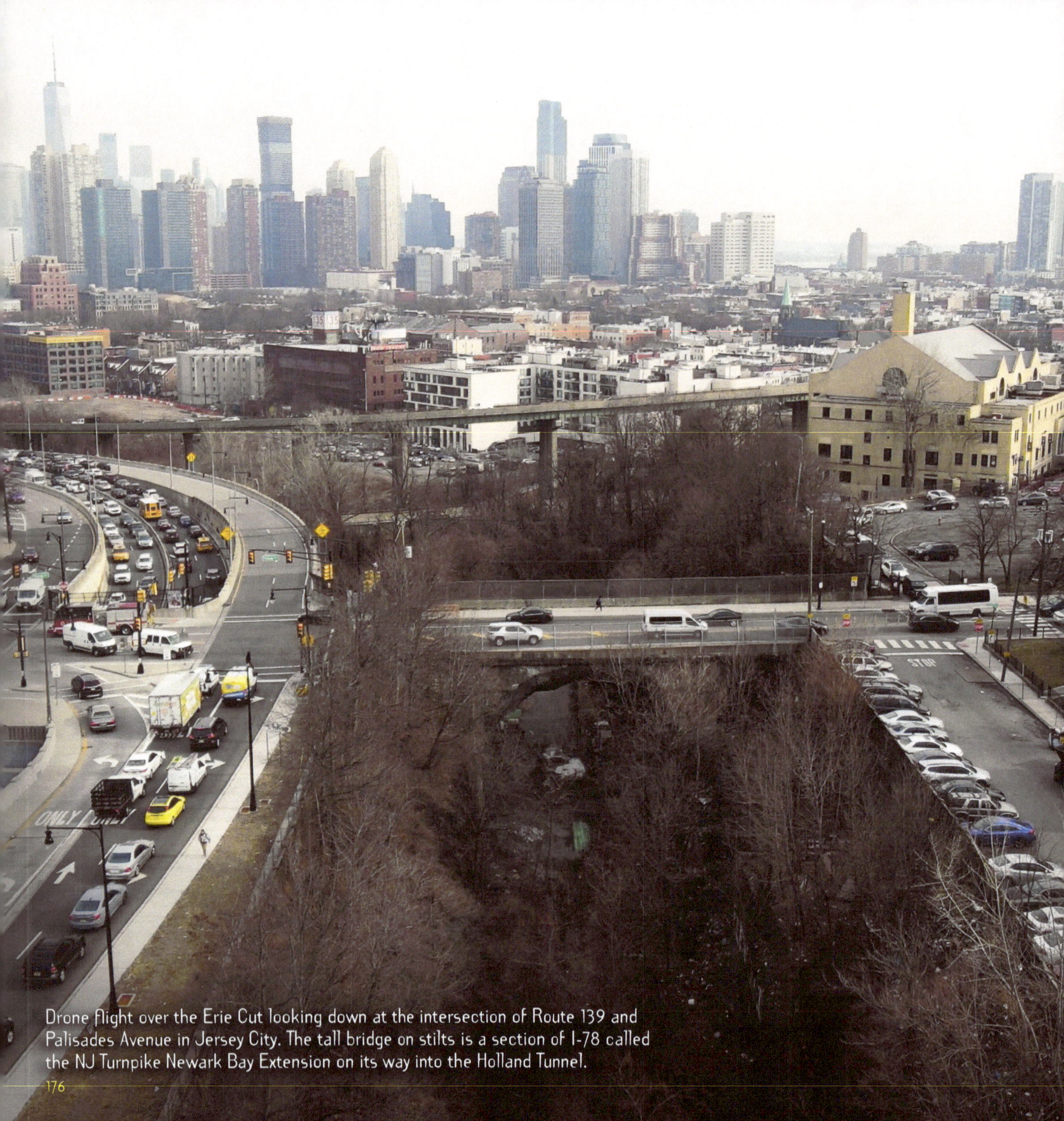

Drone flight over the Erie Cut looking down at the intersection of Route 139 and Palisades Avenue in Jersey City. The tall bridge on stilts is a section of I-78 called the NJ Turnpike Newark Bay Extension on its way into the Holland Tunnel.

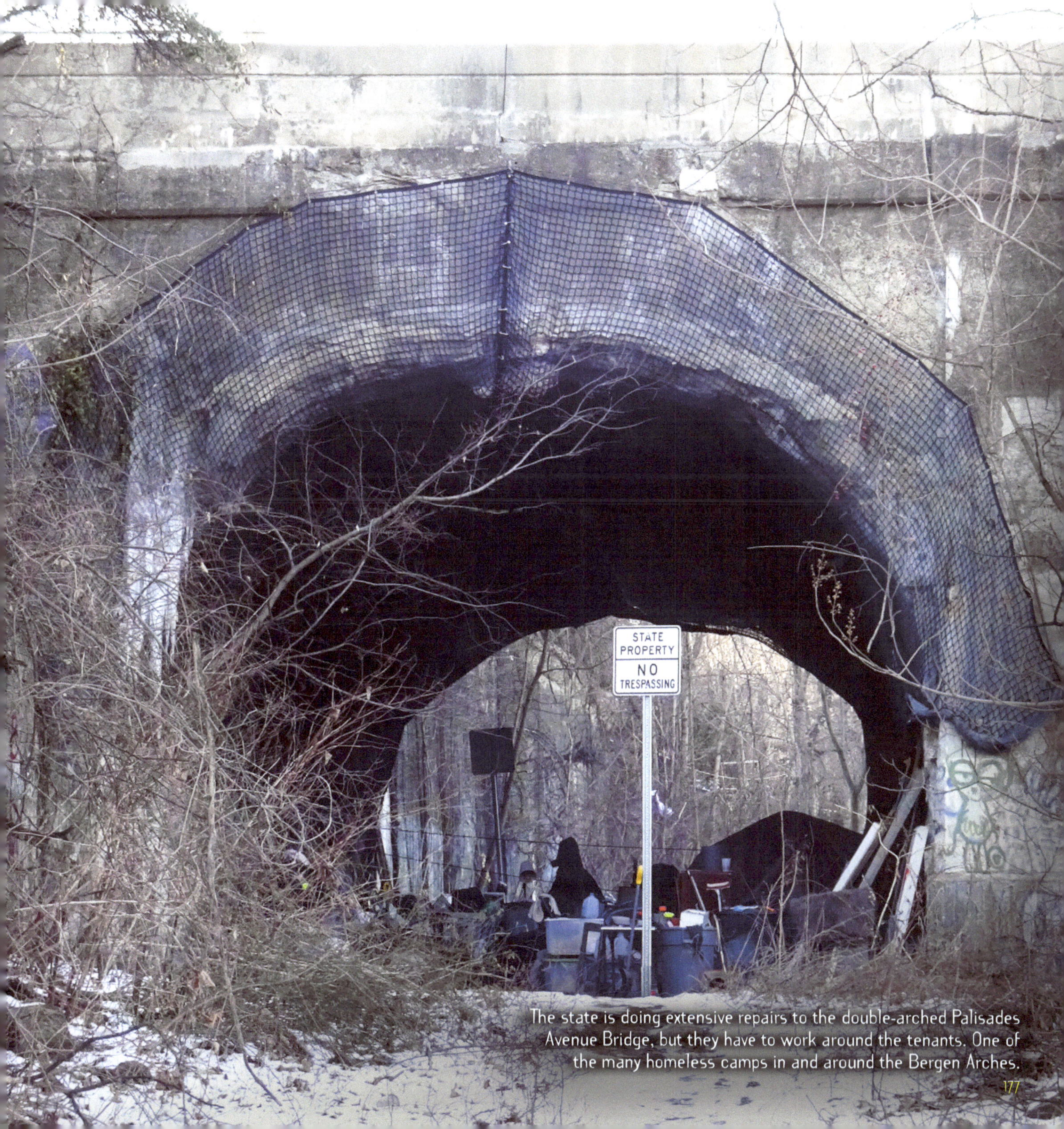

The state is doing extensive repairs to the double-arched Palisades Avenue Bridge, but they have to work around the tenants. One of the many homeless camps in and around the Bergen Arches.

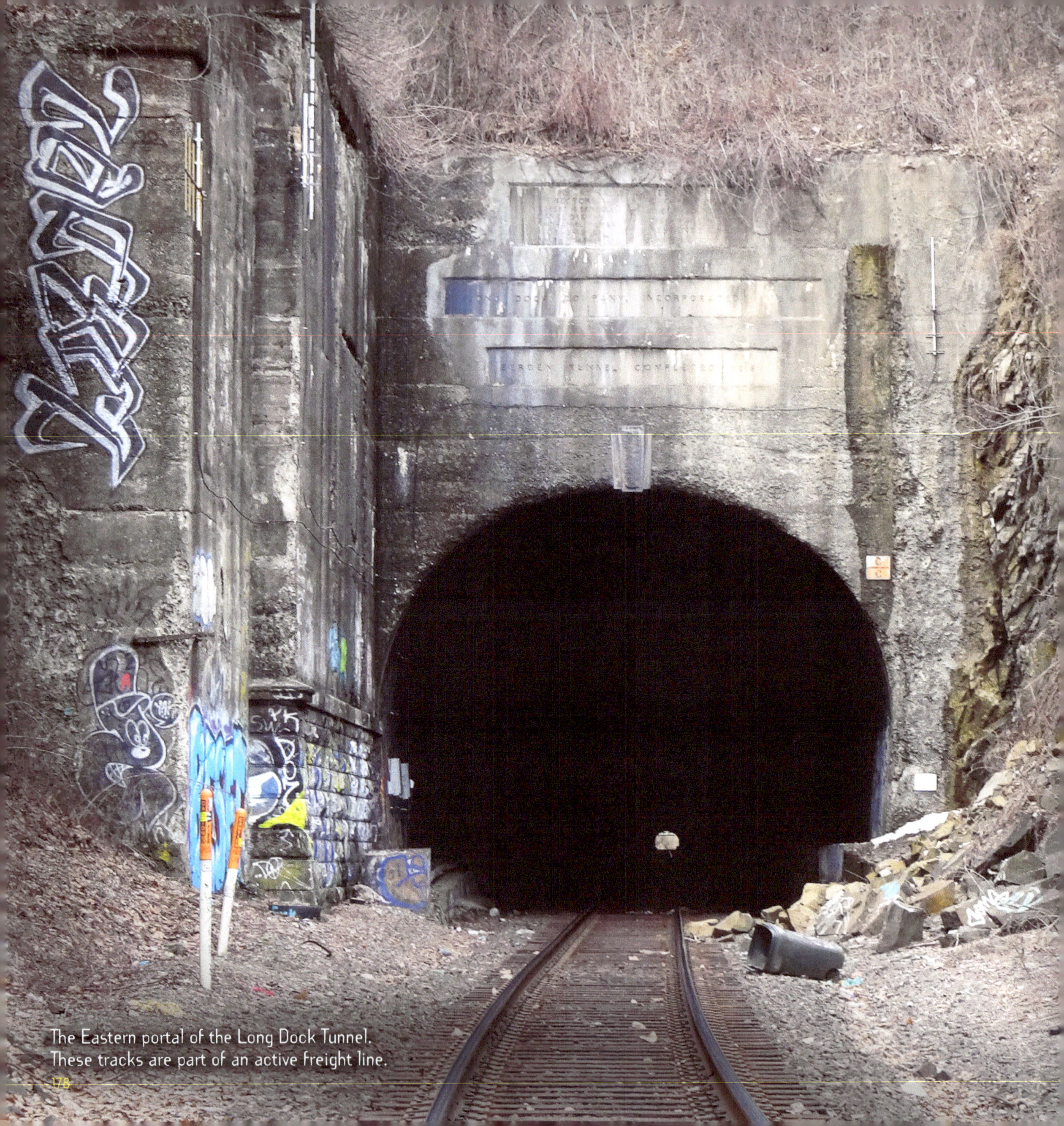

The Eastern portal of the Long Dock Tunnel.
These tracks are part of an active freight line.

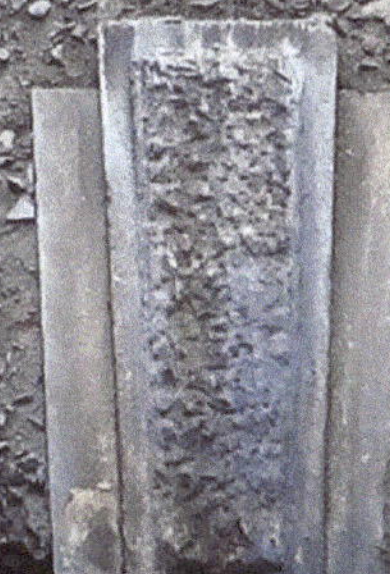

Stone tablets over the Eastern Portal of the Dead Man's Tunnel. The inscription pays tribute to the company big shots but fails to mention the fifty-seven workers that lost their lives during construction of the Long Dock Tunnel.

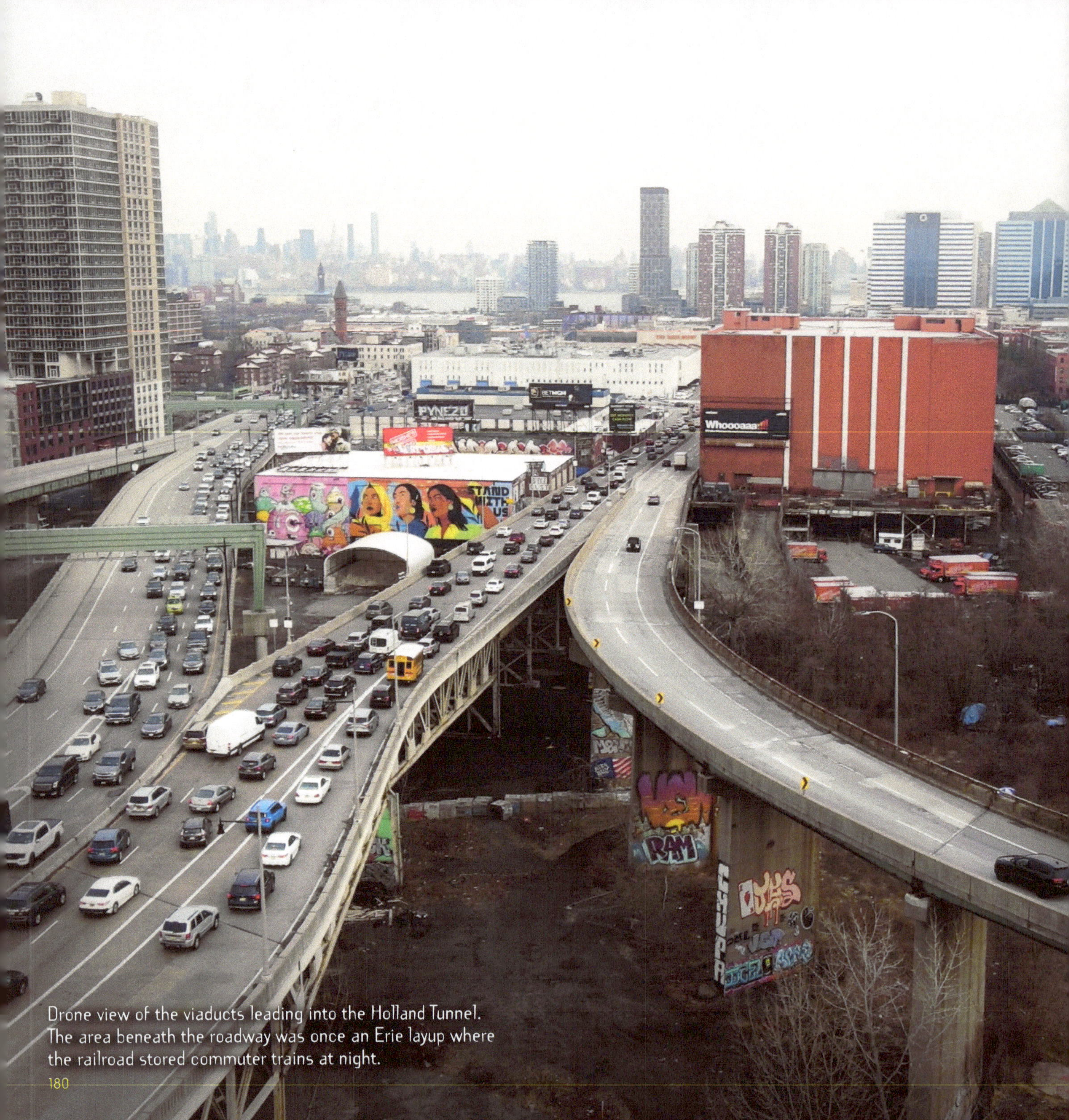

Drone view of the viaducts leading into the Holland Tunnel. The area beneath the roadway was once an Erie layup where the railroad stored commuter trains at night.

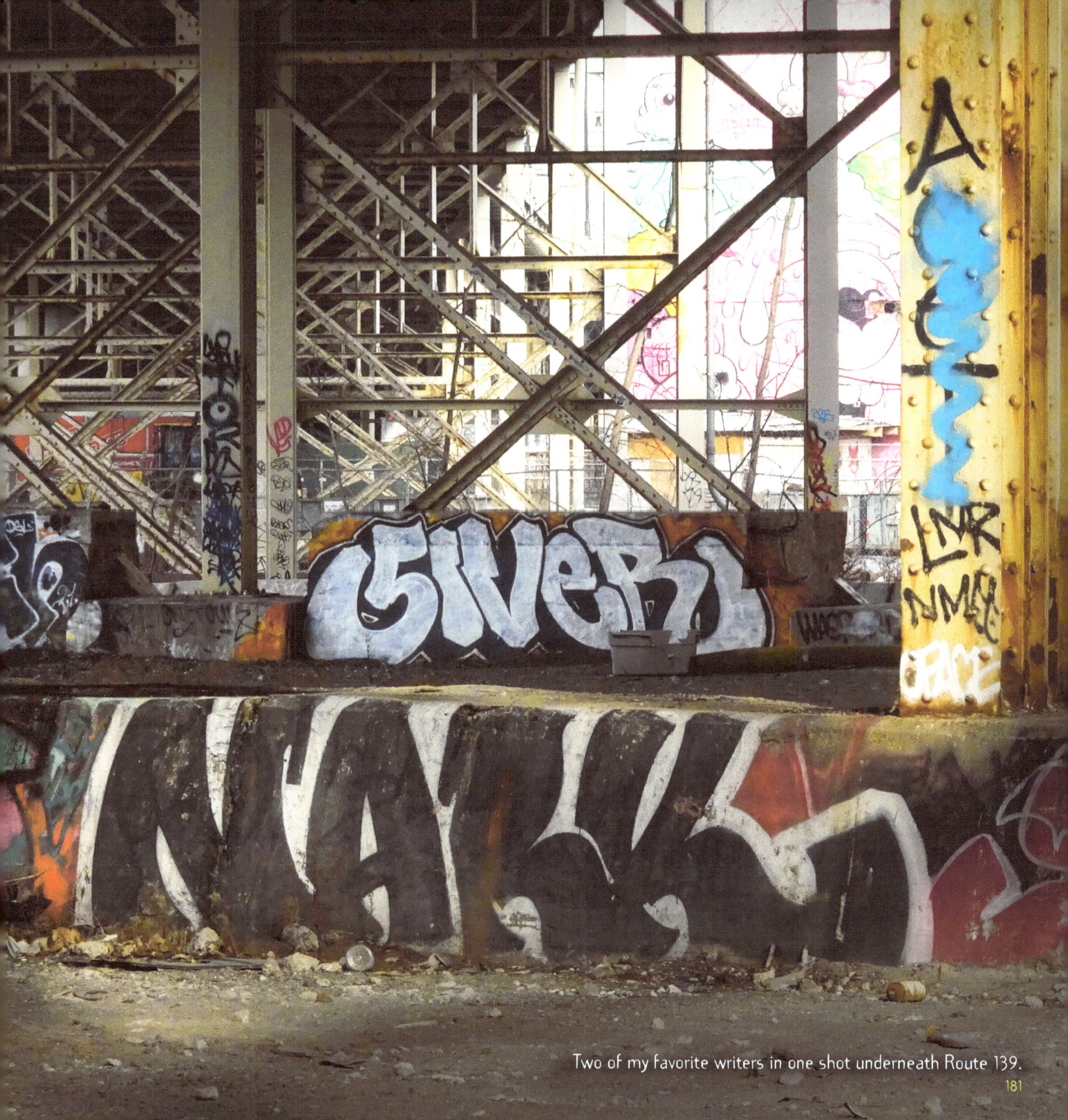

Two of my favorite writers in one shot underneath Route 139.

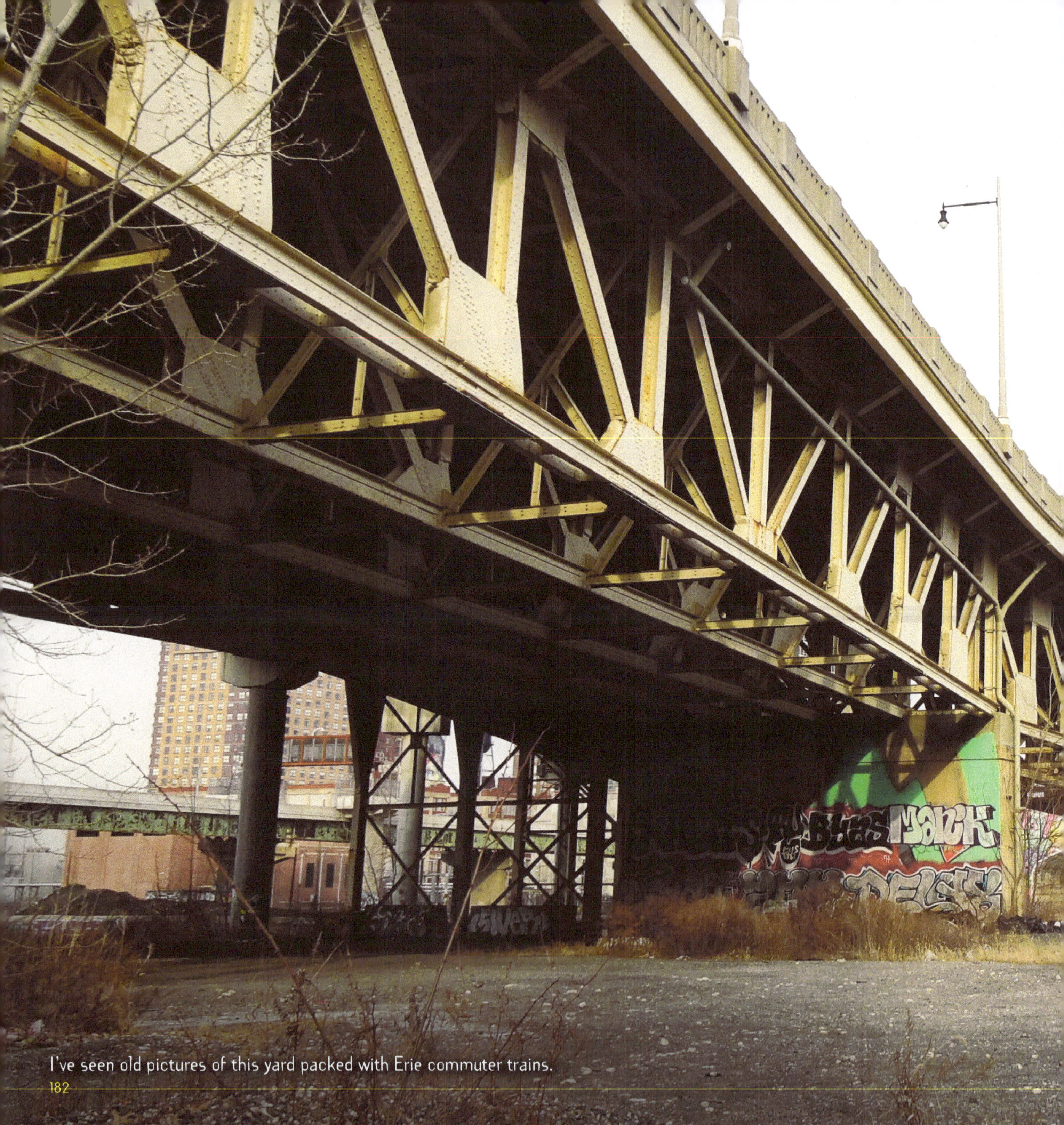

I've seen old pictures of this yard packed with Erie commuter trains.

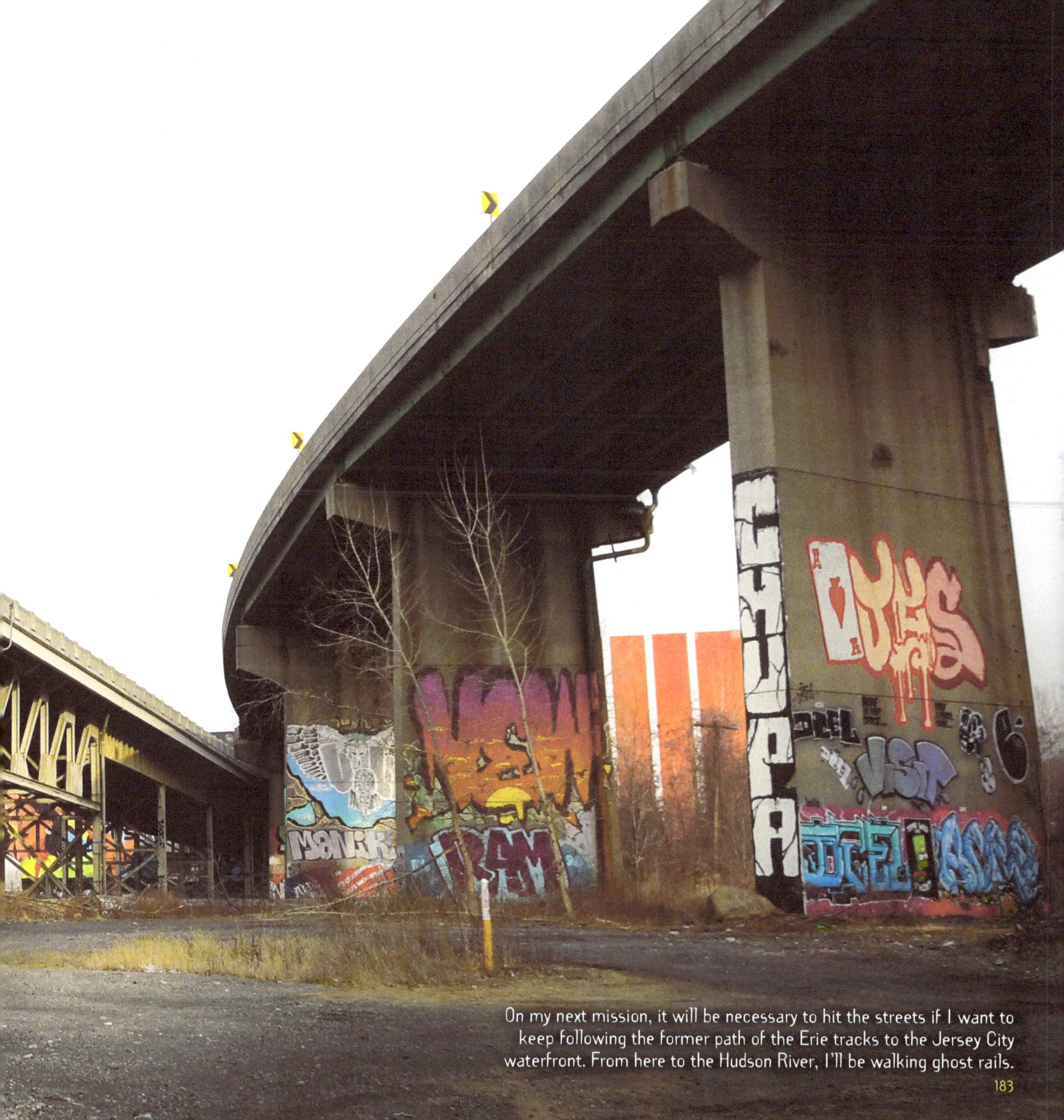

On my next mission, it will be necessary to hit the streets if I want to keep following the former path of the Erie tracks to the Jersey City waterfront. From here to the Hudson River, I'll be walking ghost rails.

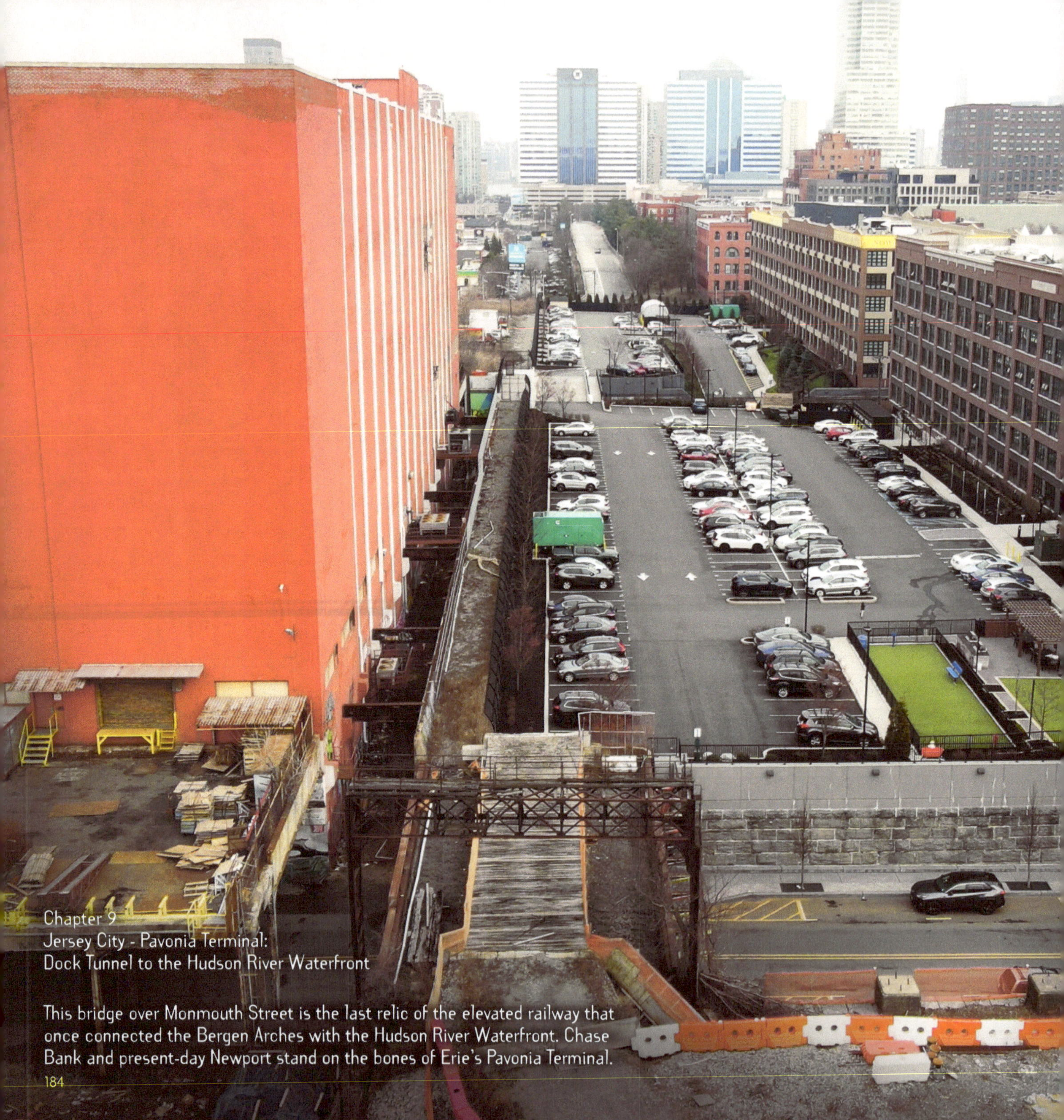

Chapter 9
Jersey City - Pavonia Terminal:
Dock Tunnel to the Hudson River Waterfront

This bridge over Monmouth Street is the last relic of the elevated railway that once connected the Bergen Arches with the Hudson River Waterfront. Chase Bank and present-day Newport stand on the bones of Erie's Pavonia Terminal.

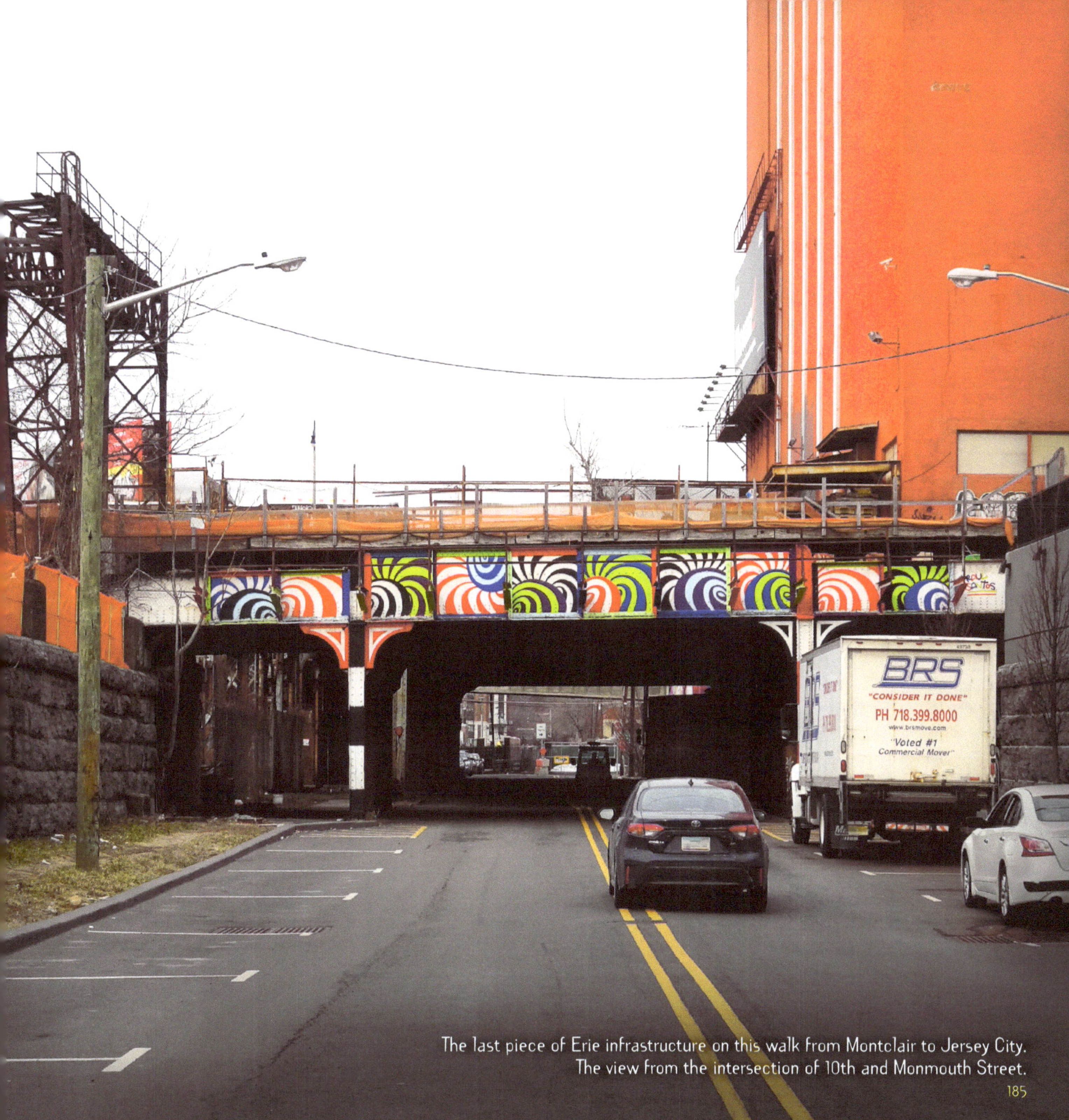

The last piece of Erie infrastructure on this walk from Montclair to Jersey City. The view from the intersection of 10th and Monmouth Street.

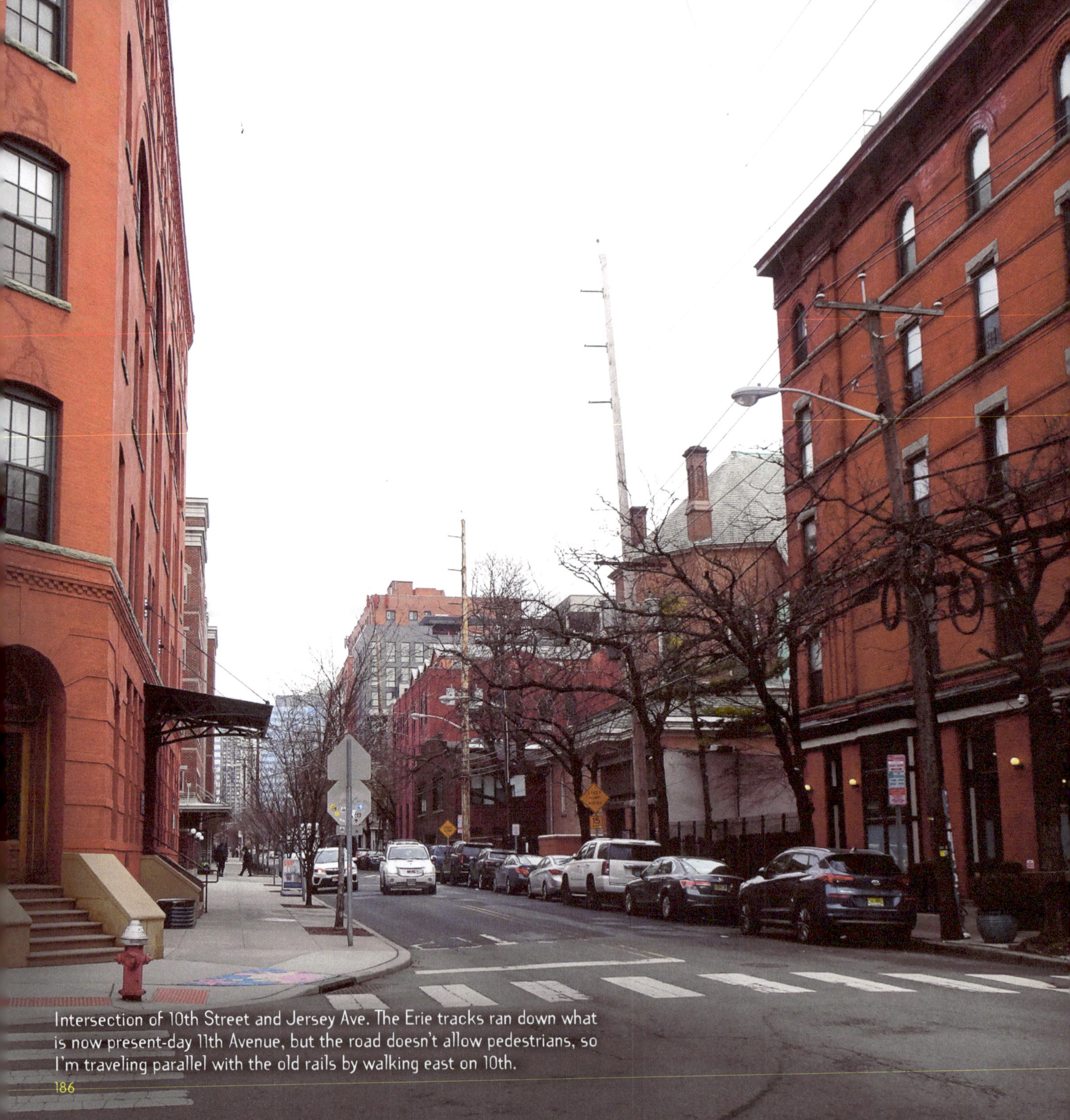

Intersection of 10th Street and Jersey Ave. The Erie tracks ran down what is now present-day 11th Avenue, but the road doesn't allow pedestrians, so I'm traveling parallel with the old rails by walking east on 10th.

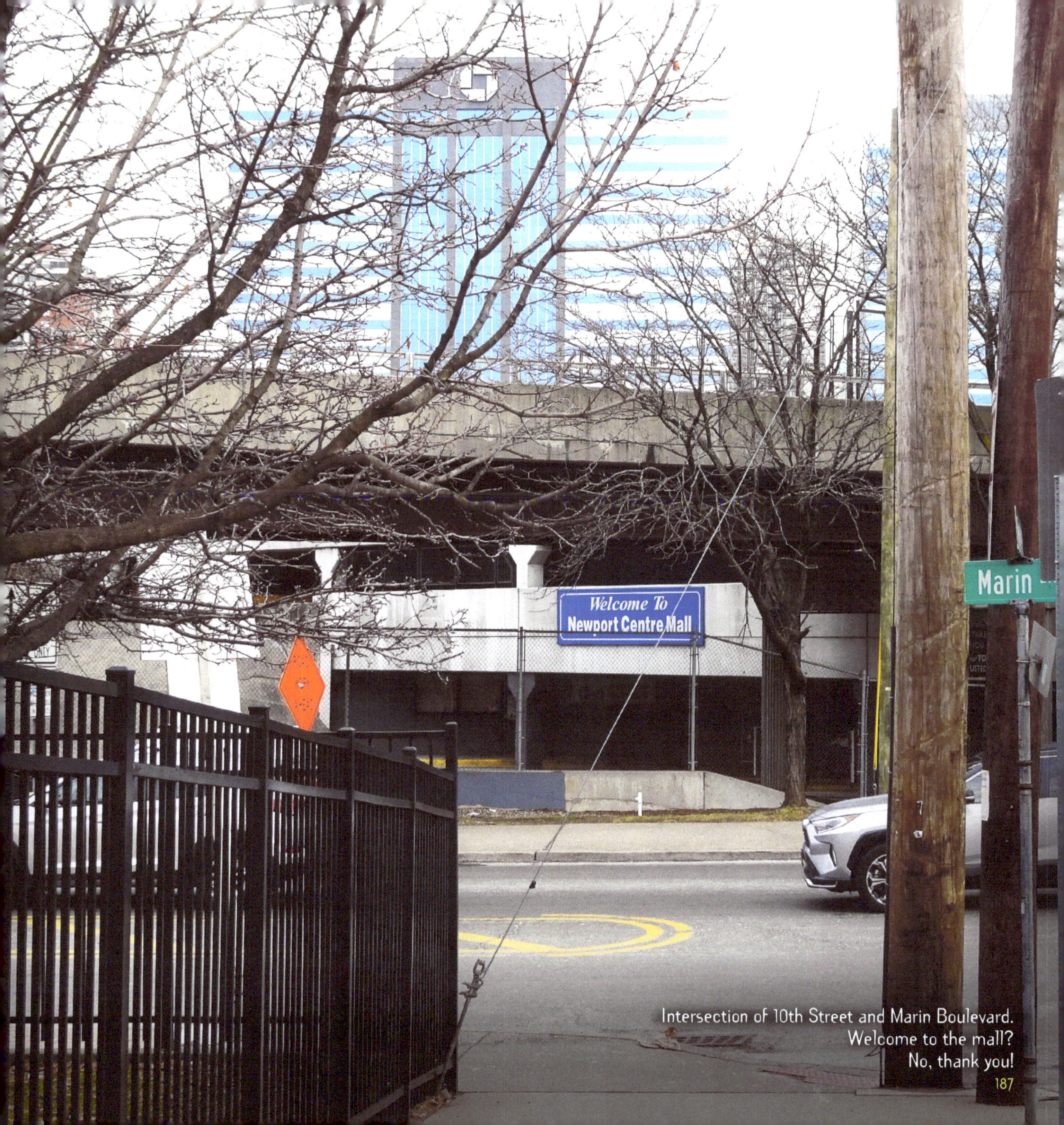

Intersection of 10th Street and Marin Boulevard.
Welcome to the mall?
No, thank you!

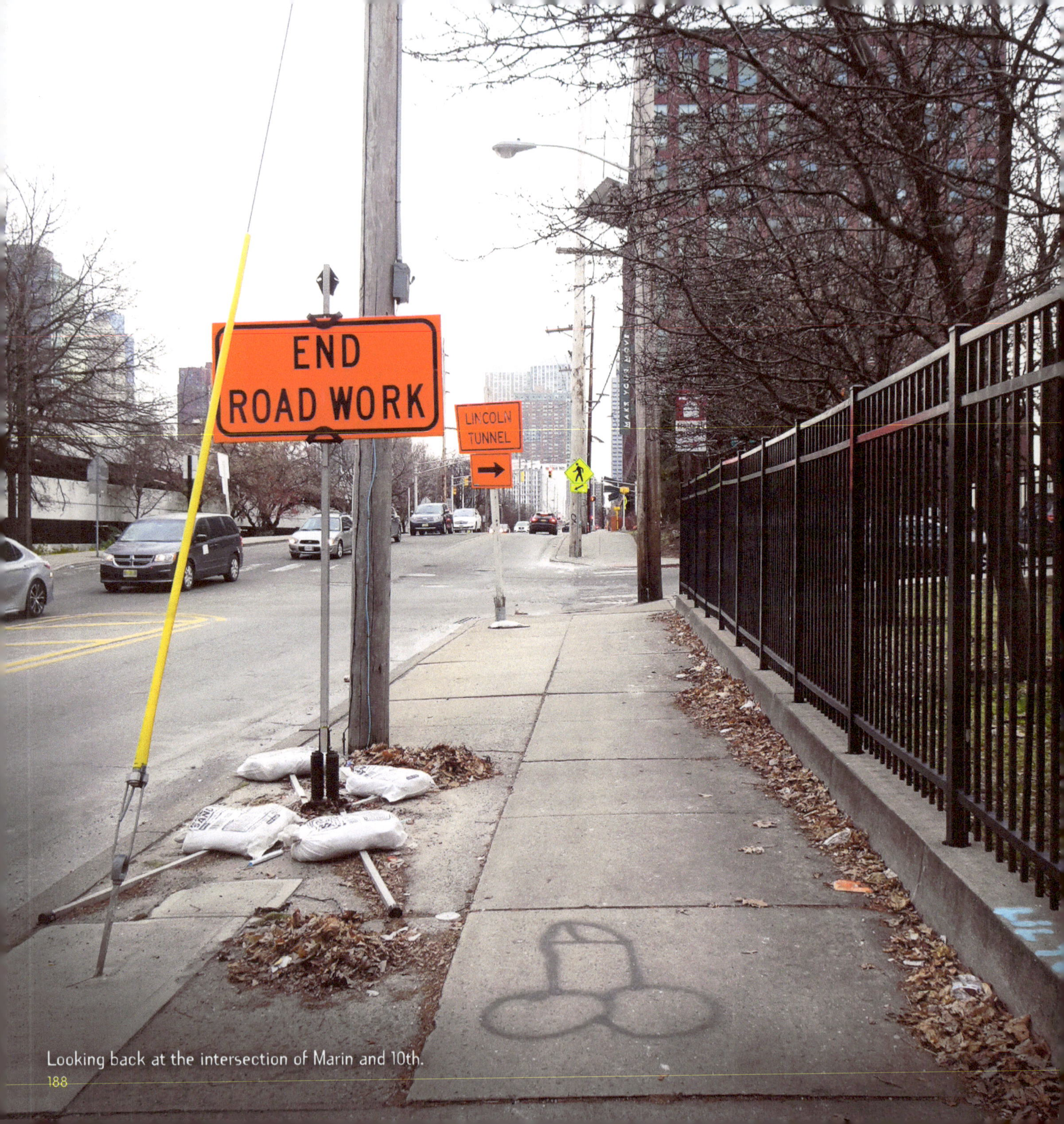

Looking back at the intersection of Marin and 10th.

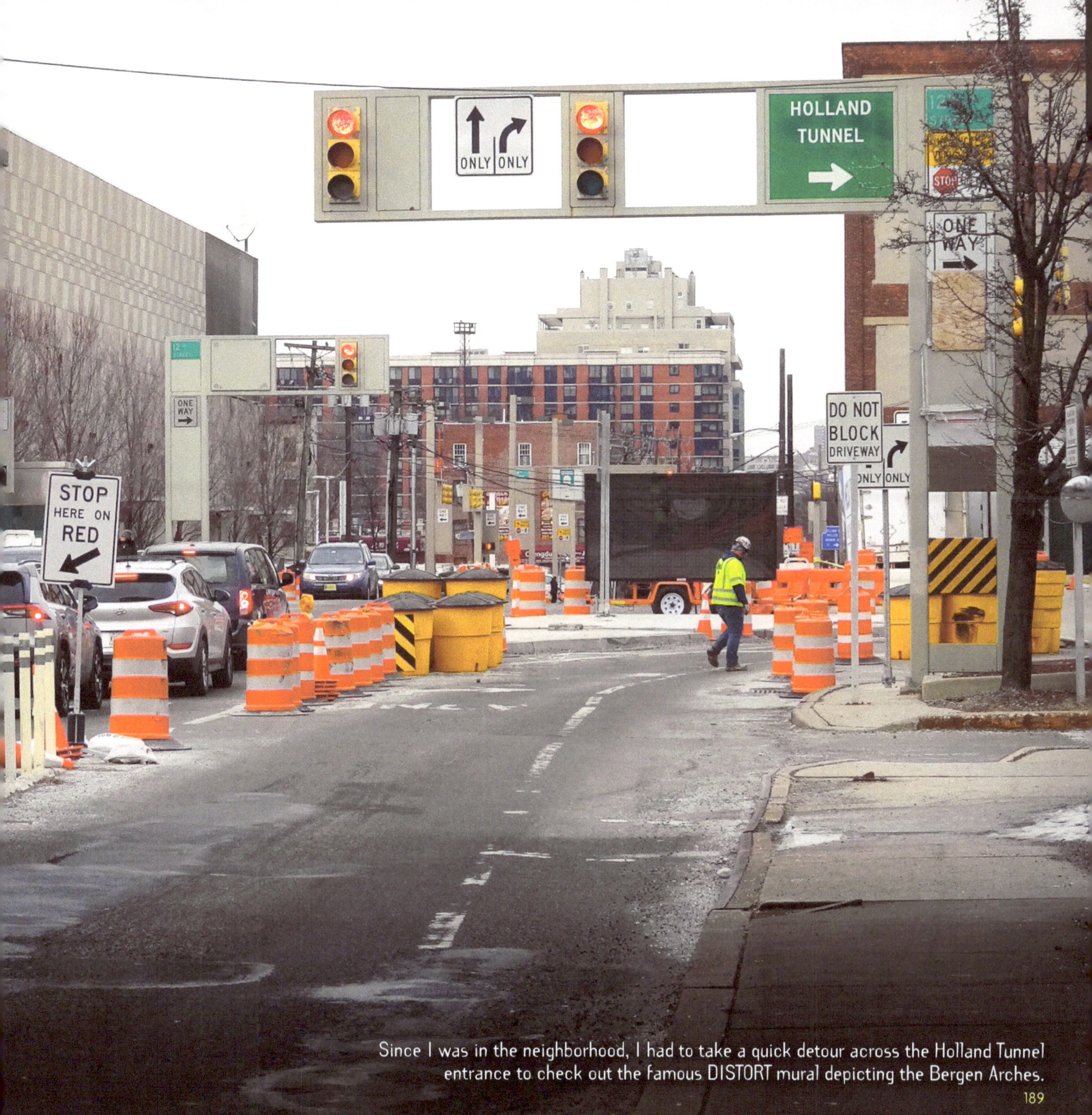

Since I was in the neighborhood, I had to take a quick detour across the Holland Tunnel entrance to check out the famous DISTORT mural depicting the Bergen Arches.

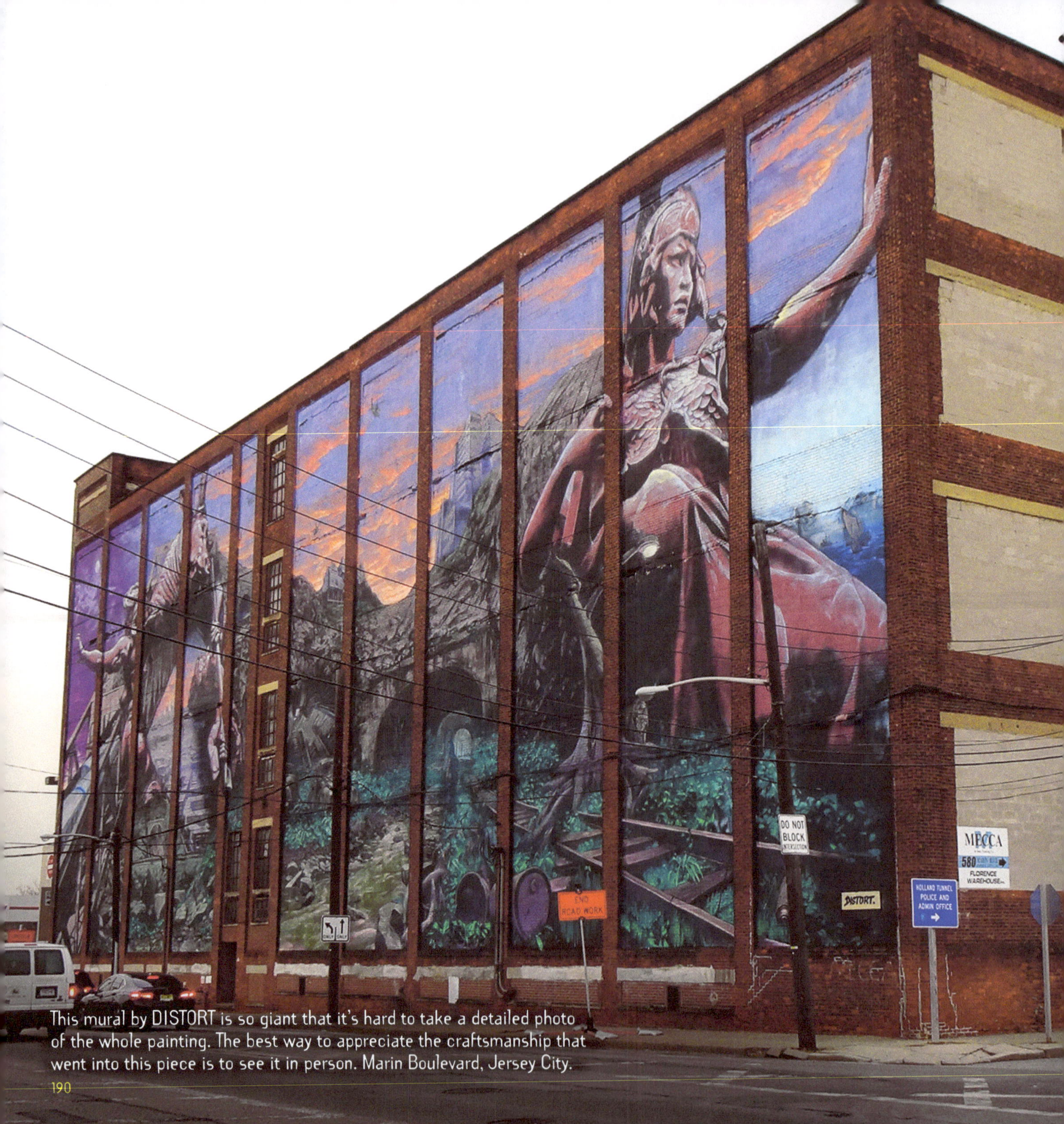

This mural by DISTORT is so giant that it's hard to take a detailed photo of the whole painting. The best way to appreciate the craftsmanship that went into this piece is to see it in person. Marin Boulevard, Jersey City.

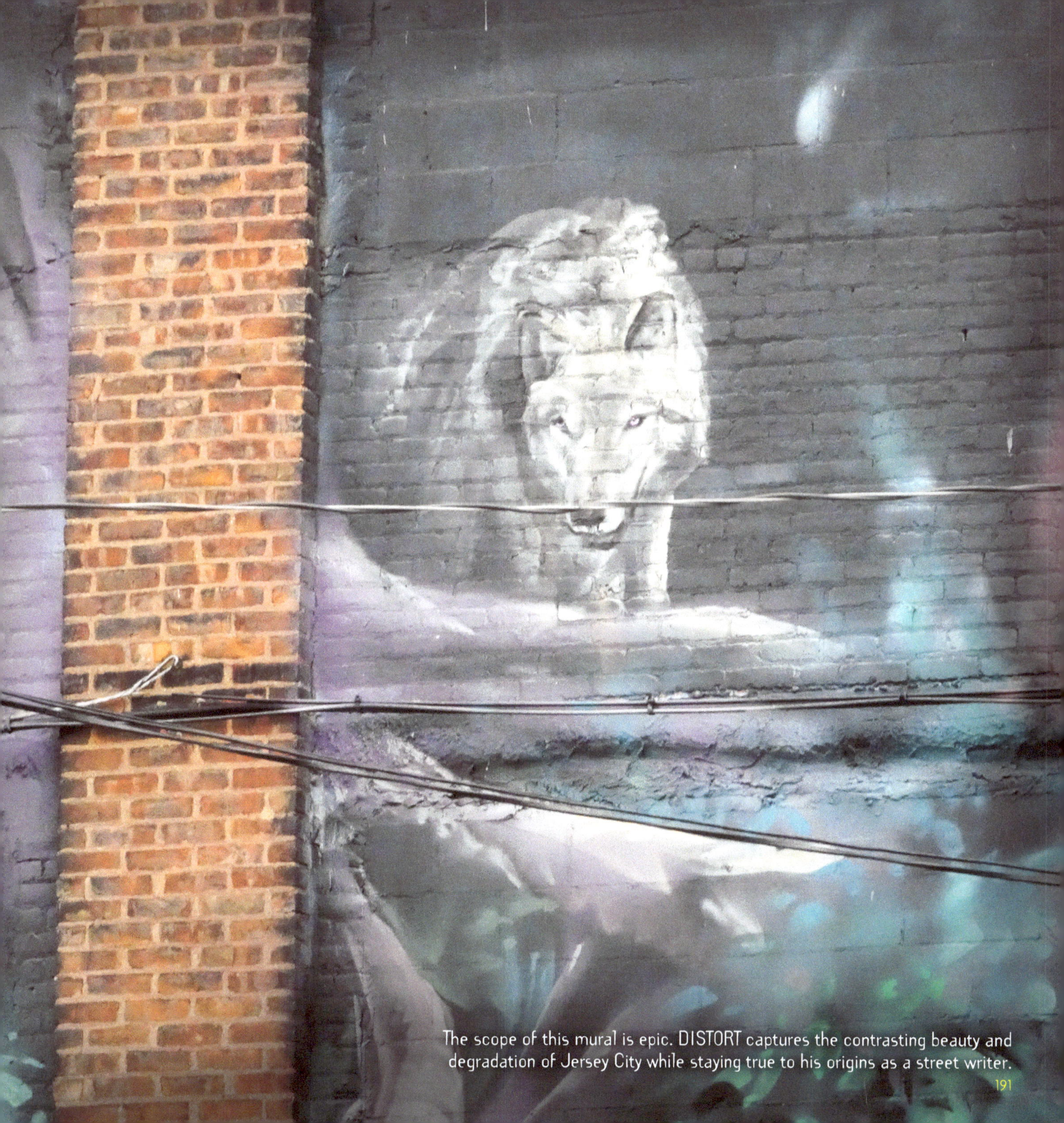

The scope of this mural is epic. DISTORT captures the contrasting beauty and degradation of Jersey City while staying true to his origins as a street writer.

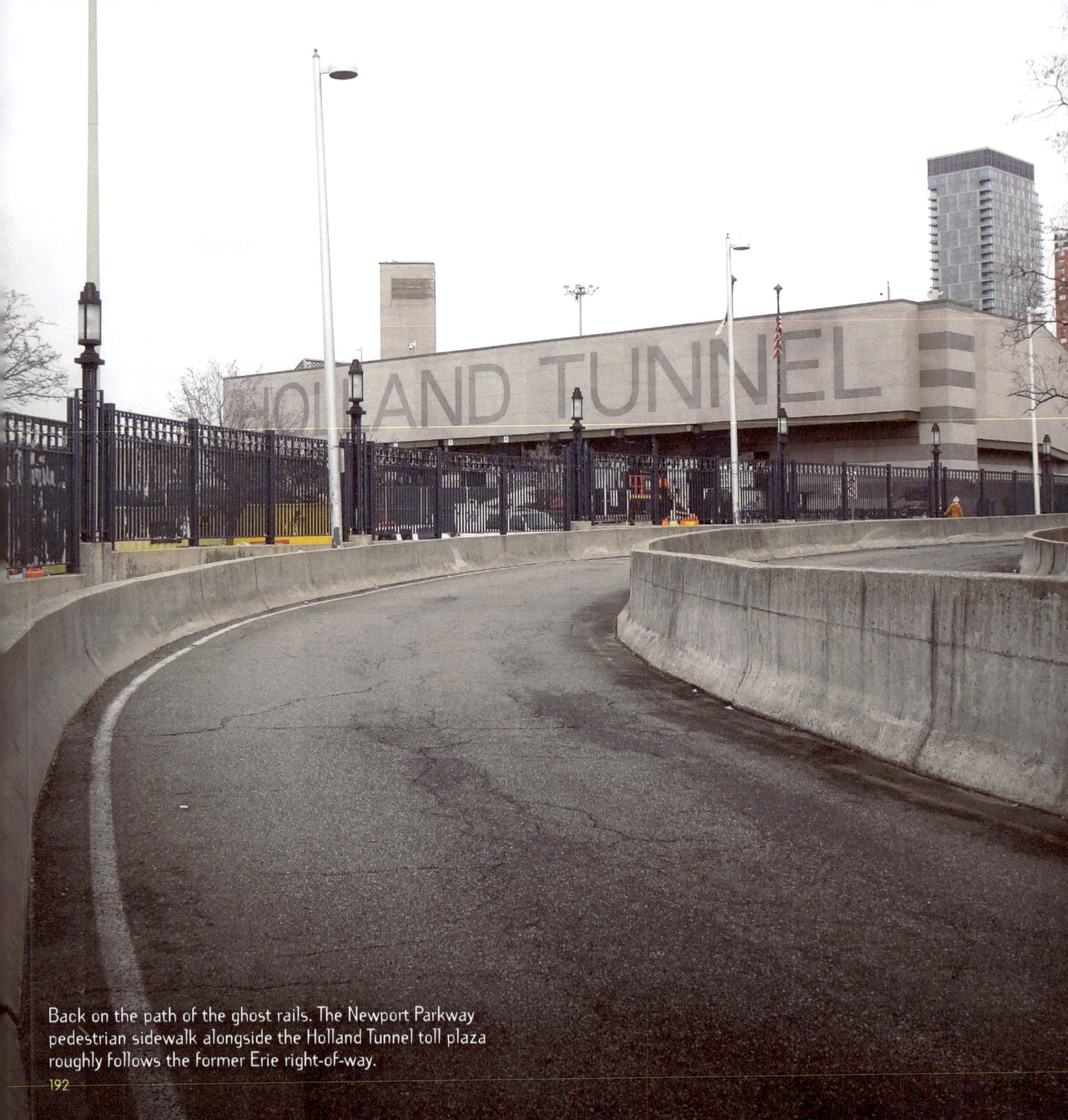

Back on the path of the ghost rails. The Newport Parkway pedestrian sidewalk alongside the Holland Tunnel toll plaza roughly follows the former Erie right-of-way.

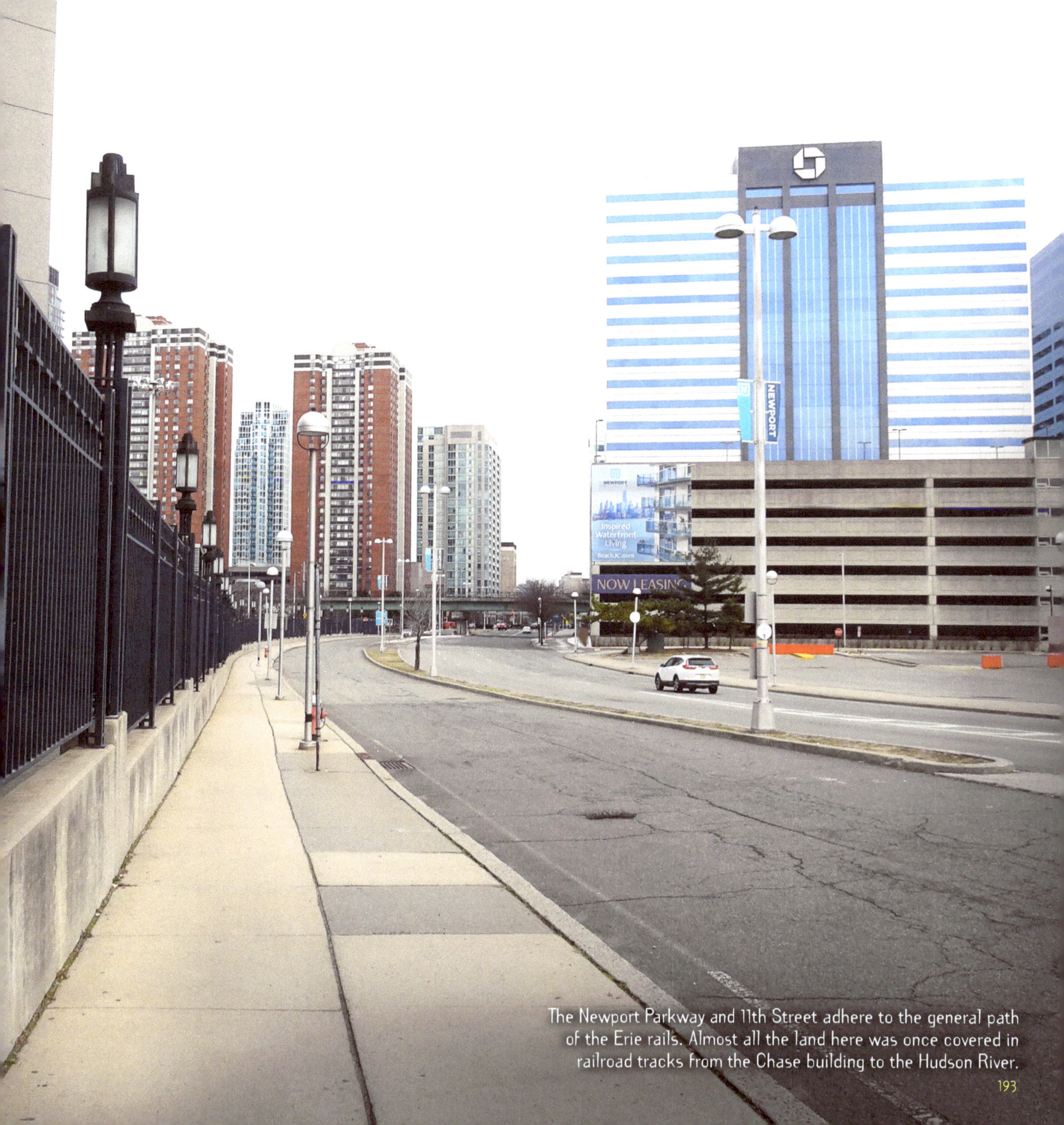

The Newport Parkway and 11th Street adhere to the general path of the Erie rails. Almost all the land here was once covered in railroad tracks from the Chase building to the Hudson River.

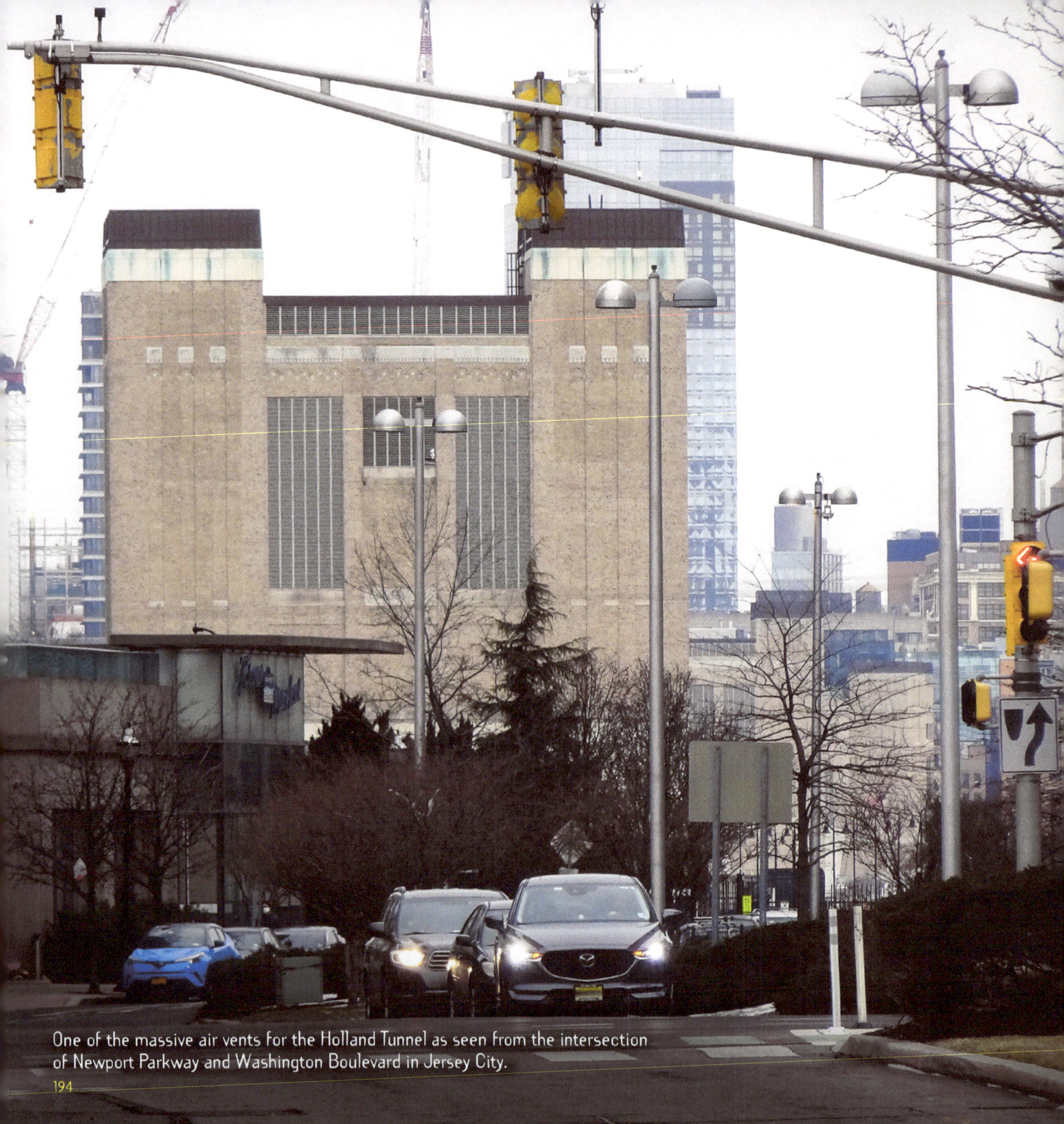

One of the massive air vents for the Holland Tunnel as seen from the intersection of Newport Parkway and Washington Boulevard in Jersey City.

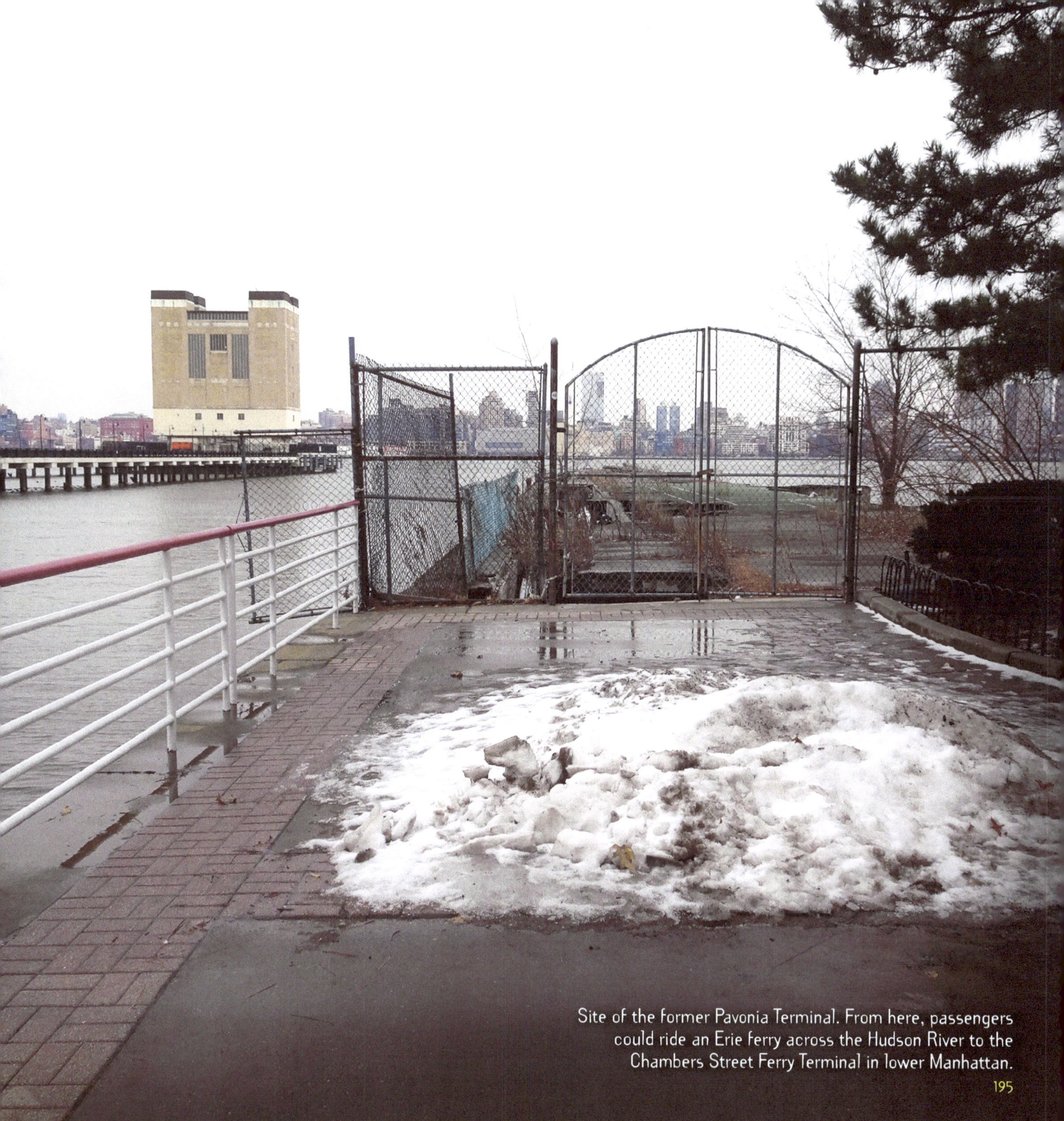

Site of the former Pavonia Terminal. From here, passengers could ride an Erie ferry across the Hudson River to the Chambers Street Ferry Terminal in lower Manhattan.

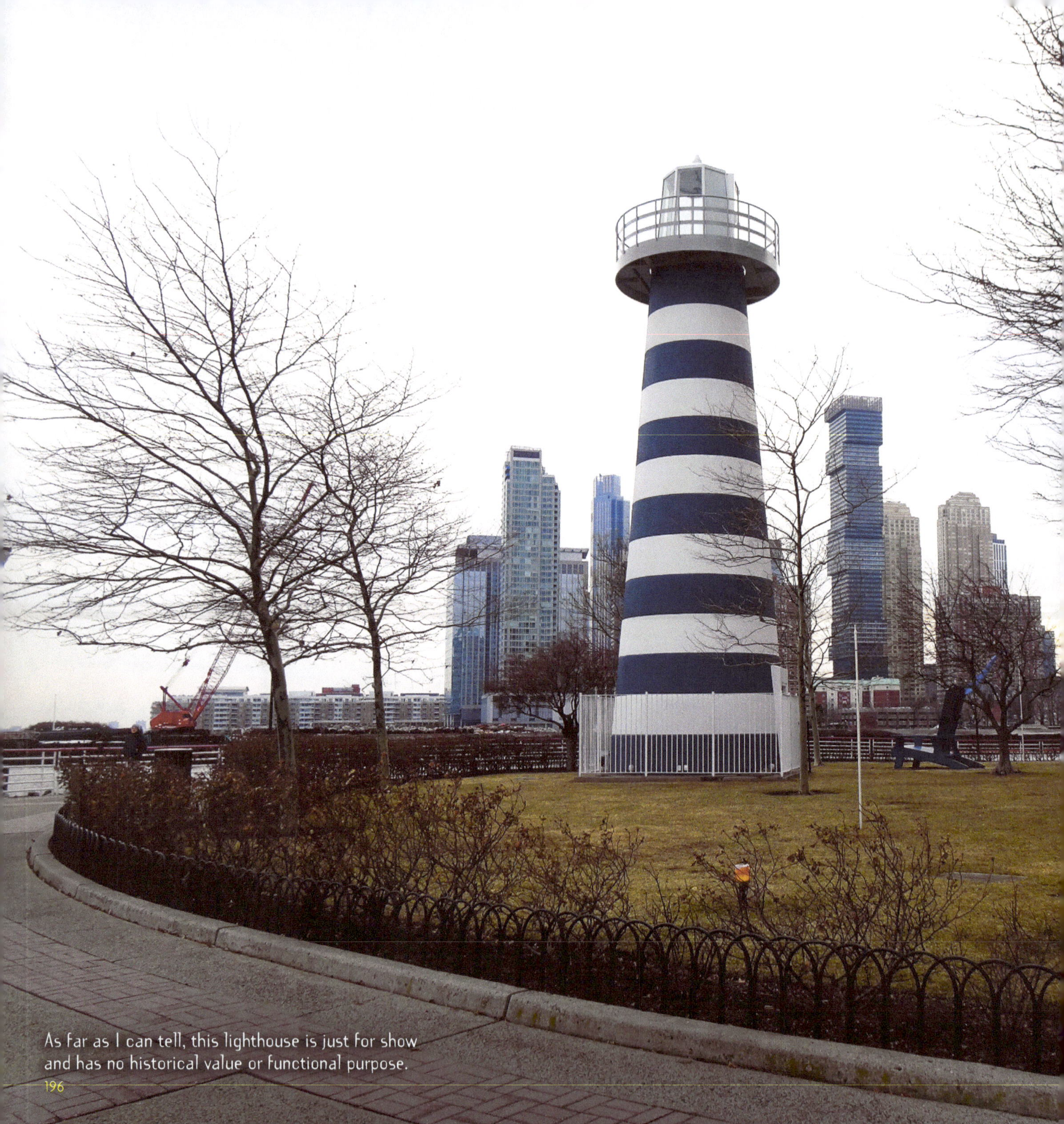

As far as I can tell, this lighthouse is just for show and has no historical value or functional purpose.

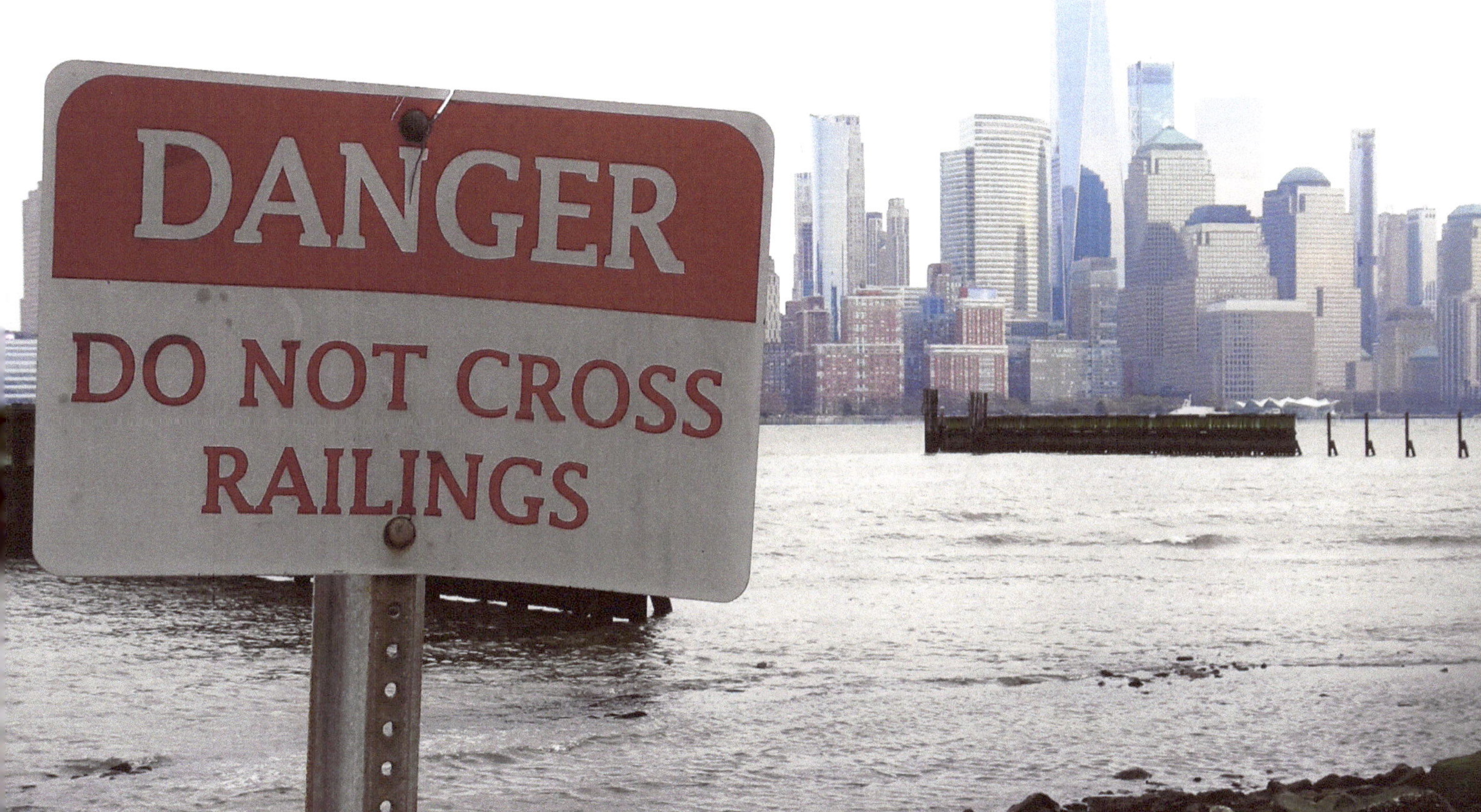

Standing on the bank of the Hudson River at the western tip of the former Erie yard. The Old Boonton Line once terminated here, but this isn't the end of the line for me quite yet.

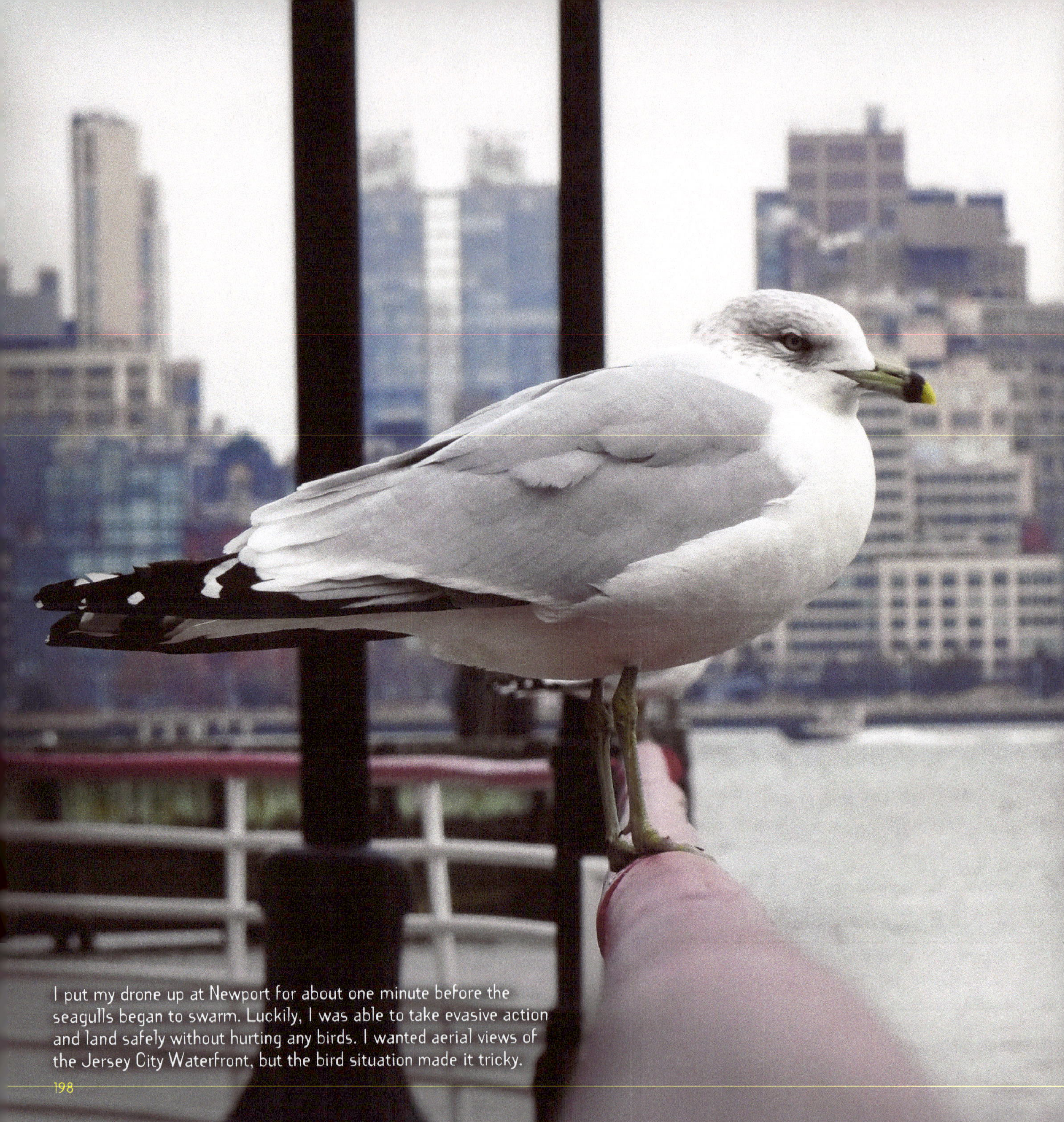

I put my drone up at Newport for about one minute before the seagulls began to swarm. Luckily, I was able to take evasive action and land safely without hurting any birds. I wanted aerial views of the Jersey City Waterfront, but the bird situation made it tricky.

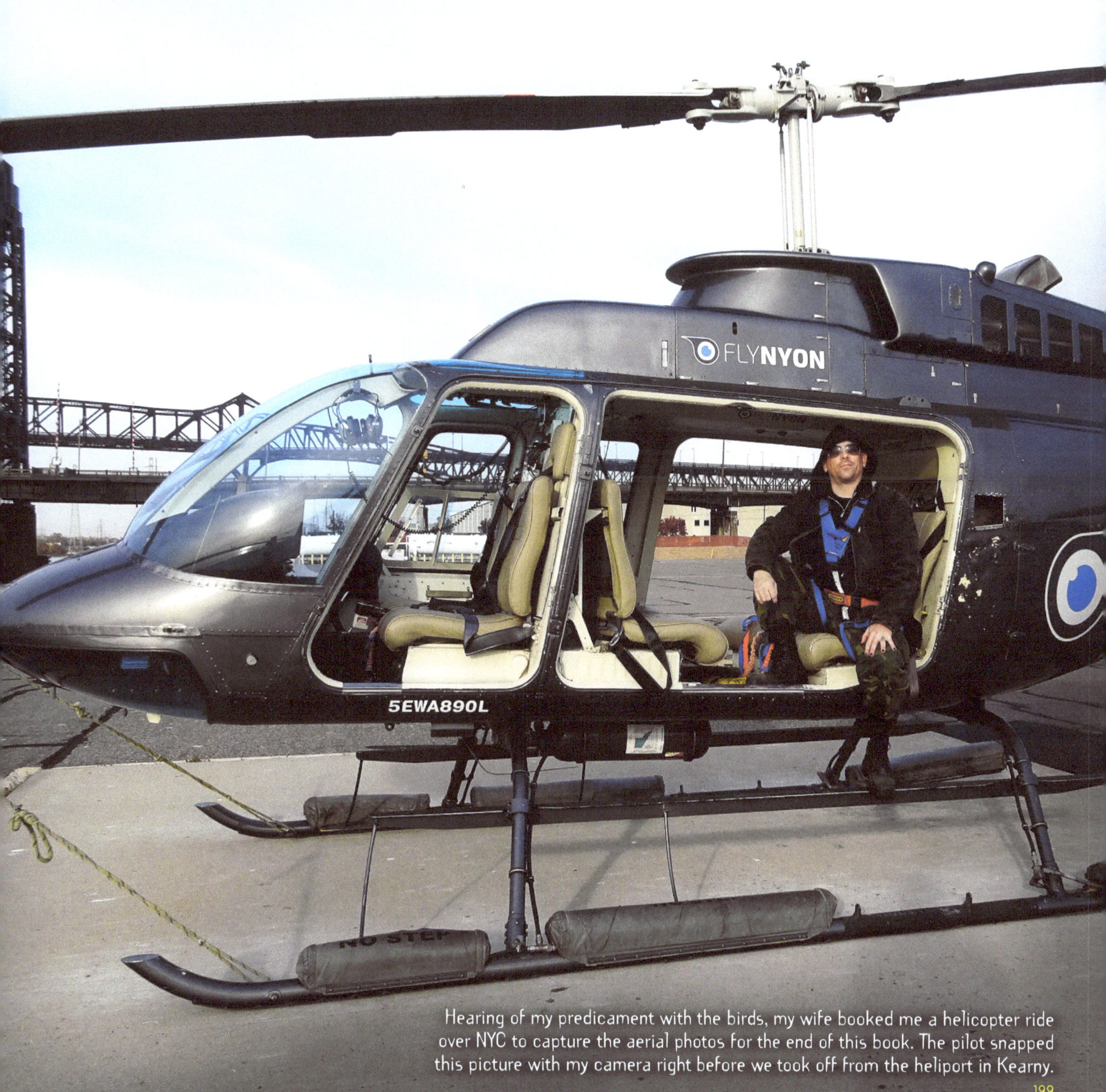

Hearing of my predicament with the birds, my wife booked me a helicopter ride over NYC to capture the aerial photos for the end of this book. The pilot snapped this picture with my camera right before we took off from the heliport in Kearny.

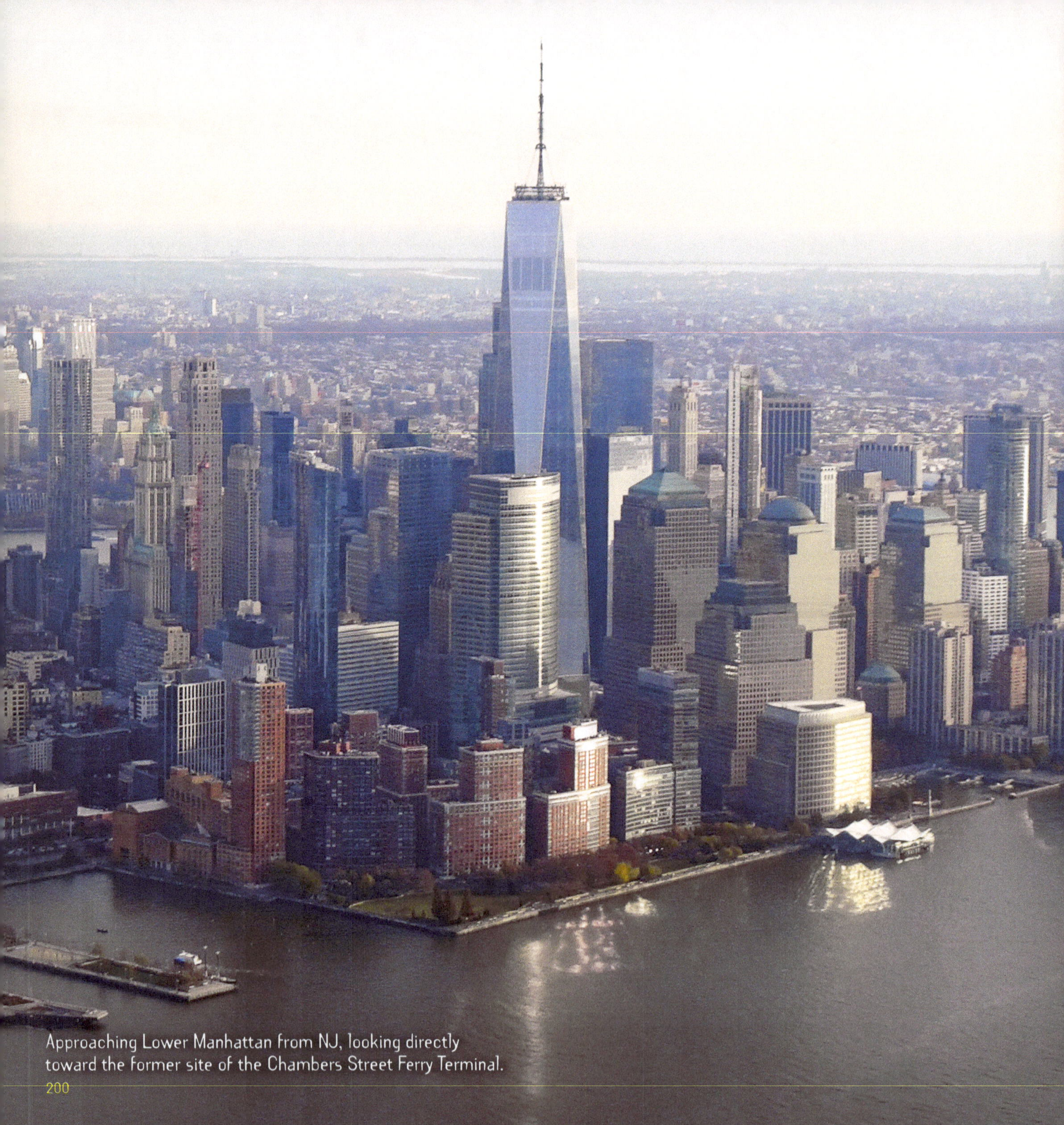

Approaching Lower Manhattan from NJ, looking directly toward the former site of the Chambers Street Ferry Terminal.

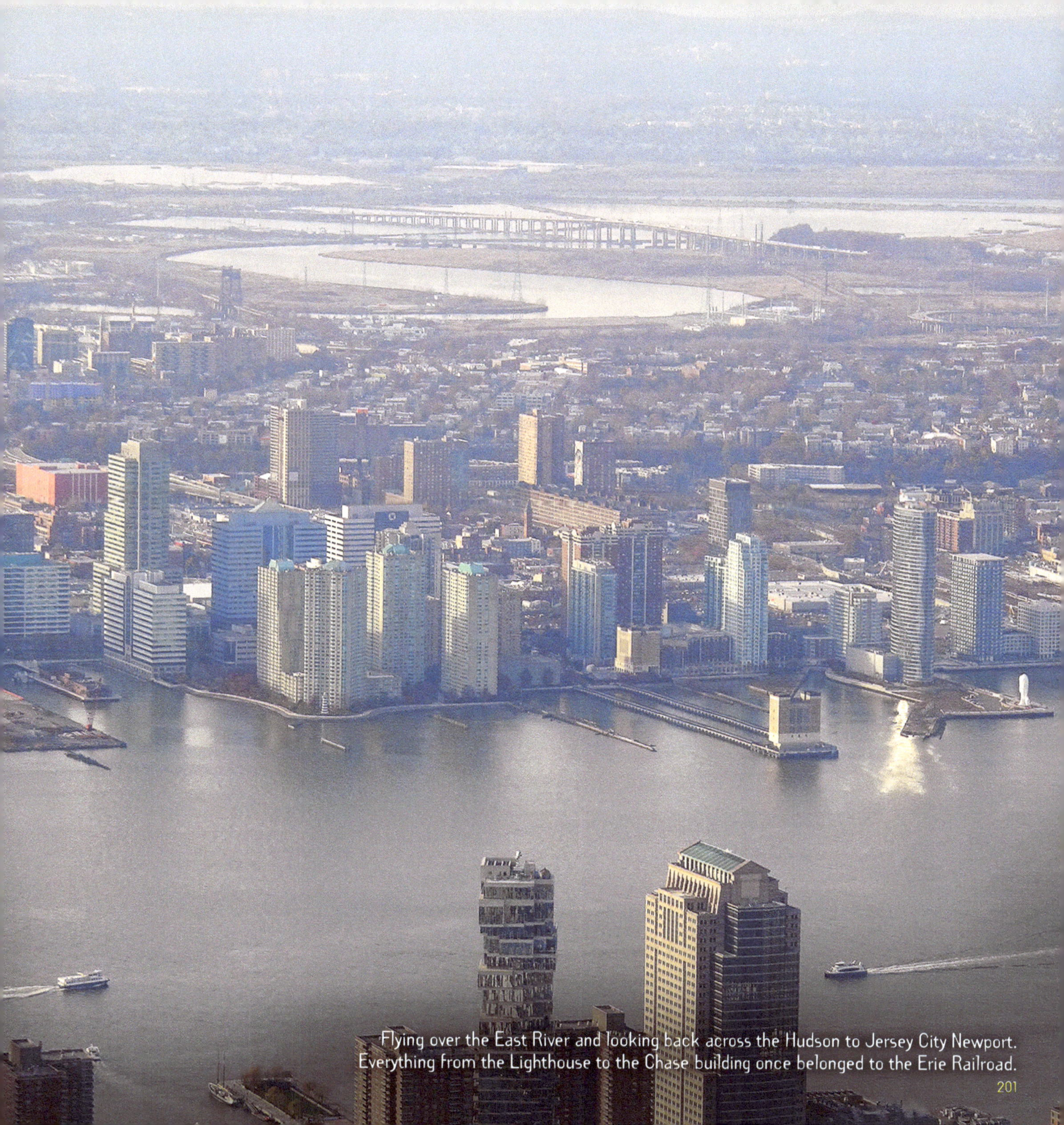

Flying over the East River and looking back across the Hudson to Jersey City Newport.
Everything from the Lighthouse to the Chase building once belonged to the Erie Railroad.

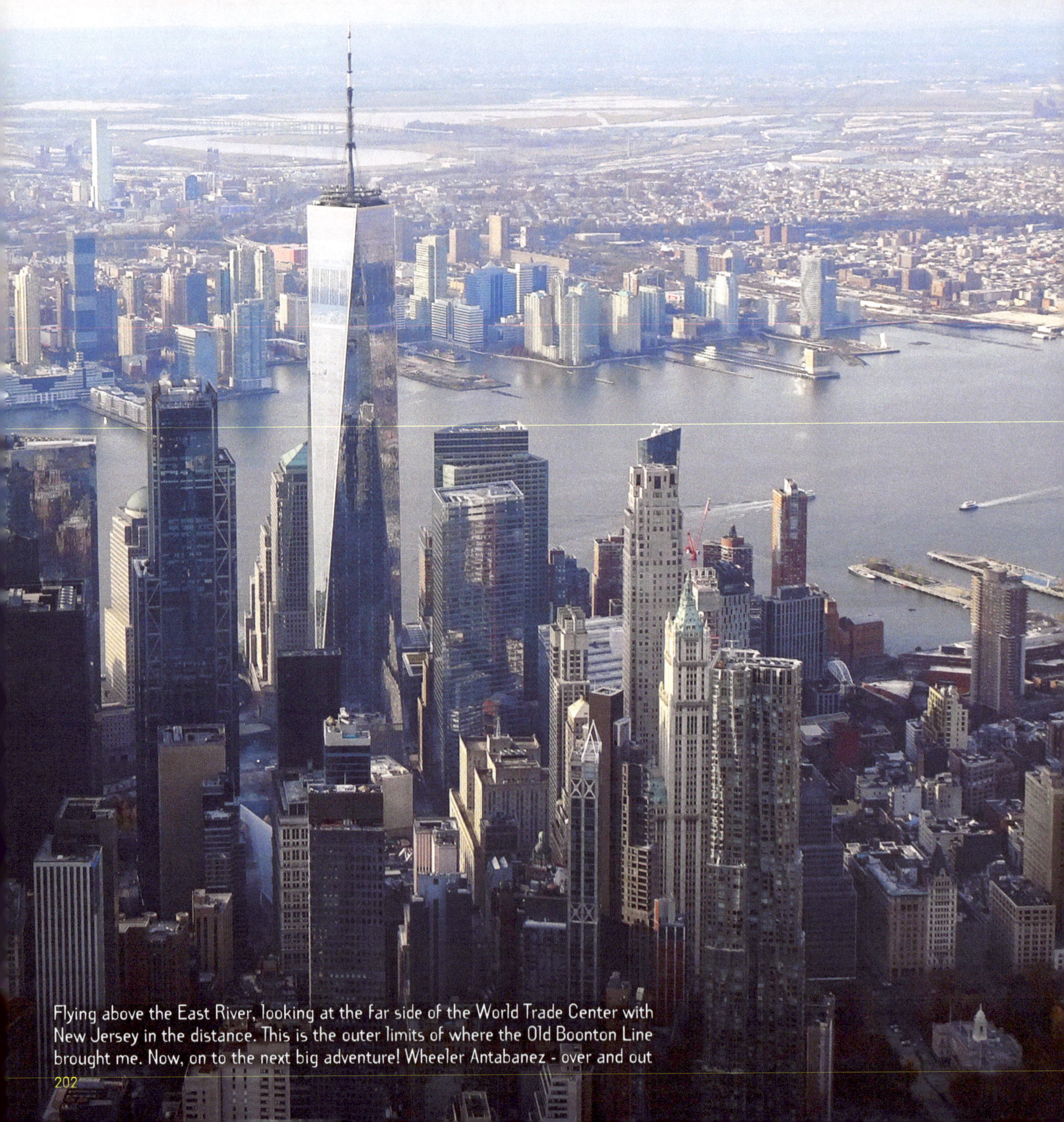

Flying above the East River, looking at the far side of the World Trade Center with New Jersey in the distance. This is the outer limits of where the Old Boonton Line brought me. Now, on to the next big adventure! Wheeler Antabanez - over and out

www.ingramcontent.com/pod-product-compliance
Lightning Source LLC
LaVergne TN
LVHW070118110826
845147LV00002B/151

* 9 7 9 8 2 1 8 0 3 3 6 3 7 *